OWNING YOUR HOME COMPUTER

THE COMPLETE ILLUSTRATED GUIDE

Robert L. Perry

DODD, MEAD & Company

NEW YORK

To Joseph Daffron and Ronald Renzulli, who,
each in his own way, made this book possible.

Published by Dodd, Mead & Company, Inc.
79 Madison Avenue, New York, N.Y. 10016

Distributed in Canada by
McClelland and Stewart Limited, Toronto

Manufactured in the United States of America

Designed by Berta Lewis

First Edition

Library of Congress Cataloging in Publication Data

Perry, Robert Louis, 1950–
    Owning your home computer.

    Bibliography: p.
    Includes index.
    1. Microcomputers. 2. Minicomputers. I. Title.
QA76.5.P3933 1984   001.64   84-10259
ISBN 0-396-08250-5 (pbk.)

CONTENTS

Acknowledgments

No one can write and then completely revise a book of this nature without the assistance, and, perhaps more importantly, the patience and willingness of dozens of people. To name any of the many considerate and helpful employees of the computer companies mentioned in this book would slight the ones not mentioned who did as much if not more than those whose names I know. But this book would not be as up to date as it is without their patient understanding of hurried last-minute calls for information and photographs almost literally hot off the presses. To the communications professionals who work for all of the companies mentioned in this book, my sincere thanks.

For the chance to gain both broad and deep insight into the future of the microcomputer industry and how it will affect each of our lives, I owe Kenneth G. Bosomworth, president of International Resource Development, my special thanks.

Revising a book of this nature in a field that seems to change daily will always occur at the worst possible moment. And thrown into the breach—as usual—was my very talented, gracious, and loving partner and wife, Bryce Webster. Without her skills as a grammarian, editor, and computer mechanic, it seemed this book would never have been completed. I can only express my deepest, most grateful love for all she has done now and in the past.

To my publisher, Lewis Gillenson, I give my most cordial thanks for allowing me to revise the successful first edition of this book and for his assistance in making the second edition an even greater success. And especially to my editor, Jerry Gross, go my thanks and appreciation for his patience, professionalism, pleasant personality, and equanimity during the five years of our association. To my literary representative, Charles Neighbors, I express sincere gratitude for his seemingly Solomon-like wisdom in working with us to make this revision possible.

Trademarks

The vast majority of the names of software packages, computer models, peripherals, information networks, data bases, and other formal names for devices, software, and services mentioned in this book are registered trademarks, trade names, corporate names and logos, or service marks of their manufacturers, producers, or dealers, or are protected by copyright.

Late News and Computer Product Developments

As this book was going to press, late-breaking news indicated that major computer companies would introduce important new products during mid- to late 1984. Given below are the initial details, as given in news stories in the computer trade press, of these developments. Some of the information is based on conjecture. Because the companies involved had made no official confirmations of these reports or announcements, this news can only be considered preliminary. But we believe it is important for you, our readers, to know of any major and impending changes in the home computer field during 1984 and 1985.

Apple Computer, Inc.

Apple is ready to introduce a portable, briefcase-sized version of its Apple IIe personal computer and a 16-bit microprocessor-based version of the same machine by summer, 1984, according to several sources. The portable briefcase-sized model is said to be similar to the Convergent Workslate model described in Chapter 10 of this book. It is supposed to be 95 percent compatible with the available supply of Apple IIe software. It is said to weigh about seven pounds, fit easily into a briefcase, have an 8-line, 80-column liquid crystal display (LCD), and cost between $700 and $800.

The second model is said to complement the 8-bit Apple IIe design, but it is supposed to weigh

about 20 pounds, be transportable, and cost about $1,500. It is also said to be able to run 95 percent of all available Apple IIe software with a compatible minifloppy disk drive. This product is supposed to have the second, 16-bit processor built in or have it available as an option. It is likely that the 16-bit processor would be compatible with the MS-DOS (Microsoft Disk Operating System).

AT&T Information Systems

Three sets of rumors are flying about AT&T's imminent introduction of personal and microcomputers during spring, 1984. One holds that AT&T is showing retail dealers a personal computer and a multi-user microcomputer system for introduction in late spring or summer, 1984. The personal computer is said to be a 16-bit personal computer compatible with the IBM Personal Computer, and the larger system was to be a multi-user system based on AT&T's own 32-bit WE 32000 computer (also called the Bellmac processor). The personal computer would be sold through computer store franchises and chain stores, such as ComputerLand, Entre Computer Centers, CompuShop, and Sears Business Centers, among others.

A second rumor has it that AT&T is going to purchase a full line of microcomputers, ranging from an under $300 home computer to a multi-user system from an unnamed Japanese manufacturer, possibly Fujitsu. The third rumor holds that AT&T really does not know what it is going to do and is also developing its own line of home computers as well as personal computers and multi-user systems.

The only confirmed announcement AT&T has made concerns an agreement with Convergent Technologies to develop microcomputer-based workstations for corporations and large organizations.

The latest reports in publications, including *Information Systems News, Computerworld,* and *InfoWorld,* show that the multi-user system would be a 32-bit system based on a small desktop box to which as many as thirty terminals and peripherals could be attached with AT&T's own highly respected operating system, called UNIX. This would require a large supply of hard disk memory—at least 36 million characters, according to one report—because a full UNIX operating system occupies about 6 million characters of computer memory. This large system is supposed to come in four models—the 100, 200, 300, and 400. It is supposed to have the ability to do more than one operation at a time—this is called a *multi-tasking capability.* It is known that hundreds of 32-bit WE 32000-based desktop computers have been in use around AT&T offices for two years, but it was not known how this model would be modified into a commercial product for small businesses and professional offices. Of course, a multi-user system is not designed for home or individual use.

It is said that the Japanese computer models will come either from Fujitsu or Panasonic's parent, Matsushita Electric Industrial Co., Ltd., both of which can and do make a wide variety of small computers and electronic devices and the components that go into them.

However, it is likely that, in late February, 1984, not even AT&T really knew what path it was going to take. Sources with close ties to AT&T said a great deal of corporate infighting was going on all during 1983 and early 1984 about determining directions in consumer computers and consumer telephones technologies. And, the multi-user system—which should be announced before this book is published—may simply represent a compromise to get something out the door because everyone was waiting for AT&T to do something about microcomputers. The true direction AT&T will take in home and personal computers is not likely to

take shape for at least a year or more, after it makes a few mistakes and the dust settles from the divestiture of the telephone companies.

None of these rumors really address what AT&T might do in home computers, or in home computers integrated with intelligent home telephones or terminals for videotex systems based on the telephone lines. Yet, as you will see in later chapters, AT&T has developed these telephone terminals for a commercial home information service in Florida and several experiments in North Carolina, Florida, and New Jersey. Thus, if the announcements have not already been made, if I were you, I would keep my ears open for announcements of AT&T home computers with built-in telephones.

IBM

Of more practical importance to individuals than the AT&T rumors is the rumor that IBM will introduce a portable model of its personal computer by the end of March, 1984. This unit will be perfectly compatible with the IBM PC and the IBM PCjr and run all of their software packages. It will use the same microcomputer "brain," have a 9-inch diameter display screen, and weight about 22–25 pounds. It will have a built-in minifloppy disk drive with a high-capacity hard disk drive option. This portable model is supposed to be the first of a series of portable models of various sizes and capacities.

Another rumor has it that IBM will also introduce a lightweight, briefcase-sized computer with a 16-line liquid crystal display (LCD) screen, and at least one microfloppy disk drive. It is possible that the Japanese parent of Panasonic, Matsushita Electric Industrial Co., Ltd., is building the briefcase-sized computer for IBM. Several years ago, an agreement between IBM and Matsushita to develop computers was announced, but by early 1984, nothing had been announced as a result of that agreement. A briefcase-sized computer could be the first product of that collaboration.

Concerning the heavier "transportable" unit, it is possible it will have 3.5-inch microfloppy disk drives. This will make the 3.5-inch drives and industry standard and end at least five years of corporate warfare about the new drive. An IBM transportable computer would also do for this part of the computer business what the IBM PC did for the personal computer—give it a tremendous boost and increase the sales of those computers dramatically.

PART ONE

THE WORLD AT YOUR FINGERTIPS

CHAPTER 1
The Home Information Explosion

Practically everyone has seen or heard about "home computers" during the past few years. Most people, however, take a look, say, "That's nice," and promptly forget about them until they see them again on television or read about them in magazines. As a friend said when I began writing this book, "Home computers? I've seen them, but what good are they?"

That phrase has echoed through history when skeptics have not seen the possibilities of inventions that we take for granted today. The world scoffed at Alexander Graham Bell—"The telephone is just a toy"—and derided Thomas Edison for the electric light, the phonograph, and the moving picture projector. But today, you can pick up the phone, dial eleven or twelve numbers, and reach any country in the world. You can flip a switch in your home and any of a dozen or more appliances you own—of more than ten thousand you might own—will automatically come on. Press another button and the appliance will perform its task quickly and efficiently without your help. And when you pull a knob, or press a button, or turn a channel, you can watch whatever is happening, while it's happening, on the other side of the moon, or in your own backyard.

You can consider that home computers are as crude today as telephones were at the turn of the century. But a major difference separates home computers from the first telephones and electric lights. No telephone network existed, no transmitters or receivers were being manufactured, no electric power network existed to carry the signals (this is the main reason that the telephone has always had an independent power supply). Edison faced the same vacuum: no generating plants, no lines, no customers, no known demand, no electrical appliances, no wall switches or outlets in the home.

At the touch of a button, however, today you can link your home computer to your telephone and "talk" to another computer on the other side of the world, or to your best friend's computer just across town. Unlike telephones and electric lights, home computers have developed from the top down. Big computers came first (as we'll see in detail in Chapter 3). Whether that helped or hindered the development of home computers incites furious debate among the experts. The fact remains, however, that IBM, Burroughs, Control Data, Honeywell, Sperry-Univac, Texas Instruments, and many others first developed big computers called *mainframes* for government and big business. That made good sense. You can't use in your home a computer as large as your bedroom, but the Internal Revenue Service and Exxon can.

Researchers then discovered how to put computer circuits on a chip of silicon smaller than a fingernail, and the current electronics revolution began in earnest. In five years, more than seventy million people bought pocket calculators, proving that adults want easier, quicker ways to do their work, and children want the same advantages in completing their school assignments. A pocket calculator was something the owner could master in minutes. Soon researchers learned to put a complete computer on an even smaller chip.

At the same time, another revolution, closely related to the calculator revolution, exploded: the Information Revolution. As almost every large and medium-sized business and government agency required computers, they learned they could generate enormous amounts of information about any subject they wanted to—and they did. Electronics companies developed incredibly sophisticated communications networks, and American Telephone & Telegraph—along with satellite companies—obligingly created millions of phone lines to carry these masses of information. Within the past several years, the tiny computers-on-a-chip have been put into numerous new types of electronic telephones and many other communications devices at very low prices.

As these trends occurred simultaneously, innovative computer engineers built the first crude home computers. The first one was little more than a plastic board with complicated circuitry and buglike chips stuck onto it. To use it, you had to know as much about computers and programming as Alexander Graham Bell knew about telephones in 1876.

But that rapidly changed as dozens of bright young men and women began making increasingly sophisticated and increasingly easy-to-use home computers. And millions of people began to wonder what they could do with these machines, although the mere word "computer" continued to strike deep fear in many hearts.

The answer to that central question began to emerge from several strange places. In Great Britain, in 1974, the British Post Office (which runs that nation's telephone system, too) began experiments with two exciting ways to put enormous amounts of information onto home television screens: teletext called CEEFAX and Oracle, and videotex, also called Prestel or Viewdata. Both heralded the first barrage in a *home* information

explosion that promises to change your life in many fundamental, yet very positive, ways.

Teletext—simple, cheap, and inexpensive or free (to the home viewer)—transmits about three hundred pages of printed material over an unused portion, or "blank space," in a television signal to a home TV. The signal, which arrives along with the regular picture, remains invisible until you punch numbers into an encoder, actually a keypad the size and shape of a pocket calculator. Then the printed material becomes superimposed on the screen, and you can read any of the three hundred pages of material and watch your favorite program at the same time. More than one hundred thousand British viewers can now choose from dozens of kinds of information: news, sports results, stock market prices, classified advertising, weather and traffic reports, real estate listings, home study courses, display advertising, and much more.

Teletext serves as an electronic newspaper, encyclopedia, dictionary, and aid to the deaf—subtitles can easily be shown through teletext for each program on each channel. Numerous U.S. television stations have tested and others are now testing teletext transmissions in this country, and major communications companies are planning to introduce commercial teletext services by the end of 1984. The first two U.S. teletext tests were broadcast over stations KMOX (a CBS affiliate) in St. Louis, and an independent station, KSL, in Salt Lake City. Both were simply engineering tests with in-house transmissions. Teletext continues to be tested in half a dozen European countries and Japan. In France, the system is called Antiope.

But teletext has one significant drawback: you cannot interact with it. Using teletext, a viewer remains passive, pressing buttons on a keypad to call up information to the screen. The viewer can not send signals back to the computer transmitting the teletext information. And in the United States, viewers can get many of the same services by turning the channels on cable television. News, weather, sports, stock market prices, television and radio program logs, and radio stations now all come over many cable channels.

Even in Great Britain, Prestel has not had the growth first predicted for it. Teletext has been held back because the quality of its graphics is poor compared to color television, and people have been reluctant to mix information with entertainment.

They do not want to be bothered with screens of text interrupting their TV show.

THE VIDEOTEX DIFFERENCE

While teletext lights a firecracker in the information explosion, videotex launches a rocket. Videotex allows viewers to call up—through a simple keyboard or typewriterlike keyboard and a telephone—any of the information a teletext system can provide, but lets the viewer respond to the information. The videotex keyboard and a telephone work through an adapter, which sits on top of the TV set (or can be built into the set, which seems more likely). Such adapters have been built by American Telephone & Telegraph, Texas Instruments, and many other firms on an experimental basis. One French expert has been quoted as saying the adapter could be built into new TVs or added to existing ones for about $100, probably less in very large quantities.

With that adapter and simple keyboard, you can order from a mail order catalog on the TV screen, vote in an instant public opinion poll (like a group did with a Columbus, Ohio, videotex system during the 1980 elections), order groceries from a local food store, do your banking and your bill paying (at least five banks now offer this service on a regular basis through home computers), and review a list of real estate offerings and ask for more information about specific houses. As the experts agree, these interactive ways to use videotex seem quite conventional and crude. Many have said they have no idea what the public will really want to do with videotex. Yet, since 1980, major computer, communications, and information companies have conducted eighty tests of videotex systems, and one commercial service began on a local basis in Texas during summer, 1983. In any case, if you can think of ways to make your life easier and save time for things you really want to do (who really likes walking up and down grocery store aisles on Thursday and Friday nights?), you can probably think of new ways to use videotex.

I believe the experiments the major corporations have conducted have tested the wrong things. Only one or two have actually charged anyone for the service, so people who use the service for free can indulge their whims. According to test results in Coral Gables, Florida, and other locations, people play with the system for a couple of weeks and use all of its services. Then, the fad wears out and they soon stop using the system. The tests have not tried to find out what services people are willing to pay for. Estimates for the cost of such videotex services as teleshopping, home banking, and so on, run to $40–$50 per month. Few people, especially those with $20–$30 per month cable TV bills, are going to double or triple their costs of TV viewing. And

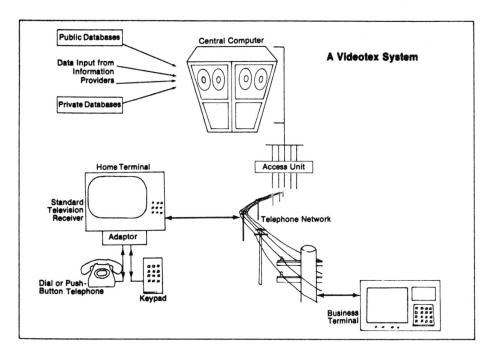

Figure 1. Block diagram of a videotex system such as one operated by Viewdata Corporation of America in South Florida. (Courtesy of Institute for the Future)

so far, the videotex companies have not created an impression that their services are going to save an average homeowner enough money each month to pay the videotex bill.

Videotex services work through the telephone lines or cables hooked up to a television set instead of through blank space within a broadcast television signal. A central company puts together a number of large computers into which "information providers"—such as TV networks, advertisers, and book publishers—feed masses of information. At home, you punch a number on the keyboard—like using a Touch-Tone phone—and make a regular phone call to the computer. The computer answers and begins sending your TV a *bit stream,* or flow of digital information. Your TV adapter receives this flow and converts it into printed text on the TV screen. Because the information comes in on the phone line, you can reply, using the keyboard to instruct the computer. In effect, your keyboard—which contains a tiny computer—carries on a computer-to-computer conversation.

With videotex, however, you cannot receive TV signals at the same time you hook up your TV screen to the videotex service. Videotex pages are shown against a blank screen, so you can't watch "Cheers" while you order milk from your grocer. But videotex has a potentially unlimited capacity to store information.

THE FIRST U.S. VIDEOTEX

Videotex was invented in Great Britain in 1970 by a British Post Office employee who wanted to encourage the British to use their telephones more often and increase the Post Office's revenues. Amazingly, the average person in Britain made only about one and a half calls a day in 1970. Most Americans make half a dozen or more calls a day, and people in business use the phones all day long.

As the British tests continued through 1977 and commercial services began in 1979 and early 1980, Warner Communications Cable Corporation (now half owned by American Express and called Warner AMEX Cable) announced the first test of a U.S. videotex-type system. Called QUBE, its testing began over Warner's cable television station in Columbus, Ohio. The cable system had one hundred thousand families as subscribers. QUBE works similarly to videotex, but it sends digital

flows of informatioin along unused cable television channels. And it uses a simple home terminal with just a few buttons. The terminal was designed to look much like a pocket calculator.

QUBE has been called "participatory television" and since 1979 has been used to test viewers' opinions on a wide variety of subjects. In 1980, QUBE viewers were polled after a debate between then-President Jimmy Carter and then-candidate Ronald Reagan. The QUBE viewers thought Reagan was a clear winner while the journalists and pundits thought it was a narrow victory for Carter. Since Reagan won the election it became clear that the QUBE viewers were reflecting the opinions of mainstream voters. Television programs like "Real People" have used QUBE audiences to test their reactions and QUBE viewers' reactions to local Columbus issues are often sought.

Another popular QUBE show is "Columbus Alive!" It carries a TV "tag sale" or "auction on the air," on which a seller can display an item for sale and get from QUBE an instant printed list of viewers who have bid on the item.

QUBE marries the TV and the computer. Four mainframe computers scan the cable system every six seconds, recording which sets are turned on and to which channels they are tuned. The computers automatically bill viewers who watch the interactive programs, which Warner calls "pay-premium" programs. The computer also instantly counts the results of any viewer survey or poll and shows them on the screen. It can also activate fire, burglar, and other emergency alarm services through additional devices, the home terminal and the main computer.

But because QUBE runs on cable television, viewers must pay for what they get. In fact, in any commercial videotex system, viewers will have to pay for many of the services, although advertising is expected to pay for many others. The exact mix of free and paid services is one of the complex marketing questions the major producers were trying to answer during 1983 and 1984. With QUBE, subscribers get regular TV and community programs for a monthly charge. They pay extra for each pay-premium program they watch. And QUBE watching can become expensive. Generally, an average monthly QUBE bill has been between $50 and $60. Since QUBE began operating, it has become clear that viewers are willing to pay for certain premium services, such as exclusive sports shows, but not many are willing to pay special fees for services which can be supported by advertising as well. The number of QUBE subscribers and actual usage has been lower than Warner AMEX expected, and the rate of cancellations has been higher.

QUBE has a further problem: compared to true videotex, its interactive capabilities are limited. Its viewers punch numbers and codes to answer multiple choice questions or signify "Yes" or "No" or "Right" or "Wrong." True videotex allows you to receive or transmit sentences, paragraphs, even long responses, batches of numbers, and computer programs.

THE 1981 KNIGHT-RITTER VIDEOTEX TEST

When Warner expanded its QUBE service to Texas in 1981, Knight-Ritter Newspapers and American Telephone and Telegraph (AT&T) were conducting in Coral Gables, Florida, what was the first and most important test of "true" videotex. From spring, 1980 until early 1981, more than three hundred families tested an AT&T home terminal and a huge information "data base" which Knight-Ritter coordinated.

Knight-Ritter rented space in its mainframe computer to an impressive array of information sources: Consumers Union, Macmillan, Inc. (a major publisher), the Associated Press, Addison-Wesley (an education and computer publisher), *The Economist* magazine of Great Britain, a Miami liquor store, local realtors, J.C. Penney, and many more.

At that time, AT&T had developed two types of terminals: a simple, hand-held, calculatorlike keypad, resembling a Touch-Tone phone, and a regular home computer typewriterlike keyboard. Both used a standard microcomputer, and AT&T made experimental adaptors which were attached to RCA color televisions.

This videotex test made available more than ten thousand "frames" of information and worked like a regular videotex system. It could test or poll consumer reaction like QUBE, but it allowed a lot more interaction. It included simple graphics so users could draw simple pictures on the screen and transmit them to the main computer. It allowed teleshopping, that is, ordering from catalogs, al-

though an AT&T official said that the Florida test did not go far beyond what British videotex had already accomplished. AT&T deliberately kept the test simple and limited to determine how the families felt about the system and what they wanted to use it for.

The potential for videotex use boggles the imagination, but that is precisely its problem. It is so new and filled with such promise that people who are not experienced with computers can not see any practical application for videotex. You need to think of videotex as an electronic Yellow Pages or a thinking telephone that never gives you a wrong number. You can send or receive messages without missing someone because of a wrong number; you can shop from catalogs, or order goods or services at your convenience; you can do most of your banking from your home; you can gain access to huge libraries of information; you can play games; you can read or see the news, sports, weather, and so on. You can do many of your daily tasks from a terminal in your home or office and save a great deal of time and money. Of course, videotex is no substitute for the pleasure of leisurely shopping for a new dress or a night on the town, but it can help alleviate a lot of drudgery.

AT&T and Knight-Ritter evaluated the results of their test in 1981. AT&T was making major changes in its terminals and in 1982 and 1983 participated in an even more significant videotex test in Bergen County, New Jersey, with CBS, Inc. Knight-Ritter, on the other hand, was so encouraged that it began an actual commercial videotex service in Texas in summer, 1983.

THE MOST RECENT AND MOST CRUCIAL VIDEOTEX EXPERIMENTS

Between late 1982 and early 1984, there were about a dozen videotex experiments under way, including these:

- *Dow Jones-Sammons, Park Cities, Texas.* A two-year-old experiment with 130 paying subscribers, this service costs just $12 a month for all services during prime hours (5 A.M. to 9 P.M.), but round-the-clock service costs $40 per month. Financial and investment information, one of the most popular types of information on any system, comes in two levels: one with stock quotations, financial news, and general information, and the second with detailed corporate information, reports from the Securities and Exchange Commission, and economic forecasts.

- *Dow Jones-Vision Cable, Clearwater and Pinellas County, Florida.* This service began in summer, 1982, and offered one free month's service to sixty-five thousand cable subscribers in Clearwater and one hundred thousand potential new subscribers in Pinellas County. A local company, Home Terminal Systems, installs and maintains the home terminals which can be rented, leased, or bought.

- *Dow Jones-Prime Cable, Princeton, New Jersey.* This three-way parrtnership is Dow Jones' showcase of videotex services, and involves Dow Jones, Prime Cable, and the family which owns the local newspaper. It involves eighty-six hundred homes and was not underway in late 1982; it was working by mid-1984. Dow Jones furnishes the mainframe computers, communications, and the marketing, technical training, and support for the system.

- *Times Mirror Cable, Los Angeles, California.* Times Mirror tested a twenty-four-hour-a-day videotex system between March and November, 1982. Of the 350 families involved, 150 used two-way cable TV and 200 used the telephone lines to obtain services such as home banking, teleshopping, airline flight schedules, Associated Press news, sports, weather, real estate listings, stock market listings, computer software, and electronic mail, that is, a direct way to send messages to other subscribers.

- *Keyfax* (*Key to the Facts*). A new national service, it is an electronic teletext (one-way) magazine provided by Keycom Electronic Publishing and Satellite Syndicated Services. Keycom is owned by Centel Corp., Honeywell (the computer and energy management giant), and Field Enterprises which owns major newspapers and TV and radio stations in and around Chicago. Keyfax was tested on WFLD-Chicago between April, 1981 and November, 1982. It delivers one hundred pages of news, sports, business, leisure information, weather and travel conditions for a monthly charge of either $10 or $19.95. It became a national service offered to cable system operators and is delivered by satellite transmission to local cable companies and then is

sent directly to homes through the cable TV wires.

- *Warner AMEX, CompuServe, Columbus, Ohio.* A small extension of the QUBE system, Warner AMEX and CompuServe have tested for a year a two-way system which gives access to CompuServe's wide range of services. These include entertainment, financial information, stock market and commodity data, and flight schedules. The service costs $5 an hour in addition to a cable subscriber's monthly charge of $12.

These tests are significant in that they take videotex one step closer toward becoming a major national service, but the one most people watched closely was the AT&T-CBS test in New Jersey.

AT&T-CBS VIDEOTEX EXPERIMENT

The AT&T-CBS test in Ridgewood, New Jersey, began in the fall of 1982 in two hundred homes and lasted seven months. CBS provided all of the information from a variety of sources, mostly from CBS's own magazines, books, and services, and AT&T provided various types of equipment. Similar to the Coral Gables experiment, the New Jersey test studied audience response to the available services. The New Jersey experiment was free of charge; many experts disagree with this approach because it does not give an accurate view of the services for which people would pay in actual practice.

AT&T decided to test various kinds of equipment. One item was a hand-held, calculatorlike numbered control pad, much like the teletext one-way systems, but with a full keyboard attached as well. This unit connected to a decoder and the home television. The other type was a full home-computerlike terminal with built-in video monitor and signal decoder. Both types handle sixteen colors and the full AT&T-CBS standard alphanumeric character and graphics sets. The information is sent to and received from a large computer through the telephone lines of New Jersey Bell.

Viewers used the system through simple, numbered menus, which helped novices learn to use the system faster, but they also could use "key words" which let you gain access to specific information by simply entering a word or series of words. This type of shortcut has been found, in similar videotex or home information systems, to be very helpful in sharply reducing the amount of time it takes to find the information you want. This rapid response time is thought to be necessary to keep people interested in using the services. Key words are easy to remember and eliminate the time-consuming task of stepping through menu after menu.

CBS offered a wide spectrum of information services, but none were out of the ordinary compared to other experiments.

THE FIRST MAJOR COMMERCIAL SERVICE

In mid-1983, Knight-Ritter, through its Viewdata Corporation of American subsidiary, and AT&T began the first major commercial videotex service in Miami based on its two-year test in Coral Gables. As this is written in early 1984, it is too early to tell exactly which services will be offered and at what price. But it surely has news, weather, sports, financial information, catalog shopping, home banking, and similar services. The cost per month to be charged is also not known.

One thing is certain: experts predict the videotex market in the home will total $10 billion a year by 1990, and that is just the beginning. By the year 2000, there will be 100 million separate households in the U.S. and almost half of them will be paying $40 to $50 a month for various videotex services, according to expert predictions. And the supporting market for information, services, equipment, maintenance, and the like will be in the tens of billions of dollars a year. As we will see later in the book, the videotex system will, however, be completely integrated into a component home computer/communications/entertainment system, and the system will be as easy to use as today's television or microwave oven. You will probably also be able to speak to it and it will speak back to you as well. And it will probably cost (in 1982 dollars) less than $500.

THE CURRENT HOME
INFORMATION UTILITIES

But you have a further surprise in store. While the communications giants tread slowly and softly into home information services, two home information utilities have offered commercial services for more than three years. In short, you do not have to wait until your cable company starts a QUBE-like system, or a large TV network offers teletext, or a communications giant mass-produces home terminals and works with major communications conglomerates to assemble huge libraries.

The SOURCE from Source Telecomputing Corporation of America (owned by Readers Digest) and Compuserv from CompuServe Information Services (owned by H&R Block, Inc.—yes, the income tax return preparation company) already provide three libraries. The SOURCE has about thirty thousand subscribers, and Compuserv has more than one hundred thousand subscribers almost all professionals, major corporations, and small business owners. The SOURCE, with a phone call and your home computer and a communications device called a *modem,* links you with national and international news, more than three thousand computer programs, a sophisticated electronic mail system, a travel club, a very large electronic shopping service, national real estate locator services, major stock and commodities market information, and access to word processing and computer languages.

Compuserv provides a nationwide community bulletin board service, dozens of computer games, shop-at-home services, corporate financial information, encyclopedia and dictionary services, airline schedules, ticket ordering, and more.

However, the main drawback of these services is the expense. They require users to pay by the minute or hour, and inexperienced users find the services quickly become expensive. Only electronic mail sent or received at off-peak hours appears to be cost effective for most people, and the traffic is heavy on both systems at 6 P.M. when the price drops more than one-third. Electronic mail is cost effective because it eliminates "telephone tag," that is, the seemingly endless round of calls business people make trying to reach each other. With electronic mail, you send a typed mesage to someone's electronic "mailbox." It waits in the box for the recipient to retrieve it. The sender only sends one message one time without busy signals, lost messages, call backs, wrong numbers, or extraneous conversation. And electronic mail costs less than one-third as much as the cheapest coast-to-coast telephone call.

Electronic mail is the perfect use for home computers and telecommunications, especially consumer-to-business communications. If you have a question about a bill or a complaint about service, you may one day be able to send electronic messages to the correct representative and get an answer without any hassles. Best of all, I believe, you will not have to "call" between 9 A.M. and 5 P.M. You can send messages at your convenience, even if that's midnight.

What's more, you can use these services with a simple home terminal and a modem. Both services work through the telephone lines and a telephone modem (short for modulator-demodulator). A modem takes a stream of digital information from a home computer, translates it into telephone signals, and transmits it to another modem inside each company's mainframe computer. The telephone networks both use are the Tymshare and Telenet communication networks and *packet-switching* services. Packet-switching services send very rapid bursts of digital information along long-distance telephone lines, microwave transmitters, or satellites. The information transmission occurs in *packets* in between the pulses of signals carrying telephone calls. In Chapter 11 you'll see how easily you can hook up to these two home information utilities and take advantage of the amazing amounts of information you can control now.

THE ADVANCED EIES TELECOMMUNICATIONS CONCEPT

People who subscribe to the two home information utilities overwhelmingly favor electronic mail and community bulletin boards. It appears that people prefer to use the services to keep in touch with their friends and colleagues in distant places rather than pay premium prices for information or computer games. Both services have recently borrowed an advanced concept which allows someone to talk electronically to someone else directly. Compuserv has a "CB" function similar to citizens band radio which allows small groups of people to establish private networks. The SOURCE has a similar, although somewhat more advanced, direct communication function.

In this case, however, EIES can do much more than a CB's electronic "ears." EIES stands for Electronic Information Exchange System, a remarkable computer network founded by Dr. Murray Turoff at the New Jersey Institute of Technology. With EIES, people can talk, leave messages, hold conferences, write articles, academic papers, and proposals, and generally carry out most normal social activities by hooking up to the computer network at the same time. EIES began, in 1977, to experiment with computerized conferencing and personal information networks among groups of people with varied professional, business, and personal interests. Each EIES user links to a minicomputer through a modem and an inexpensive terminal/printer without a videoscreen, or a personal computer or terminal with a TV screen and printer.

Since 1977, EIES has become, as Turoff says, "a blooming, buzzing garden" of social activities. Computer communication through EIES has shown that people and their natural sociability triumph over distance, time, and computers. EIES has become a microcosm of society, but it has also created new ways for people to work together and relate to each other. EIES users send birthday, wedding, and holiday wishes, share vacation plans, and announce births, deaths, and other family events through the system. And many people have checked the EIES directory to find dinner companions when they visit new cities. Inevitably, spouses and children of EIES members use the system to share ways to cope with spouses addicted to EIES.

But EIES is only the largest of dozens of electronic information exchanges which have sprung up during the past five years as home computer owners have formed small networks to share information about computers, play interactive computer games, and act as community bulletin boards for people with similar interests. In the future, I believe groups of people with similar or shared interests will form major networks. It has been shown that people with specific requirements or serious interests in information available on a network tend to use the service many times more frequently than someone who is not seriously interested in anything other than computer games. A group of five thousand stamp collectors, antique car buffs, square dancers, or any other group of hobbyists could start its own EIES network and operate it for a few dollars per member per month. Experts believe lawyers, physicians, researchers, writers, government officials, stock and bond traders, and other professionals will be the first to start EIES-like networks.

THE INTEGRATED VIDEO TERMINAL

Would you want a $1,000 machine that combines a television, videocassette recorder, cassette tape, printer, telephone modem, and a home computer? Sony, Matsushita (Panasonic and Quasar), and Zenith are well on their way to providing you with this kind of machine, but it is not one unit. The first round in the battle of the *integrated video terminal* (IVT) has been launched with the Sony-pioneered concept of component TV. These three companies now offer high-priced TV components which include a high-resolution color monitor, two stereo speakers, a unit into which plug home computers, record turntables, audio equipment, videocassette recorders, videodisc players, and much more.

A few years ago, it was thought the major TV manufacturers would incorporate all of these electronic entertainment devices into one unit. Since then, it has become clear that consumers want to pick and choose their systems, much like the stereo component business. So, manufacturers are responding with component TVs into which one can add new devices as money becomes available and interest increases. This is certainly more profitable for the manufacturers. And the price is higher than $1,000, although not that much higher if you factor inflation into the 1979 estimate of $1,000. The price of home computers is down to about $200 for a good unit, TV prices have remained stable or dropped sharply for the past ten years, and stereo prices have fallen in real terms. Technically, nothing prevents any computer, TV, or electronics manufacturer from offering these systems for $1,000 to $2,000. The IVT has begun to enter U.S. homes, perhaps a little more slowly than predicted, but the home computer boom which exploded in 1982 means you will probably own an IVT-style system by the late 1980s—sooner if the economy continues to improve in late 1984 and 1985.

COMPLETING THE CIRCLE

You will have to be patient to buy an inexpensive IVT system, but you can create your own now. Experts say that the number of computers in U.S. homes more than doubled in 1983 alone to more than 2 million. That number is expected to double again in 1984, again in 1985, and so forth until the end of the decade. Commodore International is selling more than 150,000 of its VIC-20 computers per month. Timex is getting one hundred thousand inquiries *per week* for its $79.95 Timex Sinclair 1000 computer. Atari shipped more than 500,000 home computers in 1983.

This rapidly increasing number of home computer owners is discovering they can do much more than play simple games, or keep track of recipes or a checkbook with a home computer. In fact, literally thousands of programs are available for home computers, and we list more than two thousand of them in the back of this book. Owners have realized their home computers open up doors of creativity, learning, and sharing they never knew existed.

When I think of all the fantastic ways to use a home computer I have seen or heard about during the past five years, I believe I have answered my friend's question, "Home computers? What good are they?" I will explore hundreds of other ways to answer that question in the rest of this book. We'll see how home computers and home information systems were first developed; we'll examine in detail all the home computers now on the market; we'll see how to use all the existing home information services; we'll examine 105 things to do with a home computer, including educating your children, running your business, and helping handicapped persons; and we'll peer into a crystal ball and predict how, in 1995, we'll wonder how we ever lived the way we do without our home computers.

CHAPTER 2
What Is a Home Computer?

Since 1972, the public has slowly but surely made friends with the computer. We first got acquainted with pocket calculators. The first ones introduced in the early seventies were bulky and could only add, subtract, multiply, and divide. But calculators were rapidly taught to perform dozens of scientific and financial functions, they were added to watches and clocks, and they became smaller and smaller and thinner and thinner. Today, more than 75 million people own or use pocket calculators, and even schoolchildren would not try to do their math homework or a husband or wife pay the family's monthly bills without the help of an inexpensive calculator. No one thinks of a pocket calculator as something forbidding and uncontrollable. On the contrary, calculators speed things up, allowing bookkeepers to complete more accurate figures and businessmen to study more thoroughly the financial health of their businesses. Advanced calculators, such as the programmable ones made by Texas Instruments, Hewlett-Packard, Unisonic, Casio and others, make everyone a mathematical wizard.

A programmable calculator is simply one that you can instruct—that is, program—to perform calculations. These calculations can be as simple as doing percentages or as complicated as navigating a sailboat by the stars. Both Texas Instruments and Hewlett-Packard free you from instructing the cal-culator yourself; they offer preprogrammed magnetic strips and modules. Each module (those made by Texas Instruments are called *Solid-State Modules*) comes with twenty to twenty-five different sets of instructions, or *programs,* inside. Each set is a step-by-step group of formulas designed to carry out a specific function, such as determining mortgage rates and monthly payments. To use a program, you just slip the module into the back of the calculator and follow the easy instructions. You usually press two numbers to indicate the program you want to use and enter the figures.

You can also write your own programs using a programmable calculator and permanently save them on the magnetic strips, called *magnetic cards* or *program cards* made by Hewlett-Packard. The thin strip is made of plastic coated with a thin magnetlike substance on one side. You can store your instructions on a card because the calculator very rapidly "prints" them with a magnetic footprint after you slip a card into the card reader slot. The calculator prints the instructions, or *program steps,* in magnetic pulses rather than printed numbers or letters. And the program will remain stored on that magnetic card as long as you protect it. (Rubbing a magnet over it or exposing it to a spark of electricity could, of course, damage or destroy the program.)

Now that you know just this much about pocket

Figure 2. The tiny silicon chip in the upper left corner—the little square smaller than the fingertip—replaces the large stack of transistors piled on the table. The silicon chip made possible the hand-held calculator shown in the photograph. The chip's descendants form the "brains" of the modern microcomputer. (Courtesy of Texas Instruments, Inc.)

instantly, but a computer is. Regardless of how fast a computer operates, or how large its "brain" and memory become, no serious scientists ever expect a computer to be as smart as you were the day you were born. Scientists could build a computer right now that could remember as much as one human brain. According to physicist Robert Jastrow, this computer would take up as much space as the 102-story Empire State Building, consume one billion watts of electricity, and cost more than $10 billion to build. And Jastrow says it would still not be anything like a human brain; it would be a clumsy imitation at best. A computer will never be in awe of a sunset or fall in love, despite what science fiction movies have been frightening us with for years.

In fact, any computer, no matter how large or how small, is an idiot. It's dumb, stupid, and inert until you tell it what to do, or program it just like a pocket calculator. A computer is simply a machine that can do hundreds of things for you. Unlike your coffee pot or your washing machine, a computer is a general-purpose machine, and a very versatile one at that. You might call it a jack-of-all-trades and master of none. It becomes a master only through your instructions. But because it's so versatile, a computer is not just another gadget; it's a mind appliance. Just as a simple calculator now speeds up writing checks and balancing your checkbook, your home computer will increase by many times the speed and efficiency with which you plan your household budget or enable you to prepare a household budget for the first time. Doing a budget and keeping track of it every month can be drudgery. But with an inexpensive home budget management program (dozens of good ones are on the market for the various machines), you simply enter numbers into a few columns and let the computer do the drudge work for you.

In short, your own computer can be a useful mechanical servant that can enable you to spend your time in more fulfilling and satisfying ways. It can be a home administration center, a home information service, or a home information utility. Within a few years—or right now, in some parts of the country—you can connect a home computer to your bank, grocery store, newspaper, favorite magazine, and your business, all at the same time for a price you can afford. In the past, machines have freed our muscles from unpleasant labors; in the

calculators, you already understand the basics of a home computer. In fact, a computer is nothing more than a machine that performs calculations. The primary and most substantial difference between the calculations of a home computer and a pocket calculator, or even the math you do with a pencil and paper, is speed and sophistication.

A home computer can perform thousands, even millions, of calculations in one second. A sophisticated pocket calculator can do hundreds of calculations a second, and whether you realize it or not, your brain does calculations faster than either a computer or calculator. But your brain would rather do other more useful and pleasurable things, like use your eyes to see a beautiful portrait, your hands to hold a newborn baby, or your voice to sing a song.

Your brain neither wants nor is trained to do thousands of mathematical formulas practically present, home computers can free our minds of mental drudgery; in the future, home computers will free our minds, run our machines, and much more.

FAMILIARITY BREEDS SUCCESS

A home computer is made up of elements with which we're already well acquainted, although we don't call them by these names: input/output devices, such as a video monitor and a keyboard; a mass storage device, such as a cassette tape recorder; a microprocessor and memory.

You probably know how to use a typewriter; most home computers have typewriterlike keyboards through which you tell the computer what to do, or interact with them. Telling the computer what to do or what information to store or manipulate is called *input,* and a typewriterlike keyboard is called an *input device.*

You also know what a television set is. The most common *output* device for a home computer is a home television set, linked to the computer through a radio frequency (RF) modulator, a small device that looks like a small thin box with antenna wires sticking out of it. Other televisionlike output devices are called CRTs (cathode ray tubes), and video monitors or screens. These are special televisions which cannot receive regular TV broadcasts, but which can produce high-resolution and high-quality color, black-and-white, black-and-green, or black-and-yellow video displays. The most popular monitors have color pictures while the least expensive have black-and-white displays. In fact, if you don't want to hook up your home computer to your television (to avoid family squabbles when you want to watch the Super Bowl and your daughter wants to play Space Invaders), you can buy a black-and-white monitor for less than $100, or a second television.

The third essential element is a *mass storage device.* You may own a small cassette tape recorder and a few blank cassette tapes. If you do, you already have a home computer's basic mass storage device. An inexpensive cassette tape is the easiest way to store sets of instructions—programs—and information outside of your home computer.

Most home computers do not have enough memory to store all the programs and informa-

tion—also called *data*—you want to keep. And most home computers lose their memory and all the information you have so diligently fed them when you turn them off. This occurs because information and programs you load into a home computer are stored in *temporary internal memory* called *RAM* for *random access memory.* RAM is *volatile,* that is, a steady flow of electricity keeps it "alive" or active. Remove the flow of electricity and the information and programs stored as electrical pulses disappear.

So you must preserve the information and programs outside the computer. Just as you can save pocket calculator instructions on a magnetic strip, you can save information in your home computer on a cassette tape because both the tape and the strip are made of substantially the same materials, magnetized, metallic oxide-coated plastic.

When you send data to a cassette tape from a home computer, the machine changes electronic pulses inside the computer into the magnetic signals the cassette tape can "understand." Computerized data actually turn into audio signals, but if you play the tape, you wouldn't hear anything, because the signals are not in a form that the human ear can interpret. But a home computer's brain can interpret them.

Cassette tapes, however, are not the most reliable way to store computer data for several reasons:

1. The quality of the tape manufacture does not often meet the rigorous standards required for electronic signals.
2. Static and noise easily accumulates on the tape, damaging or destroying electronic signals.
3. Cassettes are slow because they can send and receive only one signal after the other. They are *serial* storage mechanisms which means they must do one step at a time in 1,2,3, order. This is opposed to *random* storage, which means a device can receive or send information in any order one desires.

A cassette tape recorder runs 1⅞ inches per second and can store (also called *read*) or load (also called *write*) 300 pieces of electronic information per second. These pieces are called *bits,* and bits per second is called *baud,* so when you read or hear someone say a storage device reads at 300 or 4800 baud, you'll know he is discussing how fast a home computer can send or receive information.

A much faster, more reliable, and more expensive mass storage device is called a *disk,* and the device that runs the disk is called a *disk drive.* A disk looks much like a phonograph record and comes in several standard sizes: 8-inch (called a *floppy disk*), 5.25-inch (called a *minifloppy disk*), and a new 3.5-inch (called a *microfloppy disk*). These disks are called *floppy* because they are flexible and bend easily. (Sony introduced the first commercial 3.5-inch disk drive, but Hitachi and several American companies were also experimenting with 3.25- and 3-inch disks in 1984. A variation on the Sony version, however, is expected to become the standard for microfloppy disks.) It is made of metallic oxide-coated plastic and has tracks and sectors within which magnetic impulses are stored in bits.

Floppy disks store from about 70,000 to more than 3 million combinations of bits called *bytes.* A byte is nothing more than an organized group of eight bits which a standard microcomputer can recognize. In computer jargon, approximately 1,000 bytes is called 1K. (K stands for 1,024, or the number 2 raised to the 10th power, in scientific terms.) Thus, 64K is actually equal to 65,536 bytes of information.

A disk drive can read and write computer bytes at very high speeds, up to hundreds of thousands of baud. Disks also use random access to read or write information; that is, you can reach any information stored on a disk directly and quickly without the laborious and slow process of reading in a 1,2,3 or serial fashion. Using your keyboard, you can tell your computer which program you want to retrieve from the disk, and the computer will instruct the disk drive to read that particular program regardless of its location on the disk. It could be the first program or the fiftieth, or located on track one or on track seventy-eight, and the computer will, through your commands, call it up immediately. A cassette tape recorder can't do this. To get to program fifty, you have to read past or load all forty-nine other programs into the computer. This could take several minutes or longer. A random access disk drive can do it all in seconds.

Many people buying their first computer use a tape recorder because it is inexpensive (a good $50 recorder or one sold by the computer manufacturer will do well), and new cassettes cost as little as $1 each. Minifloppy disk drives start at about $279 and go up to $645, and each floppy disk costs about $4–$5.

Many home computer manufacturers, such as Atari and Commodore, use special plug-in cartridges like those used for video games, or, in the case of Texas Instruments, Solid-State Modules, the more sophisticated brothers of the modules for the TI 59 programmable calculators. These cartridges are another form of magnetic medium for storing and loading programs and data. Each one is different and cannot be used interchangeably with any other machine—at least not yet. In fact, the manufacturers do not want you to be able to exchange their programs easily because developing programs is very expensive and they seek to recover their costs and make a substantial profit. The home computer business is also becoming more and more like the razor business; the hardware (the razor) is becoming cheaper and cheaper to buy, so manufacturers must try to make their profits on the programs (the razor blades).

The cartridges do have a lot of advantages for consumers. They load very easily, and they require less knowledge of computer operations and fewer instructions to use them than either cassettes or floppy disks. They are also harder to damage than cassettes or disks.

The fourth essential element in a home computer is its *memory.* Obviously, a mass storage device is one kind of computer memory because it records and stores, in a permanent form, programs and information. But computers have another, essential kind of memory within the computer itself. This *internal memory* determines the computing power of each home computer, and there are many kinds of configurations of computer memory.

The internal computer memory cannot function without the fifth essential element, the computer's *microprocessor.* The microprocessor is simply an electronic device that receives information from the outside world, performs calculations upon it, and sends out results. Any microprocessor, made of three basic parts—a Central Processing Unit (CPU), input/output ports, and memory—performs the calculations for the computer and makes sure that information is received, processed, and returned in its proper order. To complete a home computer, you need only add a power supply—reg-

Figure 3. The parts of a computer are clearly shown in this photograph of an IBM PCjr home computer. The keyboard is the primary input device; the video display the primary output device. In the center of the screen is a single disk drive with the system's power supply in the cabinet. The printer is also an output device. The computer's microprocessor and internal memory are in the same box as the power supply and disk drive. (Courtesy of International Business Machines)

ular home electric current—and a clock, usually a tiny quartz clock, inside the microprocessor. All these elements, most of them familiar electronic objects, combine to form a home computer. The combination of elements, with the unique capability of the microprocessor, creates computer power you can easily learn about and use at home.

Comparing a computer to a human body is an easy way to understand how a home computer is put together. However, don't take the comparison literally; people are thousands of times smarter and more complex than any computer. The microprocessor is the brain; the computer memory is like our brain's memory, although much less sophisticated and smaller. The power supply is the heart pumping electronic signals, or blood. The input device is like our feet, hands, eyes, nose, and ears through which we feel, touch, see, smell, and hear the world. A computer, however, can only "see" electronic pulses. An output device is like our voice through which we speak.

When we use our hands to type or paint, they, too, become output devices. What they produce—letters or pictures—are like mass storage, which could be returned to the computer. The console or cabinet in which a computer sits and the television

set or video monitor are like our legs, upper torsos, and skulls. Although the individual parts may be interesting and useful in their own limited ways, it's the way all the parts combine, the *synergy,* that makes a human or a computer a fascinating and wonderful creation.

HOME COMPUTER, PERSONAL COMPUTER, OR MICROCOMPUTER?

As your interest in *home computers* grows, you'll soon read and hear the terms *personal computer* and *microcomputer.* And many computer owners fiercely debate which is the correct term for this new machine. The three names are essentially interchangeable: a home computer is a personal computer is a microcomputer. In this book, we'll define the terms for the sake of clarity, but we will stick with the term *home computer* most of the time.

A home computer very properly is predominantly used at home by the whole family for entertainment, home financial management, household appliance control, an information utility, home business, home administration and record keeping, home education, or any other use that occurs through the home and family. In today's rapidly changing market, a home computer is considered by industry and marketing experts to be a machine that costs less than $1,000, such as the Atari 400, Commodore VIC-20, Radio Shack TRS-80 Color Computer, the Texas Instruments 99/4A, the Panasonic 3000, and so on.

A personal computer, on the other hand, is used mainly by one individual for sophisticated computing and hobby applications, such as machine language programming, or a business person who predominantly uses the computer at his or her desk for individual job functions. Personal computers, for several years now, have been defined as the Apple II Plus, the Osborne 1, the TRS-80 Model III, the IBM Personal Computer, the Sony SMC-70, and literally hundreds of types of computers which sell for less than $2,500.

Still, tens of thousands of people use Apple IIs and IBM PCs at home, so what distinguishes the home from the personal computer is how and where an owner or family uses them.

The term *microcomputer* has a definite, technical meaning. According to Dr. Rodney Zaks, a noted microcomputer pioneer, a microcomputer is a computer whose central processing unit (CPU) works from a microprocessor. The CPU and the microprocessor are self-contained. In its simplest form, a microcomputer has its basic building blocks on a single microprocessor. Here lies the difference between a computer and a calculator: a calculator has no central processing unit or microprocessor. So within every home or personal computer there is a microcomputer.

Bell Laboratories scientists discovered that some substances, particularly modified silicon, are semiconductors of electricity—that is, they can either conduct electricity or insulate, or even raise or lower the flow of electricity, depending on temperatures, pressures, and methods of construction.

The scientists called these materials *transistors,* combining "transfer" and "resistors." They could make transistors very small. Of the first transistors, two hundred could fit inside the old radio and television tubes, called vacuum tubes. (They are called vacuum tubes because the flow of electricity occurs in a vacuum.) Semiconductor transistors are called *solid-state* because electricity flows through the semiconductor material, not across a vacuum.

Solid-state transistors have had an incredible impact. You've known about transistor radios since the late 1950s. Your television has been a solid-state one since the 1960s. In the early 1970s, watchmakers crammed two thousand transistors inside a watch face and produced the first digital watch. The first electronic calculator had more than six thousand transistors, the first electronic game more than four thousand, and so on.

As marvelous as these devices are, they are not computers. During this development, engineers were also using solid-state transistors to make computers smaller, faster, and more powerful. But the computer industry and computer users wanted ever smaller and more powerful computers. After years of effort, engineers found a way to produce thousands of transistors using wafers of silicon, the basic building block of sand.

To produce a semiconducting microprocessor with a wafer requires many sophisticated technical processes. Silicon is first purified in a hot furnace. Then, a silicon wafer is treated with certain acids, some of which create positive charges and others of which create negative charges on the wafer. This makes the silicon electrically "alive." Putting thousands of transistors into one wafer is called *large-scale integration,* or LSI. The first semiconductor transistors were SSI, small-scale integration; later ones were MSI, medium-scale integration. Today, as scientists seek the million-transistor wafer, engineers use VLSI, very large-scale integration.

You would need a powerful microscope to study an LSI circuit. But designing each integrated circuit and microprocessor starts with a huge drafting board, perhaps as large as an entire wall. In what looks like a highway system designed by a maniac, the engineers painstakingly plot each transistor and make each connection. And since each transistor and connection is dedicated to performing just one logical function, the engineers must make sure their design is perfect.

THE MICROPROCESSOR BRAIN

Years ago, one of my favorite science fiction movies was *Donovan's Brain,* in which a human brain was kept alive outside of the dead owner's body. The brain went berserk and took over the body of another human being, and in the end, both the new body and the old brain were destroyed to save mankind. Needless to say, a brain on the loose scared a lot of children and some adults.

With computer brains, however, we don't ever have to worry about their getting loose. Yet you can roughly compare the five basic parts of a microprocessor "brain" or a microprocessor-on-a-chip to the parts of the human brain. As we've noted, the five basic parts of a microprocessor are: CPU, input/output (I/O) ports (or electronic openings), memory, clock, and power supply.

The CPU can be thought of as the central nervous system monitored by the pituitary gland. The memory corresponds to our own memories. The I/O ports correspond to our nerve endings and senses. The power supply is our digestive system and blood, veins, and arteries, or circulatory system. And the clock corresponds to our internal sense of time.

Like our brains, the computer's CPU and memory cells are contained in very, very small areas. That's why these processors and computers are called *micros,* from the Greek word for small. All the parts of a microprocessor are contained on a slice, or wafer, of silicon smaller than a thumbnail.

Simple microprocessors have thousands of electronic elements—transistors, capacitors, and circuits—etched on a tiny wafer. Experts say that in 1985, a microprocessor will have 1,000,000 infinitesimal elements. Today, several Japanese companies and IBM, Bell Labs, Texas Instruments, and other American companies have perfected microprocessors with 256,000 elements, and are close to 512,000-element models, although the latter are not yet commercially available. A million-element microprocessor will be more than 250 times smarter than the smartest electronic video game, 100 times more powerful than the most popular computer on the market now, and 8 times smarter than a large IBM 370 mainframe computer.

In Agatha Christie's mystery novels, her eccentric Belgian detective hero, Hercule Poirot, solved murders by using his "little gray cells." Computer brains have little gray cells, too, but they are called *integrated circuits,* or ICs. Integrated circuits, first made in the 1960s, result when a silicon wafer is connected to a ceramic or plastic shelter. The ceramic shelter acts like a skull, and tiny paths or circuits lead from the wafer—on which sits the mi-

croprocessor or microcomputer—to pins protruding from the bottom of the ceramic piece. The pins—the wafer's nerve endings—connect I/O ports on the wafer to the outside world so the microprocessor can send and receive information.

The microprocessor on the wafer would not be possible without what has probably become the most important invention in the second half of the twentieth century: the semiconductor. Within the letter "o" in the word transistor, each semiconducting wafer has 5,000 transistors. And each wafer is less than ¼ inch square.

A completed wafer is called a *chip.* Contrary to popular belief, a chip is not the black plastic or ceramic rectangular IC which plugs into a slot inside the computer. Rather it is the piece of silicon itself. The completed object with the chip inside, the ceramic shell, and the pins is an integrated circuit.

Each integrated circuit relays electronic signals very rapidly because the tiny pathways are so very close together. With the first SSI circuits, calculations took place in thousandths of a second. In today's microcomputers, calculations are performed in billionths of a second, a time so short and in an area so small as to confound the imagination.

In 1971, Texas Instruments developed the first microcomputer-on-a-chip by placing more than fifteen thousand transistors with all of the elements of a computer onto an area less than 1/20th inch square. The first practical microcomputer, as we know them today, was not developed until 1974. By the end of 1975, the race to develop the best home computer had begun.

THE COMPUTER'S CENTRAL NERVOUS SYSTEM

If the microprocessor is the computer's brain, then its Central Processing Unit (CPU) is its central nervous system. The CPU consists of a control unit, a group of circuits which process information or data; storage registers; an arithmetic logic unit (ALU); and circuits that control the clock that makes every operation work in sequence.

The data control unit calls up—or FETCHES, in computer language—instructions called *words* from the computer's memory. The unit then figures

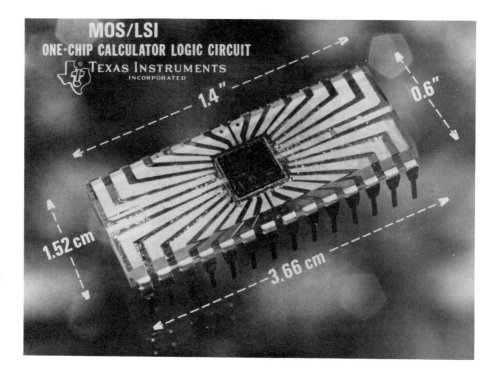

MOS/LSI
ONE-CHIP CALCULATOR LOGIC CIRCUIT
TEXAS INSTRUMENTS
INCORPORATED

1.4"
0.6"
1.52 cm
3.66 cm

Figure 4. Photograph of the first microprocessor-on-a-chip developed by Texas Instruments in 1971. The chip itself is the small square in the center of the packaging. Also shown are the wires embedded in the ceramic which lead to the input/output pins. (Courtesy of Texas Instruments)

out or interprets the instructions and follows through on, or EXECUTES, them.

A word in computer language is simply a logical set of electronic pulses which a computer treats as a single unit. For example, the English alphabet has twenty-six letters, which we organize into words. English combinations or words then mean something to anyone who speaks English. The same holds true of computer words. However, every word in a computer language is the same length.

The CPU also has many different registers. Each register holds information for the control unit and performs different tasks. The CPU moves information and instructions properly among the CPU, its individual units, I/O devices such as the keyboard, the video monitor and the disk drive or cartridge, and memory.

Of the ten different kinds of registers, the most important are the accumulator and the ALU. The accumulator does what its name implies: it accumulates each piece or pulse of electronic information before it is sent into another register for processing. When one process is completed, the new information or the old data unchanged is returned through the accumulator for rerouting. In short, the accumulator acts like the center of the nervous system.

The ALU adds, subtracts, and performs logical operations on computer information in the shape of words. The ALU places each word or operation in a different register, adds to, subtracts from, or logically compares each word to another, and then puts the results into a new register. If the addition, subtraction, or operation fills up or empties a register, the result is "carried" to the next register.

The operation inside the ALU and the accumulator is like the one that occurs when you add two one-digit numbers (7 and 8, for example) and get a total of 10 or more (15). We all learned in grade school that when you add 9 and 1, you put the resulting 0 in the ones column and carry the 1 to the tens column. That's the decimal or Base One system of mathematics we borrowed from the Arabs who developed it in medieval times. The way a microcomputer adds and subtracts is even simpler.

BITS AND BYTES TURN INTO WORDS

The microcomputer numbering system is based on the binary or Base Two system. There are only two numbers—1 and 0—when you count in binary. This is because electricity, which provides the power for a computer, can exist in only one of two states, off or on, dormant or flowing. When you add in the binary system, you always add ones to zeros. And instead of carrying to the tens column, you carry to the twos column.

For example, add 0 and 0 in the binary system. You get 0. Add 1 and 0. You get 1. But add 1 and 1. Under the decimal system, the answer would be 2, but in the binary system, the answer is 10—you carry the 1 to the twos column.

The accompanying figure shows you how to add 2 and 2 in the binary system:

		4	2	1	BINARY VALUES
DECIMAL					
2		1	1	0	10
+2	=	+0	+1	+0	=	+10
4		=1	0	0	100

Add 2 plus 1 in binary. The result is 011. Add 4 plus 4. The result is 1000, because you have to carry the 1 to the fourth column. And so on.

Microcomputers use the binary numbering system because electronic signals, like any other electric signal, can exist only off or on. When we discuss how computers conduct memory and data transfer, we use binary numbers—1 and 0—to represent off and on. A register, transistor, capacitor, or other electronic function within an integrated circuit or CPU has changed states—from on to off or off to on. These two states and the number symbols are also called *binary digits,* or *bits.*

As we noted, combinations of bits are called *words.* Words are used as a standard package or bundle for transmitting electronic information among computers and their ancillary devices. The first generation of home computers used, as their standard package or bundle, words 8 bits long. Eight-bit words are called *bytes.* The Apple II Plus and IIe, the Commodore 64, the VIC-20, the Atari 800 and 1200 also used 8-bit word lengths. This is, their CPUs could understand only packages of computer data 8 bits or 1 byte long. The second generation of home and personal computers, however, such as the IBM PCjr, the IBM PC itself, and their dozens of emulators, used 16-bit or 2-byte word lengths.

The bit and byte lengths or combinations determine how powerful a microprocessor is, how much internal memory its CPU can "address" or transmit data to, how speedily it can carry out its functions, and how rapidly it can address or talk to video monitors, disk drives, and so forth. In actuality, all the CPU can really do is add, subtract, and carry out logical operations (and, or, not and, not or) by switching bit combinations on and off. But a computer can switch thousands of bits on and off in a few millionths of a second. Further, each bit and each byte is designed to have a logical function, such as sending signals to or receiving them from a video monitor, a disk drive, a cassette tape, a plug-in cartridge, a printer, or any other I/O device. The *word length* determines how much information a CPU can receive through its I/O ports at one time. In short, a 1-byte word length can send only half as much information as a 2-byte word length. Compare this process to pouring water through a funnel. Although rules of physics are involved, obviously you can pour twice as much water, in the same time, down a funnel with an opening two inches wide as one with a one-inch-wide opening. This is basically, although technically not precisely, why a 16-bit computer has more power, capacity, and capability than an 8-bit computer.

BUS STOP

As you may have realized, because of its binary language, a CPU can perform only two basic operations, FETCH and EXECUTE. In the fetch operation, information or instructions in word length form are called up and placed in a register through the ALU and the accumulator. In the execute operation, computer words are added to or subtracted from other words and the result is returned through the accumulator and ALU to an output device through a *port.*

To get from the CPU to the output device, the signal must go through a physical connection called a *bus.* A bus is a group of circuits that make up the correct path between a CPU and an I/O device, or a CPU and other memory.

There are two basic kinds of buses: bidirectional data buses and address buses. (The plural of bus is buses, not busses, which would mean multiple kisses. I don't know of anyone who likes to kiss a computer.) The latter usually control signals between memory and I/O devices. The former, the more important, is made of the same number of lines or circuits as the word length: so, 8-bit CPUs have 8 lines, 16-bit CPUs have 16 lines. It carries data back and forth among the CPU, memory, and I/O devices.

(Note, however, that the IBM PC's CPU, the

8088 from Intel Corporation, is a hybrid 16-bit CPU. Its internal operations have a 16-bit word length, but its bus to its I/O devices is only 8-bits wide. This means it processes information faster than an 8-bit computer, but cannot transfer the information back and forth among devices much, if any, faster. Newer models of IBM PC-compatible computers made by other companies use the Intel 80186 or 80286 CPU which does have a 16-bit bus.)

If the bus were not bidirectional—able to carry messages back and forth through the same circuit—an 8-bit MPU would require 16 lines, 8 to carry information to the CPU and 8 to send it out of the CPU. Without a control line, however, back-and-forth signals would collide on the same line; for this reason, one of the 8 lines is used to tell the outside devices whether the bus is sending or receiving information.

BANKS FOR THE MEMORY

We've said a lot about how a home computer's memory does the same thing as our own memories—stores information. We know that our memories are made of "little gray cells." But what is a computer memory? A computer memory is nothing more than a semiconductor integrated circuit specifically designed to store large quantities of digital signals in an on or off state. A memory chip is largely thousands of on-off registers.

Two basic types of microcomputer memory exist: RAM and ROM. RAM is *random access memory.* It allows you to "write" data words into any memory location and to "read" data words, or receive information or instructions, from any memory location. Further, it is usually *volatile,* that is, it temporarily stores the data as long as it receives a continuing flow of electricity from a power supply; it must be constantly *refreshed.* It is also called *internal memory.* (There are nonvolatile RAMs, but they essentially have battery-backed power supplies connected to them at all times.)

ROM is *read only memory;* it permanently stores information or instructions placed in it when the chip is made. You can only "read" information or data words from it, not write or change it. You cannot write into or send instructions to a ROM memory.

RAM is the most versatile and the most commonly used in home computers because it makes a computer into a general-purpose tool. When you load programs into a computer from a floppy disk, cartridge, or cassette tape, the program instructions are temporarily stored in RAM. When you interact with, manipulate, add to, or change the programs or information, the additions or changes are temporarily stored in RAM. if you use an income tax program, for example, you will load the program first from a tape or disk. Instructions will appear on the TV or videoscreen. As soon as you hit the keyboard and enter numbers and letters, those entries not only appear on the screen, but are simultaneously stored in the temporary RAM or internal memory. You permanently store new data and changes on the tape or floppy disk.

ROM is most often used to permanently store often-used sets of instructions and programs. Each home computer must "know" how to start operating (called *booting* or start-up) and respond to your first commands. This "knowledge" is stored on ROM chips, and the computer automatically executes these programs by calling them from ROM and executing them through the CPU as soon as you turn the computer on. Programs stored in ROM are also called *firmware,* a term you'll hear more and more frequently.

In general, the more ROM a microcomputer has, the better and easier the computer is to use. ROM-stored programs often control the video screen, color graphics, the input and output among the CPU, RAM and mass storage device—tape or disk drive—and much more. If a computer does not have a large amount of ROM, it means that programs to carry out routine internal operations will use up the available temporary RAM. As you will see below, this is inefficient and makes it difficult for you to use sophisticated programs and enter a lot of information.

ROM is also the secret of the plug-in cartridges. Inside each plug-in cartridge, whether it is for a video game, such as the Atari 5200, Colecovision, or Mattel Intellivision, or a home computer, such as the VIC-20, is a ROM chip. The cartridge is little more than a plastic case protecting the ROM chip and a small plastic board with wire connections.

ROM comes in several versatile types. Standard ROM is *nonvolatile,* in that it is dedicated to one set of instructions, which are permanently etched into the integrated circuit chip. An increasingly popular variation is called PROM, *programmable read only memory,* in which you can change the internal program with a special device. PROM's cousin, EPROM, *erasable programmable read only memory,* can be changed or destroyed with ultraviolet light or electrical current and reprogrammed with a new set of instructions and informatiion. PROMs and EPROMs can make a home computer much more sophisticated, but even after seven years, few are used with home computers. They are more often used in desktop and personal computers; using them requires a lot of expertise and programming ability.

Later, we'll refer quite often to each home computer's RAM and ROM. Internal memories within a microprocessor are defined in terms of the number of words and bits which make up each word length. For example, the first generation of home computers (Apple, Commodore PET, Atari 800) had word lengths 8 bits or 1 byte long. But—and this is a very important distinction—each home computer has two types of internal memory.

First, each CPU—the microprocessor itself, not the complete computer—has an internal memory. The size of this CPU memory is determined by its word length; an 8-bit word length gives the CPU a basic internal memory of 8,192 bits, *not* bytes. This refers only to the number of bits that can be stored in the CPU's registers at one time.

Second, each computer has an internal memory which refers to its overall capacity to store programs and information, or its total RAM and ROM. This figure refers to the total number of *bytes* or words which can be stored, temporarily, in the case of RAM, or permanently, in the case of ROM. These figures are always referred to in "K." "K" refers to the number 1,024; 1,024 is equal to two raised to the tenth power (two times two times two and so on ten times). "K" is used as a convenient computer shorthand to represent 1,024. The storage capacity of almost every computer is referred to in multiples of 1,024 because two is the base number of the binary numbering system. Therefore, 8K = 8,192; 16K = 16,384; 32K = 32,-768; 64K = 65,536; 128K = 131,072; 256K = 262,-144; etc.

Thus, a computer described as a 16-bit, 128K RAM IBM Personal Computer refers to the fact that it has a 16-bit word length with a CPU memory of 16,384 *bits* and a RAM with 131,072 *byte*

storage capacity. A 64K Apple IIe has an 8-bit word length, a CPU memory of 8,192 bits, and a RAM of 65,536 bytes.

"K" has confused many computer novices, but you rarely will run into instances where the size of the CPU's memory is mentioned or important. "K" will almost always refer to the computer's or storage device's memory capacity in bytes.

ABILITY TO ADDRESS RAMS OF DIFFERENT SIZES

A key difference between generations of microcomputer CPUs is the total amount of RAM each can *address,* or access at one time. The 8-bit computer, such as the Apple II Plus or Commodore 64, can address, under normal circumstances and without special equipment and programming, only 64K RAM. The 16-bit computer, however, can address up to 1,000K of RAM. 1,000K is also called a *megabyte* of RAM. The abbreviation for megabyte is commonly given as *Mb.* or *M.* or *Meg.* In this book, we shall use the Mb. abbreviation. The third generation of microcomputers with 32 bits will address up to 16 Mb. of RAM. To the novice or non-computer owner, these capacities are enormous. In fact, to get a real sense of just how enormous they are, consider that the 8K RAM of the first microcomputers made in 1975 was greater than that of the first mainframe computers built during the late 1940s. And the 16 Mb. RAM of the 32-bit microcomputers will be greater than the current line of IBM mainframes, the 370 series and the 4300 series.

Why does one want so much RAM capacity? The more RAM a computer has, the more sophisticated programs it can use and the more information to which you will have immediate access. In general, if you want to work with a program or play a game, the program must be loaded into RAM memory. If you want to add, change, or process information, such as the categories and numbers in a home budget program, you make these additions and changes in the RAM. If you want to permanently store the additions, changes, new programs, or fresh information, you must store it, usually called "save" it, in the mass storage device—either the cassette tape or the floppy disk.

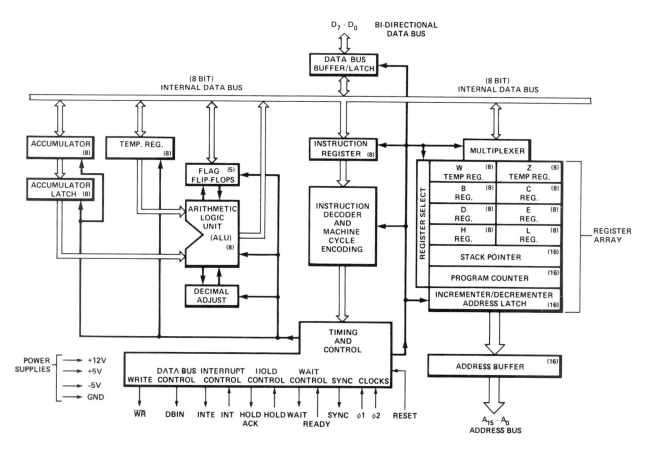

Figure 5. This block diagram shows the internal operations of the Intel 8080 microprocessor, one of the first 8-bit computers. (Courtesy of Schlumberger/Heath)

The processing that occurs between a program and information takes place between the RAM and the CPU. Of course, it happens very rapidly, and often, it may seem like the interaction occurs between the computer and the disk drive or tape recorder. What actually occurs in most microcomputers is that the computer is calling another program from the disk or tape, loading it into RAM, and processing it with any information through the CPU.

Most microcomputer programs work like this: say you have a 32K Commodore VIC-20 and a cassette tape recorder. You put a tape into the recorder and load a program. You issue a command to load a program, say Home Budget. The computer's CPU then sends a signal to the tape, telling it to "send me a copy of Home Budget." The recorder obliges, reads the program stored on tape, and dispatches the copy to the RAM. The Home Budget program was written in 8K bytes and takes up 8K of the 32K space in the RAM. And the

computer's monitor, wake up or *boot* program takes up 4K more in the RAM. Together, the two programs take up 12K of the available 32K, leaving 20K for information about your home budget.

21,000 bytes may seem like a lot of room, and for most home budgets it is, but for a small business, an at-home business, or a professional, it is not. That 20K bytes is equal to just ten single-spaced typewritten pages because 1 byte is equal to one *character*, as we noted. A character is any letter, number, or symbol a computer understands.

I will give you an actual example of my work. I have an older Apple II Plus with 48K RAM. I use VisiCalc to do my personal and professional budgets. VisiCalc and the Apple's boot program occupy about 30K of space in my RAM, leaving me just 18K or nine pages for temporary storage. My budgets, with about twenty-five or thirty categories, twelve months, and a yearly total take up the entire 18K. Further, the more space that is occupied in RAM, the slower the program executes its functions. As the RAM fills up, the computer literally has to take more time looking for empty storage space—in the shape of "open" integrated circuits—in the RAM.

If I wanted to expand my budgets, I would have to divide it into two or more parts, or add special equipment to my Apple. This special equipment adds more RAM space and allows the Apple to process more information than usual.

MEMORY CAPACITY EQUALS POWER

A larger memory capacity in RAM or ROM almost always equals more computing power and capability. This means that a computer with a 64K RAM memory will handle a more sophisticated, complex, and useful program than a 16K RAM. As you will see in the section on software and programming, exceptions to this rule exist. The usefulness of any program—set of instructions which tell the computer to execute a function—depends on how well that program is written. A program may require 64K of RAM, but be less efficient and less useful than a similar program written in 16K RAM. In general, however, given two programs written with somewhat equal efficiency, a 64K RAM allows far more versatility and storage capacity than a 16K RAM.

It is easy to see how much more useful the new computers with 128K, 256K and greater RAMs are compared to the earlier 8K and 16K micros. What's even more important is that within a year or two, the 256K RAM memories will be as inexpensive as the 16K RAMs were several years ago. AT&T, Fujitsu, and several other companies are engaged in intense competition to provide the 256K RAMs and are continually reducing prices as they increase their production capacity. By 1990, it is likely that individual RAM chips with 1 million-byte capacities will be as inexpensive as 256K RAM chips are today.

MASS STORAGE DEVICE CAPACITY

As the capacity of microcomputer RAMs increases, so do the capacity and capability of the most often used mass storage devices. As we noted, the most common today for home computers are floppy disk drives and cassette tape recorders. As the size of the RAMs increase, the cassette tape recorder becomes less desirable. It simply takes too much time to load lengthy programs. Loading a short program from standard cassette tape takes thirty seconds to two minutes. Loading a 30K program from a floppy disk drive into RAM takes a few seconds, and the disk, of course, can load any program that quickly. With the serial tape, if you want program number twenty-five, or information stored halfway through the tape, you must wait until the tape gets to that point.

Techniques have been improved to speed up the tape loading process, and "digital" tape drives are used in some personal computers which load and record fairly rapidly, but none are as fast or versatile as the disk drive. Further, the floppy disk drive is rapidly falling in price; often, as with the IBM PCjr, the floppy disk is included as part of the system you buy off the shelf. (In this section, we refer to the 5.25-inch minifloppy disk drives, not the 8-inch floppy disks used with minicomputers and some of the first generation of microcomputers.)

Floppy disks have, however, different capacities depending on the sophistication of the manufacturer. For example, the first Apple disk drive had a 70K capacity. That was doubled in 1979 to 140K. However, today, the IBM PC disk drives has a 360K capacity, the Commodore 64's disk drives have a 1 Mb. capacity, and some other personal computers have floppy disk drives with up to 2 Mb. capacities.

And as we noted above, the sizes of the floppy disk drives are changing rapidly too. The new microfloppy 3.5-inch disk drives, led by Sony, are the wave of the future. All of Hewlett-Packard's HP-150 model personal computers, the new Apple Macintosh, most of the new Japanese home computers, and the Sony SMC-70 use the smaller drives. As important, the new floppy disks have a large capacity. The Sony microfloppy has a 437K capacity, and reports of microfloppies with 1 Mb. capacities have been published. You can also expect a micro-microfloppy in the future: Toshiba is known to be developing a 1-inch floppy disk with a 100–250K capacity.

For people interested in using a microcomputer for a small business or profession, the Winchester hard disk drive will become increasingly important. Unlike the floppy disk and tape, which are *removable media,* that is, you can put them in and take them out, a Winchester hard disk is a *fixed*

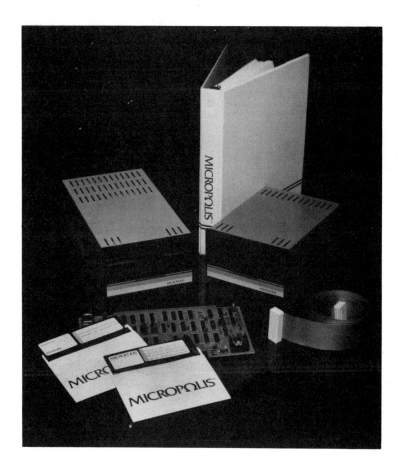

Figure 6. An early 5.25-inch minifloppy disk drive from Micropolis gives a clear picture of the elements of the drive, including the minifloppy disks themselves, the disk drive controller board, the connecting ribbons, and the cabinet for the drives. (Courtesy of Micropolis Corporation)

media. It is locked inside a small, airtight, permanently sealed box. The box contains a thin, round, stiff (which is why it is called hard as opposed to the flexible floppy), metallic disk on which data is recorded as electromagnetic impulses. Compared to a floppy disk, however, a hard disk can store millions of bytes of characters. Hard disks come in sizes ranging from as small as 3 (still experimental) to as large as 14 inches (used only on mainframe computers). Today, for home and personal computers, the most common sizes are 5.25 inches and 8 inches in diameter. The most common capacities for the 5.25-inch disk are between 5 and 20 megabytes, although experiments have raised that as high as 120 megabytes. For the 8-inch hard disk, capacities range from 20 Mb. to 200 Mb., with 20–80 Mb. the most common and least expensive.

In the future, as manufacturing techniques improve and prices go down, even for home computers, the microfloppy disk and the hard disk will become standard equipment. Yet, the home computer will not increase in inflation-adjusted price. For example, the new Morrow Computer MD-11 has a 128K RAM, an 11 Mb. hard disk, a keyboard terminal, and five free programs, yet it costs just $2,745. In 1980, the same thing would have cost more than $15,000. Five years from now, it will cost $500 in 1984 dollars.

Now you know all the basics of the hardware for a home computer, you need to realize that all this hardware is just pieces of metal and plastic, a jumble of wires and plugs without programs to run them. This is where the real "mystery" of the computer begins, and it is no mystery at all. People write programs; even computers that write programs have been programmed to people to write those programs. And whatever a computer is programmed to do requires a human programmer to tell it how and when to do it.

There is no mystery to computers. In fact, computers and how they work are easier for many people to understand than the workings of an automobile. They were for me; I still don't know one end of a spark plug from another, although I do know how to drive a car. By knowing so much more about the workings of a computer, you'll be able to put them to more and better uses.

CHAPTER 3

What Is Software and Why Is It Important?

Software seems to have mysterious properties for the computer novice. By slipping a disk or tape into a computer, and pressing a few buttons, a home computer may seem to spring to life without your help at all. Fortunately, computer software only appears to be mysterious and difficult to understand. Actually, software is defined simply as a set of instructions, prepared by a human programmer, which tells the computer what to do. It seems mysterious because it is intangible; unlike hardware which you can see and feel, or bang around if you don't like it, software is both a process and the result of a process of human thinking. Thinking is not mysterious because you have been doing it since before you were born. As you see the results of thinking, so you can see the results of software—when letters, symbols, or action scenes appear on a video screen, when the cassette tape or disk drive whirs and wheezes as it loads a program, when the printer produces text or graphics on a piece of paper. However, instead of thinking, software is the expression in electronic pulses of the set of instructions created by a programmer. That person produces each set of instructions to interact with a particular type of computer hardware. Thus, an Apple computer requires a different set of instructions from an IBM PCjr because its *architecture* differs.

Each computer's architecture is different because each one's microprocessor, memory chips, video display chips, sound and color graphics circuits, tape or disk drive differ. Although it is clear that an 8-bit and a 16-bit computer are architecturally different, it may appear that each 8-bit computer should be the same. This is not the case because many companies make 8-bit microprocessors with the internal components laid out in different configurations. Each one even has a different number of prongs or pins on the integrated circuit chip. Each microprocessor also has a unique *interface,* the electrical connection between it and the outside world.

In the 8-bit world, the most popular microprocessors are:

- MOS Technology 6502, used in Apple II Plus and IIe computers, Commodore PET, and Atari computers. Later variations of the 6500 design were used in the Commodore 64, the VIC-20, and others.

- Zilog, Inc. Z-80 and variations, Z80A and Z-80B, used in Tandy TRS-80, and more than a hundred common desktop computers which used the CP/M (Control Program/Microcomputers) operating system which will be explained later in this chapter.

- Intel 8080, the ancestor of the Z-80, also used in dozens of common computers.
- Motorola 6800, used in many common desktop computers, and some Radio Shack TRS-80 models.

In the 16-bit world, so far, the struggle has come down to these microprocessors and their variations:

- Intel's 8086, with a 16-bit internal word length and an 8-bit external word length. This is the CPU used by the IBM PC, and PC XT, the PC 370, and 3270 PC, and the PCjr, not to mention dozens of PC "compatibles" and look-alikes.
- Intel's 80186 and 80286, variations with true 16-bit external word lengths.
- Motorola 68000, used in the Apple Lisa and MacIntosh, among many others.

Others in the running in the second generation are the National Semiconductor 16000 series, the Zilog Z-8000, and the Texas Instruments 9900 series, used in TI minicomputers, the now defunct TI 99/4A home computer, and the TI Professional.

Within the next year, the 32-bit CPU will become prevalent, and Intel, Motorola, Sinclair Research, and others are racing to make the most popular models, with Intel in the lead in mid-1984.

It is important to connect software to the architectural differences because the various CPUs require different computer languages or distinct variations of computer languages in which software is written. But that's getting a little ahead of the game.

THE MYSTERY OF SOFTWARE EXPLAINED

If software is a set of instructions, what is a *program?* A program is also a set of instructions, but for one specific purpose. The term software is used several ways: first, as a set of instructions or a program; second, as a collection of programs designed to carry out a specific purpose—playing a game, writing a letter, doing accounting or income taxes, ad infinitum; third, as a term for all computer programs, that is the home computer software industry; and fourth, as a collection of programs, routines, compilers, assemblers, translators, manuals, and procedures associated with a particular type of hardware. The latter comes from the *Standard Dictionary of Computers and Information Processing, Revised Second Edition,* by Martin H. Weik, which is published by Hayden Book Company.

As it is commonly used with home and personal computers, software is used as a collection of programs which work together.

The essential part of software is the program. Every program—the intangible part of a computer system—is written by a human programmer in a form the computer can understand. We talk to one another in a common "language"—each computer has its own unique language—that is, a code that dictates how a microprocessor receives electronic pulses and transmits them out of the system. This happens, as we noted, because each computer has a somewhat different internal architecture. Even the computers with the same CPU—the Apple II and the Apple III—may not perfectly "understand" each other. Their circuitry was laid out differently, so they require a different "dialect" of the same language. This situation is a lot like an American from the Deep South visiting London, England; much of what an American says to an Englishman (and vice versa) will be understandable, but often just as much will be incomprehensible.

Computers with different CPUs trying to communicate are like English-speakers trying to speak Russian or Swahili. Thus, each computer has a unique *machine language*. A machine language is nothing more than a series of zeros and ones in binary code (using the binary numbering system described in Chapter 2) which control the registers, transistors, capacitors, and other elements within each computer's circuitry.

The computer can talk or transmit pulses in its unique language very rapidly, and this incredible speed—millions of pulses per second—is what surprises and frightens many people. This speed, in which a CPU can transfer thirty thousand characters from a disk drive to its RAM memory in a few seconds, is no more mysterious than switching on a light. Turning on a light is very familiar; after you use a computer a few times, moving the information from the disk to the RAM will seem just as normal. In fact, you will find yourself becoming impatient if your computer takes more than two seconds to do something you told it to do.

HOW WE "COMMUNICATE" WITH COMPUTERS

Relatively few people "talk" to computers in the computers' own languages because learning machine language is difficult. Fortunately, there is little need for you or even most professional programmers to communciate with a computer in its machine language. This is because in the 1950s and 1960s, it became apparent that the demand for programs for the large computers was growing faster than the supply of programmers who could write machine language programs. Computer scientists developed new languages, based on variations of English and English-like symbols, with a formal structure and hierarchy. They also developed *translators* and *interpreters* to change the English-like language into machine language and vice versa.

At the end of the scale in which the language is closest to English or most humanlike are *high-level languages*. But make no mistake; high-level languages are definitely *not* the same as a human one. They appear to be because many of the words and phrases are similar to their English counterparts. But, in a computer language, the words, their meanings, the computer's syntax and grammar, and the way they all are used are very different.

The most popular high-level languages for home computers are variations of BASIC (Beginner's All-purpose Symbolic Instruction Code). I've lost count of the variations of BASIC, but the most prevalent are those written by a major software company called Microsoft, Inc. Variations of its Microsoft BASIC are used in almost all home and personal computers, including the IBM PC.

Between high-level languages and machine languages are four types of languages that convert or translate the former into the latter. These four are:

- *Assembly language.* The symbols in the language, called mnemonics, have a one-to-one correspondence to machine language codes. This direct correspondence enables the program to run much faster than a program written in BASIC which must be translated. The translator takes time to make the conversion and slows the computer down. An *assembler* is a particular program which runs the assembly language and turns the program into machine language.

- *Compiler.* An assembler differs from a compiler in that the assembler converts each symbolic instruction independently while the compiler uses the logical structure of the program to make the conversion. Because the conversion is not a direct correspondence, a compiler's development and its use with high-level languages is more difficult at first. However, compilers are very useful in the "automatic" generation of computer programs. A compiler is more complex than an assembler and requires a lot of analytical processing within the computer.

- *Interpreter.* An interpreter is the easiest conversion program to develop, but it is also the slowest to operate. It instantly converts its instructions one at a time, whereas a compiler or assembler prepares a new group of instructions to be carried out a fraction of a second later. Compare an interpreter to a human translator: if a person were a computer "interpreter," he or she would translate one word at a time. Human translators are more like compilers or assemblers in that they usually translate sentences or paragraphs and put them in the context of what the person has already said or is about to say.

- *Translator.* A computer language translator converts the same instruction only once and stores that translation to be used every time it is encountered in a program. It is like a person who learns a foreign word or phrase once and no longer needs to deliberately translate it each time it occurs.

A COMPUTERIZED TOWER OF BABEL

As computers grew in popularity, the number of high-level languages proliferated both in the computer science labs and in actual practice. This was done mostly for competitive reasons in the days of the mainframe; the essential idea was that each company wanted its own computer to have a unique language. In that way, their customers would be forced to use their programs and their services. If you invented a computer and the only language it could use, you would have a tremendous competitive advantage until your competitors could learn how to write programs in that language.

Unfortunately, the same is true of the microcomputer industry, and the home computer world is a veritable Tower of Babel with variations or "dialects" of the most important languages for all of the most popular computers. There have evolved *de facto* standards for home computer languages (as I noted, Microsoft BASIC), but there are so many variations of MBASIC, as it is called, that the standard is practically meaningless. It simply means that it is easier for professional programmers to learn the relatively minor changes among MBASIC dialects than to learn whole new languages. This reduces the amount of time it takes to convert an MBASIC program for the IBM computer to an MBASIC program for the Compaq or Columbia Data computer. As we noted, it is far more difficult to convert programs written in BASIC for the 8-bit Apple to programs for the 16-bit IBM PC with a different BASIC.

THE MOST POPULAR LANGUAGES

The most popular languages for home and personal computers are:

- *BASIC,* developed in 1964 at Dartmouth College by two academicians looking for an easier way to teach students programming. Compared to languages for minicomputers and mainframes, BASIC is limited with a limited grammar or syntax. BASIC is almost too simple or the new 16-bit microcomputers because it is relatively slow and its commands are too limited to take full advantage of the 16-bit processing speed and memory capability. Nonetheless, IBM, Apple, and Tandy have all chosen to use the 16-bit version of MBASIC.

- *COBOL,* acronym for Common Business-Oriented Language, developed by the Defense Department. COBOL executes programs in a precise narrative resembling standard English. A COBOL program written for one computer can often be translated quickly and easily for another computer. COBOL has long been used as the most popular language for business applications for minicomputers, and it is gaining in popularity for 16-bit micros, especially the Apple Lisa. COBOL's structure requires far more memory space than BASIC, so the new 16-bit micros may allow thousands of COBOL pro-

grams written for minicomputers in the 1960s and 1970s to be used for microcomputer applications.

- *FORTRAN,* for FORmula TRANslator, was designed by IBM during the 1950s to expedite scientific and mathematical research. It allows computers to solve algebraic problems by directly converting the mathematical language into machine code. Dozens of versatile variations have been developed for almost every type of computer, but it is most useful in research applications.

- *Pascal,* named for the Renaissance mathematician, Blaise Pascal, is a relatively new and versatile language. It is based mostly on symbols and mnemonics. Popular with the Apple II computer for business applications, it is much faster than BASIC, and programs can easily be "transported" or converted from one machine to another with few changes.

- *LOGO,* a new language designed by Seymour Papert and researchers at the Massachusetts Institute of Technology (MIT), is aimed at making computers very easy for children to use. It advances new concepts in programming and human-computer interactions.

- *UNIX,* a language originally developed at Bell Laboratories for use with AT&T's internal computer systems. Noted for its ease of use, UNIX has a well-regarded built-in text editor. However, UNIX works best on multi-user systems—systems with more than one terminal and microcomputer and large internal memories. It is probable that AT&T will introduce a "personal" version of UNIX for the 32-bit personal computer it is likely to introduce during 1985. Its first foray into personal computers during 1984 (being decided while this book is being written) was likely to be a 16-bit IBM-compatible personal computer and a UNIX-based, 32-bit multi-user business microcomputer system.

BRINGING IT ALL TOGETHER

There is more to how software works than the four levels of language. Even if you understand the hardware and the types of languages, you are still missing two crucial pieces to the puzzle that makes a computer do what you want it to. The first missing piece is called the *operating system (OS)*. To put it simply, an operating system acts as the computer "traffic cop"; it controls the flow of information and programs through every part of the computer. An OS is a coordinated collection of programs and parts of programs called *routines* that do the following and more: a monitor program which turns the computer on and off, runs self-diagnostic tests, and readies the computer to accept a program; a video display routine which governs how information gets from the CPU to the video screen; a routine which accepts input from the keyboard or other data entry device; another one which regulates output through a printer or other device. The OS allocates hardware operation, memory storage, and processor time, controls information flows, and regulates all organized internal operations. The OS loads a program, enables an assembler (or other language) to convert it to machine language, and dictates how and when an *applications package* carries out its functions.

In most computers, the OS also regulates and coordinates the interaction between the computer and the disk drives. In this case, the OS is called a *DOS (disk operating system)*, which does all of the above as well as having routines to control the floppy or hard disk drives.

Each type of processor, and often each separate computer, has its own DOS. For example, the Apple IIe, the Apple III, and the Apple Lisa and Apple Macintosh have different operating systems. The Atari computers, which use the same chip as the original Apples, have different operating systems. Most of the Tandy/Radio Shack models have operating systems which differ not only from those of other computers, but from each other's. But in the 8-bit world, the most common operating system is CP/M (Control Program/Microcomputers). CP/M has been used in more than 1 million computers since it was developed in 1978 by two college classmates who were looking for an easier way to run the new microcomputer they had just bought. The company these two founded has since become one of the five largest software makers in the country.

CP/M gained its popularity and became a quasi-standard for the Z-80 and Intel 8080 microprocessors because it is relatively easy to write programs with. It is limited in that its earlier versions did not allow for very sophisticated use of color or graphics. Thus it was not very useful for games or entertainment and its popularity grew through small business and professional users. Further, it was designed to be versatile and easy for programmers, not for computer users who do not know programming.

In the 16-bit generation, the latest version of CP/M, called CP/M-86 is competing with a DOS developed by the largest independent software house, Microsoft, Inc., called MS-DOS and the variation for the IBM PC, called PC-DOS. MS-DOS is now used on more than fifty types of personal and home computers and that number will probably increase to more than 100 by 1985.

THE IBM PC COMPATIBILITY TRAP

The operating system for the IBM PC, PC-DOS, is a unique version of MS-DOS. The IBM PC also runs on MS-DOS itself and will run a subset of CP/M-86. But this can be very misleading, and computer makers often use these misleading facts in their advertising. Many vendors claim their hardware products have "IBM PC compatibility." This would appear to mean that any program that runs on the IBM PC will automatically run on the "compatible" computer. However, in most cases, this is *not* true because the IBM PC is a unique machine and has many proprietary features. These features not only protect IBM from companies that would copy their machines wire for wire, feature for feature, and chip for chip, they also make it very difficult, if not illegal, to make a machine that is completely and truly "IBM PC-compatible."

What this phrase usually means in ads and public relations is that the computer runs a version of MS-DOS. Then, programs written for the IBM PC with MS-DOS can be easily converted to run on their machines.

More important, the internal operations of the IBM PC disk drives differ from those of any other computer. Thus, at the very least, any MS-DOS program must be changed and reformatted so it will run on the disk drive used by each computer manufacturer.

There are other technical reasons for the lack of true "compatibility," but there are also some exceptions. Some IBM PC-compatible machines will run some or most of the IBM PC programs with little or no alteration, particularly computers from

Compaq and Columbia Data Systems. By and large, however, you should thoroughly investigate any computer store's or vendor's claim that their computers have IBM PC compatibility. Unfortunately no standards exist in the industry and no government regulations apply to the "compatibility" issue, so you must be an alert and watchful consumer to avoid difficulty.

THE TRUE COMPATIBILITY OF THE JAPANESE MSX

However, a new development from more than twenty Japanese home computer manufacturers may establish a new operating system standard in the U.S. during the next several years. Working with the developer of MS-DOS, Microsoft, Inc., these Japanese companies have developed MSX, an OS that does create true compatibility across a wide range of computers. For several years, the Japanese watched and waited for the U.S. computer makers to produce a standard operating system for the first and second generations of home computers. The Japanese have long believed in setting standards for each type of electronic device. For example, if the early television industry had been like the computer industry is today, you would have to buy one television to watch CBS, another to watch NBC, a third to watch ABC, a fourth to watch WTBS. Or, you would have to buy an expensive converter that would accept many different kinds of signals and change those signals into the one signal your television understands. The same would hold true for stereo record players, cassette tape recorders, AM and FM radios—in fact, for every type of electronic gadget.

Clearly, for many people, it would be just too confusing and difficult to learn all of these differences. People have a hard enough time as it is knowing the difference between the two types of video cassette recorders (VCR). Do you know the difference between the Sony Betamax standard and the Matsushita VHS system? But in home computers, you are expected to learn the differences among MS-DOS, Apple DOS 3.3, TRSDOS, PC-DOS, OASIS, TURBODOS, CP/M-80, CP/M-86, and so on for dozens of operating systems.

The Japanese have decided to end the confusion, at least as far as their home computers are con-cerned. Their standard operating system, MSX, is an outgrowth of Microsoft BASIC, the quasi-standard version of the BASIC language, and MS-DOS. But the key point is this:

Any program developed for one MSX machine, say a Panasonic, will run on any other MSX computer, say a Hitachi. Take a disk out of one machine and put it in the second and it will run, just like moving a stereo record from a Sansui turntable to a Fisher.

For six years, I and many others in the home computer business have urged American manufacturers, particularly Commodore, Atari, Radio Shack, and others, to take a similar step, but the competitive urge among American manufacturers is too strong to allow them to cooperate to this extent. However, it is likely that the Japanese standard will replace the chaos created by the American manufacturers within five years.

UTILITY PROGRAMS

Until the happy day when a standard operating system for all computers of the same generation arrives, it is important to know the basics of the inner workings of your computer. An important adjunct to the OS is a program category called *utilities.*

Utility programs are routines that can be used independently of the operating system, but make using the total system easier. Utilities can be added to the system as the need for them arises. For example, when you print out a letter or document, you use a "print" routine; when you make a copy of a program, a file, or a disk, you use a "copy" or "disk copy" routine. Many types of utility programs exist for each computer, including "copy protection" and password programs which provide security. Their importance lies in the extra functions which expand the usefulness and increase the protection of your computer.

APPLICATION PACKAGES

So far, you know what software is, what programming languages are, what operating systems are, and what part each of these plays in running various computer operations. Yet, you still do not know how to do something with your computer.

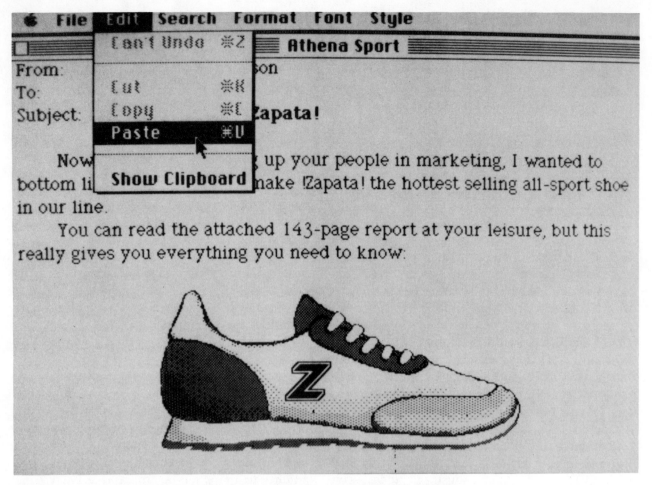

Figure 7. This reproduction of a screen display from the Apple Macintosh computer illustrates the results of applications programs. Applications programs are collections of program routines that actually carry out the tasks or play the games you want to do. In the photograph, the shoe was drawn with a graphics application program and the memo was written with a word processing applications package, and the two were merged together with programs from the Macintosh operating system. (Courtesy of Apple Computer, Inc.)

To do anything with your computer—other than write programs for which you use a programming language—you need an *applications package.* An applications package is simply a collection of programs and routines that let you do a specific task with a computer. A computer game, like *Space Invaders,* for example, is not one program; it contains numerous programs linked together. A home budget manager or a financial analysis program is divided into various sections.

Why? It is easier to write them in sections or modules, but more importantly, you rarely need to use the entire package at the same time. For example, the word processing software I use has a print routine that allows me to print letters and documents, but the "print" routine or command is now loaded into RAM while I write and edit. It would waste the amount of available storage I have. When I want to print something, I issue a "P" command, and the CPU goes to the disk, "fetches" the print routine, loads it into RAM, and shows me a "print" menu. After I finish printing, I issue another command, and the "print" routine stored in RAM disappears, leaving me more room to work.

Applications packages for personal investments, word processing, business analysis, small business management, ad infinitum all have many interrelated sections.

Applications packages are usually written or programmed in one of the high-level languages. Some parts of some applications programs are written in assembler and/or machine languages because these parts enable the computer to process information more rapidly and efficiently. As you will quickly learn, an efficiently written program can make computing a joy; an inefficiently written program will process information very slowly and make using a computer, even playing games, a chore and a bore.

CRANKING UP YOUR COMPUTER

When you put all of these "soft" functions and "hard" equipment together, you have a complete computer system. Despite the depth of this explanation, however, cranking up your computer is as easy as cranking up your car. In the early days of computers, you had to know how to flip a complex array of switches and issue a stream of commands to crank up a computer. Those days are long gone. Today, you need only know a simple procedure that prompts the cassette recorder or disk drive and the OS's monitor program to start your computer. Here's how.

First, remove your computer equipment from its boxes and packaging and make sure you have properly connected all the wires and cables and plugged them in. How you start your particular home computer will vary from computer to computer, but these general guidelines apply to most. Second, recheck the hardware setup; most service calls are made because Dad or Jane forgot to connect the computer to the television, or the disk drive to the computer.

Third, unwrap the instruction manual for the game or applications program you plan to use. Read the introductory material carefully. It should clearly explain how to start this program. There are two basic ways to get started: in one, you insert the program tape or disk *before* you turn the computer on; in the second, you turn the computer on *before* you put the tape or disk in. It varies from machine to machine and, worse, program to program.

With that in mind, let's *boot* the program, computer jargon for putting the program disk into the disk drive and activating it. To boot the program with the machine off, take the disk in your hand with the label on the disk facing up. Your thumb should rest on the label. Slide the disk or tape into the drive or recorder. Next, turn the video monitor or television on. Gently snap the lid closed and find the on/off switch and turn it on.

To boot the disk with the machine on, insert the disk or tape in the same way. (NOTE: if you use plug-in cartridges, as you can with the IBM PCjr (Peanut), the Commodore VIC-20, and the Atari 1200XL, among many others, turn the machine on and simply slip the cartridge into the correct slot. The program will automatically appear on the screen.)

When you use a disk drive, a red light located near the front of the disk drive should come on. This means the CPU and monitor program have activated the disk operating system. The disk drive will whir and click, and in a few seconds, the menu display, a command menu, or an introductory screen should appear on your video monitor or TV. During those few seconds, the DOS has run some diagnostic tests, prepared the computer to receive commands, and loaded the first sections of the applications package from the disk into RAM.

In some programs, a blinking light will appear when you turn the machine on. That light indicates the computer monitor is working and waiting for a command. The cursor will pinpoint where you must enter a command or some information. Enter an appropriate command, usually something simple like "LOAD HOMEBUDGET" or "RUN EXECDATA.SVX." Press return. You may also have to enter the date and time, and/or perhaps your name and a password or identification number. The disk should whir and click and present a menu or display on the screen.

If you use a cassette tape recorder, it is likely the start-up procedure will be slightly different. You turn the machine on first, put the tape in the recorder and close the lid. Then, you will type LOAD or something similar and press the RETURN or ENTER (carriage return) key on your keyboard. The monitor program will activate the tape and load the program into RAM. Depending on the length of the program, the tape will stop turning after a few seconds or in up to two minutes, and a blinking light—the *cursor*—will appear on

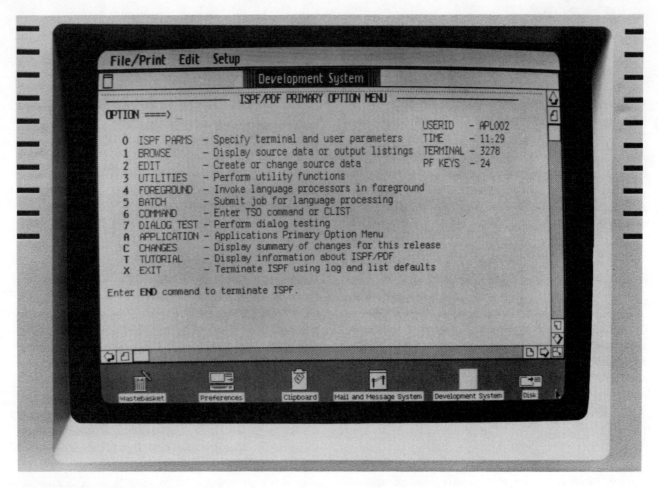

Figure 8. This photo displays a somewhat complex menu for a software development program displayed on the Lisa 2 computer. However, most menus used in home and personal computers are much shorter, simpler, and easier to use. Yet, to use even this difficult one is as simple as entering a number, a letter, or a three-letter word. How much easier can computers be to use? (Courtesy of Apple Computer, Inc.)

the screen. Then, you type RUN and press RE-TURN, and the program will appear.

In computer jargon, what these steps accomplish are called:

- Booting the disk
- Bringing up a program
- Loading a program
- Calling up a program (software, package, etc.)

All of these phrases mean basically the same thing: the procedure required to get your computer working.

All three procedures should result in getting you started. In computer games, these steps will probably lead to a basic set of instructions about how to play the game. In a more serious program, it should result in a "main menu," a list between five and twenty lines long of commands, procedures, steps, or choices you can make to work with your program. This menu is the starting point for a package and should be designed to give you easy and clear choices to get into the program's real functions.

For example, the main menu for the word processing program used to write this book consists of these commands:

"W — Write a new document
F — File this document
M — Modify a document
P — Print a document
R — Read an existing document
DE — DEstroy a document
RM — ReMove a storage medium
CA — CAtalog all documents with commands
SO — Start Over (do not file changes)
EX — EXit from Type-Rite (file document)"

Other main menus are more complex than this one; some are even simpler.

Let's summarize what software is and what it does. A human programmer writes a set of instructions, called an applications package, in a high-level language which the computer translates into its own unique machine language. The applications package, a collection of programs and routines stored on disk or tape, or inside a plug-in ROM cartridge, is processed through the computer's hardware—CPU, RAM and ROM—by an operating system. When you use a program, the whole system works together through a logical structure. It is like a very complex ballet of bytes which should work flawlessly and seemingly without effort. In this *ballet de computer*, the "ballet master" is you. Your applications are being carried out by the computer. You are the master, the computer is the servant to what you want to do. It processes your ideas and information and is under your total control.

CHAPTER 4
PERIPHERALS: Optional Equipment for Your Computer

When it comes to reading price tags, buying a home computer is a lot like buying a car. The list price, say $7,999 for a compact car, is only part of the story. Any person who has ever bought a car before knows he's going to spend a lot more for so-called optional equipment: air conditioner, AM-FM stereo cassette player, mag wheels, white sidewall tires, racing stripe, door guards, tinted windshield, leather seats, automatic transmission, and so forth. With just a few options, taxes and destination charges, the price of a $7,999 car can end up $10,000 or $11,000.

Both fortunately and unfortunately, the same holds true when you buy a computer. It is unfortunate because you are led to believe that by spending as little as $99, you will obtain a useful home computer. In almost all cases, all you can do with the $99 home computer is play simple games and do simple programming, and that is true only if you already have a spare television to use as a video display. It is fortunate because unlike some optional equipment for autos, much of which simply makes the car look better, computer options most often make a computer far more useful than it was before.

For example, adding an option called a *memory board* may double or triple the amount of RAM internal memory you can use for serious applica-

tions. Or replacing a slow cassette tape recorder with a floppy disk drive can increase the available mass storage many times *and* make a computer's operations dozens of times faster for slightly more than five to ten times the cost of a recorder. Continuing the automobile analogy, it would be like adding a device that could make a car, the old top speed of which was 55 mph, go 1,500 mph while increasing the cost of the car about $2,500. Try to buy a jet that will go 1,500 mph—more than twice the speed of sound—for $2,500 more than the cost of an automobile. Many computer accessories give similar boosts in performance and function.

To obtain a useful home computer, compared to a cheap one, you have to add accessories—optional equipment. In computer jargon, these accessories—actually practical necessities—are called *peripherals*. They got this name because they are detached from or peripheral to the CPU. The Coleco ADAM is a good example of how much you must expect to pay to get a minimally useful system: $699 plus the cost of a video display. The ADAM system includes not only a CPU and a keyboard—the same thing you can get for $99—but also a high-speed data tape cassette recorder, a large RAM memory, a large ROM memory, and a simple, though effective, letter-quality printer (that is, it types out fully formed characters like a typewriter).

Even after you obtain accessories to boost your system's speed and capacity, you must plan to spend more money for software. And as many parents discovered when they bought inexpensive home video games, they can spend far more on software than they originally spent on the machine itself. You will probably find this to be true with computers, too. The manufacturer may give you a game or two, but you must add software costs to your budget, as well.

There is one essential point about software to remember in connection with peripherals: many software packages are written to use specific types of peripherals or add-on equipment, and if you do not have these peripherals, the software will simply not work. For example, I have a home computer with which I wanted to communicate with a public information utility as well as transfer files to and from some clients. I had to add an external communications device called a modem ($200), an internal communications device ($200), and a communications software package ($95), or almost $500 more on top of a basic system cost of $3,800. Incidentally, in the $3,800 cost was included the cost of three types of add-on equipment: a video display, two disk drives, and a printer. The cost of the computer, its RAM and ROM, operating system, the keyboard was less than $1,500 at retail. It could have been bought at discount stores for less than $800, but the add-on equipment, all required if I was going to have a system I could use for more than games, added $2,300 to the system cost at the time of purchase.

At one time, some manufacturers believed they would eventually build very cheap hardware and make their profits selling software. This is known as the "razor blade" principle of marketing first perfected by Gillette—give away the razor to sell the blades. However, when Texas Instruments, Atari, Commodore, and others tried to apply this principle to home computers, they found consumers were not willing to spend $80–$100 for software to use with a computer that cost them $99. Throughout 1983 and early 1984, smart consumers refused to follow this path, but their recalcitrance had begun to turn against them. Instead of lowering software prices, computer manufacturers began to actually raise their hardware prices.

Eventually, the razor blade principle will take hold in the home computer industry, but only when home computers are so inexpensive as to be throwaway items like pocket calculators. In the meantime, computer makers are looking to make their profits by selling hardware—both computers and peripherals.

Making the situation even more complicated is the nature of the home computer. Unlike an adding machine or a car, it is a relatively general-purpose tool; any program you can squeeze into its memory, it will execute. Turn it into a satellite tracking system, and it will do it; program it to control the lights, appliances, and home energy system, and it will do it; use it one minute to play a game, and the next minute to do your income taxes, and it will do that, too. But to do each of these things and many more requires different types of equipment and software. During the rest of this chapter alone, seventeen types of peripherals will be discussed and these are by no means all of those available. They are just the most common and popular.

CASSETTE TAPE RECORDERS

The most common type of peripheral is the simple cassette tape recorder. There are two basic types, the audio cassette (like the ones you use to play music tapes), and the data cassette recorder, a special type which uses digital magnetic tape to record digital signals instead of audio signals. The tape recorder is a classic input/output (I/O) device: it inputs data stored on its tape, and it permanently stores programs and data fed it by the computer, so that it can output them later.

The audio cassette recorder converts and stores digital information from a computer through a simple cable and interface built into the computer. However, years of experience show that audio cassette tape recorders and tapes, especially ones not recommended by the computer manufacturer, are very unreliable. Unless you confine your use to simple games and programs, you will find the tapes often "drop out" data. They will often not load a program or information correctly the first time you try, and you may waste many minutes trying to salvage data or load the tape correctly. If you still plan to use a commercial, off-the-shelf recorder you have around the house, be careful. If you plan to buy one, try to get the best quality available at the most reasonable price.

The recorders and cassettes recommended or sold by the manufacturers or the computer store when you shop may, of course, be more expensive, but they tend to be more reliable. And both Atari and Commodore require you to buy their own dedicated tape recorders with some of their models, most notably, the Atari 600X1 and 1200XL, and the Commodore 64. The IBM PCjr also has a recommended tape recorder available.

Tips on Tapes

Here are several key points to remember when buying recorders and tapes for your home computer. First, use high-quality, but short (10 minutes) cassette tapes. The longer the tape, the more distortion and stretching you get on the tape, and the more problems you have with data losses. Second, do not run the recorder on batteries; always try to use an adapter and plug the recorder in. This keeps a steady motor speed, a necessity for accurate storage and retrieval of data; as batteries wear out, the motor speed varies, and this can damage data. Third, use the "auxiliary" AUX jack with your computer tapes because it best accepts computer signals.

DISK DRIVES

Although floppy disk drives have been discussed in detail above, there is more to disk drives than their size. To recapitulate, a floppy disk is a flexible metallic oxide medium on which electronic pulses are stored as magnetic signals. There are three common sizes for microcomputers: floppy or 8-inch flexible disks; minifloppy or 5.25-inch disks; and now microfloppy in a range of sizes, ranging from 3-inch to 3.5-inch. A standard size for the microfloppy is still evolving, but it appears the Sony standard for 3.5-inch disks is the most popular. Both Hewlett-Packard and Apple have adopted that standard. However, IBM has not announced its microfloppy standard, and any it chooses will likely capture most of the market.

Beyond size, however, is the question of density, that is, how many bytes or characters a disk can store. Single density implies one amount of storage for each disk—usually 250K on an 8-inch disk and

between 70K and 110K for a minifloppy. Double density generally doubles the amount of storage. There is also the question of whether a disk is single- or double-sided. If a disk is single-sided, then you are supposed to only use one side; if double-sided, you can store data on both sides. Quadruple-density floppy disks are being developed, and are available for a handful of desktop computers. But double-sided, double-density disks are available for the Commodore 8000 series floppy disk drives with a storage of up to 1 megabyte of information. The Sony microfloppy standard, for example, has an *unformatted* storage of about 500K or half a megabyte. Because it has advanced data recording techniques on the smaller disk, this capacity is considered single density for a microfloppy disk.

It is also good to know about single or dual disk drives; a single disk is simply one self-contained disk drive while a dual disk drive is two drives in one cabinet with one *controller* or disk operation board.

One should also understand the difference between formatted and unformatted capacity. Unformatted capacity is the number of characters a disk can hold *before* you run a software procedure. This procedure literally prepares the surface of the disk to accept data the way a program will transfer it to that disk. In doing so, it occupies space on the disk, reducing the actual amount of space in which you can store programs and information. To use a fictitious example, suppose a disk has an unformatted capacity of 250K; you format the disk for use with a home budget program and that procedure leaves you with a formatted capacity of 190K. That means the procedure took up 60K bytes, and you only really have 76 percent of the capacity for direct use.

When you buy floppy disks, ask about the unformatted and formatted capacities of the disks. Remember, too, the formatted capacity can differ from one program to the next.

To summarize the jargon of floppy disk drives: floppy, minifloppy, and microfloppy disks can be single-, double-, or quadruple-density, and be single- or double-sided, and either in single or dual drive configurations.

Rapid Changes in Disk Drives

Disk drives themselves have undergone rapid evolution during the past several years, too. Prices

Figure 9. The Apple Computer Duodisk is a good example of dual single-sided, single-density minifloppy disk drives. (Courtesy of Apple Computer, Inc.)

have fallen by almost half while reliability has increased dramatically. And the size of the disk drives themselves has changed. In the past, minifloppy disk drives were at least 3.5 inches tall; now, most computer and disk makers produce "half-height" drives of less than an inch and a half tall. These have more electronics and fewer moving parts, meaning greater quality, lower costs, and more reliability. For example, Apple Computer has introduced a dual floppy disk drive for its Apple IIe—a half-height, single-sided, double-density unit with two drives and one controller. The new unit costs $795; the latest purchase price for two single drives bought together is $945. In 1981, the same two drives cost $625 for the one with the controller, and $525 for the other, for a total of $1,150. This is a significant $355 drop in price. And cheaper units are available from other sources, ranging as low as $279–$309 per disk drive.

In the near future, it is likely no home computer will be produced without at least one built-in microfloppy disk drive. Most microcomputers for businesses and desktops already include two 5.25-inch drives in their standard layout or configuration and price.

It is advisable that you add a floppy disk drive to your home computer system for several reasons. First, it will speed up your computing and increase your fun by many times. Second, it will make

available a far larger range of programs for serious problem-solving tasks. Most programs on cassette tapes are games and simple home financial programs, and are not adequate for even an at-home business's needs. Third, disk drives are far more reliable and error free.

However, there are several points to remember when buying a floppy disk drive. First, you will have to obtain a disk operating system, but that should be included in the system price for most units. You can buy other DOSes, such as the popular TURBODOS for the Radio Shack line. And MS-DOS for dozens of machines, PC-DOS for the IBM PC, and Apple DOS for its machines are also examples of low-cost or free DOSes. Second, you may need to add memory capacity because the DOS may occupy some space in the RAM. For example, Apple DOS 3.3 takes up about 16K of the 48K which I have in my older Apple II Plus model. That leaves me just 32K for program and data storage. When I use VisiCalc, I end up with about 16K in RAM for data storage, not much for even my business' budget. Third, watch out for the memory requirements of and compatibility with various software packages. The package must fit into the available space in the RAM *after* the DOS is loaded into the system *and* work with the system. Thus, a program requiring 64K RAM and three disk drives will simply not work on a 48K RAM system with one disk drive. This is a far more common problem than you might expect, so keep your eyes open.

VIDEO MONITORS

The most common output device is a video display unit, most often a common television or a special video monitor. A key word of advice: Unless you have an extra television now, buy an extra or a *video monitor* when you buy a computer. Why? To avoid family quarrels. If you have one or two TVs, and you hook the computer to one, what will happen when Johnny wants to play a game when Dad wants to watch the football game, and Mom wants to watch the evening movie? You get the picture. Dedicating a television or monitor to the computer

is a good idea because it allows for more flexible use by all members of the family.

Fortunately, some computers come with their video monitors built in. This is a hallmark of the portable computers, such as the Compaq, the Kaypro series, and the Eagle. However, the most popular computers, including the Apples, the IBM PC models, the Commodore 64 and VIC-20, and the Ataris, among others, all require you to add a video display. The least expensive is a black-and-white TV to watch you add a signal convertor called an RF modulator. In fact, if you already have a video game, you probably already have an RF modulator that will work with your home computer. Of course, you can buy a color television and use the same RF modulator, but find out from your dealer first because some computers will not accept signals from those modulators. The RF de-

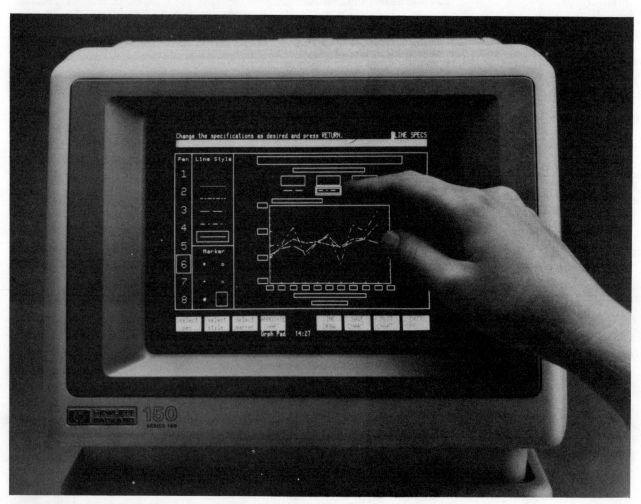

Figure 10. Hewlett-Packard's touch screen video display shows both the high resolution of and rapid evolution of modern video monitors. (Courtesy of Hewlett-Packard, Inc.)

vices send signals from the computer to the television.

Of course, the best type of display is a video monitor made especially to be used with computers. This monitor will not work as a TV, however, but it will sharply improve the reception and clarity of the computer display. Video monitors have built-in modulators and connect directly to the computer with a cable. Special video monitors come in several types. The least expensive are black-and-white monitors costing less than $200; the next type are one-color monitors—usually green phosphor or amber—costing about $300–$400. Color monitors which give brilliant, high-resolution colors—ranging from 8 to 256 or more colors—are more expensive, $500–$1,000 or more.

For computer games and some at-home programs, color TV or monitors are more enjoyable. For business applications, a green phosphor or amber monitor is more relaxing; black-and-white screens tend to worsen eyestrain when used for long periods of time. Color monitors are usually not necessary or required for business applications, and little software has been written to take advantage of color coding for business applications.

Like TVs, monitors also range in size from as small as 7-inch diagonals to 19-inch diagonals or more. The most common are 9- to 15-inch, and generally the larger the better, because size enlarges the size of the characters and reduces eyestrain.

There are two types of color monitors: one-gun or composite, which combines all three primary colors through one signal; and RGB—Red, Green, Blue—with three signals. RGB provides better displays, but costs a lot more. You can probably obtain the same quality as RGB with a more useful, high-quality component TV. After a certain point, the differences in color and quality are technical and of importance only for special business or industrial applications.

In short, to buy the right video display for your computer, determine your most common applications—games, small business, professional/career applications. Then look at your pocketbook, and consider how often you plan to use the computer. If you plan daily use for a variety of applications, get a good-quality color monitor; if occasional game playing is your intent, use an inexpensive color TV; if you'll use it strictly for business, get a

high-quality green phosphor or amber monitor. Do not cut corners if you plan to use the computer frequently. A few extra dollars for the monitor will save you many hours of eyestrain and irritation. Take the word of someone who uses a black-and-white screen every day.

RAM CARDS AND MEMORY BOARDS

I have mentioned in several places that you may have to add more internal RAM to your computer for certain applications, such as adding a DOS or a larger program. How do you accomplish this? It's simple and can be inexpensive. You add a peripheral called a *RAM card* or *memory board* and plug it into the back of the computer or an interface unit.

Inside every computer is a flat plastic board into which numerous integrated circuit chips are plugged or attached. This board is actually thin layers of plastic into which infinitesimal gold or metallic wires are laid. The wires run among the chips and enable the chips to communicate with each other and the "outside world." This central flat piece of plastic is called a *motherboard* because it contains the CPU, ROM, and standard RAM chips, among others, for video display control and other internal functions. The motherboard also has several *slots* into which other things can be plugged; these things are similar, but smaller plastic boards stacked with chips. These are also called boards, but each is dedicated to a specific function.

One type of plug-in board will contain extra memory chips which expand the memory of the computer. These are called *memory boards*. In the current home computer, memory boards range in capacity from 16K RAM to as many as 256K or more. In the future, memory boards will have capacities of greater than 2 megabytes of RAM because the cost of 64K RAM chips has fallen very low, and the new 256K RAM chips have just begun to appear on the market. A Japanese company just announced it has developed a 1 megabyte RAM chip in the laboratory. Bell Labs, Intel, and other American companies also have 1 megabyte RAM chips, and commercial versions are expected by 1987.

You can also buy single chips to plug into empty memory sockets on the motherboard, but this is not recommended for novices, only for those with a good knowledge of electronics and computer memories.

Memory boards are also called *RAM cards,* but RAM cards include more general types of plug-in boards with different functions as well.

The advantage of adding memory boards and RAM cards is that it expands the capacity and often the processing speed of your computer at relatively low cost. Most memory cards are easy to plug in, and you can do it yourself without help. This can be very helpful and even necessary with the second generation, 16-bit computers, such as the IBM PC. As we noted in Chapter 2, first generation, 8-bit computers can access, under normal circumstances, only 64K RAM. The 16-bit computers can easily access 512K, even 1 Mb. of RAM, but the normal configuration for an IBM PC is 128K RAM. However, if you want to run two popular financial analysis programs called Lotus 1-2-3 and Context MBA, you must have 256K RAM in the IBM PC. If you buy the 128K extra memory for IBM, it will cost twice as much than if you buy it yourself from a company such as AST Research or Quadram, both of which specialize in add-on memories for the PC.

Another reason you might want to maximize the available RAM is the problem discussed above: the "occupation" of memory space by disk operating systems, high-level BASIC languages and programs. Even more sophisticated programs tend to take up still greater quantities of RAM, leaving less than you expect for your information.

Of course, you need to add lots of memory if you plan to use programs and do applications that require much memory, such as a small business inventory system. But, be careful even when buying an inexpensive computer mainly for playing games: a 32K RAM will not be adequate if you want to play a game that requires 48K RAM.

PRINTERS

After the necessary video display, the most popular output device is a *printer.* In computing, there are only two basic types of printers: *line printer,* which logically enough prints an entire line at a time, and *character printer,* which prints one character at a time. The latter is also called a serial printer because it prints characters in series. Line printers are usually high-speed (100 lines per minute is considered slow) and expensive, and are used in business applications. For home computers and personal computers used at home, on managers' and professionals' desks, and in small businesses, the various types of character printers are of most immediate concern.

There are two basic types of character printers: *dot matrix* and *letter-quality,* or *daisywheel,* printers. Dot matrix printers form letters, numbers, and symbols with a configuration or matrix of wires connected to a printing mechanism. The mechanism is programmed to push forward the wires in the matrix which form the shape of the desired character. The number of wires in the matrix varies from as low as 4 across by 6 down (4 x 6) to as many as 7 x 9 or more. In general, the more wires in the matrix, or the more dense it is, the more solid the characters will appear to be. The goal of most dot matrix printer manufacturers is to produce a low-cost dot matrix printer which produces characters that appear to be solid. This is desirable because the solid characters do not look like they were printed by a computer—unlike the products of most line printers often used in high-speed bill printing operations.

Newer dot matrix models offer nearly letter-quality print in several ways, most often by striking the same character twice, or having the print mechanism print one line twice. Of course, this slows down a dot matrix printer, but unless you need the best-quality print for correspondence, a dot matrix printer is useful. This is true for most small busi-

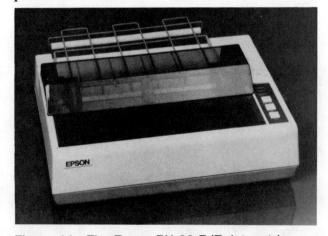

Figure 11. The Epson RX-80 F/T dot matrix printer is one of the most popular models available. It prints at a speed of 100 characters per second, has 128 type styles, and produces graphics for a less than $500 price. (Courtesy of Epson America, Inc.)

ness billing, routine correspondence, and large mailings, such as labels or envelopes.

A dot matrix printer can cost anywhere from $250 and up, but less expensive types of printers are available for hobbyists and those on a tight budget. These use heat to literally burn an impression on specially coated paper, much as the small printers on printing calculators do. One is called a *thermal printer* and the heated printing element touches the special paper and turns it a different color. A second is called an *electrostatic printer,* and its paper has two fine layers, one of which the printing element actually burns away to produce characters. The special paper for these is inexpensive, but the print quality is poor and the paper can be hard to find. They are not useful for even personal correspondence, but they are very useful for programmers and hobbyists who want to make records of their work. Today, when regular dot matrix printers are inexpensive and the required paper is simple plain paper, abundantly available and inexpensive, it makes little sense to buy a thermal or electrostatic printer. The cost savings of $50–$100 may be offset by the difficulty you have with one.

Consider here an important term in computer jargon: *hard copy.* This phrase simply means a piece of paper with information or program listings printed on it. A *printout* is simply the printed copy of an entire letter, record, file, bill, or any group of information that forms a logical unit. As you learn more about computers, you will see these terms frequently. We dislike jargon, preferring traditional words such as "a copy" or a "printed copy," but home computer jargon is flooding the language, so one needs to know what it is and how little most of it means.

Letter-Quality Printers

Letter-quality printers are not only called daisywheel printers, but also *correspondence-quality printers.* The daisywheel name derives from the shape of the print wheel used to produce the characters; the wheel has a central hub around which spokes stick out, on the end of each or which is a character or symbol. The spokes are thought to look like the petals of a daisy. Each daisywheel may have 88–96 spokes. NEC print wheels also have spokes, but they are called *thimbles* because they are shaped like an oversized thimble.

Since 1980, letter-quality printers have fallen in price, and a wide variety of models has become available from an increasing number of manufacturers. At that time, the top manufacturers were (and largely still are for top-of-the-line models) Qume, Diablo, and NEC. Most of their units are similar. They print between 40 and 55 characters per second (cps), run very reliably and quietly, and provide many important options among various units: bold face, super and subscripts, proportional spacing, and so on. However, although in 1980, these units cost $3,800–$4,500, today you can buy the same type of unit for $2,000–$3,000. Some competitors have released far less expensive

Figure 12. The Apple Daisy Wheel Printer with a helpful tractor feed mechanism. (Courtesy of Apple Computer, Inc.)

models—the Smith Corona TP-11 for $895 and the new Brother model, for example—but these models run far more slowly—12 to 15 cps. If you write letters occasionally which require letter-quality print, a slow one will be helpful, although it makes more sense to me to pay slightly more for a far more versatile dot matrix that produces near letter-quality print at a slower, although still fast (60–100 cps) speed.

However, if you print numerous letters, or if your routine correspondence is heavy, or you write articles or reports frequently and fast, the 12–15 cps speed will be far too slow. That is only about twice as fast as a typist can type. As someone who has had a 55-cps letter-quality printer for almost five years, I can testify to the virtue of the speed of getting one single-spaced page printed each minute. That's six to eight times faster than a typist and

has made a tremendous difference in my personal productivity. You will find as you become an experienced computer user that you become impatient when the computer runs slowly or the printer grinds along at a paltry 12 cps.

Remember, too, that the 12 cps is the speed you get printing regular letters; it will slow down dramatically when you print boldface, which requires double striking each character, or other special functions. The speed of the 12 cps printers may even fall below that of a human typist under those circumstances. Of course, it is still the cheapest printer choice.

Useful Hybrids
As mentioned, perhaps the most effective and cost-efficient printer for a small or at-home business, is a dual-function dot matrix printer, such as the To-

Figure 13. The Texas Instruments Model 855 is an excellent example of a hybrid dot matrix printer which also produces correspondence-quality print in a different mode. As you can see from the plug-in modules in the front of the unit, you can use three print styles within the same document. (Courtesy of Texas Instruments, Inc.)

shiba TH-2100H and a newer printer from Epson. The Toshiba model, among an increasing number of similar printers from Okidata, Epson, and various American manufacturers, runs at 192 cps for regular dot matrix and 100 cps for its near-letter-quality print. Both speeds are very fast by most standards, but these models herald what will become standard equipment on most dot matrix models during the next few years.

Coleco's slow, but very inexpensive, letter-quality printer, which comes as part of the package for the ADAM computer, may herald the day of the under $500 high-quality, letter-quality printer. If the makers can improve their speeds and product reliability at those prices, then the dual-function dot matrix may not become as popular as it would otherwise. The Coleco printer, of course, is included in the $700 total price, and cannot cost the company more than $50 to include.

Another hybrid which seems to offer a lot of value, but which is still an iffy proposition, is using an electronic typewriter as a computer printer. Many companies, including IBM for its electronic Selectrics, and Brother, offer inexpensive interfaces ($195–$395) which convert their typewriters into printers. This can be dangerous for several reasons: 1) it will wear out the internal mechanisms faster than regular typing, 2) these machines experience more reliability problems, 3) many inexpensive typewriters are not designed for heavy use, and 4) in less popular brands, the conversion mechanism may be made by an unproven company. If you already have an electronic typewriter and want to convert it, don't—unless the original manufacturer has included the capability in the original machine. Some companies sell devices which place crude mechanisms on top of the keys and which pound away at the keys. These are very hard on the typewriter. If the manufacturer built in the conversion capability, and the model you have is designed to take a constant, eight-hour-a-day pounding, you can try the conversion. If you have only an electric typewriter, don't convert it at all unless you are very handy with repairs or can afford them. Of course, some successful conversions of electrics and electronic typewriters have been made, and more will be made in the future. But before you believe a salesman's or advertisement's claims, investigate to see who has actually succeeded. It will probably be a situation in which little typing and little computer printing is done and the machine does not take a lot of rough use.

Growth of Graphics

Perhaps more important to the dot matrix printer is its graphics capability. Many dot matrix printers will print graphics from images stored in your computer. These graphics capabilities range from simple line and bar charts to high-quality color drawings. Of course, graphics capabilities add considerably to the price of a printer, but these prices too are falling in relation to the total price of the printer. For example, Printacolor Corporation produces a printer which produces multiple colors from ribbons with multiple inks that costs less than $2,000. It also produces high-quality graphics and drawings which would be acceptable to replace slides or color photocopies in presentations.

The Japanese company Matsushita, the parent of Panasonic, has developed a low-cost color printer which it has added to a home television. It has no immediate plans to introduce the color printer in the U.S., but it certainly will be available for home computers by the end of the decade, probably by 1985.

Using the graphics capability of a printer is as simple as using it to print text. A graphics printer will print any file, no matter what kind of information—text or charts or drawings—you tell it to print. However, special models of dot matrix printers with built-in graphics, of course, will give you better results than regular dot matrix, some of which will not print detailed drawings at all. For example, the popular Epson MX-80 has a sister version for graphics called the MX-80IIIF/T. The sister version costs about $100–$200 more.

A Warning on Printer Software

Getting your printer to work may not be as easy as hooking the cable to the printer port (called a *serial interface port*) and plugging it in. Your computer must have printing software designed to control your specific type and model of printer. This special program may have to be obtained separately and added to your word processing program. Often, a general printing routine is included in the word processing software, but you or your dealer will have to establish the specific layout or configuration for your computer. This will require going through a setup menu or procedure the first time you link your computer to your printer. After that, the software will permanently store it, and using the printer will be as simple as pressing one or two buttons. If you change printers or parameters, you will have to modify the software. Fortunately, more and more programs include all these elements and your involvement will diminish. But find out as you discuss buying the printer and any software package. Ask whether the package will run on your printer without any software modification, or if it doesn't, what modifications are required.

Shopping for Printers

When you shop for a printer, consider the following:

- *The nature of the job:* Consider the kinds of information you want to print and buy the kind of printer best suited for it. Dot matrix printers are best for at-home uses, occasional correspondence, small business billing, in-office reports, and draft copies. On the other hand, for frequent outside personal or business correspondence, typewriter-quality print is preferred. In many cases, the print quality you get from the two-in-one dot matrix models is good enough for regular correspondence. But for a sleek, stylish, and sophisticated look—also called manuscript quality—a full-fledged daisywheel, letter-quality printer will be required.

- *Price you can afford:* As letter-quality printers fall permanently below $2,000, and good dot matrixes below $500, price will become less important.

- *Desired printing speed:* In general, the faster the better.

- *Graphics capability:* Determine how crucial good graphs will be, and keep an eye out for low-cost, two- or three-color printers.

Printer reputation and quality of manufacture: Both are essential. Pay a little more for more quality. With a printer at home, you do not want to drag the printer back to the dealer every week or so; as a business person, you cannot afford the time lost to repairs (called *downtime* in computer jargon). Many lower-cost printers develop problems more frequently than more expensive ones. But, unlike

credit card calculators and cigarette lighters, printers are not yet disposable items.

Also, make sure you know who actually made the printer. For example, the IBM PC dot matrix printer has an IBM label, but is made by Epson. It is a high-quality printer, and is backed by both IBM and Epson, so it can be a good buy. Other companies with their logos on printers may not have been as careful as IBM.

Type of paper-feed mechanism: There are three ways to get the paper fed through your printer: friction feed, pin feed, and tractor feed. The first is the method typewriters use, as do printers which can handle only one page at a time. A pin feeding platen has a band of pins usually attached to a post at either margin of the printer. Often, these posts are adjustable. *Continuous feed* paper, which has strips with holes on each side of the paper, is rolled through the platen and the holes are slipped over the pins. The printer automatically moves the pin band which moves the paper from one post to the next. A tractor feed mechanism can be expensive ($150–$450), but it is sturdier than a pin feed and is adjustable across the width of the printer. (A pin feed platen is usually not so adjustable.) It also has at least two paper guides. The tractor feed is removable so you can use the printer for single sheet printing.

Width of printer: Another important consideration, this concerns how many columns (character widths) a printer has. The most common width is 80 columns, enough to hold a standard 8½-inch wide piece of paper. If it has a tractor feed mechanism or can accept an optional one, an 80-column printer will be slightly wider to accept the edges of the continuous feed paper. The second most popular width is 132 columns, the original standard in computer paper. Some printers are 100 columns wide, and some are 155 columns wide. The width you need depends on your applications. If you will mostly use the printer for correspondence or written reports, save the extra cost and get an 80-column. If you plan to do mostly graphics or numbers in financial work or analysis, spend the money for the 132 columns. Simply, it is hard to squeeze a lot of budgeting or financial analysis material into 80 columns and make it look attractive. With 132 columns, you can often squeeze 33 percent more columns into that space—a full year's budget with quarterly and annual totals included.

Plotters

An impressive and useful type of printing device which had long been used only in computer-aided design and manufacturing applications has made a graphic impression on the world of microcomputers during the past two years. These devices are called plotters. Using various colored pens or styluses, plotters produce striking graphs, charts, pictures, pictograms, whatever kinds of shapes can be represented in two-dimensional or simulated three-dimensional form.

More than twenty companies make plotters for microcomputers, but the best known is the Hewlett-Packard 7000 series. Plotters have dropped in price from more than $4,000 in 1978 to less than $2,000, and often less than $1,500 today. Plotters are very useful in businesses which "communicate" facts and figures with numerous charts and graphs, which summarize complex information. Plotters can even be used to create color overlays for overhead projectors and the raw material for color slides.

As important, many easy-to-use packages for common microcomputers (Apples and IBM PCs, to name a couple) have been written to take advantage of a plotter's capabilities.

Graphic artists, interior designers, decorators, and similar professionals may find plotters more useful and versatile than printers with graphics capabilities.

COMMUNICATION MODEMS

Many computer owners, particularly professionals or people with special interests, often find after they own one for a short time that they want to use it to communicate with other computers or to get quick access to public data bases and information utility services. With the rising cost of long-distance telephone calls, electronic mail, in particular, is becoming more and more popular among large groups of people. The advantage of electronic mail over the telephone is this: you never miss a phone call, and you never miss the person you are trying to reach. It's very frustrating and time-wasting calling someone over and over again—busy signals, no answer, and "Sally is not in right now." In business, an average of 40 percent of all telephone messages never reach the person for whom they are intended. I know from twelve years' experience as a journalist and author that I often have

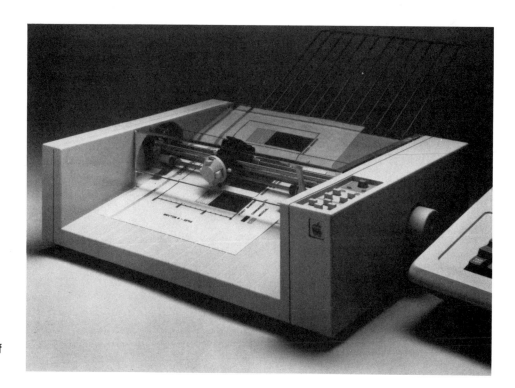

Figure 14. The Apple Color Plotter is a relatively low-cost example of these devices which produce multicolor, high-resolution charts, graphs, and drawings. (Courtesy of Apple Computer, Inc.)

to call the same person five or six times to finally speak to him.

With electronic mail, I can send a short, typed message: "Joe, please send me information on your new product line," or a long, detailed discussion. I send the message to Joe's electronic "mailbox" where he can retrieve it at his convenience. Even more advantageous, I can send the message at my convenience whether that is 1 P.M. or 1 A.M., and Joe can receive my message and reply to it at his convenience.

The usefulness of computer communications would take up a volume of its own. Suffice it to say that if it's not available now, within a few years, any type of information or service you want will be available through a computer network.

So, how do you take advantage of these immense resources? You hook up a small, inexpensive, and very simple device called a *communications modem*. Modem is jargon for modulator-demodulator, a device that transforms digital computer signals into analog electrical signals the telephone lines can transmit, and vice versa. A regular telephone cannot directly accept computer data, and the modem acts as translator for the computer and the telephone system. Although modems are available for sophisticated, very high-speed operations, home computer modems usually send signals relatively slowly—between 300-baud and 1,200-baud. Technicalities aside, a modem's

baud rate is simply how many bits per second (bps)—not bytes—can be transmitted through the modem. Now, 300–1,200 bps is slower than a snail's pace compared to a computer's internal speeds of hundreds of thousands of bps, but that is as fast as the regular telephone lines can handle. Otherwise, the computer data would be garbled by interference on the telephone lines.

Modems, too, come in many varieties, have numerous functions, and are becoming very inexpensive. There are only two basic types for our purposes: *direct connect* and *acoustic coupler*. Direct connect modems plug directly into your telephone line; they have built-in modular jacks. They tend to be far more reliable and less susceptible to transmission errors than the other type. An acoustic coupler has two rubber cups on top of it, and each end of the telephone receiver fits into one of the cups. The computer sends a signal to the modem, the modem turns it into a high-pitched sound, the telephone receiver "hears" the high-pitched sound and sends it along the telephone line to the receiving modem. The receiving modem turns the sound back into a digital signal and gives it to the receiving computer.

Acoustic couplers are susceptible to noise in the room around them as well as more transmission errors. Until 1983, acoustic couplers were the least expensive types, but new uses for integrated circuit chips brought low-cost direct connect modems. For

Figure 15. The Timex Sinclair TS 2050 Telecommunications Modem is a 300-baud direct connect modem attached to the TS 2068 Color Computer with a ribbon cable and a serial interface module. This is a typical way in which modems are connected to home computers. In the future, most, if not all home computers will have the modems built into the unit itself. (Courtesy of Timex Computer Corporation)

example, Radio Shack has a 300 bps direct connect modem for less than $120. One company advertised a similar modem for $89–$99.

However, even so-called intelligent or smart 1,200 bps modems have fallen dramatically in price, too. As recently as 1982, they cost at least $995; today, they cost as little as $395. By 1985, they should be in the price range of today's 300 bps modems. Smart modems are those with a range of computing functions included in the package.

Intelligent functions include these capabilities (with the proper software, either loaded into the computer or included in the modem's ROM [permanent] memory):

- Automatic answering
- Automatic dialing
- Automatic log-on—the ability to carry out the procedures required to make a connection to another computer or a network by remembering and sending the correct sequence of account number, passwords, and so on.
- Diagnostic and self-testing routines

There are many more available intelligent functions, and modems will become even more functional during coming years.

In fact, modems are becoming so smart and so cheap that most computers built after 1984 will have modems built in. All of the functions contained in the small box you buy today will be one integrated circuit chip in the home computer of tomorrow. Many of the computers described in the personal and portable computer sections of this book already have built-in modems; the Radio Shack Model 100, the NEC 6000, and the Texas Instruments CC-40 are just three portable computers with built-in modems.

In the distant future, modems will become obsolete because the telephone system will be an all-digital system. When that occurs—during the late 1990s, according to AT&T—you will be able to plug any computer directly into the phone lines and communicate with another computer.

Communications Software
While we wait for the computer communications millenium, we must still be concerned with mundane reality. One of the crucial aspects of this for communications is the need for *terminal emulator software*. A home computer must emulate or appear to be the same computer as the computer it is trying to communicate with. Since Apples and large mainframes and minis don't speak the same language, you must use software in your Apple that turns the Apple into a type of terminal that does speak the same language.

Communications software tends to be inexpensive, $25–$100 per package, but the cost depends more or less on its function. The software can be as functional and intelligent as the modem can be. In fact, a key point to remember is that to take advantage of the intelligence of a modem, one must buy similarly intelligent software, and vice versa. Otherwise, you have wasted your money.

The most popular modems and packages for Apple and IBM personal computers are made by Hayes Microcomputer Products, Inc., one of the amazing success stories of the microcomputer revolution. It was the first to introduce low-cost, direct-connect, smart modems with 300 bps and 1,200 bps speeds. Other leading modems are those from Novation, Microperipherals, and UDS, as well as Radio Shack's own model. Well-regarded software includes Data Capture 4.0, Softterm, Hayes's own package, and dozens more.

Study the modems and the available packages carefully and compare function and price before you buy.

INPUT/OUTPUT INTERFACES

Using peripherals with your computer can be a complex task, and if you do not know enough, you can make expensive mistakes. No information about peripherals is more important than understanding the *interfaces* your computer does or does not have.

As we noted, a computer communicates with its peripherals through *ports*. However, the ports are not necessarily alike. These ports are also called *interfaces*, more jargon for the electromechanical boundary between two computers or a computer and a peripheral. Standard interfaces have been developed and agreed upon in the computer industry (with glaring exceptions) for communications.

The most important of these interface standards for microcomputers is the RS-232 *serial* interface and various *parallel* interfaces. A serial interface transmits or receives signals in a stream of bits one after the other. A parallel interface works with one or two complete bytes at a time. A parallel interface works much like the internal CPU; it accepts bunches of bits simultaneously.

The crucial problem is whether the peripheral you buy has the same interface as your computer. If both the computer and the peripheral have standard interfaces built in, then you simply connect them with a standard cable. However, many computers, including the Atari and the Apple IIe, do not have either parallel or serial interfaces. You must buy them at extra cost. Many such interfaces have been developed for these machines, but it is annoying and costly. Many personal and desktop machines have the interfaces built in.

Many printers have parallel interfaces to increase their speed, but you must make sure your computer has a compatible parallel interface. If not, look for a printer that does. Among printers, the Centronics parallel interface is a quasi-standard.

It should be clear from this discussion that the low-cost home computers are not really such a bargain after all, if you want to do anything beyond the basics. Adding interfaces, communications capabilities, modems, and so on, can more than quadruple the total cost of the system before you know it. There are two ways of looking at this: first, manufacturers are selling computers like stereos—with components. You can buy a cassette tape deck, but not a turntable; a transceiver, but not an amplifier. In computers, you can buy a printer interface, but not a modem; a memory board, but not a printer, and so forth. Under this philosophy, you buy what you need when you need it. Second, however, the deck could be stacked against the user. A stripped down, cheap home computer could be a simple "loss-leader" to force you to buy more expensive and profitable software and accessories. It's like a grocery store's weekly special offering ground beef at three pounds for $5.00 because the store knows you'll buy a $10.00 steak as well.

BUFFERS AND SPOOLERS

A particularly annoying problem with microcomputers is that you cannot do two things at once.

The computer I use for word processing—a Jacquard J-500—lets me write on the screen while an article is being printed. I can even print, write, and make a copy of a file at the same time. The J-500 is not, however, one of the popular microcomputers. Although it is known as a micro, it has many of the capabilities of a stripped-down minicomputer. None of the popular microcomputers let you do two things at once, much less three.

However, special cards and boards have been developed called *buffers* and *spoolers* that let you print a file while working at your terminal. This is what happens: normally, the very fast computer must wait while the very slow printer works. While the computer is waiting, you cannot use it. With a buffer or spooler, the computer sends the entire file to be printed to the buffer. The file waits in the buffer, and the computer's CPU is free to be used for another task.

Buffers and spoolers are essentially RAM cards with some controller chips. When buying a buffer, the essential aspect is its capacity; if you want to print out fifty pages, each with two thousand characters, you would have to have a 128K buffer to print the entire file. Those are expensive and hard to find, so you would do best to divide the file into smaller pieces and obtain a smaller buffer—16K–64K, depending on your demand and pocketbook.

JOYSTICKS AND TRACKBALLS

For the game fans, the most important peripheral may well be sophisticated *joysticks* and *trackballs*. Many home computers come with joysticks as standard equipment, but one of the first things to break on most home computers is a joystick; children and overeager adults tend to rapidly take their toll on these devices.

Joysticks are simply electromechanical devices which send signals to a computer with a pointing device. Inside a joystick is a servomechanism and electrical contacts. Most joysticks have eight contacts or points of reference, while sophisticated ones have sixteen, thirty-two, or practically infinite points. Trackballs, developed for the NASA Apollo moon shots for guiding the Lunar Landers, are round balls sitting in a similar servomechanism. The difference is that trackballs have 360 degrees of rotation and more freedom of movement.

A very hot consumer market in home computers is the sale of advanced joysticks which are more reliable and flexible than the ones that come with the machines. Good ones are made by Wico, Kraft, TG Products, Coleco, and Atari among others. They cost anywhere from $20 to $80 each.

GRAPHICS TABLETS

Another interesting type of input device is the *graphics tablet*. Originally designed for designers, the graphics tablet is a flat plastic board with a grid of electrical contacts inlaid in its surface. You draw on the tablet with an electrical stylus, and any shape you draw with the stylus appears on the video screen and can be stored as digital data on disk. You can become a computer artist, you can use the tablets for any type of design for which drawings would be helpful, such as architecture, interior design, and graphics design. The best known graphics tablet is the Apple Graphics Tablet.

However, another type of graphics tablet has been developed for children. It is a touch-sensitive pad with which children use their fingers or a non-electrical stylus to draw on pad with the pattern shown on a video screen. Chalkboard and Koala Technologies make popular touch-pad tablets.

LIGHT PENS

Another input device with a bright future, which is also a very easy way for novices to work with a computer is the *light pen*. A light pen is essentially a type of electrical stylus, but instead of touching a pad, you touch a specially made video display itself. The special screen reacts to the electrical current coming from the pen. Light pens are most often helpful when training computer novices or people who do not know how to use a keyboard, or in business or industrial training. Instead of learning to type, the user simply chooses from menus, or answers questions presented on the screen.

Light pens are not as versatile as keyboards, but they may become more popular as a helpful aid for people who use computers at home or in business, but who do not know how to type. Gibson/Koala and Futurehouse make popular light pens.

Figure 16. The Atari Touch Tablet, which you use to draw on the video screen, can be controlled with either your finger or a touch stylus. It is an easy and interesting way for young children to work with a home computer. (Courtesy of Atari, Inc.)

THE MOUSE

The Apple Lisa and Macintosh, along with Visi-Corp's new VisiOn and Microsoft's Windows software concepts, have launched a revolution in input devices. This new device is called a *mouse,* and is actually a more or less upside-down joystick with one, two, or three buttons. The mouse is used to make it very easy for people to execute commands and functions on a computer screen. Apple uses the video screen like the top of a desk; the mouse is used to move things around on the desktop, open or remove data from files, carry out functions like a calculator, and so forth. The mouse is supposed to be the easiest way ever developed to work with computers.

There remains a great deal of controversy about the true usefulness of the mouse, and its impact on the future of human-to-computer interaction. As someone with many years of typing experience, I find using the mouse cumbersome and slower than rattling the keys. But someone who does not know how to type may find the mouse very helpful and it might make using a computer much more rewarding for him.

Apple, Mouse Systems, and Alps are important

Figure 17. The mouse pointer for the Apple Macintosh, Lisa, and Lisa 2 computers controls cursor movement on the screen and executes your commands. Other types of mouse pointers have two or three buttons. (Courtesy of Apple Computer, Inc.)

mouse makers. By the way, the device was given the name "mouse" by engineers at the Xerox laboratory when they developed it during the late 1960s. Others have volunteered less cutesy name such as "power pointer," but we are stuck with mouse. The plural is "mice."

HARD DISK DRIVES

In the very near future, even home computers will have a type of mass storage system that vastly increases your disk capacity at very low additional cost. Called a *hard disk drive,* or *Winchester disk drive,* it works according to the same principle as a floppy disk drive with notable exceptions. The disk is a rigid or hard piece of metallic oxide-coated aluminum and it has hundreds more tracks for data storage than a floppy disk. The rigid disk is contained in an airtight, permanently sealed box. It is sealed because the tracks on which data is stored as electromagnetic impulses are infinitesimal; a bit of dust, which a floppy disk would ignore, would be like a boulder in the middle of a highway for a hard disk. If the disk head, or "needle" if you will, hit the dust, it would be severely damaged and could wreck the disk.

Hard disks come with varying capacities—5 megabytes to as many as hundreds of millions; various sizes—5.25-inch, 8-inch, 11-inch, and 14-inch; and various price ranges, from as low as $1,000 to tens of thousands of dollars. For the home and personal computer world, the most important configurations are: 5 Mb. to 40 Mb.; 5.25-inch; and $1,000–$7,000. It is highly likely that by the time this book is published, a home computer with a 10 Mb. hard disk drive, a 400K microfloppy disk drive, a 32-bit CPU, 256K RAM, color monitor, and lots of software will be available for less than $2,000.

Morrow Computers, Inc., came close with its MD-11; for $2,745 you get an 11 Mb. hard disk, a 320K minifloppy, a 16-bit CPU, 128K RAM, and five software packages, including the operating system and programming language.

Small business people and professionals are being advised not to bother with 10 Mb. drives, and to go with 20 Mb. hard drives for slightly more money. Compare the $1,000 cost of a 5 Mb. drive to the $500 or so cost of the 400K Sony microfloppy; twelve times the storage for twice the price.

SPEECH SYNTHESIS AND RECOGNITION

Much has been said about talking and listening computers. Sophisticated talking computer peripherals have been available from Texas Instruments for more than four years. However, so far, no company has been able to figure out how to best coordinate the talking computer with the keyboard computer. The problem seems to be that people simply do not want to be talked to by a computer unless they can talk back.

Talking computers use techniques called *speech synthesis* which essentially store in ROM chips words broken down into their phonetic parts. The computer retrieves these parts and processes them into words and literally speaks them through audio speakers inside the computer. This technology is highly developed and very inexpensive. Texas Instruments's Speak 'N Spell toy, for example, has been very popular since 1978.

Listening computers are a different and far more complex matter. It is much easier to implant in a ROM chip the parts of speech than it is to develop chips to dissect the spoken word. There are two types of *speech* or *voice recognition*: speaker-dependent and speaker-independent. There are two methods: continuous speech and word-by-word. Many low-cost devices are available today that can understand 16–128 words spoken by the same person in a slow, distinct voice. But computers that can understand how anyone speaks in a normal conversation are just not yet available and it is unlikely they will be in the next five years. However, they almost assuredly will be toward the 1990–95 period.

You can buy these devices as peripherals for your home computer: Radio Shack has the Vox-Box, a 32-word voice recognition device, Compu-Talker Consultants has a $500 device, and a range of synthetic speech devices are available.

The most important applications for these technologies are in the military and as aids for the handicapped. Tens of thousands of people cannot speak because they are afflicted with various illnesses; computers can speak for them. Millions of blind people cannot read, but they can hear computerized devices read or speak to them. Dozens of machines have been and are being developed to help the handicapped, but the progress is slow because state and federal governments have lengthy review processes before they will agree to help pay for the devices.

MUSIC SYNTHESIZERS

Although home computers are still in the "baby-talk" stage, they are well into the symphonic sound stage already. Computerized music synthesizers and peripherals for your home computers are generally available and can be very inexpensive. You or your family can learn to read and compose music either with the computer keyboard or inexpensive add-on piano-style keyboards. The Atari and Commodore machines have very good quality sound reproduction systems. Commodore uses a special chip it developed for that purpose. The cost of these products ranges from as low as $30 to as much as several thousand dollars, but for the common home computers, the devices usually cost between $50 and $200. The functions you can get include: numerous voices, pitch, rhythm, timbre, ranges of octaves, original composition, and editing. More sophisticated systems let you compose and play multi-track recordings, store music on disk, print music scores, and study music theory with software.

For the youngsters in your family, a variety of inexpensive software is available for learning and having fun with music. Scarborough Systems has a very good package called SongWriter.

MISCELLANEOUS

Here are several other types of less often used peripherals:

RAM Disks: A special type of RAM card which emulates the operations of a disk drive. It speeds up computer operations and increases capacity.

Clock Card: A board that puts a clock with timing functions inside the computer for various uses, most importantly, the timer needed to control any computer-controlled home security or energy management system.

Touch Screens: A new type of input device—your finger—is used to literally touch the video screen.

Figure 18. The ActionCode interactive videodisc instruction illustrates the home computer of the future today: it has no keyboard. You interact with it through a touch-sensitive screen, a wand bar code reader (much like a light pen, but it reads the Universal Product Code (UPC) symbols found on packages in the grocery store), and a few simple push buttons. Its programs also interact with a laser videodisc to produce television-quality video displays combined with the power of a computer. Many experts see these or similar ways of working with a computer as what it will take for everyone to have a computer in their home. (Courtesy of ICS-Intext, division of National Education Corporation)

These are special types of video screens which either use electrical current or radiation (power too low to harm anyone); when you touch the screen, the current is broken which sends a signal to the computer. The HP-150 personal computer from Hewlett-Packard is the first machine with a standard touch screen. It is useful as an easy way to work with menus, move things around the screen, and execute commands. Whether touch screens and the finger will become major input methods is open to question. They can, however, help novices get over their fear of computing quite rapidly.

CHAPTER 5
The First Generation: Chips off an Old Block

Any technological development is both the result of thousands of years of human intellectual growth and change, and a stop along the way to further growth. Today's home computer got its start in the 0–9 numbering system the Arabs developed during the Middle Ages. (Europe did not drop the Roman numeral system and adopt 0–9 until the Renaissance.) In 1643, mathematician Blaise Pascal, after whom the Pascal computer language is named, invented an arithmetic machine that counted 0–9 with a series of wheels. In 1694, another mathematician, Leibnitz, adopted this machine so it could multiply and divide.

It wasn't for another 140 years that another improvement was made: Charles Babbidge began his "analytic engine." He borrowed an essential principle from French weavers who literally programmed mechanical looms with punched paper cards. This process was invented by a man named Jacquard and his method is still used in some areas of the world. (In fact, my "workhorse computer," which I mentioned in Chapter 4, and on which this book was written, is named after that Frenchman by its manufacturer.) Babbidge adapted the punched card idea for the instructions for his analytic engine; he also wrote about the theory of memory and output devices, but he did not have the technology to make them. Although he never finished his engine, he did achieve something more important: the attempt to use a machine to represent "pure" numbers instead of quantities or analogies like a thermometer or odometer. "Pure" numbers, of course, are the basis for digital counting.

Somewhat simultaneously with Babbidge's work (and the work of his assistant Ada Byron, the daughter of the poet Lord Byron, and the namesake for the Ada programming language) came tremendously influential developments: the telegraph in 1843–44, the telephone in 1876, the mechanical typewriter in 1874, the electric light in 1876, and many more. It was not until the late 1880s that Babbidge's work and an electromechanical device were combined into a useful instrument. This instrument, the punch card machine developed by Herman Hollerith, saved the 1890 U.S. Census from chaos.

The punch card machine used an electromechanical hole puncher on a paper card to represent the letters of the alphabet and the 0–9 digits. The rectangular card had 80 columns. To this day, Hollerith's card remains the standard for punch card technology. Hollerith's device was used by the U.S. Census for many decades, but its advancement for computing was this: when the device received a signal, it punched a hole; when it did not, it did not punch a hole. The same off-on principle was applied to binary, off-on, digital counting.

Hollerith was also the developer of the paper tape reader which used the same standard but in a continuous paper stream.

About the same time, the Burroughs electromechanical adding machine was developed, and in 1917, the first four-function electrical calculator was in operation. Many improvements were made between 1917 and 1944, but the first digital computer was not developed until American scientists needed to complete the calculations for the atomic bomb. By the way, the first practical computer was not finished in time to help with that project, but two computers were built in 1944, one at Harvard and one at Bell Labs. Both were monstrosities filled with thousands of electrical relays, and neither was fast enough to be of real use because they used electromechanical relays. They were the first machines to count numbers and not analogies and multiply 12-digit and 10-digit numbers, respectively.

In 1945, a leap forward occurred when ENIAC (Electronic Numerical Integrator and Computer) became the first computer based on vacuum tubes. Vacuum tubes make electric current flow between a filament and a plate in an open space emptied of air. This occurs very rapidly. A vacuum tube can be only in two states—off and on, the basis of the binary system. ENIAC was also huge, much greater than an average house, with eighteen thousand tubes, seventy thousand resistors, ten thousand capacitors, and six thousand switches, and it was terribly unreliable. A tube blew out once every six minutes, and the computer then made errors. But when it worked, it calculated numbers one thousand times faster than any machine had ever done before.

After ENIAC, electronic computers exploded. IBM introduced the first business computer in 1953, and Honeywell, Burroughs, Univac, and a host of long-dead companies started the race to automate major corporations and government. Meanwhile, the researchers laid more groundwork for home computers; almost simultaneously, ITT and Bell Labs discovered semiconductors—the substances, such as silicon and germanium, through which a flow of electricity can be controlled, increased or decreased, off or on. From this discovery, during the 1950s and 1960s, scientists

developed transistors that work just like vacuum tubes. However, they can be as small as millionths of an inch. Thus, transistors can move electricity around thousands of times faster than a vacuum tube can, enabling computers to do many thousands of times more calculations per second.

Of course, this technology was quickly adopted in the computer industry, by IBM to build more powerful mainframes, and by Digital Equipment Corporation to develop the first minicomputer. Most of us have lived through the incredible impact of the solid-state transistor: the transistor radios you took to the beach during the 1950s and 1960s, solid-state televisions which made color TV affordable for everyone, and particularly, pocket calculators.

THE FIRST MICROCOMPUTER

All of these precursors to the home computer age led, in 1971, to the development of the first microprocessor on a chip of silicon. Texas Instruments developed it, and, in fact that 4-bit chip remains one of TI's best sellers. However, the first microcomputer—with all of the elements of a computer on a chip—was developed in 1974 by a new New Mexico company. The 4004 4-bit microcomputer was the first in late 1973, the 8-bit 8008 model was introduced in 1974. Microprocessors quickly found their way into video games, hand-held electronic games, home appliances, military applications, industrial controls and processes.

However, the home computer revolution began in January, 1975, when the MITS Company advertised a computer kit based on the new Intel 8080 microcomputer in an electronics magazine. The company was overwhelmed by fifty thousand inquiries and cash orders, hundreds of times more than expected.

When word got out, computer engineers and entrepreneurs sensed that something of earthshaking importance had occurred. By the end of 1975, dozens of kits were for sale, although they required assembly and programming in machine language. The first computer store opened in mid-1975; the first hobby computer clubs and users groups began by late 1975; *Byte,* the first and most successful computer magazine began publishing in 1976; microcomputer fairs and festivals sprang up around

Figure 19. A rare photograph of the complete Processor Technology SOL, the first complete micro-computer system sold as a unit. Introduced in 1976, it contained all of the elements that are so familiar today. (Photo from author's archives)

the centers of development, particularly the area outside San Francisco called Silicon Valley. And the first assembled microcomputers—with everything in one container and peripherals available—were produced: the IMSAI 8800 and the Processor Technology SOL. The SOL was the first personal computer because it came with a keyboard and a video screen. A group of college students founded Cromemco, a shortened form of the names of their college dorms. Cromemco is the surviving company of these pioneers.

1977—THE WATERSHED YEAR

The next year launched the home computer revolution as a permanent aspect of American business and family life. During 1977, the early leaders—and both notable successes and failures—were introduced: Apple I, Commodore PET, Radio Shack TRS-80 Model I, Exidy Sorcerer, and Ohio Scientific Challenger. They were different from the dozens of kits which applied to hobbyists (MITS Altair 8800A and B, IMSAI 8800, Cromemco Z-1, Southwest Technical Products 6800, Polymorphic 8800, KIM-1, and Vector Graphic V-1, for example). They had a keyboard, a microcomputer, internal memory, I/O devices, mass storage, internal monitor software, and so forth all in a neat, usable package. And all of them could be used by slipping a preprogrammed cassette into a recorder and

loading a program. The microcomputer had become an appliance anyone could afford and use.

THE HOME COMPUTER ENTRENCHED

Between 1978 and 1984, an incredible business emerged from a handful of underfinanced, amateurish computer engineers to become the fastest-growing major industry in the country. About thirty thousand microcomputers were installed in 1977. The computers installed during 1984 alone are expected to exceed 2.5 million small business and desktop computers and 3–4 million home computers. By the end of 1985, the number of computers in American homes and businesses should easily exceed 15 million.

Computer pioneer and futurist Ted Nelson was ridiculed in 1976 when he predicted 10 million home computers by 1980. He was not wrong; he was simply a bit too optimistic. My own 1980 market research estimates for a multi-billion dollar software industry by 1982 were also scoffed at. My estimates were low.

In short, beginning in 1978, a machine for hobbyists was transformed practically overnight into a personal tool that will make more difference to each person's intellectual life than any tool since the invention of the Gutenberg printing press in the 1480s. Considering that, within a few years, a microcomputer will be used in or will control vir-

Figure 20. The Radio Shack TRS-80 Model I, the first inexpensive home computer, introduced in 1978. (Courtesy of Tandy Corporation)

tually every electromechanical device, the microcomputer must be equated not only with the printing press, but with the discovery of electricity and even the first use of fire. It can do more for personal freedom and expression than the mobility given us by the automobile and the political power gained by the right to vote.

Think ahead to the near future, 1990 and back six years to 1978. Consider the changes during the past six years and double the pace of change in the computer industry during the next six years. It may be daunting, but it is also exhilarating and intriguing.

THE PERSONAL COMPUTER EMERGENT

The microcomputer revolution that soared in 1978 took an unexpected direction, into the world of corporate management and small business. Pioneers thought the micro would flood into U.S. homes, but the move into the home stalled for several years for several reasons, among them, the poor economic conditions, but more important, mass computerphobia. The computerphobia was a factor simply because very little software was developed which gave anyone a good reason to use a computer at home.

The spur that boosted the personal computer to "stardom" was a program developed in 1978 by two young university students and programmers in Cambridge, Massachusetts. Called the "visible calculator" at first, the program was initially marketed by a third student. Transformed into VisiCalc, the program provided the answer to the question on every business person's lips: What do I do with a personal computer? The VisiCalc answer was: Anything you do that involves rows and columns of numbers and mathematic equations. Of course, for most business people and professionals, especially financial analysts and budget managers, numbers and figures are part of their life's blood.

VisiCalc was originally developed only for the Apple II computer, and by the end of 1979, conservative estimates showed that VisiCalc alone had been responsible for selling more than one hundred thousand Apples. As 1980 began, the wave of personal computers began in earnest as dozens of new competitors introduced new personal computers for business and a handful of powerhouses moved into the home computer field. Distracting from home computer sales was the boom in video games, but the main problem was that home computers were simply priced too high for an average family.

Apple enhanced its computer and called it the Apple II Plus. This model differed from the original in that it came with 48K RAM as standard equipment, and it adopted a new operating system called DOS 3.3. Radio Shack came out with the business-oriented TRS-80 Model II and later the home-oriented Model III to replace the Model I. Dozens of companies introduced small computers based on the business-oriented CP/M operating system while everyone waited for IBM to drop its personal computer shoe.

For the home, Atari introduced the Atari 400 and 800 models, priced at $460 and $990 respectively, and permanently established the notion of plug-in software cartridges for home computers, an idea which has not played as large a part in the home computer explosion as was originally thought. Software companies seem to find it easier to work with floppy disks, and the buying public seems much more satisfied—certainly for business programs and for most games—with a disk they may modify if they know how. Mattel, Inc., made the first of its three-year series of announcements concerning a computer keyboard for its then new Intellivision video game and launched a marketing program which eventually failed in 1983. Texas Instruments introduced a technically sophisticated home computer, the original TI 99/4, but hampered its sales with a high price ($1,000), very little

THE WORLD AT YOUR FINGERTIPS

software, a touch membrane keyboard, a negative attitude toward outside software developers, and poor marketing. As you'll see, the 99/4A—a full keyboard update of the first model—eventually sold for as little as $49 discounted and $99 at retail, one tenth its original price.

At the end of 1980, Sinclair Research, a tiny British research firm led by a genius, Clive Sinclair, revolutionized the home computer industry by introducing the ZX-81, the first under $200 home computer. It had a tiny 5K RAM and a plastic touch membrane keyboard, but it used the very latest chip and manufacturing technology and began the cutthroat competition that led to the 1983 shakeout among home computers. At the high end, Hewlett-Packard introduced a powerful personal computer, the HP-85, that foreshadowed the portable and briefcase computers of today. HP sold only tens of thousands of the HP-85s, but it made more money selling personal computers in 1980 and 1981 than either Apple or Radio Shack did by selling complete systems to engineers, scientists, and businesses, the Hewlett-Packard's traditional markets for its well-regarded line of minicomputers and engineering products.

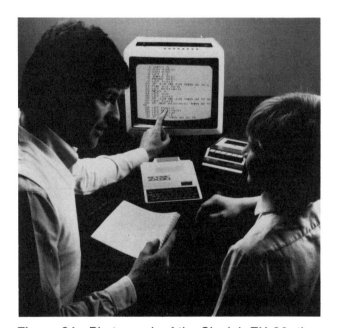

Figure 21. Photograph of the Sinclair ZX-80, the first computer sold for less than $200. Its direct descendant, the ZX-81, was the first computer sold for less than $100. (Photo from author's archives)

During that year as well, a raft of companies, which have since failed or were subsumed into larger companies, introduced home computers: Interact Electronics, APF Electronics, Compucolor Corp., Ohio Scientific, Exidy Data Systems, and more. Toward the end of 1980, Apple also introduced the Apple III, a decent computer which bombed in the marketplace for several reasons. First, it was not compatible with software for the Apple II except through a cumbersome procedure. Second, Apple tried to hog the software development for itself, so few outside software products supported it. And third, and most important, the product suffered a severe failure of quality in the manufacturing process. A very high percentage of the first few thousand units simply did not work, and the III quickly got a very bad reputation, so people stayed away in droves.

I've given this brief historical review to make several points about what it takes to succeed in the home computer market. There are three major considerations: software, software, and more software. The consumer simply is not interested in buying computers with which immediately they can do nothing. The home computer is an instant gratification machine. Another consideration was the consumer's strong bias toward typewriter-style keyboards. Any machine that came out with a touch membrane keyboard simply did not succeed as well as those that had typewriter-style keyboards. It appears U.S. families are very serious about their children learning to type and use computers correctly. Many other factors influence the success or failure of a computer, but these, plus sufficient financial backing, of course, appear to be the two most common denominators.

Enter the Colossus
Apple, Radio Shack, and Commodore vied for top place in computer sales during early 1981, and then, in August, 1981, the other shoe fell and landed square on top of Apple and Radio Shack: IBM introduced its IBM Personal Computer, and to the amazement of the entire industry, did it right. At the press conference introducing the machine, there was a very tall stack of popular and useful software ready to go with the machine: VisiCalc, EasyWriter word processing, a choice of three operating systems, Microsoft BASIC applications language, small business accounting software,

and, more important, a raft of technical manuals on how anyone could write programs for the IBM PC.

IBM had learned its lessons very well and stolen a march on Apple who had ignored its own success story by trying to keep Apple III software development in its own hands.

When the history of the IBM PC development is written, it will show an incredibly unlikely series of events within the IBM corporate structure. First, IBM dumped the problem of making the computer on a small five-person group. Second, the group was given independence from any major operating group, thus it could move quickly and make its own decisions. Third, IBM let the group not only use other companies' parts and equipment in the machine, it also chose an outside company's microcomputer as the heart of the PC—the Intel 8086 16-bit chip. Fourth, the group actively sought and encouraged outside software developers, realizing there was no way IBM specialists could develop enough software in the eighteen months they had to finish the machine. Fifth, they threw the doors open to outside dealers and put them in open competition with its sales force. All of these were revolutionary practices for IBM. Finally, from start to finish, the PC took thirteen months to get ready for introduction.

And the world of personal computers was changed overnight. IBM is said to have anticipated orders for fifty thousand to seventy thousand PCs during the first *twelve* months of production. It received forty thousand firm orders from its own employees in the first three months and more than three times as many orders from regular customers during the same three months.

IBM was taken by surprise, yet during the past three years, it has turned its company upside down to take advantage of the future of the personal computer. One of the great sea changes in modern American corporate history occurred as IBM managed to build and ship about 150,000 PCs during 1982. by the end of 1983, it had built and shipped more than 750,000, and by the end of 1984, IBM alone will ship more than 2 million personal computers worldwide.

Within a few months after the PC's debut, literally hundreds of companies were modifying their Apple II software to run on the PC or were building peripherals of every size and shape to fill the large gaps left by IBM's inability to make its product fast enough.

By early 1982, a new mini-industry had begun: building personal computers "compatible" with the IBM PC. As we mentioned, true compatibility with the PC is impossible because it would violate IBM patents and copyrights. Only a handul of computers, such as the Compaq, Columbia Data Products, and a couple more can even run any disk which you take out of the IBM PC and put in the other machine. IBM PC "compatibility" actually means the computer runs a very similar version of the MS-DOS operating system. During 1982 and 1983 and through 1984, several dozen IBM PC compatibles have been introduced. However, the most important ones were not yet available by early 1984. They are the ITT personal computer, said to be a virtual "clone" at half the price of the IBM PC, and several models being built in Taiwan. The Taiwanese computers are said to be illegal copies, but it appeared IBM might make deals with these companies to charge them a licensing or royalty fee. Apple Computer experienced a similar problem with Taiwanese, Korean, and Hong Kong ripoffs, but chose to fight in court rather than negotiate. With the exception of one $2.5 million judgment in the United States against Franklin Computer Corp., Apple fought a losing battle. IBM is expected to be more realistic in its dealings with these emerging computers.

In mid-1983, Apple's anticipated challenge to the IBM PC in the business world, the 32-bit Lisa workstation based on advanced multi-tasking software, fizzled at first. Listed at $9,999 when introduced, by 1984 its price had been cut twice to $6,500 and Apple was only making slightly more than ten thousand Lisas a month. This was said to be in line with Apple's expectations, but Lisa was plagued with some problems similar to those of the Apple III—not enough software, not enough early encouragement of outside software developers, failure to deliver promised applications, a product without a well-defined market, and so forth.

The IBM of the Home Computer

As IBM stole the headlines and an increasing percentage of the market for desktop and personal computers, Commodore introduced the low-cost $299 VIC-20 and soon thereafter, the low-cost $595

Commodore 64. And a cost-cutting war began that lasted through 1983 and shook up both the stock market and several major companies. Commodore's success—2 million home computers sold during 1983 with more than 50 percent of the market—occurred because it is a vertically integrated company. It makes everything from chips to disk drives, even monitors, and gains the vast economies of scale. It also owns the company that made the original CPU (the 6502 microprocessor) for the Apple, the Atari, and its own computers, and had pioneered in techniques to put more and more functions, which used to be executed on several chips or several units, onto one chip. Commodore also excels in aggressive marketing programs through department stores, discount retailers, toy stores, and the like. Consider the change: in 1978, there were fewer than one hundred computer stores or outlets. Today, there are at least three thousand computer stores, and more than ten thousand retail outlets for home computers. That would be like the number of automobile dealerships growing from five in 1900 to two thousand in 1905. That kind of explosive retail growth did not occur with any other twentieth-century technological development.

However, the cutthroat competition caused severe problems for many computer companies: both of Atari's main businesses—video games and home computers—were shellacked by competition at the same time, and it has yet to fully recover; Texas Instruments decided to stop making home computers at all; Mattel decided to drop its Intellivision keyboard and its Aquarius home computer; Radio Shack held its own, but retreated to its own large retail network, and kept rapidly losing its share of the sales. Even the Japanese were dismayed and chose to avoid any real commitment to the U.S. market until 1984–85. Yet, a significant advance did occur in 1983, the introduction of the Coleco ADAM, an integrated system with printer for less than $700.

As 1983 ended, two major changes occurred: IBM prematurely announced, but did not deliver, its home computer, the IBM PCjr—a technologically disappointing machine, but one that made a big impact on the public mind; and Coleco had trouble delivering its ADAM to fill Christmastime orders.

(All of the existing machines described briefly in this chapter will be discussed in detail in the next part of the book.)

The Apple Recovery

As 1984 began, Apple staked its future on the Macintosh, heralded as a revolutionary third generation personal computer. This time, Apple appears to be doing it right. The day Macintosh was introduced, Apple also announced a list of 170 software and hardware developers who either had Macintosh ready to use or would by the end of April, 1984. Apple was spending $25 million to advertise the Macintosh, and it had generated a lot of enthusiasm among dealers. The initial units appeared to be made of high-quality machines, and the price was amazing: $2,495 for a 32-bit CPU, 128K RAM, 64K ROM, a 400K Sony microfloppy disk drive, a very high-resolution black-and-white monitor, and much more. This is much cheaper than the regular IBM PC, but Apple has decided not to take IBM head-on among large corporations. Apple is appealing, as its ads imply, to "the rest of us," the people who don't know how computers operate or even care very much to find out.

Whether the Macintosh heralds a millenium in home computers or is a stepping stone to the truly useful computer remains to be seen, but it should certainly guarantee Apple's second place in the microcomputer sweepstakes for two or three more years.

As this book was completed during February, 1984, several crucial developments were awaited:

- The public response to the IBM PCjr, IBM's first foray into consumer electronics
- The entry of numerous low-cost Japanese home computers based on the MSX operating system with truly compatible and interchangeable programs
- American Telephone & Telegraph's first line of personal and small business computers
- The ITT Personal Computer
- A new generation of software which would dramatically encourage the average home owner to buy a home computer
- The emergence of home videotex systems in several communities around the country, including Coral Gables, Florida.

- The beginning of computer game playing by telephone as envisioned by Coleco and AT&T, and several cable-based game systems, including PlayCable.

Of course, these developments during the first decade of the microcomputer revolution are just the highlights. In between, an amazing industry has grown up with thousands of programs, hundreds of computers, thousands of peripherals, and fortunes made and fortunes lost (for example, the Osborne 1 computer, the first personal computer with built-in disk drives and software for under $2,000, went bankrupt during 1983). To those on the inside and those of us reporting developments from the outside, the first decade has been the most exciting period of our lives. The pioneers trekking westward in the 1870s and 1880s must have felt a lot like this; their eagerness to conquer new territory and to overcome seemingly impossible challenges is shared by today's microcomputer pioneers. Fortunately for them, their pioneering is done in Mercedes and BMW autos instead of Conestoga wagons, but the risks appear to be just as high. The microcomputer revolution is still a sparsely settled territory, a combination of welcoming soil and hostile climates. Fewer than 10 percent of all families and less than one quarter of all businesses have a microcomputer. Compare that to the telephone—99 percent of all households have at least one; the television—97 percent with at least one; and the radio—98 percent with at least one, usually five or six. The home computer revolution has just begun.

CHAPTER 6

How to Buy a Home Computer

While home computers are getting easier to use, they aren't necessarily getting easier to choose. Among inexpensive home computers, personal computers, and desktop small business computers, more than two hundred kinds of microcomputers line store shelves, and more than three hundred companies actively market microcomputer accessories and components through more than four thousand computer stores, more than ten thousand department stores, and thousands of discount stores, electronic outlets and boutiques, systems houses, computer specialty houses, mail order houses, and distributors. Yet, each fully assembled microcomputer differs from the next in many ways. Most models—even those that claim to be compatible with the IBM PC—cannot be hooked up to another computer without special equipment and software; they are truly incompatible.

So, you can easily become confused when you begin looking for your first home computer. And spending $100 to $5,000 for the best microcomputer for your needs should make even the most confident consumer stop and think before buying. If you go into a computer store or electronics outlet without really knowing what you want and need, you could easily make a bad and costly choice and be forced to unhappily coexist with the wrong home computer.

THE VARIOUS STORES EXPLAINED

Even if you have a firm idea of which make and model you want, choosing the right store from which to buy it may present another bewildering problem. There are eight different ways to buy microcomputers, and each has its own strengths and weaknesses. You can match your desires, knowledge, and strengths with a store that's "compatible" with you and begin a healthy, cooperative relationship that may help you get the best results from your first computer.

Here's a rundown of the basic places to buy microcomputers and ways to buy them:

Computer Retail Stores are dedicated exclusively to selling and servicing many different microcomputers with each one's peripherals, programs, books, and manuals. Some also offer consulting, education, and training classes. Most offer basic repair services for popular products and basic support for popular software. During the past two years, computer stores have divided into two basic subdivisions: 1) strictly business-oriented stores which sell more expensive micros—the Apple IIe, IBM PC, Compaq, DEC Rainbow—to corporations, professionals, and small businesses; and 2) consumer-oriented stores, which sell some models to small businesses, but concentrate on sales of home and game software and moderately priced home computers to individuals and families. They may also emphasize sales of educational software and computers to schools.

The weaknesses of computer stores, in general, center on the strong pressures they are under. Their high-volume, low-margin nature means they are caught in a very tight vise between customers who need and demand a lot of support and service, and the pressure from competitors to lower prices while offering more products. They therefore tend to push off on you their most profitable products whether those products meet your needs or not. Computer stores have faced a real shakeout and face more rough times: the store that is here today may be gone tomorrow. Shop only at a reputable store that can show you it will be there in the future to provide support. Unless you are an immediate prospect for buying lots of equipment, you are unlikely to receive the service you should expect. And a shortage of knowledgable salespeople means you are likely to get worse service than you need, especially if you are a novice. If you want to spend a few hundred dollars on a home computer, a computer store is not the right place to go. If you plan to spend several thousand dollars for a small desktop computer for general applications—word processing, budgeting, accounting—a computer store is a good place to go. However, if you have a specific need for unusual applications, most computer stores will not be able to best handle your requirements.

Retail Franchises operate as retail stores, but follow the standard operating procedures established by a national franchise company. They have national marketing power and use the management expertise of the national franchise headquarters. Many also tend to be company owned and managed. The strengths of this type originate with the management whip the national company can wield, but the weaknesses are the same as for any retail store. Although about a dozen franchises have begun during the past three years, ComputerLand, with more than 350 stores, remains the largest. Another type of franchise, led by Businessland, sells all types of business equipment and services—computers, copiers, telephones, electronic typewriters, calculators, and office supplies—to small

companies in their areas. And their are also software-only franchises, such as Programs Unlimited and Software City, which mostly sell games and "generic," that is, the most common, types of programs.

Small Retail Stores may sell home computers in addition to a large variety of electronic equipment—audio, video, videotapes, calculators, digital watches, clocks, electronic gizmos of every kind. Some are hobby shops that have added a line of home computers and software. Others include electronic boutiques, audio stores, television stores, stereo shops, even small toy stores. Their strength is primarily low prices on common hardware and game software. Their weakness is support. It is very unlikely anyone in the store knows anything at all about how the software works or the machine operates beyond plugging it in and turning it on. Only use this type of store for the least expensive and easiest-to-use computers like the Commodore VIC-20 and the Sinclair series.

Manufacturers' Stores, exemplified by Radio Shack's 7,700-plus outlets, sell the company's own computers exclusively. This was supposed to be the wave of the future in computer retailing in 1980 and IBM, DEC, and Xerox made heavy commitments opening about 35, 25, and 45 stores respectively. But with the exception of Radio Shack, this approach has been very unsuccessful. Xerox has sold almost all of its stores, and both IBM and DEC stores have slowly turned into little more than unprofitable window displays for their products. Some have become mere extensions of the company's direct sales and support force, a method the major companies have helped perfect. The problem is that the major manufacturers know little about the ins and outs of retailing and did not expect retail operations to take so much money and deliver such small margins.

Computer Shopping Centers form a marketing concept pioneered by Radio Shack. Radio Shack has opened more than 250 Computer Centers, which provide everything a buyer or owner would ever need or want in the company's hardware, software, maintenance, support, repairs, professional advice, and training. A one-stop computer shopping center would carry: microcomputer, terminals, printers, documentation and manuals, floppy disks, ribbons, papers, printer wheels, cassettes, storage baskets, disk packs, accessories, peripherals and samples of spare parts, memory boards, and components. Sears Business Centers and Control Data Corporation's similar stores are prototypes of this type of store. Another prototype is the specific product shopping center; for example, one store sells and services only printers and printer-related supplies and services.

Computer shopping centers have proven they can be helpful for the small business person, but so much of their activity comes from service and support, they are not really the best place for a consumer to buy. Small business people or people who work at home should find them useful if they insist on good service.

Department Store Chains and Large Toy Stores like Macy's, which started the ball rolling in its California stores in 1978—a lead that had been followed by every major retailer in the country. Department stores, discount stores, and large toy stores are all high-volume, low-margin operations, so most of them will sell you a computer at a low price and have a variety of games and simple software. But do not expect much support or service. Buy only the least expensive and simplest computers through these stores unless you plan to become a hobbyist and dedicate yourself to doing it yourself. One exception to this rule is the department stores which have leased their computer sales space to local computer stores or computer franchises. At these locations, professionals and individuals with serious applications can find much better service and support, but will still have to contend with a lot of curious shoppers and children.

Mail Order-Houses and Distributors often intrigue novices with the lure of significant price savings by buying computers and software by mail order. The greatest weakness of mail order sales is the lack of service and support; you either have to arrange a service contract with a local dealer—who may be very reluctant to provide it since you won't have bought the system from him—or ship any broken computers to the factory for service. Mail-order houses are often criticized for being fly-by-night operations; however, it appears mail-order

houses are no more fly-by-nights than any other type of business. You, the buyer, are responsible for checking the mail-order house's reputation and financial status before you buy. *Caveat emptor* for any type of computer store or outlet. Make sure any mail-order house offers money-back guarantees on delivery, warranty and service, and do not hesitate to complain to the proper authorities in the mail-order house's home state and city if you encounter any serious difficulty. (A one-week delay in shipment is not a serious difficulty; an unanswered or disconnected telephone number, a two-week shipping delay, and a cashed check or credit card charge without delivery soon thereafter are all signs of serious trouble.) You could also make any mail order purchase C.O.D. (cash on delivery) to avoid some of these problems.

Software service will have to come through the software house's hot line or a local user's group.

However, if you can find good service for your system and software, then by all means use mail order if the discounts are substantially better than you can do at a local store. But stick with well-known equipment and software from well-known companies: products for the Apple, the IBM PC, Commodore models, and Atari series. Then, even if a mail-order company does disappear, you will find many other sources of assistance.

Systems Houses and Street-Front Sales Organizations are dedicated to providing essentially "turnkey" computer systems for small businesses, corporations, and professionals such as attorneys, physicians, accounting firms, and other specific industries and service businesses. A systems house packages all of the hardware, software, service, support, and training and sells that package to one or more specific types of businesses in which they specialize. Systems houses developed during the minicomputer era to provide software and sales to medium-sized organizations. In the microcomputer era, they have found a home in those industries where the buyers need assistance, but want less personal involvement in computing than a dedicated hobbyist. If you are in a specific type of business, know little about computers, and do not really want to become a dedicated computerist, using a systems house to develop and install a complete system is the best way for you to go.

Many computer stores, which began trying to

sell to consumers and professionals, have abandoned consumers and become, in effect, street-front systems houses. Another approach, exemplified by Morris Decision Systems in New York City, is a street-front sales and service organization. Morris Decision Systems provides sales, service, support, and training only to professionals involved in financial analysis and decision support. Its clients are almost always managers and professionals in very large and important banks, stock brokerages, investment houses, financial institutions, and major corporations located in or with its headquarters in New York City. If you are a financial analyst or strategic planner for a corporation, an organization like Morris Decision Systems is the best way for you to go.

The weakness of this approach is that systems houses must often compete against the direct sales forces of major manufacturers, such as IBM, DEC, and Data General, and the only way they can compete successfully is to offer a full range of services that the major manufacturers simply are not interested in. They must carve a niche out of a local or regional market, and many are often financially weak. Before you buy from a systems house, make sure it is financially secure and find another one that can give you service and support if the one you buy from should go out of business a few years after you install the system. However, for the best service and support, systems houses and organizations like Morris Decision Systems are the best available.

I bought my computer from a systems house, and for three years, service and support were superb. When I moved from one region to another, the original systems house recommended some friends in my new area; they were even better than the first systems house and have stayed with me through thick and thin and several more changes of address. My experiences with computer stores have been less positive.

Each type of store has its own advantages and disadvantages. To make the best buying decision, you need to know how to be alert to and compensate for weak areas and use the strengths to your best advantage.

First, learn about the fascinating panoply of home computers and pick the one that best suits your needs and increases your enjoyment. After all, you expect a computer for the home to be as convenient to use as your automobile, your television, your videocassette recorder, your food processor, your video game, or any other expensive, but enjoyable home appliance.

WHAT DO YOU WANT TO DO WITH YOUR HOME COMPUTER?

Here are some basic guidelines to help you answer the most important questions about buying your first computer.

Decide What You Want To Do With It. First, and most important, carefully decide *exactly* what you want to use your computer to do. It is easy to buy a hammer; you buy it to drive and remove nails. Just because you occasionally use a hammer to drive screws, bend bars, or break windows does not mean that is the purpose for which you bought it. The problem is that a home computer is a general-purpose tool. The concept of the microcomputer offers hundreds of different choices or applications for the technology. But each computer has its own limitations of memory capacity, processing power, speed, and capacity, types of peripherals it can accommodate, and so on. A computer like the 16K RAM Timex Sinclair 1000 series will let you balance a simple home budget, learn simple BASIC programming, and play games. It will not control a 3,000-item inventory for a small store, althought an IBM PC or Apple IIe with a hard disk will do it easily. Thus, the general type of computer you buy will largely be determined by your applications.

Although you can buy hundreds of programs on cassettes, cartridges, or floppy disks for the most popular computers, more advanced applications, such as word processing, will involve studying instructional manuals. Or, with some study and effort, you can learn to program your computer yourself. A very high percentage of the millions of people who have already bought computers have learned some of the basics of programming. However, some studies have shown that an even greater percentage of computers are sitting on shelves or in closets gathering dust because their buyers simply could not find enough to do with them. This will happen if you consider a home computer a fad or the thing to do, or even if you buy one because you are afraid your children will not be as smart as the other kids in school. Computers and kids appear to go together very well, but only for short periods of time; few children develop long-lasting and serious "relationships" with computers, or become whiz-bang programmers with futures at MIT or Harvard. What happens when the kids grow out of their computer phase, or the fad dies, and the kids chase after the next fad? You could easily waste hundreds of dollars if you look at a home computer as only something for the kids.

So ask yourself what *you* and your family will want to do with your home computer now and say two to five years from now. You may become so fascinated and involved that you'll want a more versatile computer while giving your first one to your children or grandchildren. Do you want your children to play games, improve their learning skills, boost their grades in their subjects at school, or learn the basics of computing? Do you want to manage your family finances, bring home work from the office to do at home, better serve local community, church, or volunteer groups, do more and better coursework for your college or post-graduate courses? Do you need to operate a home business or improve the management of your professional practice? Do you have an investment portfolio over which you would like to exercise more control? Do you want to manage professional research projects or schedule projects on your job? Do you want to learn programming and languages quickly for your own interests?

Each of these applications requires different computer capabilities. For example, to run a simple monthly household budget of twenty or so expense categories, a cartridge for the Commodore 64 or VIC-20, or the Atari 1200 will do nicely with a cassette recorder for data storage. If you own a portfolio of fifty stocks and bonds and want to keep track of them each day, you'll need the Dow Jones Portfolio Manager, a subscription to the Dow Jones News & Information Service, and a communications modem with the proper software for an Apple IIe, an IBM PC, a TRS-80 Model III, or any of many other similar computers with 64K RAM and two disk drives. The basic investment for the home budget would be less than $500; for the stock and bond manager, up to $2,500.

If you draw up a detailed list of what you want to do with your computer, you will save yourself a lot of time and trouble. Make a side-by-side list: a "must" list—the things you must do with the computer; and a "wish" list—the things you would really like to do with the computer. Then, look for a computer that will do everything on the must list, but can be expanded to accommodate most of the applications on the wish list.

But decide from the start that buying a home computer will be the result of a serious, thought-provoking process involving the whole family. Too often, a father will spend $1,000 for a computer because his teenaged son told him the machine would do everything he wanted. The problem is the "he" in question; it is likely the computer will handle the son's game playing and dating schedules, but not the father's mail-order business budget or mailing list.

What Can You Or Will You Pay For Your Home Computer? Finding the answer to this question is the second important step. If you're willing to pay $79 for a video game, paying $100–$200 for a simple home computer to play games and do some other fun things makes good sense. If your children's game playing is secondary to their education and your professional or business tasks, then spending several thousand dollars or more for a good personal computer makes even better sense. You can even deduct that portion of the cost of the computer dedicated to business use; if you spent $2,500 for a computer, and use it for business half the time, you can deduct $1,250 of the purchase price from your taxes. If you have an office at home, or keep the PC in your office most of the time and game playing is incidental, you may be able to deduct the entire cost. (There are IRS rules regarding these deducations, so check with your accountant before you take the deduction on your income tax return.)

Between the extremes of the $79 home computer and the $5,000 desktop computer with peripherals lie dozens of models, configurations, and variations of available microcomputers. And that variety and choice increase every month.

If you decide your uses will be mostly game playing and you have $500 to spend on a computer, your choices will be narrowed to a handful of machines: Commodore VIC-20 and 64 and a couple of new Commodore models; Atari 1200XL (at a discount in stores); Spectravideo models; Radio Shack Color Computer series; and several Japanese models. If you can afford $5,000 for a sophisticated business machine, the whole world opens up to you: the Apple Macintosh; the IBM

PC XT with a 10 Mb. drive, a host of IBM compatibles—Compaq, Columbia Data Systems; Tandy 2000; Radio Shack Model 16B; Hewlett-Packard 150; and on and on. We'll give a good idea of how to distinguish among business machines below.

Construct A Budget. When thinking through the total costs of a home computer, remember that buying the machine is just the beginning. Build a budget and include these extra *operational* costs you need to anticipate:

- *Maintenance costs.* Very little for small machines, basically throwaway machines if they break down; as high as 8–15 percent per year of the purchase price of a personal computer. You will need a hardware and software service contract for business computers after the warranty (usually ninety days to one year) expires.

- *Software costs.* Some companies throw in a variety of software with their machines. Morrow Computer, for example, throws in five packages, including three languages, a word processor, and a spreadsheet, with its very inexpensive $2,745 MDS-11 with a built-in 11 Mb. hard disk. However, additional programs add up rapidly. Game cassettes cost from $4.95 to $19.95; game floppy disks cost from $14.95 to $79.95 or more. Small business programs start at $49.95 and rapidly climb to the hundreds of dollars, although the prices for "generic" or common standard programs are falling rapidly to the $50–$75 level. Consider, too, the out-of-pocket expense of buying new games for yourself and your children as they are introduced.

    Computer and software vendors base a lot of their business on how much money you spend on software. Although software development costs are high—$250,000 for a new game is not unusual—the production costs are minimal, less than $1 each for games on cassettes or floppy disks. Thus, a game selling for $29.95 will turn a handsome profit if more than ten thousand copies are sold.

- *Peripheral costs.* Required or desirable peripherals will quickly add to your costs as well. Often, you want to add disk drives to replace a cassette recorder, but disk drives cost $279–$625 each. Or you may want to add a printer. The simplest printer starts about $89, but good dot matrix printers run from $249–$1,000, and letter-quality printers range from $595–$3,500. More important will be memory boards and RAM cards required to run specific types of software. The cost of additional memory is falling like a rock, but the temptation is to buy more than you need because the incremental price is so low. A 16K RAM board may cost less than $100, so you may think, why not buy 128K for $300? These are false economies of scale if your computer cannot use the additional 112K, or none of your applications could really benefit from the extra capacity. And remember my earlier comment about the need for an extra video monitor to prevent family arguments over who gets the family TV for the evening—the TV watcher or the computer user.

- *Supplies.* The most often overlooked cost of a computer is that for supplies. If you do not have printers or disk drives, these will be low; you may buy inexpensive cassette tapes to store programs, but that's about it. However, if you use even the simplest printer, such as the Coleco ADAM printer, you will need to buy ribbons and paper. If you use your computer in your business or profession every day, you can expect substantial annual supply costs.

For example, I use my Jacquard J-500 computer practically every day in my profession as an author, consultant, and market researcher; my supply costs—floppy disks, letter-quality printer ribbons, print wheels, and continuous-feed printer paper, for the most part—run about 6–8 percent of the cost of the hardware itself. I also have spent $200 for a modem and $100 for a cable and terminal emulator software, so my peripherals cost beyond the original letter-quality printer and two disk drives has been minimal, but the supplies cost has been high. This has occurred despite the fact that the ribbons, and floppy disks, and the print wheels, are about 20–30 percent cheaper today than when I bought the machine four years ago. Of course, I use my computer more often than I did at first. It has become indispensable.

So beware of the *hidden* costs of buying a microcomputer.

Buy Software First. Only one absolute rule exists when buying a microcomputer, especially for business, but often for home use as well. That rule—which you ignore at your own peril—is this: FIRST, find the software which will execute the application you want to accomplish and only then buy the hardware that runs the program. Why? Today, most computer hardware is pretty much the same; one 8-bit CP/M-based or one 16-bit MS-DOS computer is pretty much as good as any other 8-bit or 16-bit computer. But, because of the architectural and disk drive compatibility problems we explained, not all software for all applications have been adapted to every available machine.

Even today, well-known programs like VisiCalc, 1-2-3, or even WordStar word processor, do not run on every machine. So, you cannot expect any lesser-known program to run on every machine. Often, the only program that fits your special needs may operate on only one or two types of machines. If you buy the hardware first, how will you know whether the software you must have will run on it? Of course, you could ask the salesman, and he will give you an answer; of course, it may or may not be the right answer. Hardware salesmen have been known to make many promises—some delivered and some not delivered. Play it safe and avoid the agony of desperately searching for essential software that simply may not be available for the hardware you bought.

Here are two examples, one very close to home: First, as a senior editor for two medical newsletters, I know of at least three physicians who bought IBM PCs because they knew colleagues who had done so. All three PCs were still sitting on the floor in their offices after six months because they didn't know what to do with them and had not had time to find out. Second, my own accountant's firm had a client who sold a certain type of computer. To do the client a favor, the accounting firm bought several of the machines. Within three months, the computer manufacturer had entered bankruptcy proceedings, and my accountant, a partner in the firm, was on the phone asking me to tell him where he could find accounting software for the computer.

This principle even applies to games. If you only want to play games, you still have to make sure the computer you buy plays the kinds of games you want to play. Suppose you prefer adventure games, or war games, or games of strategy. The best of these games require large RAMs—often 48K and 64K—and many are only available for the most popular computers, such as the Apple IIe and the IBM PC. The game software house may not find it worth the effort to make its games run on Commodore or Atari computers, much less on the less well-known computers and IBM PC compatibles.

The good news is that as the number of home computers sold increases to the 10 million range, more and more software companies find it profitable to adapt their software to all of the most popular computers: Apple IIe, Commodore 64 and VIC-20, Atari 1200, IBM PC, sometimes the Radio Shack TRS-80 series, and a few others.

Remember: Computer software is not like an audio record, which will run on any stereo or hi-fi record player, or VHS standard videotapes, which run on any VHS videocassette recorder. Because no standards exist for microcomputers and their storage media, each software package you want must be exactly compatible with the computer you plan to buy. So I repeat: Ignore the first rule of computer purchasing at your peril. Appendix A gives you a checklist of questions to ask when buying software.

Examine And Compare Your Initial Choices. Using this book and computer magazines (many of which are listed in the Bibliography), begin studying your software requirements and the available computers which may match those requirements and your budget. Visit the types of stores where you are most likely to find the software, hardware, support, and service you need: computer stores, computer shopping centers, department stores, discount stores, wherever you can buy computers.

A good idea is to develop a written checklist to take with you, and go through that checklist point by point with the salesman. If a salesman will not cooperate with you in filling out the checklist, buy somewhere else—with the possible exception of a $79 computer. If they won't be helpful when you are trying to buy something from them, they won't be helpful after they already have your money.

Find the software which best matches your application(s). Ask what software is available for applications on your wish list, the things you would like to grow into. Study the manuals and documentation. Can you understand their instructions on the first reading? If not, be careful. Manuals should be written so any novice can grasp the meaning, if not leap right into the application.

Then, compare the features of each machine which will run your application(s): RAM capacity and expandability; mass storage medium; keyboard and its "feel"; video monitor and the screen—is it comfortably placed, is it color, green phosphor, amber, or black and white; number of peripheral ports and types (parallel, serial, or dedicated to one type of peripheral); available peripherals and their costs; and so forth.

Next, look at the hardware user's guides and make sure they, too, are well-written and easy to understand. Many novices believe it's their fault if they don't understand a manual. However, that is simply not true. It is the company's responsibility to provide a good manual.

Carefully compare the hardware's features, without comparing apples and oranges. Don't expect a 16K machine to do the same things as a 128K machine, or cost the same amount of money.

"Test Drive" The Computers. Although many people scoff at test-driving cars before buying one, "test driving" a home computer before you buy it is essential to making the best decision. Just as intangibles influence buying a car—seat comfort, windshield angle, knee and leg room—similar intangibles should influence buying a home computer. You can buy any car and get an engine, four wheels, seats, and a steering wheel. With any computer, you can get a CPU, RAM, input/output, and so forth. The options and the "standard" features make the difference in cars *and* computers. If two computers have similar features and prices, but you don't like the keyboard or the color of the one the dealer favors, don't buy it. The idea is to buy a computer that makes *your* life more pleasant, and that includes esthetics.

During the past several years, too, the so-called intangibles have been shown to have a great deal of real effect on how people use computers and what people think of them. For example, it has been proven that black-and-white video screens can be more tiring to the eyes than green phosphor or amber; the effects of color screens vary with application. Keyboard configurations directly affect how fast and how accurately you can type or enter data. The height of the video display and where you place your chair in relation to that height has

been shown to cause back aches and neck pain. These so-called human factors are also known by the scientific name of "ergonomics," but human factors are both science, in that some effects can be studied and quantified, and art, in that the effects of many factors depend on an individual's unique reactions. Keyboards are very much in this category: how well one uses them depends not only on the physical makeup, but on the size of each operator's fingers and hands, whether the person is a speedy touch-typist and uses all ten fingers, or, like me, uses eight, seven, six, five, or four fingers depending on what I'm typing.

These variables and the known facts about the effects of computers make it imperative for you to test drive each model.

Test Drive The Software. If you are buying a business computer, there is an even more compelling reason to test drive the machine. It gives you the chance to test the software you have chosen with "live" data, that is, information you actually use in your business. Before you buy any software and computer, take a batch of whatever it is you do—balance sheets and general ledgers if you are an accountant, standard or flexible contracts if you are a lawyer, a manuscript if you are a writer—and use the software to execute those tasks. This is the very best way to find out whether the system—the synergistic results of the software and hardware—does what you want it to do in the ways you want it to do it, and whether you (and your employees or your family) are comfortable with the system's operations.

During the test drive, deliberately make mistakes and see how the system responds. Do anything short of damaging the equipment and software to try to make the system crash. The dealer may exhibit signs of nervousness, but do it. It's your best protection before the computer arrives in your home or office.

If you are looking for a home computer, expect to take a couple of weekend afternoons or weekday evenings searching the department stores before you get a clear idea of the computers available in your area. Buying a machine for business and professional uses will take much longer if you do the proper search for software first and then hardware. Most of that time should be spent planning and deciding just what your applications will be.

Study Warranties and Service Contracts. Once you've narrowed your choices down to two or three machines, get a copy of the manufacturer's or software producer's warranty and read it carefully. Most home computers and software come with complete ninety-day warranties that cover everything; some contain partial warranties on certain parts or peripherals for up to a year or more. In general, the longer the warranty, the better it is.

Software warranties often are difficult, however, because they often offer you little or no protection. Many often do not even warrant or guarantee that the program will run at all, much less do what the vendor claims it will do. Software warranties are a legal mine field, and should be read carefully. The plastic-wrapped package or binder will often have printed warranty sheets warning you to "READ THIS FIRST" with explanations of the dire things that will happen if you open the package and then decide you don't want the software. I strongly feel this all-or-nothing, and everything-is-in-my-favor attitude of the software companies is a serious detriment to the industry. And instead of discouraging software piracy—a person making illegal copies of a program and giving them away or selling them at a profit—this stiff-necked attitude actually encourages it.

Before the warranty period expires, maintenance and service can be handled in several ways:

1. The dealer may often offer warranty service, if the vendor has designated them as authorized service centers.
2. You may have to return the defective equipment or disks to the factory or vendor for repair or replacement. Most companies promise quick turnarounds on service; Radio Shack has been offering twenty-four-hour turnaround for several years. Often, this means you have to take the equipment to the dealer who ships it to the factory. At the factory, they diagnose the problem, and if it can be fixed on the spot, they do so and ship it back to the dealer. Or, if it can't be fixed, they'll ship a replacement to the dealer or authorize the dealer to give you one from his inventory.
3. If you arrange for it, on-site service will bring a repairman to your door to fix the problem on the spot. But you almost always have to pay a monthly fee for on-site service. It's almost always best to do this if you are in a small business and cannot wait even twenty-four to forty-eight hours for a problem to be fixed. You may believe you can wait, but remember this example: For two years in a row, I had a severe problem with my system on a Friday afternoon in July. One of those days was Friday before Fourth of July weekend. If I had had to ship my computer out, I could not have done so until the next business day, Monday. I could not have had my computer back before Wednesday, at best. But, with on-site service, I called the serviceman Saturday morning at home. Over the phone, he walked my wife (the mechanical genius in the family) through dismantling the disk drives where she, and he, thought the problem was. She then put the faulty drive in the car, drove to his house forty-five minutes away, and exchanged it. She had the new one back home in another hour, into the machine fifteen minutes after that, and we were in business to meet the deadline that fell on the Tuesday after the holiday. Only because we were then living so far from the repairman did we have to deliver; in the other case of holiday *downtime,* because we lived very close, the repairman was at my door on July Fourth, Monday morning, and gone before early afternoon, the problem fixed. On nonholiday weekends, the serviceman arrives within twelve hours after our call. Period.

Only once, in four years, was I unable to reach a repairman when I had a critical system crash. What that cost me was a summer weekend shot to pieces because I had to borrow electric typewriters and my wife, my assistant, and I spent all weekend typing, editing, and retyping by hand—a torturous, expensive, and wasteful process I had willingly given up years before.

During the early days of microcomputers, obtaining service for the inexpensive machines was difficult, if not impossible. Now, all of the major companies and most smaller ones, including Atari, Commodore, Radio Shack, and Apple either have their own service personnel, or have made arrangements with national service companies as have Atari with Control Data Corp., dozens of companies with TRW Service, and dozens more with Sorbus, Inc. Apple now has instituted authorized service centers, and IBM has its own and authorized service centers to fix machines.

A good and less costly strategy for service, if you don't want to spend the money for on-site service (8–18 percent of the purchase price per year, depending on machine and manufacturer), is to divide the service arrangements according to the most crucial components of the system. Have on-site service for the microcomputer itself and any software bugs, and use drop-off service (you do the hauling and picking up) for printers and peripherals. But be sure to have a spare printer or disk drive around you can just plug in and go. You can even get a very inexpensive printer to keep you in business while your best one gets fixed. In this way, you can save up to hundreds of dollars a year in service charges, while making sure the key elements are repaired as quickly as possible. And you can pay for the inexpensive replacement printer and drive in a year or two with your savings.

One development I anticipated in 1980 has not happened yet, although I still think it will happen: small computer repair shops that resemble or are offshoots of TV repair shops. TV repair shops are already doing VCR repairs, so it is just a matter of time before small computer repair shops become feasible.

An Important Note On Programs. Some software companies will replace program disks if they wear out, but usually place a small charge on the replacement, usually 20–30 percent of the original cost.

More important, however, are a company's policies on software updates and changes. Most software companies are constantly changing and improving (*upgrading* in computer jargon) their packages. In the past, many companies gave buyers these improvements free of charge; however, those days are ending for software sold through computer stores. Software producers now usually charge a nominal fee—as low as $10 to as high as 50 percent of the original purchase price—to provide you with an updated copy of the software. Many other vendors charge full price for improved versions.

However, there is a way around this if you deal with a systems house. Often, if you are a good customer, your systems house will willingly give you software updates. My experience with repairs on

holiday weekends and obtaining software updates has led to a Golden Rule of computer service:

*A Good Relationship with Your Serviceman
Is Worth Your Weight In Gold*

Determine the Normal Start-up Problems. Like a car, some computers will have "kinks" when you break them in. Fortunately, there appear to be fewer and fewer kinks in the hardware because quality control standards in the industry are so high; companies like Apple have found out how fast a product can fail if the product is not well made. Most kinks will occur in the software because most are complex and it is difficult for a team of programmers to eliminate all the bugs before the product is sold. Ask your dealer what start-up problems you may expect, and don't believe him if he says there are none. Talk to other people who already own the kind of computer you plan to buy and ask them. They will already know.

Check the Manufacturer's Reputation. While you determine these other factors, you should also look into each manufacturer's reputation, financial status, and staying power. As unfortunate as its competition thinks it is, among all the reasons IBM can expect to sell almost two million PCs this year, one is often overlooked: buyers know IBM will be around to support its products. Buyers do not have to fear IBM's imminent bankruptcy or inadequate service. If you want to buy a computer from a less well-known company, be careful. Osborne was the highest flying company around for a year, and then, in a space of six months, it went under. Check with user's groups and hobbyist clubs, read magazines, check with friends, and even ask the Better Business Bureau to see if you can find a chink in the company's public relations armor. Do NOT trust the word of the machine's dealer. I know two people who bought Victor computers because high-pressure salesmen talked them into the purchase although I am almost sure that the salesmen already knew Victor was in financial trouble. Be very skeptical of a dealer offering any surprisingly large—40, 50, or even 60 percent—discounts on hardware or software. It means the manufacturer or software vendor or the dealer himself is in serious trouble.

The only time I've seen a real bargain was the

last few months Apple made the Apple II Plus. Listed at $1,495, you could buy an Apple II Plus with two disk drives for as low as $599 in New York City as dealers cleared out their stocks. This was an exceptionally good deal because there are thousands of programs available for the II Plus, hundreds of service centers, dozens of peripherals and components, and dozens of books and magazines with things to do. The same was not true of Osborne or Victor before they entered bankruptcy proceedings.

Manufacturers' reputations are not usually as big a problem as they were in the early days when weak companies opened their doors, advertised a product, and folded the next week, but you still need to stay on your toes. For example, who would have thought Texas Instruments would stop making home computers? If you had known that Texas Instruments invented the digital watch in 1972, but stopped making them in 1979 because of competi-tive pressure from cheaper Japanese and Hong Kong watches, you could have at least been suspicious. In early 1984, Mattel stopped selling home computers, and it was an open question whether Atari would stay in the field. However, as with Texas Instruments, there is no reason not to buy an Atari now if it suits your purposes because a lot of software, service, and support is available for Atari computers.

If you want to buy from a mail-order house, ask it for at least five to seven references in your area, and follow them up. If a mail-order outfit balks at your request, you might want to try somewhere else.

By following this buying plan, you can make a satisfying and intelligent decision. After all, micro-computers should entertain and enlighten, and make life easier and more profitable, not waste your money on a bum steer, or your time in a re-pair shop.

PART TWO
THE NEW GENERATIONS— 1984 AND BEYOND

Home computers have rapidly reached millions of homes in the United States and abroad. When the first edition of this book was published in 1980, only 350,000–400,000 microcomputers were being used in the home. Yet, the figure was ten times the number sold in 1977. More than four million home computers were sold during 1983 alone, and that figure does not include the almost 1.5–2 million microcomputers sold to businesses and professionals. During 1984, the sales figures doubled, and in 1985, the figures may double again.

Microcomputers had grown from nothing to what was, for the year 1983, an $11 billion industry. This was more than consumers spent for black-and-white televisions, dishwashers, washer-dryers, food processors, microwave ovens, hairdryers, and similar home appliances combined.

Truly, a remarkable change in our way of life continues to gather momentum. Part Two, "The New Generations," describes all of the newest microcomputers in three price ranges—under $1,000 for the basic system; under $2,500; and more than $2,500—and examines the phenomenal and powerful portable and briefcase-sized computers that portend the watch-sized computer of the future. Here you will find out in detail what all of the popular and many not so well-known computers can offer you. You will also find out how you can turn your home computer into a thoroughly reliable electronic post office, a personal information utility, and a "window of the world." Yet, you will find all of these computers as easy to use as your stereo equipment or pocket calculator.

CHAPTER 7

Home Computers for Less than $1,000

During the heady and very competitive days of 1983, home computer prices fell below $100 for very powerful and useful machines. The severe price reductions had serious side effects, pushing Texas Instruments out of the market, threatening Atari, and preventing many other companies from introducing new machines. By early 1984, however, the dust had begun to settle, although prices had stabilized at a higher $229–$669 level for the inexpensive home computer.

The current generation, along with new, inexpensive home computers introduced during 1984, packs an amazing punch in smaller and smaller packages. And, now more than ever, people with no knowledge of computers, keyboards, programming, or typing can use these machines and a wide variety of software packages.

However, the most important thing to remember about these inexpensive computers is that the low prices, in most cases, buy only a computer, a keyboard, and sometimes a cassette recorder. The low price does *not* usually include the cost of peripherals, especially printers and floppy disk drives, and software. Often, assembling a useful system will cost more than $1,000, if not $1,500. Generally, with the exception of Coleco, computer makers are selling their systems like stereo equipment—a basic unit with lots of options. So be prepared to spend

more, often a lot more, than the low price given in a newspaper ad.

How to Use This Guide

This and the next three chapters use a standard format so you can easily and quickly find out the most important facts about each computer. The essential information is given so you can do some comparison shopping before you start visiting stores. Our discussion of each computer begins with a brief description of the company and the computer. Next are given thirteen categories of information which will be repeated in the same order for each computer. A brief discussion of the anticipated future development and evolution of the computer and its manufacturer will end each section.

To give the most objective viewpoint of each computer, they are given in alphabetical order according to manufacturer's name.

But remember that the home computer industry changes every day. New microcomputers, dozens of software packages, new peripherals for existing machines, all this and more happens every day in this incredibly fast-changing world. Rapid, unpredictable, and intriguing changes will remain the hallmark of home computing for years to come.

Fundamental change, however, does not come

every day, merely new products. It takes at least two or three years for a fundamentally new type of machine to reach the market. For example, the new Apple Macintosh was in development for three years and for most of that time, experts knew it would have a hybrid 16-bit/32-bit microprocessor brain. The first 16-bit microcomputer was introduced in 1978, but the IBM PC, an 8-bit/16-bit hybrid was not introduced until 1981, and the wave of 16-bit machines did not hit until mid-1982.

The same kind of thing is happening now with 32-bit microcomputers. The Macintosh is the first popular use of the technology, yet Bell Laboratories has used a 32-bit Bellmac CPU for its internal purposes since 1981, and it had developed the 32-bit processor in 1979. Announcements of new, expensive, sophisticated 32-bit micros are being made regularly in the computer magazines, but the wave of popular 32-bit machines will not reach the store shelves until 1985. For example, Sinclair Research, a British firm, introduced its $500 32-bit Sinclair QL computer in the United States in late summer/early fall, 1984. And the very inexpensive (under $200) 16-bit computers from Japan did not reach the United States until the 1984 Christmas season. So, although the next four chapters do not and cannot discuss every computer that will be available, they will give you a very good picture of the most popular and proven computers and point you in clear directions for what to look for in the future. (Basic system prices will be given in its own category. Prices for peripherals and software, if known, will be given in parentheses next to each one's name, like this: Dot matrix printer ($395).)

ATARI INCORPORATED

Atari 600XL

BRIEF SUMMARY: After years as the hottest video game and home computer maker, Atari fell on very hard times during 1983–84. Despite a wave of TV ads with Alan Alda, it was in doubt during mid-1984 whether Atari would be able to stay in the home computer business. Yet, the company produces several very good and easy-to-use computers. It was buffeted by the competitive price wars and internal dissension.

Figure 22. Illustration of using the Atari Touch Tablet with the AtariArtist program on the Atari 600XL computer. Note the plug-in cartridge in the top of the unit and the cable between the computer and the tablet. (Courtesy of Atari, Inc.)

CPU: 8-bit 6502 family.

RAM/ROM: 16K RAM, expandable to 64K with 1064 Memory Module.

OPERATING SYSTEM: Atari DOS 3.0, replacing Atari DOS 2.0.

MASS STORAGE: Atari 1010 Program Recorder or Atari 1050 disk drive, and ROM Program Cartridges.

VIDEO DISPLAY: 40 characters by 24 lines (40 x 24), but user must provide television or monitor.

KEYBOARD: Typewriterlike keyboard with four function keys, and superior sound and color graphics capabilities, including a three-and-a-half octave range for four voices.

I/O SLOTS/INTERFACES: Three, one RS-232 standard interface, one for program recorder, and one for disk drive.

SYSTEM PRICE: $200.

PROGRAMMING LANGUAGE: Atari BASIC; Atari Pascal 2.0 ($69.95); Atari Super PILOT ($39.95) for educational programs; Atari Player Maker ($39.95) for video games; and Atari Screen Maker ($39.95) to combine text and graphics for customized displays.

PRINTERS: Atari Dot Matrix Printer and Atari 1027 Letter-Quality Printer.

MODEMS: Atari 1030 300-baud direct connect modem.

OTHER PERIPHERALS: Very wide variety available from both Atari and many outside manufacturers. Atari's newest peripherals include: *Atari Touch Tablet* ($89.95) for use with AtariArtist software; *Atari Light Pen* ($99.95) with AtariGraphics software that lets you draw directly on the screen in 128 colors; *AtariLab* ($49.95–$89.95) plug-in screen lab kits; and many others.

AVAILABLE SOFTWARE: Literally thousands of games of all types for all Atari computers. Atari is very popular for educational programs and hundreds of those in most subjects are also available. Atari itself has made a concentrated effort during 1983–84 to improve its software with: AtariMusic I and II ($39.95) each; Atari Translator (requires a disk drive, 64K RAM, and costs $9.95) which converts outside software for the Atari DOS; home management software—SynCalc, an easy spreadsheet, SynFile, a personal data filer, and SynTrend, a graphics and statistics package ($99.95 each); Typo Attack ($39.95); Atari/Walt Disney Learning Series for children; and a variety of others.

WARNING: Many of Atari's peripherals and software require more than the minimum 16K RAM. You will have to buy extra RAM boards or modules for this software to run. Be sure to check the required RAM before you buy.

SALES OUTLETS: Thousands of department and discount stores, computer stores, toy stores, electronics, and stereo outlets.

SERVICE AND SUPPORT: More than one thousand authorized service centers and a toll-free number (800) 538-8543, or (800) 672-1404 in California to find the one nearest to you.

FUTURE DEVELOPMENTS: Atari is also making a major push into converting its software for other computers, such as Commodore's VIC-20 and 64, Apple II Plus and IIe, the IBM PC, and even the TI 99/4A. Atari seems dedicated to recovering its position in the field, but must introduce a new, low-cost 16-bit computer if it expects to compete with the Japanese during 1985. Such a product is under development and was scheduled to be introduced during late 1984.

Atari 800XL

BRIEF SUMMARY: Basically the same machine as the 600XL, but with the 64K RAM included.

CPU: 8-bit 6502.

RAM/ROM: 64K RAM.

MASS STORAGE: 1050 disk drive and one plug-in cartridge slot.

VIDEO DISPLAY: Sophisticated color graphics, but user must provide television or monitor.

KEYBOARD: Typewriterlike with four function keys.

I/O SLOTS/INTERFACE: Three, including one for disk drive and one for RS-232 serial interface.

SYSTEM PRICE: $399 list, but widely discounted.

PROGRAMMING LANGUAGE: Same as 600XL.

PRINTERS: Atari 1025 Dot Matrix Printer, Atari 1027 Letter-Quality Printer (at $350, a real buy), and Atari 1020 Printer/Plotter ($300). Variety of other printers will run with the 800XL with minor software/system modifications.

MODEMS: Atari 300-baud direct connect modem.

Figure 23. The Atari 800XL and its peripheral 1050 disk drive, 1030 communications modem, and the 1027 letter-quality printer. (Courtesy of Atari, Inc.)

OTHER PERIPHERALS: Same as for 600XL.

AVAILABLE SOFTWARE: Same, but with more emphasis on personal computing applications, such as AtariWriter for word processing.

SALES OUTLETS: Same as 600XL.

SERVICE AND SUPPORT: Same as 600XL.

FUTURE DEVELOPMENTS: A more advanced Atari 1450XLD was shown at two consumer electronics shows, but it was not known in mid-1984 whether Atari was going to make it or not. It was more likely the 16-bit computer—not the 1450XLD—would replace the 600 and 800XL series. One should also look for a portable version of the Atari computers.

Atari 1400XL and 1450XLD

BRIEF SUMMARY: Advanced 64K versions of the same computer but with built-in modems, a real plus, and more features. The 1450 version may not be produced.

CPU: 8-bit 6502.

RAM/ROM: 64K RAM.

MASS STORAGE: Built-in disk drive, double-sided with 254K capacity per side.

VIDEO DISPLAY: 80 x 24, more useful for business and professional applications.

KEYBOARD: Row of eight function keys above the typewriterlike keyboard.

I/O SLOTS/INTERFACES: Same.

SYSTEM PRICE: $799, designed to compete with IBM PCjr.

PROGRAMMING LANGUAGES: Same as above with Atari CP/M and Microsoft BASIC options.

PRINTERS: Same.

MODEMS: Built-in modem obviates need for extra one.

OTHER PERIPHERALS: Same.

AVAILABLE SOFTWARE: Same.

SALES OUTLETS: More emphasis on computer store with these products.

SERVICE AND SUPPORT: Hardware service through same channels, software through vendors and Atari itself.

FUTURE DEVELOPMENTS: Actual production of 1450XLD to be determined by success of IBM PCjr and similar competitors.

COLECO INDUSTRIES, INC.

Colecovision ADAM

BRIEF SUMMARY: After the IBM PCjr, the ADAM was the most eagerly awaited home computer of 1983, and once it was finally shipped in late 1983, it proved to be among the most successful. During 1984, it was giving the IBM PCjr a real run for the money. ADAM is simply less expensive and more functional than the PCjr, plus Coleco—with years of successful experience with hand-held electronic games and the Colecovision video game, which gave Atari and Mattel fits dur-

Figure 24. In the top photograph is the ADAM-Colecovision family computer system complete with its letter-quality printer, keyboard, game paddles, and dual cassette tape drive. In the bottom photograph is the module which plugs into the Colecovision video game unit and turns it into the home computer. The module also allows ADAM owners to play all Colecovision game cartridges. (Courtesy of Coleco Industries, Inc.)

ing 1982 and 1983—knows a lot more about selling home computers than IBM thinks it does. The advantage of the ADAM is its six processors, each of which handles separate functions, and makes available lots of RAM for program and data storage. They work through a controller system called "ADAMNet."

CPU: One 8-bit Z80 CPU, one MC6801 master controller CPU, and three more MC6801 CPUs to drive the digital data cassette, the printer, and keyboard.

RAM/ROM: 80K RAM (64K user RAM and 16K video RAM) expandable to 144K RAM, and 40K ROM (24K ROM word processor, 8K ROM OS, and 8K ROM for peripherals).

MASS STORAGE: C-250 digital data cassette with preformatted 256K capacity. Plug-in cartridge port that accepts *all* Colecovision game cartridges. Optional second digital data cassette and 360K-byte-capacity 5.25-inch disk drive.

VIDEO DISPLAY: 36 x 24, with 80-column optional available, sixteen colors.

KEYBOARD: Seventy-five-key typewriter keyboard including six color-coded function keys, ten word processing command keys, and five cursor control keys.

I/O SLOTS/INTERFACES: Four slots through Memory Console for printer, modem, disk drive, video game adapter for Atari 2600, and other peripherals.

SYSTEM PRICE: About $700–$750, with discounts available. Includes SmartWriter word processing program, two multi-function ColecoVision game controllers, SmartBASIC, and an arcade game.

PROGRAMMING LANGUAGES: 56K Smart-BASIC included in system price; Personal CP/M optional for business programs.

PRINTERS: Slow 10 cps, but good SmartWriter Printer included in system price, a packaging and manufacturing breakthrough in the computer field. Slow, slightly noisy, and somewhat difficult to use, but it is very useful for students and people who do occasional correspondence at home. Uses standard daisywheels.

MODEMS: Optional ADAMLink 1200-baud direct connect modem.

OTHER PERIPHERALS: 64K RAM Memory Expander; Tractor Feed device for SmartWriter Printer; Atari 2600 video game adapter; Adapter that turns a Colecovision game into an ADAM computer; and more to be introduced by Coleco and independent hardware makers throughout 1984 and 1985.

AVAILABLE SOFTWARE: SmartWriter word processing is included in 24K ROM and it's a good, versatile program for use at home, but not for professionals. ADAM was introduced with 170 software programs under four headings: Family Learning, Languages/Programming Aids, Home Information Management, and Entertainment. See Appendix B for a complete list of these and more programs. More are being introduced all the time.

SALES OUTLETS: Hundreds of toy, department, discount, mass-market, electronics, stereo, and similar retail outlets.

SERVICE AND SUPPORT: Honeywell Information Systems' Customer Services Division has established a nationwide network of service centers for ADAM, with thirty-five in operation by early 1984. Software support comes directly from Coleco or the software house. Toll-free number: (800) 842-1225.

FUTURE DEVELOPMENTS: ADAM clearly looks like a winner which will put Coleco in good stead for its competition with Commodore and Atari. Coleco is well aware that it must encourage software developers to provide more and better things to do with the system, and its early 1984 announcement of 120 new software titles (added to 50 in late 1983) shows its commitment. New software for the ADAM will emerge throughout 1984 and 1985, and one can expect Coleco to add more peripherals, such as touch tablets and light pens, by 1985, and go out of its way to encourage other hardware firms as well. Look for Coleco to introduce another home computer toward the middle of 1985 which is compatible with, but extends the ADAM concept.

COMMODORE INTERNATIONAL
Commodore VIC-20
BRIEF SUMMARY: Commodore is by far the leader in the under-$1,000 field, and its success

took the industry by storm during 1982 and 1983. Commodore was a brand new company making low-cost pocket calculators in 1977 when it introduced the Commodore PET (Personal Electronic Translator). At $750, the PET was the first home computer priced lower than $1,000, it had the best keyboard of any of the first generation, it had exceptional graphics capabilities for a black-and-white machine, and it all came in one convenient box, including the monitor. The PET did well and was the leading educational computer, but Apple stole the media show with its success among trendy professionals. However, as Atari made headlines with its video game craze, Commodore positioned itself to steal the home computer market. Commodore's key advantage is that it is "vertically integrated," that is, it builds all of its chips and processors and most of its own equipment. Thus, it can build larger quantities of computers at lower prices much more quickly than its competition. In fact, Commodore owns the company that makes the 6502 series of chips that control the Apple II series, the Atari series, and several other computers. Commodore dropped the other shoe on the industry in 1981 when it announced the VIC-20, the first under-$300 home computer. In 1982, it announced the Commodore 64, the first under-$600 computer with 64K RAM. With these two, Commodore also began slashing prices, forcing the price down from $299 for the VIC-20 to less than $100 in many instances, and as low as $199 for the Commodore 64. By the end of 1983, Commodore had sold more than two million computers, and had prospects for selling more than that during 1984.

In early 1984, Commodore experienced an internal shake-up, but it was not clear how that might affect the company's future growth. However, it also introduced several new computers in January, 1984, with plans for several more. Commodore appears to have the strength to match wits with IBM, Coleco, and the Japanese; it has already outwitted Atari, Texas Instruments, Timex, and a host of others.

The VIC-20 is a nice little home computer with a limited RAM and memory capacity. It is a good way for you and your family to be introduced to home computing concepts, and its home management programs can be helpful in most straightforward home financial tasks.

CPU: 6502 and Video Interface Chip for sound and graphics.

RAM/ROM: 5K RAM, expandable to 32K RAM.

MASS STORAGE: Plug-in cartridge port standard; C-1530 Cassette Recorder optional; C-1541 disk drive with 174K optional.

VIDEO DISPLAY: 22 x 23 with sixteen colors.

KEYBOARD: Typewriterlike with four function keys.

I/O SLOTS/INTERFACES: Three—Commodore serial bus port for printer, port for cassette recorder, and port for joysticks. Special interfaces required for other equipment.

SYSTEM PRICE: $199 list, discounts widely available.

PROGRAMMING LANGUAGES: Commodore BASIC 2.0.

PRINTERS: Two optional dot matrix and one letter-quality printer.

Figure 25. The Commodore VIC-20 keyboard unit. Note the four function keys on the right hand side. (Courtesy of Commodore Business Machines)

MODEMS: One 300-baud direct connect VIC-MODEM ($60), and one 300-baud direct connect modem with automatic answer and dial intelligence ($100), both optional.

OTHER PERIPHERALS: Optional RAM cards and memory boards, joysticks, light pen, voice or speech synthesizer, game controller paddles, and more, including memory and I/O expansion and interface boards, available from a wide variety of manufacturers as well as Commodore.

AVAILABLE SOFTWARE: Hundreds, if not thousands, of arcade games, educational programs, home finance and management programs. But be aware that the limited 32K RAM does not allow for much sophistication. See Appendix B under various headings and Commodore for available software.

SALES OUTLETS: Thousands of retail outlets. This is the computer you are most likely to find sold anywhere and everywhere.

SERVICE AND SUPPORT: Many authorized service centers, but you may have to ship the computer back to a Commodore factory to get it fixed. Software support from Commodore or the individual software houses.

FUTURE DEVELOPMENTS: Commodore has de-emphasized the VIC-20, but will continue to make, sell, and support it. After all, it still makes the PET, now three generations old, eight years after it was introduced.

Commodore 64

BRIEF SUMMARY: The Commodore 64 (C-64 for future reference) is the flagship of the current Commodore line. It has taken the home computer market by storm. Commodore continues to introduce improved software and more peripherals and accessories for the C-64 both independently and in conjunction with others. However, the low list price of the C-64 belies the additional cost you must pay for a storage device, a monitor or TV, a printer, and so forth. So be aware that a usable C-64 system could easily cost more than $1,000. In fact, Commodore is the master of low-priced CPUs and high-priced and often necessary peripherals.

CPU: 6510 and two special variations for graphics and sound.

RAM/ROM: 64K RAM (only 38K for user programs).

MASS STORAGE: C-1530 Cassette Recorder or C-1541 174K-capacity disk drive, both options.

VIDEO DISPLAY: 25 lines by 40 columns with graphics and special video game characters called "sprites." 128 color variations.

KEYBOARD: Standard typewriter-style with four function keys, very similar to, if not the same as, the VIC-20.

I/O SLOTS/INTERFACES: Commodore Serial Bus for printer, joystick port, disk drive port, optional IEEE-488 cartridge interface for parallel printers.

SYSTEM PRICE: Can be found many places for under $300.

PROGRAMMING LANGUAGES: Commodore BASIC 2.0. Logo and PILOT educational software languages, optional CP/M expansion module, and

Figure 26. The Commodore 64 keyboard unit. Note that the function keys can handle up to eight programmable functions instead of the VIC-20's four functions. (Courtesy of Commodore Business Machines)

other options for business software. Inexpensive $30 PET emulator lets you run thousands of programs originally written for the Commodore PET.

PRINTERS: C-1520 printer/plotter; C-1525 80-column dot matrix; C-1526 80-column dot matrix; C-4023 80-column parallel printer; and C-6400 daisywheel printer, all optional.

MODEMS: Same as VIC-20 models.

OTHER PERIPHERALS: Magic Voice speech synthesizer with talking software modules ($59.95); several music synthesizer keyboards; and others from outside vendors.

AVAILABLE SOFTWARE: Hundreds of games and home programs, and numerous interesting programs for small business and professionals including word processing and electronic spreadsheets, including integrated software packages such as 3-PLUS-1, a cartridge with a word processor, electronic spreadsheet, file manager, and graphics package. Commodore has also announced more than one hundred templates to run with its MANAGER 64 home information management package.

SALES OUTLETS: Thousands of locations in every type of retail store selling computers. Many mail order distributors for software and peripherals as well.

SERVICE AND SUPPORT: One of the few shortcomings. With comparatively few authorized service centers, one must often ship the computer back to Commodore, and all software support will come from the company or the independent vendor.

FUTURE DEVELOPMENTS: The C-64 has been very successful, but it is being succeeded by the Commodore 264 described below. With almost 1 million Commodore 64s already sold and thousands more sold each day, the supply of software and accessories will remain plentiful for the next several years.

Commodore 264 and CV-364

BRIEF SUMMARY: Commodore's newest microcomputer is the C-264, and its most important advance is built-in software (as options), eight function keys, four cursor keys, and a variety of other features and functions. A sister product to the C-264 is the CV364 which adds 16K more

Figure 27. The Commodore 264 keyboard unit. Note the changes in style from the C-64. The cursor keys are full arrows at the bottom right hand side and the programmable function keys have been moved to above the keyboard. (Courtesy of Commodore Business Machines)

ROM and an optional 48K ROM with the built-in software options. It implements a much larger keyboard with a 19-key numeric keyboard. It builds in speech synthesis with a 250-word vocabulary.

More important than the features is the strategic change in direction for Commodore. This new series is the first in a new way to introduce microcomputers to family groups, according to Commodore officials. This means Commodore believes the company can sell more computers by offering variations from a basic model, much like General Motors sells automobiles with various options. But it bodes ill for C-64 and VIC-20 owners and software developers because neither new machine is compatible with the software for the older machines; and Commodore has announced no plans to sell emulator programs or plug-in adapters. Commodore has done this before, but it does not seem to adversely affect the company's sales or fortunes.

CPU: 6510 and a special chip called TED.

RAM/ROM: 64K RAM (60K available for programs), 32K ROM standard for C-264, and 48K ROM standard for CV-364. 32K–48K additional ROM for 264 and 364 respectively with built-in software options.

MASS STORAGE: All optional—SFS-481 fast disk drive, C-1542 disk drive, and an improved C-1531 cassette recorder.

VIDEO DISPLAY: 40 columns x 25 lines, 121 colors.

KEYBOARD: Sixty-seven keys on C-264, eighty-seven keys on CV-364 with eight user-definable function keys and four cursor keys. Upper and lower case.

I/O SLOTS/INTERFACES: 264 Modem port; serial port for printers; ROM cartridge and parallel disk drive port; two joystick ports; and cassette interface port.

SYSTEM PRICE: $500 or less for 264; slightly more for CV-364.

PROGRAMMING LANGUAGES: Commodore BASIC 3.5.

PRINTERS: Same as for C-64 with added MCS-801 color dot matrix printer.

MODEMS: 264 Modem, 1200-baud direct connect option.

OTHER PERIPHERALS: None at present, but many should be introduced during 1985.

AVAILABLE SOFTWARE: Announced software emphasizes home and personal productivity products and includes 3-PLUS-1 integrated package, a built-in word processor, "Scripsit 264," and a business product called Magic Desk. The concept is to sell fast ROM-based software to match a person's greatest need—word processing for a writer, spreadsheet for personal or business finance—and sell cartridges to handle any desirable, but less crucial, applications. Commodore said in mid-1984 that it expected to have thirty packages on sale by the end of 1984, with that number to double during 1985.

SALES OUTLETS: Same as VIC-20 and Commodore 64.

SERVICE AND SUPPORT: Same.

FUTURE DEVELOPMENTS: Commodore appears to have no plans to abandon any of its machines as long as they sell, and since the C-64 is selling in the several hundred thousand a month range now, it is unlikely to abandon it. Commodore seems to be trying to develop a whole range of hardware to appeal to everyone's interests. The C-264 and CV-364 are also clearly responses to what Commodore thought the IBM PCjr was going to be. Yet, the C-264 has its shortcomings compared to the C-64; its sound and graphics are not as good,

for example, but the C-264's BASIC is much better than the C-64's. With any Commodore product, expect to make trade-offs.

Miscellaneous Commodore Computers

Following is a short description of older or not very popular computers Commodore continues to manufacture. Two portable computers made by Commodore—the Portable 64 and the Executive 64—are discussed in Chapter 10.

Four Commodore PET Models

The original PET computer comes in four variations: PET 64, PET 4032, CBM 8032, and Super-PET.

PET 64: It has 64K RAM, comes in an all-in-one cabinet with a green-and-black monitor, has eight function keys, a 40 x 25 display, a typewriter keyboard with a full set of graphics characters, a slot of plug-in cartridges, and cassette and printer ports. Peripherals include four printers, disk drive or cassette, two modems, and more. Software is very plentiful, although you'll have to check software house backlistings for it.

PET 4032: The original PET comes with just 32K RAM, a 40 x 25 display, 18K ROM, 256 characters, serial and parallel printer ports, a separate numeric keypad, a variety of single and double disk drive options, and five printers. Software must be programmed in Commodore BASIC 4.0. Hundreds of educational programs are available and this machine remains popular in the schools.

CBM 8032: The PET designed for business and professional use with 32K RAM expandable to 96K RAM. It adds an 80-column display to essentially the same machine as the PET 4032.

SuperPET: The 96K version comes with a high-speed RS-232 interface for a printer or modem, an IEEE-488 printer bus, compatibility with 8032 software, and five programming languages (APL, BASIC, COBOL, FORTRAN, and Pascal). It includes built-in dual CPUs, and works with either cassette recorder, floppy disk drives, or hard disk drives, and any of five printers.

Commodore also makes two other computers for small business: the B128-880 and BX256-80.

B128-80: It comes with 128K RAM, expandable to 256K internally, and up to 704K in an outside memory bank for 960K RAM total. It comes with a 6509 CPU, and optional processors include the Z-80 for CP/M and 8088 for CP/M-86.

BX256-80: The differences between these two include the latter's 256K RAM as standard, the green-and-black monitor is included as standard equipment, and it has built-in dual processors, the standard 6509 and the 16-bit 8088. Both work on the full line of Commodore peripherals and storage devices. But by mid-1984 neither machine had become very popular compared to major competitors.

IBM

IBM PCjr Personal Computer

BRIEF SUMMARY: Did IBM stub its toe on the home computer market when it announced its $669 IBM PCjr on November 1, 1983, but did not begin delivering them until February, 1984? Did IBM make serious technical and consumer mistakes with the PCjr? If the answer to both these questions is yes, does it make any difference to how many IBM will sell? The answers are yes, yes, and no. The experts, including me, are not fond of the PCjr. It is outdated technology and overpriced for what it gives the consumer, but we are equally convinced that IBM will sell the heck out of the machine because of the name and the company's marketing clout. But be forewarned that I found it difficult to put the PCjr in the under $1,000 category because it is not very useful for most applications unless you add a floppy disk drive, and the disk-based system starts at $1,269. Another IBM shortcoming is that its peripherals, too, will run up the cost substantially. One joystick is $40, for example.

The best thing IBM did was to make the disk drive version compatible with most of the existing programs for the IBM PC, opening the door for extensive use of the PCjr in business and professional offices. Whether a program is directly disk-to-disk compatible with the PCjr will depend on how the program was written to take advantage of machine language and architectural arrangements and disk drive formatting procedures. Another advantage is a 12-month warranty, one of the best in the industry, a key IBM quality difference.

CPU: Quasi-16-bit 8088 processor.

RAM/ROM: 64K RAM and 128K RAM respectively, 64K ROM for both.

MASS STORAGE: Cassette recorder for 64K version; one 360K double-sided disk drive standard with 128K version, optional for 64K version.

VIDEO DISPLAY: 40 x 24 with 64K version; 80 x 24 for 128K model.

Figure 28. The IBM PCjr with its cordless keyboard and optional one 320K minifloppy disk drive. The IBM monitor and the dot matrix printer are also options. (Courtesy of International Business Machines)

KEYBOARD: Sixty-two-key cordless typewriter keyboard which operates through infrared radiation signals. All keys are programmable as function keys, but the unit is battery-operated on four "AA" batteries. (WARNING: If you use the cordless keyboard, get used to difficulty with dying batteries causing keyboard errors.)

I/O SLOTS/INTERFACES: Two plug-in cartridge slots; interface for cassette recorder; slot for disk drive adapter and cable; serial interface for printer or modem; 64K RAM expansion memory board ($140); parallel printer attachment ($99); two joystick ports ($40 for each joystick); cable for TV connection; cable for video monitor connection, connectors for light pen and audio output. Same interfaces and slots for both models.

SYSTEM PRICE: $669 for 64K version; $1,269 for 128K version.

PROGRAMMING LANGUAGES: IBM PCjr BASIC cartridge with supports enhanced video and sound, light pens, joysticks, three-voice sound, and communications; and IBM DOS 2.1, variation of MS-DOS, for the disk-based versions. DOS 2.1 works on all IBM PCs and is the secret to program compatibility.

PRINTERS: IBM PC Compact Printer ($175), but it's a thermal printer; and IBM PC Computer Color Printer ($1,995) which works at 200 cps in up to eight colors, and also works as a 35-cps letter-quality printer.

MODEMS: Optional auto-answer, auto-dial, 300-baud integral modem ($199) which plugs into back of either model.

OTHER PERIPHERALS: Hundreds are available from independent vendors in every category.

AVAILABLE SOFTWARE: Hundreds of programs are available now as every major software company has joined the bandwagon, but be careful; most of this software will only run on the 128K model. A list of PCjr software with the IBM label is given in Appendix B.

SALES OUTLETS: More than one thousand authorized dealers across the country, with hundreds more following during 1984–85. IBM also sells the PCjr through its National Accounts and National Marketing Divisions, which sell mainly to major corporations and large organizations. It is highly likely you may be able to buy a PCjr at a discount through your corporation if you work for one of the Fortune 2000 firms. Software is available through authorized IBM PC software dealers.

SERVICE AND SUPPORT: Dozens of authorized service centers across the country. Software support through service centers, IBM, or through independent vendors. Check with your dealer to find out how each package is serviced.

FUTURE DEVELOPMENTS: The PCjr should be viewed as IBM's initial thrust into the marketplace. Its introduction was timed strangely for IBM: it was the first time in IBM history that it officially introduced a consumer product it was not delivering at the same moment. It was done this way to accomplish two aims: 1) cut short a planned Japanese invasion of the U.S. home market, and 2) hamper sales of Apple IIe, Coleco, and Commodore computers during the holiday season. IBM will make a lot of money with the PCjr, but it is basically a toehold in the home computer market which IBM expects to total in the tens of millions by the end of the decade. IBM will come out with a full line of new computers based on true 32-bit technology during 1985, and a more sophisticated and less expensive home computer will be in that line. Despite its reputation with the public, IBM is not technologically superior in its computers; its superiority comes from marketing—identifying who wants to buy what and when—and making it available to them at a slightly premium price. IBM does not yet appear to understand the consumer marketplace, but it is learning rapidly, and it is seeking to take over the upper-middle-class home/professional computer market long controlled by Apple. It seems to have ceded this stage of the very low-end family computer to Commodore.

RADIO SHACK/TANDY CORPORATION

Micro Color Computer MC-10

BRIEF SUMMARY: Radio Shack sells the largest line of microcomputers of any manufacturer, with systems ranging from a $79.95 toy to $6,000 small business computers in addition to a line of portable and pocket computers. Its 300-plus Computer Centers and 7,700 Radio Shack stores also give it the largest single sales network of any company. However, Radio Shack has traditionally of-

Figure 29. The Radio Shack Micro Color Computer MC-10 model, the least expensive Radio Shack computer. (Courtesy of Radio Shack/Tandy Corporation)

fered poor service and support, and does not give much space to outside software vendors in its stores. At least in Computer Centers for business, this trend is changing, and its new System 2000 discussed in Chapter 9 is IBM PC-compatible. Radio Shack also tends to have problems with inexperienced personnel in its Computer Centers and the company puts its store managers under intense pressure to meet sales quotas. These pressures may be easing as Radio Shack slows the frantic pace at which it was adding new computer centers, and store personnel are allowed to stay in the same store and learn their jobs. But Radio Shack still has trouble shedding its middle-class, medium-quality image, and has watched IBM scoop up the corporate marketplace, and Commodore dominate the home market. The first three computers discussed are Radio Shack's least expensive computers.

CPU: 8-bit 6803.

RAM/ROM: 4K RAM, expandable with 16K module to 20K RAM.

MASS STORAGE: Optional 1500-baud cassette recorder and plug-in cartridges.

VIDEO DISPLAY: 16 lines x 32 columns, upper case only.

KEYBOARD: Typewriterlike, but plastic membrane, not full travel.

I/O SLOTS/INTERFACES: Serial port for printer, cassette port, port for 16K RAM module, port for TV or monitor.

SYSTEM PRICE: $79.95.

PROGRAMMING LANGUAGES: Radio Shack BASIC.

PRINTERS: TP-10 Thermal Printer with 32 columns ($99.95).

MODEMS: Micro Compac interface required ($29.95) with any of three Radio Shack modems: AC-3 Acoustic Coupler ($149.95); Direct Connect Modem I ($99.95); and Direct Connect Modem II (auto answer/dial) ($199.95).

OTHER PERIPHERALS: 16K RAM Module ($49.95), joysticks ($24.95 each or $39.95 per pair), and Color Mouse ($49.95) for art and graphics.

AVAILABLE SOFTWARE: Compared to most home computers, a limited selection of games and educational programs.

SALES OUTLETS: All 7,700 Radio Shack outlets in U.S. and Canada.

SERVICE AND SUPPORT: Only through Radio Shack factory service.

Figure 30. The Radio Shack TRS-80 Color Computer 2, the top of the line model for Radio Shack's under $1,000 computers. (Courtesy of Radio Shack/Tandy Corporation)

FUTURE DEVELOPMENTS: Likely to be replaced in near future.

TRS-80 Color Computer 2

CPU: 8-bit 6809E processor.

RAM/ROM: 16K RAM in two versions, one standard and one extended, expandable to 64K in extended version only. 8K ROM in standard, expanded to 16K ROM in extended version.

MASS STORAGE: Cassette recorder, or Color Computer 2 disk drive ($399.95, with additional drives $279.95 each) for extended version only.

VIDEO DISPLAY: 16 x 32 upper case only. Extended version has much higher color resolution of eight available colors.

KEYBOARD: Fifty-three-key typewriterlike full-travel keyboard including four cursor keys.

I/O SLOTS/INTERFACES: One plug-in cartridge slot; an RS-232 port for printer or modem; two joystick connectors; optional multi-pak interface lets you plug in four "Program Pak" cartridges at a time and connect hardware peripherals as well ($179.95).

SYSTEM PRICE: $159.95 for standard and $199.95 for extended versions.

PROGRAMMING LANGUAGES: Standard Color BASIC and Extended Color BASIC. Optional OS-9 DOS ($69.95) and BASIC-09 ($99.95).

PRINTERS: Variety of dot matrix printers, two-color graphics printers ($199.95 and $699 respectively); and letter-quality printers for extended version; simple thermal printers for standard versions.

MODEMS: RS-232 Program Pak ($79.95) acts as serial interface for modem with built-in communications software. It leaves the regular serial port open for printer connection.

OTHER PERIPHERALS: 16K RAM Kit ($49); 64K RAM Kit ($69.95); Extended Color BASIC ROM Kit ($39.95); Low Profile Keyboard ($39.95); an X-Pad Graphics Input Tablet with stylus for easy drawing and input ($349.95).

AVAILABLE SOFTWARE: Dozens of programs for games and simple home management available from Radio Shack, hundreds of others through mail order distribution through magazines.

SALES OUTLETS: Radio Shack's 7,700 stores.

SERVICE AND SUPPORT: Same as for Micro Color Computer.

FUTURE DEVELOPMENTS: Likely to be replaced or supplemented by 1985.

SINCLAIR RESEARCH LTD.

Sinclair QL

BRIEF SUMMARY: Clive Sinclair, the founding genius of Sinclair Research, has done it again, with a $500 32-bit home computer. Sinclair is the father of the pocket calculator, the pocket television, the under-$100 miniature microcomputer, and now the miniature 32-bit microcomputer. After being pushed out of the pocket TV and pocket calculator markets by Sony and Texas Instruments, respectively, Sinclair struck gold with his Sinclair ZX-81, and sold more than five hundred thousand of them through mail order sales in the U.S. alone during 1982. In late 1982, Timex Corp., the world-famous watchmaker, bought Sinclair's U.S. marketing rights; Timex was already assembling the hand-sized computers in a plant in Scotland. Sinclair's genius lies in his ability to cram more and more transistors and integrated circuits onto one chip of silicon with very cheap mass production techniques. His new 32-bit computer should be the first of the wave of 32-bit home computers that should become standard for U.S. home computers during 1985.

CPU: Motorola 68008 32-bit.

RAM/ROM: 128K RAM, expandable to 640K RAM.

MASS STORAGE: Two 100K digital microcassette drives built in.

VIDEO DISPLAY: Not fully known, but 25 x 80 is likely with color graphics capability.

KEYBOARD: Sixty-five-key typewriter, full travel keyboard.

I/O SLOTS/INTERFACES: Serial slot, tape drive slots.

SYSTEM PRICE: $499–$559.

PROGRAMMING LANGUAGES: Not fully known, but likely a very fast BASIC.

PRINTERS: At least one dot matrix likely.

MODEMS: Probably compatibility with current Timex/Sinclair modem.

OTHER PERIPHERALS: Unknown in mid-1984.

AVAILABLE SOFTWARE: Range of home and business software, including four free application programs.

SALES OUTLETS: Mail order at the end of 1984, probably through Timex distribution by the end of 1985.

SERVICE AND SUPPORT: Factory service at first, Timex service centers later.

FUTURE DEVELOPMENTS: Keep an eye on Sinclair. He is likely to be the first to develop a 64-bit home computer for less than $300 in 1986–87. The Sinclair QL line will evolve into a series of powerful computers, but Sinclair has been historically weak in software development and support.

SPECTRAVIDEO CORPORATION

Spectravideo SV-318
BRIEF SUMMARY: This is a small company making its products in the Far East, and its ma-

chine, delivered in mid-1983, has not had great success in the market. Whether it will still be available during 1985 is an open question in mid-1984.

CPU: Zilog 280A CPU.

RAM/ROM: 32K RAM, expandable to 256K with modules with bank switching; and 32K ROM.

MASS STORAGE: Optional cassette recorder or 170K minifloppy disk drives.

VIDEO DISPLAY: 24 x 40 with only 24 x 32 in graphics mode.

KEYBOARD: Seventy-three-key with typewriter-like, but plastic touch keyboard.

I/O SLOTS/INTERFACES: Built-in joystick; slot for cartridges; and optional expansion box for serial or parallel ports.

SYSTEM PRICE: $299 list price.

PROGRAMMING LANGUAGES: Microsoft BASIC with a word processor and a telecommunications program in ROM. CP/M available with expanded memory module, 80-column display cartridge, dual disk drive controller, and two disk drives.

PRINTERS: Two dot matrix models.

MODEMS: Have to purchase from independent vendor.

OTHER PERIPHERALS: None known.

AVAILABLE SOFTWARE: Home finance and management programs, variety of games.

SALES OUTLETS: Limited number of discount stores and electronics boutiques.

SERVICE AND SUPPORT: Ship hardware back to factory, use hot line for software support.

FUTURE DEVELOPMENTS: This company was struggling to establish itself during 1983–84, but it seemed to have gotten a foothold by mid-1984.

TANO CORPORATION

Tano Dragon
BRIEF SUMMARY: Tano Microcomputer Products Corp. has introduced two products: a relatively low-cost, but more than adequate home computer, and an Apple-compatible personal computer. Introduced in late 1983, the Dragon has an unfortunate toy store look, but it appears to

Figure 31. Tano Dragon home computer. Note the simple keyboard. (Courtesy of Tano Corporation)

function better than that. Tano will have a difficult time carving a niche for itself in the crowded low end of the home computer market. But its machine at least deserves some consideration from those who want a simple home computer, but do not plan to use it or expand it for serious business applications. The Apple-compatible Tano AVT-2A may have better luck since it is priced lower than the Franklin ACE Apple-compatible.

CPU: 6809 CPU, compatible with the same one for Radio Shack Color Computer.

RAM/ROM: 64K RAM, 32K ROM.

MASS STORAGE: Radio Shack cassette recorder, or 184K single or double disk drive ($359.95 for one drive, $529.95 for two).

VIDEO DISPLAY: 32 x 16, nine colors, upper case only, good resolution.

KEYBOARD: Sixty-four-key full travel keyboard.

I/O SLOTS/INTERFACES: Two joystick slots; plug-in cartridge slot; serial port; parallel port.

SYSTEM PRICE: $249.95.

PROGRAMMING LANGUAGES: Microsoft Extended Color BASIC, practically the same as the one for Radio Shack's extended color computer model.

PRINTERS: Optional 80 cps dot matrix printer from Mannesmann Talley ($349.95).

MODEMS: Requires independent vendor's device and interface.

OTHER PERIPHERALS: None at present, but with near-TRS-80 Color Computer compatibility, some should become available.

AVAILABLE SOFTWARE: Included in base price are eight software programs: Color Computer Writer, Mail, Merge, Filer, Calc, Courier Pilot game, Dragon Quest, Tower of Fear, and CVT, which allows the Dragon to run Radio Shack cassette BASIC programs. About thirty games, children's packages, utilities, and self-help, home business programs.

SALES OUTLETS: Discount stores, toy stores and electronics outlets.

SERVICE AND SUPPORT: Factory service only. Corporate number is (800) 327-7671, or (504) 254-3500 in Louisiana.

FUTURE DEVELOPMENTS: Tano's should be able to make a dent in the Radio Shack enclave if it can get wide enough distribution.

Tano AVT-2A

CPU: 6502 CPU.

RAM/ROM: 64K RAM.

MASS STORAGE: Single floppy disk drive included in purchase price. Apple-compatible cassettes or disk drives supplied by outside vendors.

VIDEO DISPLAY: 24 x 40 and amber monitor included in system price.

KEYBOARD: Detached, typewriterlike keyboard.

I/O SLOTS/INTERFACES: Cassette; game paddle/joystick; serial slot for serial card; parallel slot for parallel card; slot for 80-column display.

SYSTEM PRICE: $549 for model without disk drive; $849 with disk drive.

PROGRAMMING LANGUAGES: Apple BASIC, Apple-like DOS.

PRINTERS: Same as Dragon.

MODEMS: Obtain from other vendor.

OTHER PERIPHERALS: 80-column Card ($149); Serial Card ($119); Parallel Card ($99); AVT-120 Amber Monitor ($99); and same disk drives as Dragon; Dragon joysticks ($19.95 per pair).

AVAILABLE SOFTWARE: Small number of Dragon packages, but large supply of Apple software.

SALES OUTLETS: Mail order or small number of distributors and dealers in mid-1984.

SERVICE AND SUPPORT: Factory service after ninety-day warranty.

FUTURE DEVELOPMENTS: Tano has its work cut out for it in this very competitive business.

JAPANESE MSX HOME COMPUTERS

The first of the wave of MSX standard home computers reached our shores in mid-1984. The Panasonic JR-200 led the way, and U.S. home computer makers are reported to be trembling in their chairs as the wave grows. However, there are many reasons the Japanese MSX computers may or may not have the expected impact. And much of their success or lack of success will directly depend on the reaction of the U.S. manufacturers.

By mid-1984, twenty-one Japanese manufacturers had endorsed the MSX operating system and programming language standard. To recap an earlier discussion: MSX is a version of Microsoft BASIC written as a standard language and operating system for 8-bit home computers. Japanese manufacturers apparently decided they would step in where U.S. companies refused to tread and agree to a common standard for software and hardware interfaces. They reason—I believe correctly—that more home computers would be sold in the U.S. and around the world if they all spoke the same language, or in other words, were compatible like televisions, stereos, and radios. Another reason they are taking this step is that the Japanese have had a very hard time developing software for the machines they have already introduced in the U.S., and their sales have suffered in competition with U.S. models. The standard will short-circuit the entire software development cycle, and make it much easier to introduce hardware. If they are all producing the same basic components, they can produce them in much greater volumes with more automated techniques at much lower costs and for much higher profits.

The developer of MSX, the U.S. software house Microsoft, Inc., maintains the new language standard will make home computers much like stereo components and allow consumers to buy computer components that will work together although they may have separate functions and be made by different manufacturers. Microsoft also believes the MSX standard is sophisticated enough to turn any home computer into a legitimate small business computer with 64K RAM, disk drives, and so forth.

Inside the MSX Standard

The MSX system for 8-bit computers is based on the Zilog Z80 microprocessor. The operating system will be a truly compatible version of CP/M-80 and the programming language will be MSX BASIC. A standard machine itself has standardized slots for plugging in cartridges to accept either software cartridges or peripheral interfaces and a standard expansion module plug. The RAM maximum capacity (without special bank switching ROM) is 64K, and it is likely that in the face of competition like Commodore, most MSX computers will have the maximum available. It is likely that basic MSX computers will sell for about $200 with single-sided, single-density floppy disks with about 175K capacity as low-cost ($100–$130) options.

But the Japanese and Microsoft are well aware the age of the 8-bit home computer is giving way to the 16-bit machine, so they are almost ready to introduce a 16-bit MSX standard based on MS-DOS; the new standard version is MSX DOS and is compatible with CP/M-86 and MS-DOS, already a *de facto* standard among 16-bit personal computers. Microsoft has developed MSX versions of its popular software, including Multiplan, Multiplan WORD, BASIC, FORTRAN, and COBOL.

A Slow and Difficult Path

In early 1984, two factors had held the MSX wave at bay: 1) Unexpected MSX success in Japan, the Far East, and Europe which soaked up all the computers they could make; and 2) the lack of Federal Communications Commission approval for the standard. The FCC regulates the radiation and electromagnetic emissions from all "class B" devices, such as computers, and its approval is required for any manufacturer to actually ship computers to customers.

More important, the Japanese and U.S. companies are still unsure whether a large market (tens of millions of home computers) exists in the U.S., so they are proceeding very slowly until trends become clear. Ken Bosomworth, president of International Resource Development, a well-respected authority, says that U.S. manufacturers are worried about the market's long-term viability and must remain incompatible so they can survive in a very unstable market. So, any move to an MSX standard or any standard is plagued by numerous difficulties.

But the problem is a chicken-and-egg question. If there is no market, no one will develop a standard; if there is no standard, there is no consumer market. As you have read in this book, the choices you have to make among incompatible hardware, operating systems, programming language variations, and so on, are very confusing. Sales of videocassette recorders were slowed because there were two standards—Sony Beta and Matsushita VHS; only when VHS gained more than 70 percent of the market did VCR sales really soar; the same happened in the personal computer market. Sales did not skyrocket until IBM established MS-DOS as the quasi-16-bit standard operating system; now there are dozens of MS-DOS computers with more than half the market.

I firmly maintain that the U.S. home computer market will not become as large as the market for TVs, stereos, and radios until a standard is adopted. And some major manufacturer—IBM or Matsushita are large enough—must force a standard on the marketplace. And the sooner the better.

Spectravideo Steals A March

In the United States, the first manufacturer to provide an MSX computer is Spectravideo with the Spectravideo SVI 728. It is a CP/M-80-based machine with MSX BASIC built into its ROM memory. Current SVI 318 and SVI 328 owners can upgrade their systems with a $50 adapter. Spectravideo will also introduce a floppy disk system for all MSX machines that will support CP/M-80 and MSX DOS, a new disk operating system Microsoft has developed. Spectravideo also showed a new MSX machine in June called "The Sting."

The Japanese companies which have entered the U.S. market, or will before the end of 1985, include such well-known consumer electronics giants as:

• Matsushita, better known in the U.S. as Panasonic and Quasar. Panasonic already produces a leading hand-held computer, a small non-MSX computer, and computers at the industrial level.

Its MSX machine is said to have only 16K RAM and is priced in Japan at a high $236; it is likely to be upgraded and sold in the U.S. for about $150.

• Sharp already makes Radio Shack's line of pocket computers as well as its now, and a new, impressive PC-5000 portable, all of which are described in subsequent chapters.

• Toshiba has an MSX machine with 64K RAM which sells for $286 in Japan.

• Kyocera, which makes the Radio Shack Model 100 briefcase computer and an integrated voice-data terminal, among other products for U.S. vendors. It would not sell under its own name in this country.

• Casio, which has a briefcase computer, also is the world's largest maker of calculators and could easily produce a very small MSX pocket computer.

• Sanyo, which already produces a line of desktop computers, clearly can compete with any other home computer.

• Others with MSX machines already in production in Japan are: Sony Corp., Hitachi, JVC (Japan Victor Corp.), Sord, Mitsubishi, Yamaha, and Pioneer Electronics.

Will the Japanese MSX standard sweep the American market? If U.S. manufacturers do not learn the lessons of the past, the Japanese manufacturers will again scoop up the major share of a low-end, inexpensive consumer electronics market. But although that may be bad for U.S. industry, it is good for you, the home computer buyer. It means that within a short period of time, you will find more software and more lower-priced components than ever before, and you will have the support of some of the world's largest companies.

Should you wait and buy an MSX computer when it becomes available during 1985? It will take two or three years for the MSX machine makers to set up national distribution, have an adequately large supply of software, and arrange for service and support on a large scale. If you want an inexpensive computer now, there's no reason to hold back; you almost certainly will outgrow it and be ready for a more powerful machine. You may feel patriotic and want to buy American; by all means, do so. It will be years, if ever, before strong American companies such as Radio Shack, Apple, and IBM are threatened by the MSX computers. In fact, Apple and IBM may have tacitly ceded the $200 market for home computers to the Japanese; the IBM PC starts at $669—three times as much—and Apple IIe starts at $1,495, seven and a half times as much.

OTHER MANUFACTURERS OF UNDER-$1,000 HOME COMPUTERS

As of mid-1984, several other companies were manufacturing home computers, but they had not established themselves very well, and their positions in the field were tenuous. Brief summaries of their products are given below.

BBC Acorn Computer

The British Broadcasting Corporation, which has brought us everything from *Monty Python's Flying Circus* to *All Creatures Great and Small,* now brings us an inexpensive computer aimed at the educational market. Called the Acorn (from which BBC must hope mighty oaks do grow), the computer has a full travel keyboard, ten function keys, a substantial 48K RAM, sixteen colors, and a good 8-bit processor. This under-$600 computer is being sold to schools both on its own and as part of a local area network called "Econet" which is said to link as many as 254 Acorns in a single system. Most of its software offerings are games and educational programs.

Jupiter Ace

Introduced by Computer Distribution Associates, this is another very inexpensive Z80 computer with a minimal 3K RAM, expandable to 53K, and 8K ROM. It has two slots for memory boards in the back, and uses a cassette recorder as its basic storage system. This $150 machine's only new innovation is that one programs it with FORTH rather than BASIC. FORTH is a good, versatile language, but it is not very popular, and this machine will have limited appeal. The computer is available by mail.

Tomy Tutor

Made by Tomy Corp., the successful toy and electronic game maker, the Tomy Tutor is a 16-bit computer, which has: a 32 x 24 video display with sixteen high-resolution colors; with 16K RAM, expandable to 64K RAM; and a plastic keyboard with a typewriter layout. It is based on the highly regarded Texas Instruments 9995 CPU, but Tomy does not seem to make good use of its capabilities with just 16K RAM. It uses an optional cassette recorder for mass storage. Although this machine was announced during 1983, it had not had much impact by mid-1984.

Video Technology

Video Technology makes two home computer models, the VZ200 and the VT2001. The company itself is a Hong Kong manufacturer. Both computers are inexpensive, the former less than $100 and the latter less than $300. The VZ200 has a rubber-key keyboard in a standard layout, but no spacebar. It has a Z80 CPU and 4K RAM with optional 16K and 64K expansion cartridges; uses a cassette recorder for mass storage; has Microsoft BASIC; and 16 x 32 video display with eight colors. The VT2001 is designed to accept optional modules, which let you play either Atari 2600 or Colecovision video games. It has a 24 x 36 video display with eight high-resolution colors and uses the same Microsoft BASIC with good graphics programming capability. It uses the 6502A CPU. It has ports for a TV, video monitor, cassette recorder, and printer and the optional adapter for Atari and Coleco cartridges. The basic system has 64K RAM. Software for both machines has been developed by the company; little outside software is available.

CHAPTER 8

Personal Computers for Less than $2,500

During 1983 and early 1984, the market for personal computers divided into two directions: one toward the less expensive portable and briefcase-sized computers, and one toward the more expensive (above $2,500) personal and desktop computers for professionals and small businesses. And as we have seen, obtaining a powerful and useful home computer system with disk drives, a printer, a monitor, and so forth was difficult to accomplish for less than $1,000. So, with a few notable exceptions, the middle of the free-standing personal computer market dropped away. The under-$2,500 personal computer market is dominated by Apple and Radio Shack with a few others participating with compatible machines.

During late 1984 and 1985, however, significant developments can be expected in this price range: it appears that at least half a dozen Taiwanese and Hong Kong manufacturers will introduce low-cost IBM PC-compatible machines. These will not be the quasi-compatible devices so often touted in the U.S., but actual IBM PC "clones" which will accept the same floppy disks and operating system as the IBM PC itself. At the under-$1,000 end, you can expect similar treatment for the PCjr if it is successful.

By the way, although it has a list price of $2,495, the new Apple Macintosh is not included in this section because it not only is based on a new and advanced processing technology, it is also designed as a small business and professional tool, and adding necessary components pushes the price far beyond $2,500. This "add-on" syndrome is a serious problem with many of the other under-$2,500 computers as well, but their base prices are well under $2,000.

Here are brief descriptions of the relative handful of under-$2,500 freestanding personal computers. Each description is based on the same categories of information so you can compare the models feature for feature if you like.

APPLE COMPUTER INC.

Apple IIe

BRIEF SUMMARY: Apple Computer is, of course, one of the success stories of the late 1970s and early 1980s. What began as two guys building computers for friends in a garage has turned into a $1 billion-plus company doing battle with the IBM colossus and winning its share of the encounters. Apple sold more than one million Apple II and II Plus computers between 1978 and 1983. Apple was the darling of Wall Street and the stock market until the IBM PC was introduced in 1981, after

Figure 32. The Apple IIe personal computer with a single minifloppy disk drive, a monitor, and the ProFile 5 megabyte hard disk. (Courtesy of Apple Computer, Inc.)

which it encountered some difficult times. But it seems to be recovering well with both the new Macintosh and the older replacement for the Apple II Plus. This is the Apple IIe, described below.

The key facts about the Apple IIe are these:

— It is directly compatible with about 90 percent of Apple II Plus software. But be aware that you must determine whether the software you want actually works on the IIe. Don't make any assumptions about compatibility and look for software that has been modified to run with the IIe's new custom chips.

— There are twelve extra keys on the keyboard with larger and better positioning for important keys, such as control, shift, and reset.

— Upper and lower case letters are standard; with the II and II Plus, you have to buy expensive options.

— Numerous minor changes make it easier to program and operate than the II Plus.

CPU: 6502A microprocessor.

RAM/ROM: 64K RAM, 16K ROM with built-in AppleSoft BASIC.

MASS STORAGE: Optional Apple DOS 3.3- and ProDOS-based floppy disk drives and optional cassette recorder.

VIDEO DISPLAY: 24 x 40 regular; 24 x 80 with optional card and monitor; sixteen low-resolution colors and six high-resolution colors.

KEYBOARD: Sixty-three keys, typewriter-style; four cursor keys and two function keys.

I/O SLOTS/INTERFACES: Seven general-purpose expansion slots; cassette interface; multiple-purpose video and memory expansion slot; two joystick ports; numeric keypad interface for optional keypad.

SYSTEM PRICE: $1,995 with one disk drive and Apple IIe monitor.

PROGRAMMING LANGUAGES: Apple ProDOS now standard; others optional include DOS 3.3 BASIC, Pascal, CP/M with special card, COBOL, FORTRAN, MUMPS, and more.

PRINTERS: Optional Apple Color Plotter for charts, graphs, and drawings ($995); 180 cps Imagewriter dot matrix printer (under $400); Apple Daisywheel Printer ($1,995); and dozens more, including Okidata and Epson models of dot matrix printers, and NEC, Diablo, Qume letter-quality models.

MODEMS: Dozens of optional 300- and 1,200-baud direct connect and acoustic coupler. Many DC models have intelligent features. The most popular are Hayes MicroModem I and II and SmartModem. Must have an Apple Super Serial Card or similar for printers and modems.

OTHER PERIPHERALS: Literally hundreds for every conceivable application: ProFile 5 Mb. hard disk, graphics tablets, light pens, disk drives, video interfaces, and so on.

AVAILABLE SOFTWARE: At last count, by Sofsearch International, more than 5,500 separate packages, including 1,000 games and 2,200 educational programs.

SALES OUTLETS: Thousands of authorized dealers, major department stores, computer store chains, and franchises.

SERVICE AND SUPPORT: Hundreds of authorized service centers across the country. Ninety-day warranty and a low-cost extended service contract after that.

FUTURE DEVELOPMENTS: Apple IIe should be available until 1986 when the 8-bit line is likely to be phased out. Somewhat overpriced by today's standards, you still cannot beat the Apple II family for versatility; with seven I/O slots, Apple IIe allows you to execute more applications than any other computer. Of course—and unfortunately— many of those slots are necessary for some things that are standard equipment on other computers: 80-column video displays, and printer and communications interfaces. But Apple leaves the slots available so you can decide—and it can profit from the decision. Of course, with so many programs available, you will almost surely be able to keep adding applications for years to come.

FRANKLIN COMPUTER

Franklin Ace 1200

BRIEF SUMMARY: Franklin Computer has done a very successful and credible job of making Apple II Plus "clones" since 1980. Apple did get $2.5 million from Franklin for patent infringement in a settlement of a court suit, but that did not deter Franklin from continuing to make the clones and even improve on what Apple offers. Franklin also managed to push the higher-priced Apples out of numerous retail locations. In our opinion, the growth and financial stability of Franklin—as it appeared to be in mid-1984—make its products worth serious consideration. There are two models—the Ace 1200 with two microprocessors, and the original Ace 1000. They'll be discussed separately.

CPU: 6502A and Z80A for CP/M OS.

RAM/ROM: 128K RAM, up to 72K ROM; 64K

Figure 33. The Franklin ACE 1200 with two built-in floppy disk drives, dual microprocessors, and numeric keypad. (Courtesy of Franklin Computer Corporation)

RAM for Apple mode, and 64K RAM on Ace 80 Z80 CPU board.

MASS STORAGE: Two 143K byte single-sided, single-density disks built in the part of system price.

VIDEO DISPLAY: 24 x 40 with Apple mode; 24 x 80 in CP/M mode.

KEYBOARD: Seventy-two keys full travel with upper and lower case; cursor keys, operational keys, and function keys with standard typewriter layout.

I/O SLOTS/INTERFACES: Eight slots including serial and parallel interfaces, and a joystick/paddle connector; five slots available for peripherals.

SYSTEM PRICE: $2,295.

PROGRAMMING LANGUAGES: BASIC and CBASIC included along with WordStar word processing, MailMerge file merging, and ACECalc spreadsheet, all part of system price; Four operating systems available: Apple DOS 3.2, Apple DOS 3.3, Apple Pascal, and CP/M-80.

PRINTERS: Dozens from independent vendors work with the system.

MODEMS: Dozens from independent vendors.

OTHER PERIPHERALS: Same variety as for Apple and CP/M machines. Ninety percent compatibility among Apple and Franklin peripherals.

Franklin has own disk drives, CP/M 80-column card, and monitor.

AVAILABLE SOFTWARE: Same availability, and many programs are disk-to-disk compatible for Apple and Apple CP/M programs, but not all are, so be careful. Make sure you check this before you obtain so-called compatible software.

SALES OUTLETS: At least several Franklin dealers in most cities, but it is also sold frequently through mail order.

SERVICE AND SUPPORT: Individual authorized dealers or factory service; Franklin supports software with its name; otherwise, software vendor gives support.

FUTURE DEVELOPMENTS: Franklin has a winner with this machine in that it undercuts Apple's prices and offers many features that are superior to those of the Apple II Plus and IIe. It is likely it will stick with the product for at least several more years and make the transition to IBM and MS-DOS clones during late 1984 and 1985.

Franklin ACE 1000

CPU: 6502.

RAM/ROM: 64K RAM, 16K ROM, with Apple DOS 3.2 or DOS 3.3 standard, and Apple Pascal and CP/M optional, the latter with the ACE 80 CPU card.

MASS STORAGE: Ace 10 143K floppy disk drive, optional on basic ACE 1000 model, but included in ACE 1000 Family Pack and ACE 1000 Pro Plus model.

VIDEO DISPLAY: 24 x 40, or 24 x 80 with optional 80-column screen card or CP/M board.

KEYBOARD: Seventy-two keys, including twelve numeric pad and special function keys.

I/O SLOTS/INTERFACES: Eight peripheral slots and a joystick/paddle connector.

SYSTEM PRICE: $1,495 for Family Pack and $1,795 for Pro Plus package.

PROGRAMMING LANGUAGES: Apple DOS 3.2 or DOS 3.3 standard, and Apple Pascal, and CP/M options. Franklin BASIC standard built-in ROM.

PRINTERS: Any Apple-compatible.

MODEMS: Any Apple-compatible.

OTHER PERIPHERALS: With Pro Plus, Frank-

Figure 34. The Franklin ACE 1000 personal computer was the most successful Apple-compatible model sold during 1982 and 1983. (Courtesy of Franklin Computer Corporation)

lin monitor, and 80-column card included in price. Also, any Apple-compatible peripheral.

AVAILABLE SOFTWARE: With Family Pack, home finance program, checkers, two games, and a joystick are included in price; with Pro Plus, AceWriter II word processor, Data Perfect information manager, and Eagle Software Personal Financier are included. Any Apple-compatible software.

SALES OUTLETS: Same as ACE 1200.

SERVICE AND SUPPORT: Same as ACE 1200.

FUTURE DEVELOPMENTS: Likely to upgrade to new Apple ProDOS operating system by 1985.

HEWLETT-PACKARD PERSONAL COMPUTER GROUP

BRIEF SUMMARY: Hewlett-Packard was the first company to introduce an all-in-one portable computer that included display, mass storage, printer, and keyboard in one 20-pound package. Its HP-85 was the ancestor of the wave of portable computers sweeping the personal computer market segment today. This machine sold very well in terms of income, but it was aimed at scientific and technical users. It did not sweep the mass market or make an impact on the consumer. HP has more recently had that impact, but that story is told in the next chapter. Here we are concerned with the descendants of the HP-85, and the less expensive and equally functional HP-86 and 87.

CPU: Custom HP 8-bit microprocessor.

RAM/ROM: 128K RAM, expandable to 640K, and 32K-64K ROM depending on models.

MASS STORAGE: Ranges from built-in high-speed 200K digital cassette to high-capacity 540K dual disk drives, depending on model. HP-85B also has a RAM disk drive option in which a RAM card emulates a disk drive and program pack cartridges.

VIDEO DISPLAY: Ranges from built-in 5-inch 16 x 32 to optional 24 x 80-column monitor.

KEYBOARD: One of the series' best features with sixteen-key numeric and function keypad; more than twelve more function keys across top of keyboard; full travel typewriter keyboard.

I/O SLOTS/INTERFACES: Varies from four slots to an optional HP-1B interface expansion box for up to fourteen peripherals.

SYSTEM PRICE: As low as $1,795 for HP-86 basic model.

PROGRAMMING LANGUAGES: HP BASIC standard with CP/M and UCSD p-System Pascal as options.

PRINTERS: HP's own line of four dot matrix, two daisywheel, and two thermal printers, and two color plotters. Its HP-7470A plotter is the most popular of its kind.

MODEMS: HP's own 300- and 1,200-baud direct connect and acoustic coupler models, and many others.

OTHER PERIPHERALS: Five varieties of disk drives, seven varieties of hard disks (4.6 Mb. to 14.5 Mb. capacity range), and many HP scientific and technical instruments, including multimeters and memory expansion modules.

AVAILABLE SOFTWARE: Dozens of program cartridges and disk-based programs from HP for accounting, engineering, finance, project management, real estate, statistics, tax planning, and word processing as well as vertical market programs for specific industries from systems houses.

SALES OUTLETS: Hundreds of HP dealers and distributors in most cities, also large HP direct sales force to corporations.

SERVICE AND SUPPORT: HP has excellent reputation for service and support with dozens of authorized and company-run service centers.

FUTURE DEVELOPMENTS: HP will continue to be a powerful force in the technical, scientific, and engineering professional community with its HP-80 series for years to come. These fields cover what HP does best.

MORROW COMPUTER

Morrow MD2 and MD3 Computers

BRIEF SUMMARY: Morrow Computer is well respected within the microcomputer industry, but it has not been well known among consumers. Yet, it has consistently produced high-quality microcomputers at very low cost since 1980. Its latest coup, the MDS-11, is discussed in detail in the next chapter, and its very good portable is discussed in Chapter 10. Given below are its two basic models which are well worth consideration if you are interested in a fine machine which runs the CP/M operating system. However, the difficulty with the Morrow in the past has been its concentration on small business system dealers, and the need to assemble an entire package of components before it is sold. For example, the basic system prices given below do not include the cost for a monitor; of course, the same problem is found with the Apple and similarly popular machines.

Figure 35. The Morrow Micro Decision MD2 computer with 64K RAM, dual built-in disk drives, and a bundle of applications programs is a powerful computer for under $1,500. (Courtesy of Morrow Computer Corporation)

One of Morrow's strengths has been bundling good, useful software with its systems. For example, the MD2 model comes with a word processor, spelling checker, spreadsheet, information manager, CP/M 2.2, Microsoft BASIC, and an educational language, PILOT.

CPU: Z80A.

RAM/ROM: 64K RAM, 4K ROM.

MASS STORAGE: Price includes two 186K minifloppy disk drives for Model MD2; MD3 model includes two double-sided disk drives with a capacity of 348K per disk. Can also read and write the formats of eight other disk drives for the MD2 model, and ten for the MD3 model.

VIDEO DISPLAY: Optional monitor with 24 x 80 display in black and green phosphor ($400).

KEYBOARD: Detachable keyboard with typewriter full travel and thirty definable function keys.

I/O SLOTS/INTERFACES: Centronics standard parallel port and two RS-232 serial ports.

SYSTEM PRICE: $1,199 for MD2 and $1,499 for MD3. The latter includes the double-density, double-sided minifloppy drives, and Quest Bookkeeper software.

PROGRAMMING LANGUAGES: CP/M 2.2 operating system with Microsoft BASIC 80 programming language and Morrow PILOT for educational applications.

PRINTERS: Morrow letter-quality printers and dot matrix printers as options.

MODEMS: Morrow 300- and 1,200-baud direct connect modems optional.

OTHER PERIPHERALS: Local Area Network available, and range of independent vendors' products.

AVAILABLE SOFTWARE: New Word word processor; Correct-It spelling checker; Logicalc spreadsheet; Personal Pearl Data Base Manager; Quest Bookkeeper with MD3 model; and three OSes and languages described above, all come with the system. Of course, thousands of CP/M 2.2 programs run on both models with little change.

SALES OUTLETS: Dozens of dealers and systems houses around the country. Call toll free (800) 521-3493 or in California, (415) 430-1970.

SERVICE AND SUPPORT: Authorized dealers

or eighty Xerox third-party service centers around the country.

FUTURE DEVELOPMENTS: Morrow seems to have found a solid niche in the market among small businesses and is poised for steady growth in the future.

RADIO SHACK/TANDY CORPORATION

Radio Shack TRS-80 Model 4

BRIEF SUMMARY: The TRS-80 Model 4 picks up where the Model I and III left off; both the I and III are no longer being produced. The advantage of the Model 4 is that it is one of the few all-in-one personal computers left: in one cabinet, Tandy has placed a black-and-white monitor, the CPU, 16K RAM and BASIC in ROM, a full keyboard with cursor keys and numeric keypad, and two I/O ports for a price of $999. The same cabinet has space for two disk drives, floppy or hard. This is the basic starter system designed to appeal to novices who want to grow into more serious professional applications. Of course, Radio Shack also offers various upgraded models with disk drives and added memory as options. These will be discussed below in the appropriate category. At present, the Model 4 is the only Radio Shack model between its very inexpensive color computers and its more expensive small business machines.

CPU: Z80A 8-bit on all models.

RAM/ROM: 16K RAM minimum, expandable on various models from 64K to 128K. 128K accessed through bank-switching technique. 14K ROM with TRS-80 BASIC built in.

MASS STORAGE: Low-end optional cassette recorder ($60); 184K double-density minifloppy disk drive, one or two ($649 for first internal drive, $240 for second internal; and $320 for third drive and $280 for fourth drive, both external); and 5 Mb. hard disk drive ($1,999 for first, $1,799 for second).

VIDEO DISPLAY: 24 x 80 black-and-white standard; optional high-resolution graphics card with 32K RAM and BASIC included ($250).

KEYBOARD: Seventy keys, including twelve-key numeric/function pad, four cursor keys, three function keys.

I/O SLOTS/INTERFACES: Parallel printer port

and cassette port standard; RS-232 port optional for all but two-drive version.

SYSTEM PRICE: $999 for starter setup without cassette recorder; $1,298 for 16K cassette-based model with color graphics printer; $1,797 for 16K cassette-based system with 80-column dot matrix printer; $1,699 for 64K, one-disk model; $1,999 for 64K two-disk model with RS-232 port; and $4,736 for hard disk system with 64K, two floppy disks, 5 Mb. external hard disk, and 80-column dot matrix printer.

PROGRAMMING LANGUAGES: TRS BASIC included in ROM; TRSDOS 6 OS and Microsoft Disk BASIC for disk drive versions; and LDOS for hard disk system all included in applicable systems. All truly compatible with all TRS-80 Model III TRSDOS programs, running in optional Model III mode; Optional languages included: Alcor Pascal ($250); COBOL-4 ($199); Compiler BASIC ($149); CP/M Plus ($150); CBASIC ($99.95); BASCOM-4 ($195); FORTRAN-4 ($99.95); Assembly Development Language ($149); and LDOS ($129).

PRINTERS: Full line of Radio Shack dot matrix, color, letter-quality, and plotter printers available and compatible.

MODEMS: Four Radio Shack modems from 300-baud to 1,200-baud.

OTHER PERIPHERALS: Memory expansion and upgrade kits for Model III conversion to Model 4 ($799), Model 4 from 64K to 128K RAM ($80); RS-232 Communications Board and Cable ($99); and more.

AVAILABLE SOFTWARE: Variety of personal finance, professional, and small business, and family entertainment packages for disk and cassette at Radio Shack stores. Many more available through mail order and distributorships. But the wealth of programming languages for the Model 4 is a clear indication Radio Shack intends to broaden the base of available software and widen the computer's appeal.

SALES OUTLETS: 7,700 stores and 300-plus Computer Centers, and selected distribution and private label channels.

SERVICE AND SUPPORT: Service contracts through Computer Centers or factory service.

FUTURE DEVELOPMENTS: The Model 4 will be available until mid- to late 1985 when it will be replaced with another machine. But Radio Shack will make the next one compatible and it will continue to support the Model 4 for years to come. The Model 4 series that appears to be the best buy is the $1,999 64K RAM with dual disk drive version. The cassette-based versions are overpriced and practically worthless for even serious game playing.

CHAPTER 9

Desktop Personal Computers for Less than $5,000

The most prevalent type of microcomputer available today is the desktop personal computer for executives, professionals, managers, and small-business people. Many of them, such as the IBM PC and the Apple Macintosh, are often used as home/business computers, but the price ranges, power, and software packages all emphasize that these are not game machines for children. They are serious business tools for adults, with entertainment software available on the side. Although the list price of most of these machines is more than $3,000, in many cases, the price is not as high as it seems. Most of these systems include *bundled* disk drives, video monitors, large amounts of RAM and ROM, DOSes, programming languages, and applications software. In most lower cost personal computers, these features are often options that can drive the cost beyond that for a desktop machine. For example, if you had paid the retail list price for a 48K Apple II Plus, two disk drives, an Epson MX-80 dot matrix printer, and an Apple III monitor, the cost would have exceeded $4,100, not including any software at all.

Before you dismiss these desktop computers as too expensive, compare what their systems give you compared to the necessary "extras" you may have to buy with some personal computers.

The desktop computers discussed below are just the tip of an enormous iceberg of more than 150 8-bit and 16-bit computers. These were selected for discussion largely because of their manufacturer's reputation and staying power, their popularity in the general market or specific market niches, or their innovations, like the Hewlett-Packard HP-150 touch screen display.

Before you buy any of these, however, read Chapter 10 to see if you can find a less expensive, though truly compatible, portable version of the same desktop computer, or a similar one.

APPLE COMPUTER, INC.

Apple Computer revolutionized the technology for personal and desktop computers in mid-1983 with its Lisa 16/32-bit computer. Using a full megabyte of RAM, Apple displayed the concepts of "windows" and a pointing device called the "mouse" to the world. The technology was developed in the late 1960s at Xerox research laboratories, and was first introduced in the $16,000–$18,000 Xerox Star 8010 office workstation. With Lisa, Apple brought the price down to below $10,000 and popularized the two concepts. The window concept allows users to overlay one screen display on another up to a total of four displays on the same screen, and

Figure 36. The Apple Lisa 2 screen illustrates the windows concept and the use of the mouse pointer device. Count the separate functions on the screen: there are four of them, including word processing, spreadsheet, graphics, and information management. (Courtesy of Apple Computer, Inc.)

merge the contents of those files by simply using the mouse point device.

The Lisa and Apple 32 Supermicro series were developed to emulate the process of working at a desk. They de-emphasize the use of the keyboard and numeric keypad for entering commands, executing system operations, or moving data around within the system. Keyboards and pads are relegated strictly to data entry. The mouse and the screen windows work together to emulate the same types of tasks any person who works at a desk does: pull out, use and put back file folders; shuffle papers and files; use a calculator; dispose of things in a trash can; write and edit memos, letters, and reports; send and receive mail; access essential information from a variety of sources—books, files, computer terminals, and stacks of papers. The Lisa technology organizes the system around symbols

called *icons*, which stand for each of these activities. Using the mouse pointer, you choose each task or activity and move through simple, short menus with the click of a button on the mouse. To move the mouse pointer (or cursor) on the screen, you slide the mouse around on the desktop, and its movements on the actual desk are duplicated within the context of the screen.

This window-and-mouse technology is supposed to enable users to access information and help novices understand how the system works much more quickly than ever before. Personally, as an experienced typist and computer user, I find the mouse pointer slow and annoying; I can type two or three command keys and hit "return" faster than I can move a mouse across a desktop and find the right icon. Hitting a "1" for a menu selection is easier for me, too. I also believe that it is a waste of computer power to take up hundreds of thousands of bytes in RAM to emulate the organization of a desktop. A computer keyboard is not a piece of paper and a pen; a disk drive is not a filing cabinet; a screen is not a desktop. They are hundreds of times faster and more versatile; and it would be a greater service, in my opinion, to develop new concepts of interacting with a computer. It seems to be like trying to put a horse's head and tail on an automobile and telling the driver that he is still riding a horse. However, I know I am bucking the great tide of mouse technology, but I firmly believe it is a transitional technology between the poorly designed software that used strange and difficult keyboard commands and the elegant yet simple structures that can be developed by combining the window technology with preprogrammed function keys. One programmed keystroke to execute a series of commands makes more sense to me than moving a mouse pointer in four or five directions. And there is no reason the window technology cannot be integrated with keyboards in this or similar manners. It is *not* a hardware problem; it is a problem of software designers and programmers who do not know how to develop new programming concepts.

Be all this as it may, discussed below are Apple's evolutionary window/mouse computers, Mcintosh, Lisa 2 (three models), and Lisa itself, which appear to be staking out positions as the first and leading third generation personal computers.

Apple Macintosh

BRIEF SUMMARY: Apple Macintosh is a low-cost version of the Lisa window/mouse/icon technology. At $2,495, Macintosh is to be sold to what Apple calls 25 million "knowledge workers" in careers, professions, and education. As noted, Macintosh uses the built-in mouse interface and high-resolution black-and-white display to simulate an actual desktop working environment: built-in notepads, file folders, a calculator, and other office tools. Apple firmly believes the mouse/icon technology represents the future for all personal computers as a third industry standard. The most significant difference between the Macintosh and other computers may be the marketing campaign and hoopla surrounding it: Apple spent $25 million during the first 100 days after its introduction to storm the marketplace. It appeared that the strategy worked. Apple also gained a foothold with

Macintosh in universities by setting up an Apple University Consortium in which twenty-four top schools agreed to buy up to $60 million worth of computers within five years and develop and share educational software applications for Lisa technology.

Is Macintosh useful to you? If you are a professional, a manager, or an office worker unfamiliar with keyboards and computers, yes. Macintosh and Lisa can provide a comfortable introduction to personal computing. Apple estimates that a conventional computer takes up to forty hours to learn to use with up to an additional ten hours to learn each software package. I suspect these are high ranges and largely depend on how easy it is to use the software designed for the computer. I bought my computer long before I was an expert, and it did not take me nearly that long to learn its operations, and the software I learned by progression—I learned functions as I needed to learn them. Apple claims Macintosh takes only a few hours to learn, and Macintosh dealers confirm it appears much easier for their clerical and office workers to learn than the conventional computers they sell. Apple predicted it will sell 350,000 Macintoshes during 1984, with 35,000 of them going into home uses, with that number tripling to more than a million during 1985.

The main difference between Macintosh and Lisa, besides price and functions (Lisa has more) is the availability of software. When Lisa was introduced, only four software packages were available with very few planned, and Lisa sales suffered dramatically. Macintosh was announced with two packages from Apple, word processing and graphics, and more than 170 more packages available by June, 1984. It is clear that the software tail wags the hardware dog. By the end of 1984, almost 500 Macintosh software packages were available.

Apple emphasized communications with Mac-Terminal to emulate DEC VT-100/52 and TTY terminals, and IB 3277 and 3278 terminals with a new peripheral called AppleLine. It also released MacPascal, MacAssembler, MacBASIC, MacProject, MacLogo, MacDraw, and more. Among the leading software houses releasing software for Macintosh were: Microsoft with Multiplan spreadsheet; Lotus Development with integrated spreadsheet 1-2-3; Ashton-Tate with dBase II information manager; BPI Systems with accounting software

Figure 37. The basic Apple Macintosh computer with mouse pointer, keyboard, and built-in microfloppy disk drive. Icons on the screen show how easy it is to grasp Macintosh's integrated functions. (Courtesy of Apple Computer, Inc.)

for small business; Blue Chip Software for stock market software; Continental Software for home and business accounting; numerous educational and game software houses; and various programming language companies.

Macintosh is not compatible with either the Apple IIe or the Apple III, although Apple promises an Apple network which allows interconnection and communication of all Apple products.

The Macintosh does have numerous new and advanced features which make it stand out from other computers. Among these are:

— Very compact size: 10-inch square main unit with video display; 17-pound weight; and typewriter-style, but uncluttered and detached keyboard.

— Very high-quality manufacture: Apple builds the Macintoshes in a highly automated factory that rivals anything the Japanese have perfected, and has instituted the best and latest quality control techniques. If you get a bad Macintosh, it will be a rare occurrence.

— Microfloppy disk: Apple includes a built-in 400K 3.5-inch microfloppy in its unit, another

strong endorsement for the Sony microfloppy standard.

CPU: Motorola 68000 16/32-bit microprocessor.

RAM/ROM: 128K RAM standard, expandable to 256K, and 64K ROM. The ROM includes all Lisa window, pull-down menu, and graphics functions, most DOS functions, and many others which formerly occupied space in RAM, leaving almost all of the RAM available for programs and data storage.

MASS STORAGE: A built-in 3.5-inch Sony microfloppy disk drive with 400K formatted capacity. Apple is the second, behind the HP-150, to use the Sony 3.5-inch drive.

VIDEO DISPLAY: Very high-resolution 9-inch black-and-white monitor included in the price. Apple no longer gives its display specifications in lines and columns because the size of the characters varies according to your desire. You can change font and character sizes at will on the screen with the mouse.

KEYBOARD: Standard typewriter keyboard *without* the normal function keys. It does not have

Figure 38. The Apple Macintosh with many of its peripherals: numeric keypad, external microfloppy disk drive, Imagewriter dot matrix graphics printer, and direct connect modem. (Courtesy of Apple Computer, Inc.)

cursor keys, leaving all of those functions to the mouse pointer.

I/O SLOTS/INTERFACES: Two RS-232/RS-422 serial ports for a printer and a modem; a port for an optional second microfloppy disk drive or hard disk; an audio slot for a 12-octave range; and an internal hardware bus for an Apple-to-Apple interconnect system, which will allow all Apple computers to communicate with each other and with peripherals.

SYSTEM PRICE: $2,495, includes video monitor, one microfloppy disk drive, 64K ROM, 128K RAM, keyboard, Lisa operating system, and mouse pointer.

PROGRAMMING LANGUAGES: MacBASIC, MacAssembler, MacPascal, and others from independent vendors.

PRINTERS: Apple Imagewriter dot matrix printer which also prints correspondence quality ($595). A wide variety of compatible printers from independent vendors.

MODEMS: Apple 300-baud modem ($225) and 1,200-baud direct connect modem ($495); Hayes Microcomputer Products SmartModem and SmartModem II software; and many others, all optional.

OTHER PERIPHERALS: Numeric Keypad ($129); AppleLine for IBM 3277 and 3278 mainframe terminal emulation; external 3.5-inch microfloppy disk drive ($495); dozens more from variety of vendors.

AVAILABLE SOFTWARE: From Apple,

MacWrite, MacPaint, MacDraw, MacProject, MacLogo, MacTerminal, and programming languages. More than 100 software houses already have programs. A partial list is given in Appendix B.

SALES OUTLETS: Three thousand authorized Apple dealers, and Apple direct sales force.

SERVICE AND SUPPORT: Authorized Apple dealer service centers and Apple factory support for hardware, and Apple hot line support and dealer support for software.

FUTURE DEVELOPMENTS: Macintosh is Apple's answer to the IBM PC. It could be a very impressive answer, and be the first in what will be a series of lower and lower cost microcomputers using the Lisa-style technology. It will be difficult for Macintosh competitors to beat Apple's price; it is known that Apple could cut the price of the Macintosh and still make a profit on each machine. Apple, of course, will not try to sit still and wait for the market to attack its position; expect a truly portable Macintosh, and a series of impressive peripherals to go with the system, along with huge amounts of software. In 1986, Apple will probably introduce a new technology to replace or, at least, supplement the Macintosh.

Lisa 2 Models

BRIEF SUMMARY: The Lisa 2 series computers are less expensive, higher performance versions of the original Lisa and complete the Apple 32 Supermicro family. The series is Apple's response to the public's negative response to Lisa's $9,995 price. There are three models, the features of which will be discussed in each category below.

CPU: Motorola 68000.

RAM/ROM: All three models have 512K RAM, three times more than Macintosh. It is expandable to 1 megabyte of RAM.

MASS STORAGE: Lisa 2 has one 400K 3.5-inch microfloppy drive; Lisa 2/5 adds an external 5 Mb. hard disk; but Lisa 2/10 has a built-in 10 Mb. hard disk. KEY FACT: All Macintosh software is disk-to-disk compatible with Lisa 2 series.

VIDEO DISPLAY: High-resolution Lisa bit-mapped, not character-oriented, display on a 12-inch display.

Figure 39. The basic Lisa 2 configuration with mouse pointer, microfloppy disk drive, and a built-in 5 Mb. hard disk drive. (Courtesy of Apple Computer, Inc.)

KEYBOARD: Standard typewriter keyboard with 18-key numeric and function keypad.

I/O SLOTS/INTERFACES: Two RS-232 serial ports for printers or modems; one slot for external hard or soft disk drive; plug for mouse pointer.

SYSTEM PRICE: Lisa 2, $3,495; Lisa 2/5, $4,495; and Lisa 2/10, $5,495. Frankly, it may be a good strategy to buy a less expensive 10 Mb. hard disk and add it to the Lisa 2. Ten megabyte hard disks for the Lisa are available for about $1,000.

PROGRAMMING LANGUAGES: Pascal, BASIC-Plus, COBOL, and programming tools— QuickPort for the three languages, and Toolkit/32 which uses Lisa to develop fully integrated software. The UNIX operating system and the Microsoft XENIX variation are also available. Ryan-MacFarland, a major programming language developer, offers RM/COBOL and RM/FORTRAN; they run under Microsoft XENIX or Unisoft UniPlus+ operating systems for the Lisa. But they require the full 1 Mb. RAM. Also offers MS-DOS as a plug-in board option.

PRINTERS: All Apple printers and compatible models by other vendors.

MODEMS: Two Apple modems and variety of other vendor's models.

OTHER PERIPHERALS: 512K RAM expansion board ($1,495); Lisa 2/5 Upgrade Hard Disk ($595); Lisa 2/10 Upgrade ($2,495); Lisa external microfloppy disk drive ($495); others announced by independent vendors.

AVAILABLE SOFTWARE: From Apple—Lisa Office System ($295) requires 1 Mb. RAM, Lisa-List ($195), LisaWrite ($295), LisaCalc ($295), LisaTerminal ($295), LisaGraph ($295), LisaProject ($395), LisaDraw ($395), and Macintosh Operating System for Lisa ($195). More than 175 software houses are delivering software for the Lisa series, so a more than adequate supply should be available.

SALES OUTLETS: Three thousand authorized Apple dealers.

SERVICE AND SUPPORT: Authorized Apple

service centers and Apple for both hardware and software.

FUTURE DEVELOPMENTS: Further variations with greater storage capacities and more software and peripherals from a variety of vendors are inevitable. One major Apple dealer, Morris Decision Systems, has commented that the Macintosh has helped sell Lisas; when buyers see what the Lisa can do better than the Macintosh, they buy the more expensive Lisa series.

Lisa

CPU: Same as Lisa 2 series.

RAM/ROM: 1 million bytes of RAM, 128K ROM.

MASS STORAGE: One double-density minifloppy disk drive and a 5 Mb. hard disk.

VIDEO DISPLAY: Same as Macintosh and Lisa 2.

KEYBOARD: Same as Lisa 2.

I/O SLOTS/INTERFACES: Same as Lisa 2.

SYSTEM PRICE: $6,995.

PROGRAMMING LANGUAGES: Lisa Office System, and all others available for Lisa 2 series with 1 Mb. RAM.

PRINTERS: All available Apple printers.

MODEMS: All Apple modems and other vendors' compatible models.

OTHER PERIPHERALS: Same as Lisa 2 series.

AVAILABLE SOFTWARE: Same as Lisa 2 series and packages from 175 software developers.

SALES OUTLETS: Same as Macintosh and Lisa 2.

SERVICE AND SUPPORT: Same as Macintosh and Lisa 2.

FUTURE DEVELOPMENTS: This will remain the flagship of the Lisa family.

Apple III Business System

BRIEF SUMMARY: The forgotten sister in the Apple family, the Apple III, was the company's poor attempt to release an 8-bit small business computer. The III, introduced in 1980, had many early manufacturing problems and suffered from them. But Apple still manufactures them and has upgraded the system with more RAM, a hard disk, and improved operating system and hard disk software. The problem today is the Apple III Business System list price of more than $5,300, especially when it is not upgradable to the Lisa nor can it run most Apple II Plus or IIe programs without special emulators. The good things about the III are that it is an adequate small business machine and you can find it priced at good discounts.

CPU: 8-bit 6502 variations with multiple chips.

RAM/ROM: 256K RAM, not expandable.

MASS STORAGE: Built-in single-sided 140K minifloppy and 5 Mb. ProFile hard disk, both included.

VIDEO DISPLAY: Apple Monitor III, 12-inch, 80 x 24 screen display with green phosphor and black, also included.

KEYBOARD: Typewriterlike, with 19-key numeric and function keypad, better laid out than the Apple II Plus and IIe keyboards.

I/O SLOTS/INTERFACES: Disk drive port; RS-232 serial port; Silentype interface for Apple Silentype dot matrix printer; two plug jacks for monitor and joystick; four additional peripheral slots.

SYSTEM PRICE: $5,330.

PROGRAMMING LANGUAGES: Apple SOS (Sophisticated Operating System) disk operating system; Apple Business BASIC; COBOL; Apple III Pascal; CP/M with Apple III Softcard optional board. Quark Inc.'s "Catalyst" program allows switching among programs stored on hard disk without restarting the computer.

PRINTERS: All Apple printers and compatible models from other vendors.

MODEMS: Apple modems and compatible modems from other vendors.

OTHER PERIPHERALS: Apple II emulator card; Apple III terminal emulator for mainframe terminals; Apple Serial Card III ($225).

AVAILABLE SOFTWARE: More than four hundred business software programs, and all CP/M programs formatted in Apple III disk drive formats with optional Apple SoftCard III. Most Apple II programs in emulation mode.

SALES OUTLETS: All authorized Apple dealers.

SERVICE AND SUPPORT: Ninety-day warranty and $288 annual service contract with

AppleCare, or RCA third-party service contract arrangement.

FUTURE DEVELOPMENTS: Apple III is a machine of the past, not of the future. Apple will sell a few tens of thousands a year, but does not emphasize this line. It is a maintenance product, not a growth one.

CORONA DATA SYSTEMS

Corona PC

BRIEF SUMMARY: Corona Data Systems is one of a number of companies making IBM PC-compatible computers. It makes two models, one a desktop discussed here, and another a portable discussed in the next chapter. Corona Data was founded by Robert Harp, one of the founders of Vector Graphics, a successful maker of 8-bit small business and desktop computers. Harp left Vector Graphics after he and his wife, founder and still Vector Chairman, Lore Harp, divorced.

Corona is generally rated one of the top five IBM PC-compatibles because it adds RAM expandability, more user-friendliness, and more features, and includes applications software in the total system. Perhaps its major advantage is its high-resolution, two-color display with good contrast. However, this high-contrast, high-density screen is also its major incompatibility with the IBM PC. Its second major advantage is price: it is about $800–$1,000 cheaper than the IBM PC on a point-for-point comparison. Taking advantage of some software for the IBM PC may require some slight program changes to avoid conflict with the differing graphics character sets. To solve this conflict would require: 2) Using an IBM Color Graphics Adapter; 2) Buying already modified programs; or 3) Using the GSX graphics interpreter for the CP/M-86 OS.

In short, be careful when selecting IBM PC software to run on this good, low-cost machine. But all in all, this PC-compatible lives up to its name better than most.

CPU: Intel 16-bit 8088.

RAM/ROM: 128K, expandable on the motherboard to 512K RAM without using up any peripheral slots, a real advantage.

Figure 40. The IBM PC-compatible Corona Personal Computer is one of the best of many computers which claim to be compatible with IBM PC software. (Courtesy of Corona Data Systems)

MASS STORAGE: One 320K minifloppy drive included. Optional second floppy drive or 10 Mb. hard disk drive ($2,695 for external version of $2,295 for internal version, although it is available at lower prices.)

VIDEO DISPLAY: 25 x 80 in character mode; 640 x 325 pixels in graphics mode, black-and-green phosphor only. Color adapter for IBM PC optional for color.

KEYBOARD: Eighty-three keys, very similar to IBM PC keyboard.

I/O SLOTS/INTERFACES: One parallel printer port; one RS-232 serial port; and four IBM PC-style peripheral slots.

SYSTEM PRICE: $2,595 for one-disk version; $2,995 for two-disk version; $4,495 for version with 10 Mb. hard disk and one minifloppy drive.

PROGRAMMING LANGUAGES: MS-DOS 2.0 OS ($60); GW BASIC from Microsoft included; UCSD p-System Pascal ($845); and FORTRAN ($245).

PRINTERS: IBM-compatible printers from other vendors.

MODEMS: IBM-compatible from other vendors.

OTHER PERIPHERALS: Additional minifloppy

disk ($450); 128K RAM memory cards ($295 each); amber monitor ($50 over system cost); 8087 floating point math coprocessor ($295); and range of IBM-compatible products from other vendors.

AVAILABLE SOFTWARE: With the system come MS-DOS 1.25; GW BASIC interpreter; PC-Tutor; and a good word processor, Multimate. Thousands of IBM PC programs, 90 percent of which should run on the Corona without modification.

SALES OUTLETS: Dealers and distributors around country, often sold through mail order. Call (800) 621-6746 for nearest dealer.

SERVICE AND SUPPORT: Xerox third-party service contract available after warranty period ends.

FUTURE DEVELOPMENTS: Corona is making an IBM PC-compatible computer for Docutel/Olivetti called the Olivetti PC. Thus, its short-term future as a maker of compatibles is basically assured.

CROMEMCO, INC.

Cromemco C-10MPC

BRIEF SUMMARY: Cromemco is one of the oldest and best survivors of the personal computer wars. It was founded by three college classmates in 1976, and has prospered by aiming at niche markets in small business and by producing high-quality, reasonably priced computers. It has been one of the Top Five manufacturers of Z-80- and CP/M-based systems for seven years. Its produce line includes thirty-five interfaces and peripherals and dozens of software tools for programmers. It has been one of the rare companies that has made it easy for professional programmers and systems houses to develop applications packages for vertical industries and professions, such as accountants.

Now, it is also selling an inexpensive and attractive personal computer with a great deal of popular, "bundled" applications software. This PC, however, is just one of twenty-four models it makes ranging in price from $995 to $10,995. If you are interested in a Z-80 PC, or one with a dual 16-bit, 8-bit microprocessor for an industrial, commercial, or small business application, you could do a lot worse than buy a Cromemco product.

Figure 41. The low-cost, high-function Cromemco C-10MPC. (Courtesy of Cromemco, Inc.)

CPU: 8-bit Z-80A microprocessor.

RAM/ROM: 64K RAM, 24K ROM.

MASS STORAGE: One 390K double-sided, double-density minifloppy included with system.

VIDEO DISPLAY: 25 x 80 with black-and-green phosphor monitor included in price. Rests on a swivel stand for easy adjustment.

KEYBOARD: Detached, ergonomically good keyboard with numeric keypad. 20 predefined or programmable keys using control or shift key, four cursor keys. Among the better keyboards.

I/O SLOTS/INTERFACES: One floppy disk port; one RS-232 serial port; one parallel printer port; one serial printer port.

SYSTEM PRICE: $2,990 with two disk drives.

PROGRAMMING LANGUAGES: Cromemco CDOS, a CP/M variation, as OS; Structured BASIC standard in ROM; RATFOR, COBOL, FORTRAN, LISP, and Macro Assembler as options.

PRINTERS: 120-word per minute letter-quality printer ($795, a good price).

MODEMS: 1,200-baud direct connect modem ($1,495, expensive).

OTHER PERIPHERALS: Optional connection to Cromemco multi-user systems with dual processors.

AVAILABLE SOFTWARE: Included with system are CDOS, WriteMaster word processing, PlanMaster spreadsheet, MoneyMaster financial analysis, Chess, Screen Editor, WordStar word processing, InfoStar information manager, CalcStar spreadsheet, and MailMerge file merging, and, of course, Structured BASIC. Hundreds of programs available through systems houses and dealers for Cromemco systems and other programming languages.

SALES OUTLETS: Sold through more than 40 ComputerLands, 55 industrial distributors, and more than 115 dealers in the U.S. and Canada.

SERVICE AND SUPPORT: Through local dealers and factory service.

FUTURE DEVELOPMENTS: Cromemco seems to be pleased with the results of its foray into the personal computer competition, and it can be expected to follow the pack in introducing low-cost 16-bit computers during 1985. It will continue to concentrate its strength in its commercial multi-user and industrial markets.

EAGLE COMPUTER CORP.

Eagle PC Plus

BRIEF SUMMARY: Eagle is another of the better IBM PC-compatible computer manufacturers started during 1982–83. It suffered a tragedy when its founder was killed in an auto accident in mid-1983, but its management has pulled the company through the transition. Its product line includes two desktop compatible models and two portable models described in the next chapter. The differences between the two desktop models will be described in each category below, and the compatible software for the Eagle—which Eagle has tested and approved—is listed in Appendix B.

CPU: Intel 8088 quasi-16-bit microprocesor.

RAM/ROM: 128K RAM, expandable to 640K RAM.

MASS STORAGE: Two double-density, double-sided 360K disk drives with PC Plus; and one 360K

Figure 42. The Eagle PC Plus (Photo courtesy of Eagle Computer Corporation).

disk drive and one 10 Mb. hard disk with PC Plus XL model. Included in each model's system price.

VIDEO DISPLAY: 25 x 80, with bit-mapped high-resolution green phosphor and black; very high-quality color RGB monitor optional.

KEYBOARD: Eighty-four keys with ten function keys and numeric keypad standard; optional keyboard with 105 keys, including 24 function keys.

I/O SLOTS/INTERFACES: Two serial ports and one parallel port, both on main board; four peripheral slots on IBM-compatible expansion board; options include: color graphics adapter board; monochrome graphics adapter; Local Area Network adapter; video cassette recorder adapter board for mass storage backup; and hard disk controller board.

SYSTEM PRICE: $2,995 for PC Plus and $4,995 for PC PLUS XL.

PROGRAMMING LANGUAGES: MS-DOS 2.0 and CP/M-86 operating systems and GW BASIC included: MS-DOS 1.25 and Eagle LAN OS optional.

PRINTERS: IBM-compatible models from other vendors.

MODEMS: IBM-compatible models from other vendors.

OTHER PERIPHERALS: RGB color monitor; 10

Mb. hard disk (optional for PC Plus); expanded keyboard option.

AVAILABLE SOFTWARE: Most major IBM PC-compatible software. See Appendix B for complete list, but none beyond BASIC and operating systems provided with system.

SALES OUTLETS: Dealer and distributor networks across country; many computer stores carry as IBM PC substitute.

SERVICE AND SUPPORT: Limited ninety-day warranty on labor, and one-year warranty on parts from day of purchase. Authorized dealer service or factory service for hardware; individual software vendors for software support.

FUTURE DEVELOPMENTS: Eagle seems to be able to hold its own in the IBM PC-compatible market as long the IBM PC is in short supply. It will have to diversify its markets, however, when IBM gears up enough production to meet the demand, something IBM is doing now (late 1984–1985).

EPSON AMERICA, INC.

Epson QX-10

BRIEF SUMMARY: Epson America is part of a major Japanese conglomerate formed around the Seiko Watch Company. It launched its first foray into the computer market with the Epson MX-80 printer in 1979; it became an overnight sensation and quickly captured almost half of the market for dot matrix printers. In fact, the IBM dot matrix printer for the IBM PC is an Epson with an IBM label on it. In 1982, Epson launched two personal computers, one a highly rated portable called the HX-20, discussed in the next chapter, and the equally high-quality personal computer, the QX-10. Epson has also expanded its line of printers with a strong series and should maintain a major presence in the U.S. market for years to come.

CPU: Zilog Z80A microprocessor.

RAM/ROM: 64K standard, expandable to 256K with bank switching.

MASS STORAGE: Two 380K double-sided, double-density minifloppies included.

VIDEO DISPLAY: 25 x 80 12-inch high-resolu-

Figure 43. The Epson QX-10 includes many "friendly" features including English-like command structures for many software programs. (Courtesy of Epson America, Inc.)

tion green phosphor and black. KEY: The display unit has its own large 32K–128K RAM memory to store information as it is scrolled off the screen.

KEYBOARD: Major difference with a HASCI keyboard in which fourteen function keys are labeled in English as are four operation keys. Also has full numeric keypad; two tab keys, four cursor keys, and special word/document processing keys. Also has conventional keyboard for regular operations available. Both detachable.

I/O SLOTS/INTERFACES: One RS-232 serial port; one parallel printer port; light pen plug; five peripheral slots built in.

SYSTEM PRICE: Under $3,000.

PROGRAMMING LANGUAGES: CP/M and BASIC.

PRINTERS: Whole line of Epson's own fine printers are plug-compatible with no modifications.

MODEMS: Any compatible model from independent vendor.

OTHER PERIPHERALS: Any CP/M-compatible from outside vendors.

AVAILABLE SOFTWARE: Very highly regarded VALDOCS 1.18 integrated software/OS with word processing, calculator, graphics, appointment schedule, personal filing, and electronic mail, all done with English commands which are specified on the HASCI keyboard. Also more than three hundred CP/M packages have been specially formatted for the QX-10 by a software distributor.

SALES OUTLETS: Computer stores, major department stores, home appliance stores through twelve independent regional distributors.

SERVICE AND SUPPORT: Standard warranty, factory, and authorized dealer service.

FUTURE DEVELOPMENTS: Epson will introduce a 16-bit computer to stay competitive in the booming professional and small business computer market. It can be expected to introduce a 32-bit desktop by 1986, possibly a portable model as well.

FUJITSU MICROELECTRONICS, INC. PROFESSIONAL MICROSYSTEMS DIVISION

Fujitsu Micro 16s

BRIEF SUMMARY: Fujitsu is one of the world's largest makers of mainframes and minicomputers as well as semiconductors and electronic equipment for industry. The Micro 16s is its first foray into the U.S. personal computer market.

CPU: Dual microprocessors—8-bit Z80A and Fujitsu-made 16-bit 8086 licensed from Intel.

Figure 44. The Fujitsu Micro 16s has two microprocessors for both 8-bit and 16-bit operations. One can use a wide variety of standard software on this imported machine. (Courtesy of Fujitsu Microelectronics, Inc.)

RAM/ROM: 128K RAM, expandable to 1 megabyte.

MASS STORAGE: Two built-in 320K double-density minifloppy disk drives; three options—dual 8-inch external floppy with 1.2 Mb. each, and two 5.25-inch hard disks, one 10 Mb. or a 20 Mb. capacity.

VIDEO DISPLAY: 25 x 80 or 40 x 25 with monochrome monitor standard and high-resolution color RGB monitor optional. 48K display RAM included.

KEYBOARD: Ninety-eight keys with ten function keys, predefined editing keys, typewriter layout, and numeric keypad.

I/O SLOTS/INTERFACES: RS-232 serial port; parallel printer port; color monitor plug; light pen plug; floppy disk controller port; monochrome monitor plug; and four-channel analog/digital convertor port, all standard. Five expansion slots built in.

SYSTEM PRICE: $3,995 includes monitor, keyboard, 128K RAM, dual CPUs, and WordStar and SuperCalc 2 applications software.

PROGRAMMING LANGUAGES: CP/M and CP/M-86 included; MS-DOS and Concurrent CP/M-86 optional. The latter allows a user to do more than one task at a time.

PRINTERS: Any compatible from other vendors.

MODEMS: Any compatible from other vendors.

OTHER PERIPHERALS: Corvus Omninet local area network compatible with Micro 16s, and any other compatible equipment from other vendors.

AVAILABLE SOFTWARE: SuperCalc 2 and WordStar included; company has tested and approved more than seventy other business packages.

SALES OUTLETS: Computer stores and dealers across country, including forty-three Genra computer stores (former Xerox stores), selected ComputerLand franchises, and BusinessLand franchises.

SERVICE AND SUPPORT: Standard warranty and factory and authorized service.

FUTURE DEVELOPMENTS: Fujitsu is likely to adapt this machine to be a Motorola 32-bit 68000-based computer during 1985. This machine is Fujitsu's toe-in-the-water in the U.S. retail market, so look for the company to ease slowly into the water, but continue to expand its presence.

HEWLETT-PACKARD CORP.

Hewlett-Packard HP TOUCH 150

BRIEF SUMMARY: Hewlett-Packard, one of the five largest computer companies in the world, produces several very high-quality series of portable and personal computers. Until 1983, its thrust had been at the industrial, engineering, and commercial markets. Then, in a bold stroke to attack IBM's place in the corporate world, it introduced the first personal computer with a touch-sensitive screen. Basically, the special screen of HP-150 reacts to a touch or near-touch. Hewlett-Packard uses the touch power to let you select items on a menu, execute preprogrammed functions and commands, and move information around without typing on a keyboard or using a mouse pointer device. You do *not* try to touch-type on the screen or do complicated data or number entries. There is also some question as to whether the touch method is any better or more efficient than a keyboard or a mouse; the people who advocate the mouse pointers say touching a video screen tires out the arm. Keyboard advocates say it's a waste of time and effort to move your hand from the keyboard to the screen. Touch screen advocates reply that the touch screen—in these simple menu and command

Figure 45. The Hewlett-Packard HP-150 was the first popular personal computer with a touch-sensitive screen. One touches the screen to make selections from program menus and enter commands in a natural and easy fashion. (Courtesy of Hewlett-Packard Corporation)

operations—makes a computer a personal and comfortable tool for a novice computer user. The HP Touch 150s were selling briskly in mid-1984, so it appears the touch approach appeals to many.

Perhaps more important than the touch screen is the HP 150's compatibility with the IBM PC and MS-DOS operating system.

CPU: Intel 8088 16-bit microprocessor.

RAM/ROM: 256K RAM, expandable to 640K RAM.

MASS STORAGE: Dual 3.5-inch microfloppy disk drives with 400K capacity each. HP was the first major company to endorse the Sony microfloppy standard and spent $20 million for them during 1983–84.

VIDEO DISPLAY: Bit-mapped green phosphor 25 x 80 monitor included.

KEYBOARD: Large keyboard with twelve function keys, eighteen-key numeric keypad, fourteen operation keys, four cursor keys; and typewriter layout.

I/O SLOTS/INTERFACES: Two RS-232 serial ports; HP's own HP-1B interface; parallel printer port; built-in intelligent terminal features; and two expansion ports.

SYSTEM PRICE: $3,995 for keyboard, dual microfloppy drives, 256K, MS-DOS 2.0, HP touch features, and 9-inch monitor.

PROGRAMMING LANGUAGES: MS-DOS 2.0 and BASIC standard.

PRINTERS: Low-cost dot matrix printer can be built into the top of the unit, a very unique and interesting concept, for less than $500. Or, eleven HP printers and two HP plotters optional.

MODEMS: Two HP modems or variety of compatible ones.

OTHER PERIPHERALS: Three RAM expansion boards ($610–$1,120); 5.25-inch hard disk with built-in microfloppy ($3,040); 15 Mb. hard disk ($3,345); and variety of HP-built industrial measuring and monitoring equipment.

AVAILABLE SOFTWARE: Thirty-five major programs adapted for HP touch capabilities by mid-1984; hundreds of MS-DOS 2.0 programs available for conversion to 3.5-inch disk format.

SALES OUTLETS: Contact any local Hewlett-

Packard authorized dealer in the local area. Also forty-three Genra computer stores.

SERVICE AND SUPPORT: Extensive authorized dealer network and HP and vendor support for software.

FUTURE DEVELOPMENTS: HP will continue to support the touch screen concept and will introduce a very interesting 32-bit supermicro to take even better advantage of the technology. HP has long been a technological and quality leader, although its prices tend to be slightly higher than others. For serious applications, the whole HP family is among the top three best.

IBM

IBM Personal Computer

BRIEF SUMMARY: IBM did not revolutionize the personal computer industry when it introduced the IBM PC in August, 1981; it legitimized the phenomenon and gave it the ultimate stamp of approval. IBM, of course, is the world's largest computer company and has made its success by being the shrewdest marketer in the world. Its products are rarely the most technologically advanced, but they do seem to have the features and functions most people want at the time they are introduced. This is certainly the case with the IBM PC and the family of PC products. IBM was very surprised by the PC's success (the details of this surprise and its effects on IBM have been discussed

in an earlier chapter), but it has turned its organization upside down to take advantage of it. Given below is a detailed description of the IBM PC and PC XT. After that are brief descriptions of the rest of the IBM PC family, products which appeal mostly to major corporations and specialized users, not professionals or managers.

The most important information for you concerning the IBM PC is the booming industry surrounding it: More than five thousand programs are available to run on one version of the PC or the other; hundreds of disk drives, monitors, hard disks, printers, plotters, light pens, memory expansion boards, communications modems, *ad infinitum* are also available. These products already fill more than a dozen magazines and thick reference books, so it is not feasible to repeat them here. Consult Appendix B and the Bibliography for some sources of more information about the IBM PC.

Concerning the PC itself, remember that it is a relatively mediocre, but known technology produced with high-quality and good, but not great, service and support. The IBM name and reputation means a lot; you can be sure IBM will be around to make you feel secure for years to come, but you will pay for that feeling of security. I can understand that approach: seven years ago, when I bought my first professional typewriter, I spent far too much money and bought an IBM Selectric because I wanted good quality and fast service. I still use the same machine, and have not had a service call in more than three years. Even by mid-1984,

Figure 46. The basic IBM Personal Computer with two 320K minifloppy disk drives, the IBM Dot Matrix Printer, and the IBM monochrome monitor. This configuration brought widespread public acceptance to the personal computer revolution in addition to causing a revolution within the company itself. (Courtesy of International Business Machines)

however, IBM's service and support organization had not caught up with the incredibly fast growth of PC sales; IBM just could not hire and train enough service people fast enough to keep up. But this condition is temporary and it is likely IBM will provide its customary superior service for the PC in the future—at a price.

CPU: Intel 8088 quasi-16-bit microprocessor.

RAM/ROM: 256K standard (minimum 64K; maximum 512K).

MASS STORAGE: Dual double-sided, double-density 320K minifloppy disk drives standard.

VIDEO DISPLAY: 25 x 80 green phosphor; optional color RGB monitor with optional color graphics adapter board.

KEYBOARD: Eighty-three keys with ten function keys and ten for numerics and cursor control. One of the weakest points of the IBM PC is the layout and use of symbols for some common English words on the keys.

I/O SLOTS/INTERFACES: Optional RS-232 asynchronous communications adapter required; game paddle and joystick port; five other slots for adapters. Requirement to add optional adapters for serial and parallel printers make IBM one of the least functional PCs in its price range.

SYSTEM PRICE: $3,995 for 128K system, dual 320K double-density, double-sided disk drives, monitor, keyboard, and PC-DOS operating system.

PROGRAMMING LANGUAGES: PC-DOS 1.1 standard; MS-DOS 2.0, and CP/M-86 ($240) optional operating systems: IBM BASIC; UCSD p-System Pascal ($625); UCSD Pascal Compiler ($175); UCSD p-System with FORTRAN 77 ($625); UCSD FORTRAN Compiler ($175); IBM APL; IBM COBOL Compiler ($700); IBM PC Macro Assembler ($100); IBM FORTRAN Compiler ($350); and many more from outside vendors.

PRINTERS: IBM PC Graphics Printer ($595) is IBM-supported; dozens of others of every type from outside vendors.

MODEMS: Variety from outside vendors, but asynchronous adapter and asynchronous communications support peripherals required for modem operation.

OTHER PERIPHERALS: Wide variety to support IBM-related mainframe and minicomputer systems. Binary Synchronous Communications Adapter ($300, software $700); with asynchronous or bisynchronous communications adapter, the following software is available: SNA 3270 Emulation and RJE Support ($700); IBM 3101 terminal emulation ($140); Asynchronous Communications Support 2.0 ($60); Synchronous Data Link Control (SDLC) Communications Adapter ($300); and communications adapter cable for attachment to modem ($75). 64K/256K RAM Memory Expansion Option ($475); 64K Memory Module ($190); Prototype Card for software engineers and hobbyists ($45); Intel 8087 Math Co-Processor microprocessor for high-speed mathematics and statistical applications. Also for mainframe terminal emulation—IBM PC 3278/3279 Emulation Adapter ($905, software $235) and IBM 3279 PC attachment to the terminal turns the terminal into an IBM PC ($1,950).

AVAILABLE SOFTWARE: Thousands of programs from more than 150 software houses. List of IBM-supported software given in Appendix B.

SALES OUTLETS: More than 1,000 authorized dealers, National Accounts Division, National Marketing Division, many Value-Added Resellers who repackage the PC and add more functions and software.

SERVICE AND SUPPORT: IBM service staff in major cities, and authorized IBM dealers service for both hardware and software.

FUTURE DEVELOPMENTS: The IBM juggernaut will continue to roll on and on. Its 32-bit computer for business will be introduced during mid-1985.

IBM PC XT

The IBM PC XT is the hard-disk version of the IBM PC. It simply adds a 10 Mb. hard disk and other improved features to the basic machine. It costs $4,995. The added features worth notice include:

- Communications adapter included as part of system price.
- Eight expansion slots instead of five (with three used for the adapter, minifloppy disk, and hard disk adapters, so five remain available).

- Optional expansion to 640K RAM instead of 512K RAM.
- XT mass storage capacity can be expanded to 20 Mb. with a second 10 Mb. hard disk.
- IBM PC-DOS 2.0 instead of IBM PC-DOS 1.0 or 1.1 to operate the hard disk.

IBM 3270 Personal Computer

In late 1983, IBM released its version of the "windows" concept for a desktop computer. Called the IBM 3270 Personal Computer, this machine allows seven windows to be shown on the screen at one time—four from information stored in a mainframe computer, two electronic notepads, and one from on-line computing. The 3270 PC is designed to be integrated directly with IBM mainframe computers and emulate and share the serious and

Figure 47. The IBM 3270 Personal Computer illustrates IBM's concepts for using multiple "windows" to display and combined information from various programs and storage devices. Unlike Apple, IBM's windows concept uses the keyboard and not a mouse pointer to enter commands and use the system's functions. (Courtesy of International Business Machines)

complex applications now performed on an IBM mainframe. It can retrieve information from several sources—IBM mainframes, minis, or other PCS, display it in windows on the screen, and combine it into one file. It can be processed, printed, or swapped between windows. However, IBM's window concept uses the keyboard, not a mouse pointer. This is a very powerful tool that has grabbed the attention of many major corporations. List price for a basic 3270 PC is $5,585 including a high-resolution color monitor and an operating system and control program.

IBM PC XT/370

The IBM PC XT/370 puts all of the computing power of a very expensive IBM 370 mainframe—for fifteen years the mainstay of corporate and governmental computing—onto three microprocessors. This machine is truly a major evolution in microcomputers. The IBM PC XT/370 works as three units in one: a regular PC XT, a workstation for an IBM mainframe running a language and control system called VM/CMS (Virtual Machine/Conversational Monitor System), and an IBM 3277 terminal linked to a mainframe computer. It is controlled by a VM/PC operating system and control program. This computer configuration appeals to mainframe programmers, professionals, scientists, engineers, and so forth who want to run mainframe applications on a desktop computer. Consider this carefully. Programs which used to run only on computers costing hundreds of thousands of dollars can now be modified to run on a personal computer system costing $8,995. This version of the PC sent shock waves through the industry. It allows users to transfer programs and information from a mainframe to the workstations where they can change files, run applications, generate reports, change programs, and send the new information back to the mainframe. Most of the VM/CMS programs run *unchanged*, a remarkable feat of software and hardware technology.

The hearts of the XT/370 are three microprocessors based on the Intel 8088 and Motorola 68000 and three plug-in boards, each of which handles one of the three applications. One board contains the three CPUs; a memory card adds 512K RAM, expanding the regular RAM for the PC XT to 640K RAM and provides 4 *million* characters of virtual memory; and the third board includes an attachment that lets the XT 370 act like a IBM 3277 Model 2 terminal linked to the mainframe.

With these superpowerful extensions of the IBM PC and the various adapters for sophisticated applications, IBM is sure to capture two-thirds of the huge market for personal computers in corporations and large organizations. No other company comes close to these interactive capabilities at this time.

MONROE SYSTEMS FOR BUSINESS

Monroe System 2000

BRIEF SUMMARY: Monroe Systems for Business is the well-known maker of office calculators, electronic banking and accounting systems, and business machines. It introduced a good, though poor-selling, Occupational Computer 8820 in 1982. But in mid-1983, it replaced this unit with the System 2000 which has dual coprocessors. Monroe has added a number of interesting features and kept its

Figure 48. The Monroe System 2000 is a desktop computer with two microprocessors and a well laid out keyboard. It is also stylishly and "ergonomically" designed. (Courtesy of Monroe Systems for Business)

strengths, including a superior word processing program that is a virtual clone of the Wang word processor. It is not billed as an IBM PC-compatible because its disk drives have twice as much capacity and it uses a slightly different and more advanced 16-bit processor. However, it does use the same standard MS-DOS operating system.

CPU: Both Z-80A 8-bit and Intel 80186, a more advanced and faster true 16-bit version of the original 8086.

RAM/ROM: 128K RAM standard, expandable to 896K RAM.

MASS STORAGE: Two minifloppy disks with 720K capacity each, double that of most 16-bit computers; 640K capacity in 8-bit mode. This greater capacity is a real advantage, although it means applications software must be converted to run with these disks. Optional hard disks with up to 20 Mb. available.

VIDEO DISPLAY: 12-inch amber with 25 x 80 and bit-mapped for graphics. Anti-glare filter included, a nice user touch. Optional 14-inch color monitor with sixteen high-resolution colors.

KEYBOARD: Low profile, detached unit with numeric keypad, separate cursor pad, four application-definable function keys, and ten user-definable function keys. Versatile and well laid out.

I/O SLOTS/INTERFACES: Two RS-232 ports; one IBM-compatible parallel printer port; five expansion slots for RAM cards, modems, external interface devices.

SYSTEM PRICE: $3,695 for basic unit, $7,225 maximum.

PROGRAMMING LANGUAGES: MS-DOS 2.0, CP/M-86 DPX, and GW BASIC included in price. CP/M-80 for 8-bit applications is optional as are Pascal, FORTRAN, COBOL, C, and others.

PRINTERS: Any available from outside vendors.

MODEMS: Any available from outside vendors.

OTHER PERIPHERALS: Memory expansion boards; RS-232 interface boards; and internal or external hard disk drives.

AVAILABLE SOFTWARE: Selection of word processors, data base managers, graphics, spreadsheets, communications available.

SALES OUTLETS: Direct sales force and

Monroe branch offices. Monroe aims its efforts at accounting, wholesaling, finance, and health care industries.

SERVICE AND SUPPORT: Through Monroe field service force.

FUTURE DEVELOPMENTS: Monroe appears to have a good product, but it is not likely to capture much of the PC market. It seems to be trying to sell to the fields in which it already has a good reputation for business equipment.

MORROW COMPUTER CORP.

Morrow MDS-11

BRIEF SUMMARY: Morrow was described in Chapter 8, but an explanation of why the MDS-11 is discussed here is needed. When it was introduced in late 1983, the MDS-11 caused a major stir when it reduced the cost of a powerful, complete system with an 11 Mb. hard disk to below $3,000. It also bundled eight software packages into the same price. And it appears the MDS-11 has made a real hit among professionals and small businesses. This is a machine well worth your consideration if you are on a tight budget, but still want the advantages of a hard disk system. Of course, by the end of 1985, someone else will have introduced a system of the same kind for less than $2,000, but no one should wait if they have an application they need to do now.

CPU: 8-bit Z80A.

RAM/ROM: 128K RAM, 8K ROM.

MASS STORAGE: 11 Mb. hard disk and 400K minifloppy, both included.

VIDEO DISPLAY: 12-inch, two-color, 24 x 80 display.

KEYBOARD: Detachable ninety-one-key keyboard; nine function keys; numeric keypad. Well laid out configuration.

I/O SLOTS/INTERFACES: Two RS-232 serial ports; one Centronics-compatible parallel printer port; third serial port with either RS-232 or RS-422 connector.

SYSTEM PRICE: $2,745, very reasonable for a very good package.

PROGRAMMING LANGUAGES: CP/M Plus 3.0 for hard disk access and bank-switching tech-

Figure 49. The Morrow MDS-11 is a low-cost desktop computer with an 11 Mb. hard disk drive packaged with eight programs included in the purchase price. (Courtesy of Morrow Computer Corporation)

niques; Microsoft BASIC 80; and BaZic, compatible with NorthStar BASIC.

PRINTERS: Any compatible from outside vendors.

MODEMS: Any compatible from outside vendors.

OTHER PERIPHERALS: Many available from Morrow and other CP/M equipment vendors.

AVAILABLE SOFTWARE: Six applications programs included with three languages in purchase price: New Word word processor; Correct-It spelling checker; LogiCalc spreadsheet; Personal Pearl information manager and applications generator; Quest Bookkeeper; and WordStar word processor.

SALES OUTLETS: Morrow distributors and independent dealers and computer stores.

SERVICE AND SUPPORT: Authorized dealers and factory service.

FUTURE DEVELOPMENTS: Morrow appears to be ready to continue to pace the industry in low-cost, high-capacity and -performance micro systems.

NEC INFORMATION SYSTEMS

NEC Advanced Personal Computer

BRIEF SUMMARY: NEC Information Systems is the business computer and printer division of one of Japan's electronics giants—Nippon Electric Company. It is one of the top five makers of microprocessor and semiconductor chips in the world, it is one of the top three makers of letter-quality printers, it is one of the top five makers of telephone PABX systems in the world, and so forth. After several tries at introducing personal computers between 1980 and 1983, none of which had much impact, NEC seems to have learned its lessons. The Advanced Personal Computer (APC) is a versatile 16-bit machine based on a NEC-produced chip based on the Intel 8086. Thus, with minor changes, software for the IBM PC will run on the APC. It is *not*, however, directly compatible with the IBM PC like the Corona or Eagle PCs.

CPU: NEC 8086 true 16-bit microprocessor.

RAM/ROM: 128K, expandable to 256K; 8K

ROM for booting and system diagnostics, and an interesting feature of 4K CMOS battery-powered RAM used to retain software which defines function keys.

MASS STORAGE: Interesting variations here. APC disk drive will use either 234K single-sided, single-density 8-inch floppies or double-sided, double-density 8-inch floppies with 500K storage per side for a total of 1 megabyte. Only one disk drive comes as standard equipment; a second is optional.

VIDEO DISPLAY: 12-inch 25 x 80 upper/lower case green phosphor standard, and color monitor with graphics subsystem both optional. 4K RAM display buffer.

KEYBOARD: Detachable with twenty-two user-definable function keys, twenty-five-key numeric keypad with arithmetic calculator keys, and four cursor keys.

I/O SLOTS/INTERFACES: 8-bit parallel printer interface with controller included; RS-232 serial interface; and optional second RS-232 interface. Serial interfaces designed to allow communication with IBM mainframe terminals and controllers. Also to use NEC-made printers.

SYSTEM PRICE: $2,748 for 128K RAM; one 1-megabyte disk drive; monitor; serial, parallel, and data communications controllers, keyboard, and CP/M-86 and MS-DOS 2.0 software. Systems bundled with letter-quality printer, color monitor, and word processing software cost as much as $7,398.

PROGRAMMING LANGUAGES: CP/M-86 and MS-DOS included in system. Concurrent CP/M-86 ($150) and UCSD p-System OS ($100) optional. Also optional are RM/COBOL ($795); MS-BASIC ($395); MS BASIC Compiler ($350); MS-FORTRAN Compiler ($495); and MS-Pascal Compiler ($495).

PRINTERS: NEC Spinwriter letter-quality printers, among the best available (about $1,700–$3,000); and APC Dot Matrix Printer ($695). NOTE: NEC discourages use of other printers and warns that standard APC software may not drive other printers. Make sure your dealer properly configures the printer and word processing software to handle the APC and the printer connection correctly.

Figure 50. The NEC Advanced Personal Computer provides an interesting choice of floppy or minifloppy disk storage drives. It also has a large number of programmable function keys. (Courtesy of NEC Information Systems)

MODEMS: Any compatible modem.

OTHER PERIPHERALS: Monochrome graphics subsystem ($448); Color graphics subsystem ($648); 128K RAM memory board and mono-chrome subsystem ($598); same with color subsystem ($798); Numeric Data Processor ($395); Optional Communications Controller/Serial Interface ($335); 10 Mb. hard disk and controller ($2,698); 128K Expansion Memory Board ($540). NOTE: two communications subsystems to allow APC to communicate with IBM mainframes— SNA/SDLC 3270 Emulator ($795) and COAXXSYS Subsystem which emulates an IBM 278 terminal through a direct co-axial cable connection ($1,295 includes software, cable, and plug-in circuit board).

AVAILABLE SOFTWARE: Twenty-seven NEC-endorsed business packages. Includes three communications packages: ASYNC-86 ($245), BI-SYNC-86/3780 ($990), and BISYNC-86/3270 ($990), of which the latter two are for IBM terminal emulation.

SALES OUTLETS: Computer stores, NEC direct sales force, dealers, and distributors.

SERVICE AND SUPPORT: Authorized NEC dealers and factory service.

FUTURE DEVELOPMENTS: NEC is in the personal computer business for the long haul, and its emphasis of communications with IBM mainframes shows it is trying to get a toehold in the IBM corporate market for future growth. This is a difficult path to follow, but NEC is having some success with it. See the next chapter for even more interesting NEC portable computers.

NORTH STAR COMPUTERS, INC.

North Star Advantage 8/16

BRIEF SUMMARY: North Star is one of the oldest microcomputer makers, and has long been known for quality products, but poor marketing. It began in 1976 and has introduced a wide range of innovative micros for small businesses during the past nine years. It offers an IBM-compatible local area network, multi-user systems, and more for businesses which require a variety of terminals, printers, and workstations. For individuals or professionals, its current desktop micro, Advantage 8/16, is a very good product. But North Star software usually comes from systems houses and dealers and is not easy to find in a computer store.

Figure 51. The North Star Advantage 8/16 has dual microprocessors and very good high-resolution graphics. (Courtesy of North Star Computers, Inc.)

CPU: Dual 8-bit Z80A and optional 16-bit Intel 8088-2 processor.

RAM/ROM: With Z80A—64K RAM, 2K ROM, and 20K video display RAM; with 8088-2—64K, expandable to 256K RAM, rest same.

MASS STORAGE: Two double-density, double-sided minifloppy disks with 360K capacity each. Optional 5 Mb. or 15 Mb. hard disk drives to replace a minifloppy.

VIDEO DISPLAY: 24 x 80 green phosphor with high resolution graphics.

KEYBOARD: Eighty-seven keys—fourteen-key numeric pad; fifteen function keys with three levels of functions; and nine control keys.

I/O SLOTS/INTERFACES: RS-232 serial port; 8-bit parallel port; and four slots for: LAN workstation board; LAN server board; 16-bit processor board (it has three slots for RAM cards); and hard disk controller board.

SYSTEM PRICE: $2,999 for dual-floppy disk version; $4,499 with 5 Mb. hard disk; and $5,999 with 15 Mb. hard disk.

PROGRAMMING LANGUAGES: North Star Graphics CP/M ($149); Total Business Solutions Operating System ($149); Graphics DOS/BASIC (8-bit, $149); Graphics MS-DOS (16-bit, $149); Graphics MS-DOS and Graphics CP/M ($249);

and NorthNet operating system with Graphics CP/M ($349). Also five applications languages with Graphics MS-DOS as options.

PRINTERS: Any compatible from outside vendors.

MODEMS: Any compatible from outside vendors.

OTHER PERIPHERALS: 5 Mb. Hard Disk ($1,499); 15 Mb. Hard Disk ($3,399); 8/16 Upgrade Board ($399); 8/16 64K RAM Board ($349); Parallel Interface Board ($200); and Serial Interface Board ($175).

AVAILABLE SOFTWARE: ACCPAC accounting series; PROPAC; InfoManager II DBMS; NorthWord I and II; NorthSpell; NorthPlan; four graphics programs; and a line of CP/M-based software endorsed by NorthStar, but made by other companies.

SALES OUTLETS: Network of dealers and distributors throughout the United States.

SERVICE AND SUPPORT: Hardware service provided by MAI/Sorbus Service Division, one of the largest computer service firms in the country.

FUTURE DEVELOPMENTS: North Star reported financial difficulty during 1983, but it appears to have scaled back its ambitious plans. It should continue to provide good products with limited amounts of software. One will continue to obtain other software through dealers and systems houses.

SANYO BUSINESS SYSTEMS CORP.

Sanyo MBC 550/555

BRIEF SUMMARY: Sanyo, well known for its audio and video equipment and televisions, has a line of 8-bit and 16-bit computers which is gradually becoming more popular. In this brief look at Sanyo computers, I will discuss only one of their machines, a 16-bit MS-DOS machine, because of its very low cost for a dual drive system. Sanyo also offers four relatively low-cost 8-bit Z80A-based machines and several more 16-bit machines, but the MBC 550/555 models offer an apparent bargain for a 16-bit machine. The whole line also comes with at least six well-known integrated software packages from MicroPro International.

CPU: Intel 16-bit 8088.

RAM/ROM: 128K RAM, expandable to 256K, 8K ROM.

MASS STORAGE: MBC 550 has one single-sided, double-density 160K minifloppy drive; MBC 555 has two with 320K.

Figure 52. The Sanyo MBC 550 (the 4050 model shown here is similar in appearance) is a relatively low-cost desktop computer from a company trying to increase its presence in the industry. (Courtesy of Sanyo Business Systems Corp.)

VIDEO DISPLAY: 25 x 80 green phosphor; RGB high-resolution color monitor with eight colors optional.

KEYBOARD: Detachable with five function keys, numeric keypad, total of eighty-five keys.

I/O SLOTS/INTERFACES: Joystick port; Centronics parallel printer port; RS-232 serial port; port for optional floppy or hard disk.

SYSTEM PRICE: $1,399 for MBC 555 with two disk drives; $999 for one-drive MBC 550, amazingly low price.

PROGRAMMING LANGUAGES: MS-DOS 1.25 as OS and Sanyo BASIC with Graphics (Microsoft BASIC variation) included.

PRINTERS: Two low-speed Sanyo letter-quality printers and one Sanyo 120 cps dot matrix printer.

MODEMS: Any compatible from other vendors.

OTHER PERIPHERALS: Sanyo PR-100XY Plotter ($995–$1,095). Hard disk drive from ThoughtWorks works with Sanyo MBC 550/555.

AVAILABLE SOFTWARE: Included in price are—IUS EasyWriter 1.3 word processor. And from MicroPro: WordStar word processor, CalcStar; InfoStar; MailMerge; and SpellStar.

SALES OUTLETS: Dozens of dealers in various states across the U.S.

SERVICE AND SUPPORT: Software support from vendor; hardware service through more than fifty authorized service centers in the United States. Contact Sanyo at (800) 526-7043. Also a one-year warranty on RAM memory board.

FUTURE DEVELOPMENTS: Sanyo has aggressively priced its products and is trying to gain a strong foothold in the U.S. market. It should introduce an IBM PC-compatible machine to keep up with the market trends in that direction. Expect Sanyo to follow the trends with machines priced far under U.S. manufacturers.

TANDY CORPORATION/RADIO SHACK

Tandy 2000

BRIEF SUMMARY: The Tandy 2000 is Tandy Corp.'s first thrust into the quasi-IBM PC-compatible marketplace. It is most significant in that the parent company abandoned the use of the name

Radio Shack in a computer for the first time. Obviously, Tandy recognized that the Radio Shack name had too many negative connotations to sell desktop computers into the IBM corporate and professional environment. The Tandy 2000 even looks like an IBM PC and not the stolid gray and black Radio Shack models. There are many good things about this machine: it's more powerful than the IBM PC; it runs faster because it uses a true 16-bit CPU; its floppy disk capacity is greater; at $2,750, it's priced much lower than the IBM PC; and more. But it has its problems as well: it is only quasi-compatible with the IBM PC. Because its floppy disks have more tracks per inch, all software must be converted to run on the System 2000. Unlike the Corona or Eagle PCs, to name just two, you *cannot* take a disk from the IBM PC and put it in the Tandy 2000. It also has a different and proprietary internal bus structure, further reducing its compatibility. Thus, the standard version of MS-DOS will not run on the machine. It appears

Figure 53. The very powerful and low-priced Tandy Model 2000 personal computer packs 1.4 megabytes of storage on two minifloppy disk drives. It also has superb business graphics capability. (Courtesy of Radio Shack, a division of Tandy Corporation)

Tandy will sell some of the machines through its outlets, but again has not learned the lessons Apple and IBM have taught the market.

CPU: Intel 16-bit 80186.

RAM/ROM: 128K RAM, expandable to 768K RAM.

MASS STORAGE: Included in system price are two double-sided, double-density minifloppy drives with a very large 1.4 Mb. capacity.

VIDEO DISPLAY: High-density monochrome monitor *not* included ($249); Also optional is a 14-inch high-resolution color monitor with eight colors ($799).

KEYBOARD: Large keyboard with twelve function keys, numeric keypad, and various operational keys. Also has mouse pointer option ($100 and controller board $120) for use with MicroSoft "Windows" software.

I/O SLOTS/INTERFACES: RS-232 port; four expansion slots for various peripheral interfaces.

SYSTEM PRICE: $2,750 without monitor, $2,999 with monitor, and $4,250 for version with one 720K floppy and a 10 Mb. hard disk.

PROGRAMMING LANGUAGES: MS-DOS and GW BASIC included. MS-Pascal Compiler ($300); MS-GW BASIC Compiler ($300); MS-FORTRAN ($350); MS-Assembler ($100); and COBOL ($595), all optional.

PRINTERS: Compatible with full line of Radio Shack printers.

MODEMS: Compatible with full line of Radio Shack modems.

OTHER PERIPHERALS: High-resolution Monochrome Graphics Adapter ($449); Color Graphics Chip Kit ($200); Joystick/TV Adapter ($250); Internal 128K Ram Expansion Kit ($299); External 256K RAM Expansion Board ($499); 128K RAM Upgrade with expansion board ($299); Internal 10 Mb. Hard Disk ($1,699).

AVAILABLE SOFTWARE: Forty-two business programs run on both Tandy 2000 and IBM PC. Software endorsed in Radio Shack catalog includes PFS series; MicroSoft Windows, Multiplan, Word; dBase II, MAI/Basic Four accounting series; MultiMate word processor; and some games.

SALES OUTLETS: Almost 1,100 Tandy Computer Centers and Radio Shack stores with computer departments, and third-party OEM systems houses.

SERVICE AND SUPPORT: Authorized Radio Shack service centers and factory service. Tandy software service through local stores, but its quality may be low, so use the software vendors' service.

FUTURE DEVELOPMENTS: It appeared Tandy would have some success with the System 2000 model, but its lack of true compatibility indicated it really did not want to clash with IBM on IBM's own turf. This is a machine small businesses can buy and feel like they are buying an IBM PC. Tandy will continue to introduce numerous products for different markets.

It already produces for small business and professionals numerous varieties of two other systems:

1. The Motorola 16/32-bit-based $4,699 TRS-80 Model 16B, an office machine with 256K, dual 8-inch drives with 1.2 megabyte capacity each. It also has a dual Z80A CPU as well. It can function as a three- or six-workstation multi-user system with TRS-XENIX operating system or its own TRSDOS.

2. TRS-80 Model 12 Z80A-based desktop with 80K RAM and two 1.25 Mb. 8-inch double-sided, double-density disk drives for $3,499. It can be upgraded with an $899 Upgrade Kit to become a Model 16.

There are many peripherals and software packages available for both of these systems.

TEXAS INSTRUMENTS

TI Professional Computer

BRIEF SUMMARY: Texas Instruments was long a technological pioneer in the development of semiconductors, the first microprocessor, the first inexpensive digital watch, the first portable data terminal, the first 16-bit microprocessor, and many more. However, Texas Instruments has stubbed its toe several times in marketing its products: it stopped making digital watches when it could no longer compete with Japanese models and it stopped production of its 99/4A home computer after selling more than a million computers, but losing hundreds of millions of dollars doing so.

However, TI's minicomputers and desktop computers for small business have done well in a very quiet way. While the world heard a lot about DEC, Data General, IBM, and Wang minicomputers, Texas Instruments did well with its 990 family. Now, in the wake of the IBM PC's dominance, TI has produced a very successful personal desktop computer for professionals and small business. Its strength is that it is highly compatible with the standard MS-DOS and CP/M-86 software, and most of it can be used off the shelf. Other strengths

Figure 54. The Texas Instruments Professional Computer is highly compatible with most standard business packages which use the *de facto* MS-DOS operating system. It is also reasonably priced and has available a good-quality stock of software and peripherals. (Courtesy of Texas Instruments, Inc.)

are a "natural language" software interface and a voice management system. The natural language interface allows users to combine common words and phrases into command sentences to tell the computer what to do. The phrases and words are posted in windows on the display screen, and the user combines those available to create plain command sentences. One of the first and most interesting applications of the "NaturalLink" is an interface to Dow Jones News/Retrieval service. It makes a very easy English-like connection to the complex financial and information services available through Dow Jones News and Stock Quote Reporter, Wall Street Journal, Barron's, and other publications and data base services. And it is very inexpensive, $150.

The voice management system combines TI's strengths in speech synthesis, voice recognition, and telephone management functions to provide voice store-and-forward, automatic dialing, telephone answering, and true voice recognition of an unlimited number of spoken words and phrases. Both are major steps forward in desktop computer technology. Of course, both require additional hardware and software.

The TI Professional's basic system is inexpensive, $2,195, but that is a misleading figure. It includes only 64K RAM and one disk drive, not adequate for any MS-DOS applications programs, so the actual useful system price is much higher as given below. Despite this advertising "quirk" on the price, the Professional is well regarded as a top-quality machine with plenty of software.

CPU: Intel 8088, quasi-16-bit processor.

RAM/ROM: 64K standard, expandable to 256K; 8K ROM, expandable to 16K ROM; and 4K video display RAM.

MASS STORAGE: One 320K minifloppy disk drive included; second internal 320K or 5 Mb. or 10 Mb. hard disks can be added to unit.

VIDEO DISPLAY: 12-inch green phosphor 25 x 80 with high resolution; color monitor with sixteen colors optional.

KEYBOARD: Ninety-seven keys, grouped by function with twelve function keys; eighteen-key numeric keypad; separate five-key cursor pad; five operations keys.

I/O SLOTS/INTERFACES: Expansion RAM interface; standard parallel printer port; five expansion slots (one used by video display controller).

SYSTEM PRICE: $2,195 for basic system—64K RAM, one 320K floppy drive, keyboard, CPU, and monitor.

PROGRAMMING LANGUAGES: MS-DOS 2.1 ($75); CP/M-86; Concurrent CP/M-86; and UCSD p-System Pascal, all optional DOSes. Applications languages included MS-BASIC, MS-COBOL, MS-FORTRAN, MS-Pascal, CBASIC-86, and Concurrent CBASIC-86. All are optional.

PRINTERS: TI Omni 800 Model 850 dot matrix printer ($599) with two speed modes—150 cps for draft quality and 90 cps for higher quality. Other compatible printers from dealers.

MODEMS: Two internal direct connect modems—one 300-baud and one 1,200-baud, both with interface included.

OTHER PERIPHERALS: Two memory expansion kits ($795 and $695); Intel 8087 math coprocessor ($325); 10 Mb. hard disk drive ($2,295, only $100 more than the $2,195 retail list of TI's 5 Mb. hard disk); mouse pointer for MicroSoft Windows system and VisiOn series; graphics video controller; clock and analog interface for joystick or light pen; synchronous/asynchronous communications board for variety of mainframe communications (TTY, 3780, 3270 SNA freestanding or cluster), 3270 BSC, and 3101 emulation; Baby Tex Z80-board for CP/M-80 program options.

AVAILABLE SOFTWARE: More than 125 important programs for business and professionals. See Appendix B for details.

SALES OUTLETS: Authorized Dealer Program with dozens of dealers in cities across the country. Strong dealer program in agricultural areas. Also TI direct sales force.

SERVICE AND SUPPORT: Twenty-five TI service centers in major cities for regional service; support for TI-made software through hotline, other support from individual software houses. On-site service, carry-in service, and a spare parts program are available.

FUTURE DEVELOPMENTS: TI has given its PC tremendous boosts with the natural language interface for software and the voice management system. TI is doing well with the Professional and its portable version, and it should be among the first to introduce a 32-bit supermicrocomputer family.

XEROX CORPORATION

Xerox 16/8 Professional Computer

BRIEF SUMMARY: Xerox, which developed the mouse technology more than seventeen years ago, developed the first local area network standard, is responsible for xerography, and has many other technological firsts, has not been able to do well in selling its personal computers. However, its Xerox Memorywriter 620 electronic typewriter is doing very well, outselling any other U.S.-made model. It is trying to recover from the doldrums in PCs with its Xerox 16/8 dual processor model and the Xerox 1800 line of good-quality portable printers. The 1800s are discussed in the next chapter.

The 16/8's main strength is that both processors can operate at the same time, that is, concurrently.

Figure 55. The Xerox 820-II personal computer is a free-standing system and acts as a professional workstation with Xerox's local area network system. (Courtesy of Xerox Corporation)

They have separate RAMs so separate applications can be executed. You can be entering data into a 16-bit spreadsheet while the computer is manipulating an 8-bit information base, or communicating with another computer. Even better, users of the Xerox 820-II, its 8-bit PC, can upgrade to the 16/8 model with a 16-bit processor card and expansion modules. And the price is reasonable for the concurrent processor models: $3,395 to $5,295.

CPU: 8-bit Zilog Z-80A and Intel 8086 16-bit processors.

RAM/ROM: 64K for 8-bit; 128K, expandable to 256K for 16-bit.

MASS STORAGE: Single- or double-sided minifloppy or floppy disk drives with 155K to 322K capacity per disk. 10 Mb. hard disk is optional.

VIDEO DISPLAY: 12-inch, 24 x 80 green phosphor screen.

KEYBOARD: Low-profile with eighteen function keys—twelve programmable; ten-key numeric pad; and cursor and help keys.

I/O SLOTS/INTERFACES: Five or ten depending on expansion module chosen.

SYSTEM PRICE: $3,395 to $5,295 depending on disk drives, expansion modules, RAM size, and so on, chosen.

PROGRAMMING LANGUAGES: CP/M for 8-bit CPU; CP/M-86 and MS-DOS included in system price. Applications languages, MS-BASIC and others, are optional.

PRINTERS: Two daisywheel printers—20 cps and 40 cps—are available.

MODEMS: Compatible models from dealers.

OTHER PERIPHERALS: Communications interfaces available.

AVAILABLE SOFTWARE: Wide range of software running on any of three operating systems.

SALES OUTLETS: Xerox direct sales force, dealer network and computer stores.

SERVICE AND SUPPORT: Xerox field service, authorized dealers with service centers.

FUTURE DEVELOPMENTS: Xerox's place in the PC market continues to be shaky, and it appears it needs an IBM PC-compatible product to remain viable.

WANG LABORATORIES

Wang Professional Computer

BRIEF SUMMARY: Wang has long been the leader in the dedicated word processor field and one of the top five minicomputer makers with its Wang VS 2200 series. Its Wang Professional Computer is designed to be both a freestanding PC and an intelligent link in the Wang office of the future. The Wang PC cannot be beaten for the easy way in which it and its applications blend right into the entire Wang family of word processors and minicomputer networks. And it has the added advantage of its own WangWriter word processing software, considered an industry standard for that kind of program.

CPU: Intel 8086 quasi-16-bit processor.

RAM/ROM: 128K, expandable to 640K RAM.

MASS STORAGE: Single or dual 360K capacity minifloppy disk drives; 5 Mb. hard disk optional.

VIDEO DISPLAY: Wang very high-resolution (800 x 300 dot) green phosphor monitor.

KEYBOARD: 101-key detachable unit with 16

Figure 56. The Wang Professional Computer is very well designed and is directly compatible with all of Wang Labs' word processing, office information, and office automation systems. (Courtesy of Wang Laboratories)

programmable function keys; 5 cursor keys; and numeric keypad. This is a good keyboard.

I/O SLOTS/INTERFACES: Eight-slot expansion slot standard. Slots for workstation connections to WangNet LAN, Remote WangNet, or direct cable connection to VS 200 series minicomputers; OIS (Office Information System) word and data processing; and Alliance 250 office automation system. Also RS-232 port; parallel printer port; communications interface port for mainframe and terminal emulation.

SYSTEM PRICE: $2,945 to $5,330 depending on configuration. Smallest is 128K RAM, keyboard, one 360K disk drive, and operating system software; largest adds a 10 Mb. hard disk drive and MS-DOS software.

PROGRAMMING LANGUAGES: MS-DOS standard and CP/M-80 emulation with software. Microsoft BASIC, Compiled BASIC, COBOL, FORTRAN, and Pascal are optional. Also PC BASIC-2 compatible with VS 2200 BASIC ($395); Advanced PC BASIC Compiler ($295); and CP/M-80 emulation software ($240). And Level II COBOL ($1,500), COBOL Animator ($500), and COBOL Forms 2 ($150), or all three for $1,750.

PRINTERS: One slow 20 cps letter-quality printer (not recommended because it is single sheet feed only, very slow and boring); and one 80 cps dot matrix printer. Get the printers from other sources with printer software. Wang's weakest point.

MODEMS: Compatible modems from dealers, and most have optional communications interface boards.

OTHER PERIPHERALS: Wide variety of memory expansion boards, LAN connections, communications boards, and boards for workstation connections to other Wang product lines as given above.

AVAILABLE SOFTWARE: PC Multiplan and Wang Word Processing included; PC Multistation with multiple-window capability for VS 2200 integration and MicroSoft Windows for freestanding window capability; complete lines of accounting and professional software. See Appendix B for details.

SALES OUTLETS: All Wang dealers and direct sales force.

SERVICE AND SUPPORT: Wang field service and authorized dealers with on-site and carry-in service.

FUTURE DEVELOPMENTS: Wang will continue to be a leading and powerful force in office automation. Even small businesses should consider the benefits of using Wang workstations to create automated offices. Expect a 32-bit workstation/PC during 1985, if not sooner.

MISCELLANEOUS 16-BIT DESKTOP COMPUTERS

The following is a list of other 16-bit desktop computers now available.

- *Durango Poppy* computer with true 16-bit 80186 CPU, priced at $4,395, for dual 800K minifloppies, 128K RAM, and MS-DOS. Not very compatible with IBM PC.
- *Leading Edge PC,* from a company that began as a distributor of printers and floppy disks, has an Intel 8088 quasi-16-bit CPU, 128K RAM, built-in RS-232 port, and seven expansion slots, two 320K minifloppy drives, MS-DOS 1.25, and GW-BASIC applications language for $2,895. Respected Leading Edge word processor bundled into system, too. A great deal of IBM PC compatibility with major application packages.
- *MAD Computer-1,* with very stylish slim-line look with 80186 16-bit CPU, and a good deal of IBM PC compatibility for the top selling software packages such as Lotus 1-2-3, dBase II, WordStar, SuperCalc, and more. The basic system costs $4,195.
- *Olivetti PC,* made by Corona Data Systems, for

Docutel/Olivetti. Just like the Corona PC with minor changes.

- *Olympia People Microcomputer,* with industry-standard 8086 CPU and MS-DOS, but the company handicaps itself with nonstandard 655K capacity disk drives. Not directly IBM PC-compatible.
- *Pronto Series 16,* from a Canadian company, priced at $3,750 with 16-bit 80186 processor with two minifloppies and 128K RAM.

Two other 8-bit desktop processors worth interest are:

- *Sony SMC-70,* as the first machine to introduce the company's increasingly popular and useful 400K 3.5-inch microfloppy disk drives. Based on the 8-bit Z80A CPU, it has 64K RAM, two Sony microfloppy drives (800K total capacity), CP/M, Sony BASIC, Sony Word Processing, Super-Calc, and a dot matrix printer bundled into a $3,451 system called the Generalist. A less expensive bundled system called The Manager with a Sony Trinitron color monitor and Record Management software, but *no* printer costs $3,036.
- *Visual Technology 1050* is a low-cost, good-quality 8-bit Z80A computer at a very low price, $2,650 complete. It comes with 128K RAM standard with bank switching, and four built-in ports for serial and parallel communications. Two 400K minifloppy drives are built in, and a 25 x 80 green phosphor monitor is included with $1,800 worth of programming and applications software: Multiplan, WordStar, MailMerge, DR Graph, Terminal Emulator, C-BASIC, CP/M Plus OS, GSX Graphics CP/M, and Utility Manager.

CHAPTER 10

Portable and Briefcase-Sized Personal Computers

Portable computers have a long history, beginning in the 1970's with the Texas Instruments Silent 700 portable intelligent terminal, which weighed 50 pounds, but had a carrying case and a handle. In microcomputers, the history does not begin until 1981 when the peripatetic British-born entrepreneur Adam Osborne introduced the Osborne 1 at the unheard-of price of $1,795 for two minifloppy disk drives, Z-80 CPU, 64K RAM, and five major software packages, themselves worth a total of $1,500 in retail value.

The instant success of the Osborne 1, a simple, no-frills machine, has spawned a very rapidly growing segment of the personal computer industry. But portable computers like the Osborne make up only one part of the personal computer industry. Developed at the same time as the Osborne 1 were *pocket computers;* complete microcomputers the size of a large pocket calculator. The Radio Shack Pocket Computer (made by Sharp in Japan) was the first one, also introduced in 1981. Within a year, several dozen portable computers and half a dozen pocket computers (led by those from Radio Shack, Sharp, Panasonic, and Hewlett-Packard) were available. Then, in 1982, Radio Shack, and soon thereafter Epson, created a third type of portable computer—the *briefcase computer*. This is a small lightweight computer that easily fits into a standard briefcase and not only contains all the

elements of a powerful microcomputer, but also includes its own power supply, bundled applications software, and built-in communications modem at a very low price. For example, the Radio Shack Model 100—by far the most popular—the Epson QX-10, the NEC PC 8001, the TI CC-40, and others each cost less than $800.

Briefcase computers are also called *lap computers* because they do just that, sit in your lap. They are more popular than pocket computers because they have full typewriter keyboards instead of calculator-style keypads which make typing and data entry more difficult.

At this juncture, the generic name for portable computers like the Osborne 1 has been changed from portable to *transportable* computers for several reasons:

1. They are relatively heavy and bulky. They usually fit under an airplane seat, but they weigh more than 15 pounds. This is still less than one third the weight of the TI Silent 700, but twice the weight of the 8-pound Model 100.
2. They do not carry their own power supplies. They must be plugged into a wall socket or special battery pack.
3. They have full 24 x 80 screens, more RAM memory, and built-in disk drives, while briefcase computers have 8- or 16-line by 32-column

liquid crystal display (LCD) screens, plug-in software modules, and small RAMs (8K to 32K is usual).

A standard transportable includes a built-in CRT screen of at least 7- or 9-inch diameter, two mini- or microfloppy disk drives or one floppy and one hard disk, a full typewriter keyboard, and bundled operating and applications software. But the software is on disk and must be loaded into the machine. It has a detachable keyboard and a carrying case with a handle.

Although the first wave of transportables were 8-bit, Z-80-based machines, most of the ones available today are 16-bit 8086 or 80186-based machines with MS-DOS operating systems. Many are portable clones of IBM PC-compatible desktop computers; in some cases, the desktop units are larger clones of the original portables. They offer IBM PC features at half the price and many are very successful, especially Compaq.

The briefcase computers' software varies from proprietary packages on modules to variations of standard OSes and languages. Most of the software must be plugged into cartridge slots in the back of the unit. The Panasonic Hand-Held Computer first perfected this approach, but the TRS-80 Model 100 was the first to succeed in the market.

Various other features found on some transportable models include built-in printers, built-in acoustic coupler modems, hard disk drives, and light pens. Mouse pointers for transportables are becoming available now.

Discussed below are most of the important transportable and briefcase personal computers. At the end of this detailed discussion are given brief listings of other available portable computers.

BYTEC-COMTERM, INC.

Bytec Hyperion

BRIEF SUMMARY: The Hyperion was the first truly IBM PC-compatible transportable computer. Introduced in 1982, its parent company has had rough going, but a recent merger seems to have stabilized the situation. It is a very powerful, reasonably priced transportable with dozens of available software packages. It includes "IN:TOUCH" instant telecommunications and "IN:SCRIBE" word processing and has an amber screen. It is

Figure 57. The Bytec Hyperion portable computer was the first truly IBM PC-compatible portable model made. (Courtesy of Bytec/CommTerm, Inc.)

lightweight at 18 pounds and 18 x 11 x 9 inches in size.

CPU: Intel 8088 16-bit processor, with socket for optional 8087 math coprocessor.

RAM/ROM: 256K standard, 8K ROM.

MASS STORAGE: One double-sided, double-density 320K minifloppy, disk drives built in. Second minifloppy optional. Virtual 160K RAM disk standard.

VIDEO DISPLAY: 7-inch amber phosphor screen with 25 x 80, and very high resolution for graphics.

KEYBOARD: Detached low profile compatible with IBM PC keyboard layout; eighty-four keys with ten function keys.

I/O SLOTS/INTERFACES: Serial RS-232/RS-423 port; IBM and Centronics-compatible parallel port; video output jack for optional larger monitor. Options include a 7-slot, IBM PC-compatible expansion chassis, but this adds 38 pounds to the weight.

SYSTEM PRICE: $3,195 for one-drive system, Advanced Disk BASIC and Aladdin Relational Database software. $3,690 for two-drive model.

PROGRAMMING   LANGUAGES: MS-DOS,

Advanced Disk BASIC, and ADI Aladdin Relational Database, all standard.

PRINTERS: Compatible models from other vendors.

MODEMS: Compatible models from other vendors.

OTHER PERIPHERALS: 10 or 20 Mb. hard disk drive; streaming tape back-up storage drive.

AVAILABLE SOFTWARE: Hundreds of applications programs tested and approved by Bytec. IN:SCRIBE word processor, Multiplan, Lotus 1-2-3, IN:TOUCH telephone manager with built-in modem and telephone cable ($395), and DEC VT-100 terminal emulator ($95).

SALES OUTLETS: National network of dealers and distributors.

SERVICE AND SUPPORT: One-year warranty; authorized dealer and factory service.

FUTURE DEVELOPMENTS: If Bytec can stay financially sound, the Hyperion will be superseded by improved 32-bit models in the near future. This is a very nice IBM PC-clone at a fairly good, though not bargain-basement, price.

COMMODORE BUSINESS SYSTEMS

Commodore Executive SX-64

BRIEF SUMMARY: This is the Commodore 64-compatible portable model introduced during 1983. It has been a very popular seller.

CPU: 8-bit 6510.

RAM/ROM: 64K RAM.

MASS STORAGE: One 174K minifloppy disk drive built in, second optional.

VIDEO DISPLAY: 6-inch, 25 x 40 with upper and lower case; graphics and sprite characters as options.

KEYBOARD: Detachable keyboard like the one on the C-64 model.

I/O SLOTS/INTERFACES: Cartridge slot for games; two joystick ports; one printer port but useful for only some Commodore printers; optional interface required for other printers.

SYSTEM PRICE: $995 for one-drive unit.

PROGRAMMING LANGUAGES: BASIC included; LOGO, PILOT, COMAL, Pascal, and others available from Commodore as options.

Figure 58. The Commodore Executive 64 portable is a popular portable clone of the C-64 model. (Courtesy of Commodore Business Machines)

PRINTER: Several Commodore models plug-compatible; interface required for others.

MODEM: Interface required for all models.

OTHER PERIPHERALS: Same wide variety as for C-64.

AVAILABLE SOFTWARE: Same wide variety as for C-64, especially educational and games.

SALES OUTLETS: Almost all stores and dealers that carry the C-64.

SERVICE AND SUPPORT: Some authorized service centers, but usually have to send back to factory.

FUTURE DEVELOPMENTS: Commodore carved itself a nice niche in the low-end personal computer market with this portable model, and it can be expected to introduce a 16-bit portable with any 16-bit line it produces.

COMPAQ COMPUTER CORPORATION

Compaq and Compaq Plus

BRIEF SUMMARY: Compaq Computer Corp. was founded in 1982 by several former Texas In-

Figure 59. The Compaq and Compaq Plus portable computers were the most popular IBM PC-compatible portable models sold during 1983. (Courtesy of Compaq Computer Corporation)

struments and Mostek Corp. executives who tired of waiting for TI to get its personal computer act together. With a huge venture capital war chest, they quickly produced the most popular IBM PC-compatible portable computer. In mid-1984, the Compaq and Compaq Plus were the darlings of the portable computer market and the company had more than 750 dealers nationwide. Compaq was aggressively selling its machine to corporations and businesses which could not find an adequate supply of IBM PCs. The Compaq is among the two or three most consistently compatible portables, and it runs most MS-DOS software with no changes. The only difference between the original Compaq and the Plus model is a built-in 10 Mb. hard disk. The size is 20 x 8.5 x 16 inches; the regular model weighs 28 pounds, the hard disk model weighs 31 pounds.

CPU: Intel 8088 16-bit processor, with plug-in socket for 8087 math coprocessor.

RAM/ROM: 128K, expandable to 256K on main board, and to 640K with internal expansion boards.

MASS STORAGE: One 320K double-sided mini-floppy; second floppy optional on regular unit; one 320K minifloppy and 10 Mb. hard disk standard on Compaq Plus.

VIDEO DISPLAY: 9-inch, 25 x 80 high-resolution, green phosphor.

KEYBOARD: Identical layout to IBM PC.

I/O SLOTS/INTERFACES: Three IBM PC-compatible expansion slots, interface for RGB color monitor, and parallel printer interface, all built in; Serial RS-232 interface optional.

SYSTEM PRICE: $2,995 for 128K, one-drive system; $4,995 for Compaq Plus.

PROGRAMMING LANGUAGES: MS-DOS and BASIC 2.0 and 2.0 BASICA, built in, highly IBM PC-compatible.

PRINTERS: Compatible parallel or serial from dealers.

MODEMS: Compatible models from dealers.

OTHER PERIPHERALS: Optional asynchronous serial communications interface.

AVAILABLE SOFTWARE: Hundreds of off-the-shelf MS-DOS programs, including all major ones for professionals and small business.

SALES OUTLETS: More than 750 dealers across the country.

SERVICE AND SUPPORT: Authorized dealer service centers, standard 90-day warranty.

FUTURE DEVELOPMENTS: Compaq will probably sell several hundred thousand models during 1985, so it is poised for entry into the 32-bit portable computer field during 1985-86.

CONVERGENT TECHNOLOGIES CORP.

Convergent WorkSlate

BRIEF SUMMARY: Convergent Technologies was best known for its technologically advanced and high-quality executive and professional workstations. It was selling its products to the heavyweights of the industry—Burroughs, AT&T, and

Figure 60. The Convergent Technologies WorkSlate is a small, briefcase-sized portable with integrated electronic spreadsheet, built-in telephone and communications modem, telephone answering device, and more. (Courtesy of Convergent Technologies)

many more. In late 1983, it introduced its first personal computing product, a remarkable briefcase computer that included a built-in speakerphone, a 300-baud auto answer/dial modem and a new kind of software storage medium, called "taskware." Taskware is integrated applications packages stored in ROM. These built-in packages include a fair-sized electronics spreadsheet, personal information storage, and telecommunications program. Recorded on small, digital microcassettes are Taskware templates—electronic applications packages with ready-made formulas for specific jobs. You use the microcassettes like regular cassettes, but they load much faster. A lot of integrated applications software is also stored in the machine's ROM memory. Other ROM Taskware includes a calculator, calendar, address book, and telephone. That's correct: the microcassettes have two tracks—an audio one for a telephone answering machine and a digital one for software storage.

Although not billed as such to avoid scaring customers, the WorkSlate was the first truly integrated computerized telephone. As such it is a remarkable product for its size and price. It is the same size as a piece of typing paper, 8.5 x 11 inches, and is one inch thick. It weighs less than 3.5 pounds and runs off of an alkaline battery, yet uses only one watt of power, less than one-hundredth of a normal computer's power consumption.

Of course, to make it that small and light, something had to give: It has only a 16 x 46 LCD flat display and the keyboard does not have full travel keys, although its layout is standard.

CPU: 8-bit CMOS,

RAM/ROM: Large 64K ROM with all of the Taskware integrated software, 16K RAM.

MASS STORAGE: Two-track audio/digital microcassettes which can store up to five worksheets on each side or 30 minutes of recorded audio.

VIDEO DISPLAY: 16 x 46 LCD display.

KEYBOARD: Plastic touch keys with standard typewriter layout and numeric keypad. Five one-stroke applications buttons allow quick movement from one application to another.

I/O SLOTS/INTERFACES: Microprinter interface; modular phone jack; A/C adapter/battery recharger; built-in 300-baud auto answer/dial modem. Optional CommPort RS-232 serial and Centronics parallel printer interface for variable configurations of communications among Work Slates and other computers ($200).

SYSTEM PRICE: $895.

PROGRAMMING LANGUAGE: Taskware templates; otherwise, proprietary operating system.

PRINTERS: 46-column Microprinter ($250).

MODEMS: Built-in 300-baud auto answer/dial unit.

OTHER PERIPHERALS: None available in mid-1984.

AVAILABLE SOFTWARE: More than 50 applications templates for many business uses. See Appendix B for partial list.

SALES OUTLETS: Growing dealer network or directly from the company.

SERVICE AND SUPPORT: Factory service and small number of authorized dealers.

FUTURE DEVELOPMENTS: If WorkSlate succeeds, as it appears it is doing, it will be just the first of a series of imitations and improved versions from both Convergent and many other companies. However, my concerns include: lack of programmability; proprietary operating system; poor keyboard; and inadequate video display. It is a much more versatile machine than the Model 100, but it was poorly designed and is unattractive. It looks like an engineer designed the case rather than a consumer packaging expert. This seems trivial, but it is what makes the serious difference between succees and failure.

CORONA DATA SYSTEMS

Corona Portable PC

BRIEF SUMMARY: We discussed Corona Data Systems in Chapter 9. This discussion concerns the portable model of the company's IBM PC-compatible machine. It is basically the same machine with these exceptions: 9-inch green monochrome screen; smaller size—about 10 x 19 x 20; and lower price, $2,945 for the dual disk drive model. Again, remember that the graphics display differs from the IBM PC, and either model requires an IBM color graphics board to run some software.

CPU: Intel 8088 quasi-16-bit.

RAM/ROM: 128K standard, expandable to 512K.

MASS STORAGE: One or two dual 320K double-sided disks, and an optional integral 10 Mb. hard disk.

VIDEO DISPLAY: 25 x 80 with very high monochrome resolution.

KEYBOARD: IBM PC look-alike.

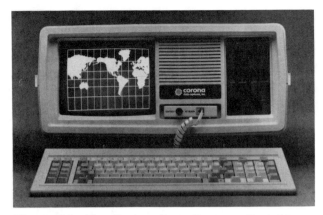

Figure 61. The Corona Data Systems Portable PC is a good-quality IBM PC-compatible machine with its own high-resolution graphics capabilities. (Courtesy of Corona Data Systems)

I/O SLOTS/INTERFACES: Four IBM PC-compatible open expansion slots; serial and parallel ports, disk drive interfaces, and video display interface all on main CPU board.

SYSTEM PRICE: $2,945 for two-drive model; 10 Mb. hard disk adds $2,695.

PROGRAMMING LANGUAGES: MS-DOS, GW-BASIC.

PRINTERS: IBM PC-compatible models.

MODEMS: IBM PC-compatible models; no peripherals interface required.

OTHER PERIPHERALS: Variety of IBM PC-compatibles.

AVAILABLE SOFTWARE: Multimate word processing and PC Tutor training disk included in system price; most IBM PC and MS-DOS software disk-to-disk compatible. Be sure to try the software first to make sure of its compatibility before you buy.

SALES OUTLETS: Same as regular Corona.

SERVICE AND SUPPORT: Same as regular Corona.

FUTURE DEVELOPMENTS: Same as company as a whole.

EAGLE COMPUTER CORP.

Eagle PC Spirit and Spirit XL

BRIEF SUMMARY: These are the portable versions of the Eagle PCs described in Chapter 9.

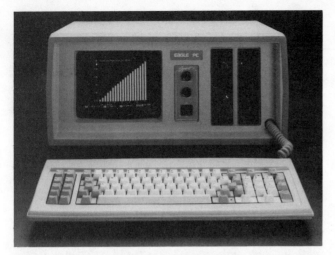

Figure 62. The Eagle PC Spirit and Spirit XL are two of the better IBM PC- and PC XT-compatible models available. (Courtesy of Eagle Computer Corporation)

They are 19.5 x 8.5 x 15.5 inches and weigh 30 pounds with two floppy disk drives each. They have 9-inch green phosphor screens. Otherwise, they are the same as the desktop models; that is, they are two of the better IBM PC-compatible models.

CPU: Intel quasi-16-bit 8088.

RAM/ROM: 128K RAM, expandable to 640K.

MASS STORAGE: One or two 320K double-sided, double-density disk drives.

VIDEO DISPLAY: 9-inch green phosphor screen.

KEYBOARD: 84-key IBM PC look-alike and 105-key optional keyboard.

I/O SLOTS/INTERFACES: Built-in color/graphics board; floppy disk controller included; four-slot IBM PC-compatible board; and optional videocassette recorder adapter and LAN adapter.

SYSTEM PRICE: $2,995.

PROGRAMMING LANGUAGES: MS-DOS and CP/M-86 OSes and GW BASIC applications language included.

PRINTERS: Any IBM PC-compatible from outside vendor.

MODEMS: Any IBM PC-compatible from outside vendor.

OTHER PERIPHERALS: Videocassette recorder for mass storage backup is optional as is LAN adapter.

AVAILABLE SOFTWARE: Hundreds of IBM PC-compatible programs.

SALES OUTLETS: All Eagle PC dealers and distributors.

SERVICE AND SUPPORT: Ninety-day labor warranty, one year parts warranty; authorized service centers and factory.

FUTURE DEVELOPMENTS: More of the future of Eagle hangs on the portable models and they seem to do all right, but not as well as Compaq.

EPSON AMERICA INC.

Epson HX-20 Notebook Computer

BRIEF SUMMARY: The Epson HX-20 is no clone of the QX-10. It is an agressively priced competitor with the TRS-80 Model 100 that has numerous interesting features. Like the Model 100, it has a proprietary word processing program stored in ROM, and like the WorkSlate, it uses microcassettes for program and information storage in either digital or standard ASCII format. It also has a built-in 24-line thermal printer.

It does have two shortcomings, however: 1) it lacks a built-in modem and users must buy an optional acoustic coupler modem, good for use in telephone booths, but not for modular phones; and 2) its display is a very small 4 lines by 20 characters

Figure 63. The Epson HX-20, which has built-in word processing, a thermal printer, and micro-cassette information storage, is a briefcase-sized portable computer. (Courtesy of Epson America, Inc.)

and hard-to-see LCD (on the good side, the display acts as a window and scrolls up and down and side to side to 255 characters wide).

It, too, is small and battery-powered—11 x 8.5 x 1.75 inches, four batteries with a normal 50-hour operating time, less when you use the printer and microcassette recorder frequently. It has an external power adapter and battery recharger. All in all, this can be a useful tool for business people who move around a lot and want to write memos on the go.

CPU: 8-bit CMOS microprocessor.

RAM/ROM: 16K standard, expandable to 32K with expansion unit; 32K ROM, expandable to 40K internally, 64K with expansion unit.

MASS STORAGE: Microcassettes with about 10K storage per side; optional regular audio cassette interface included.

VIDEO DISPLAY: 4 x 20 with virtual width to 255 characters.

KEYBOARD: Sixty-eight-key standard typewriter keyboard with five function keys and eight preprogrammed operational keys.

I/O SLOTS/INTERFACES: Included are RS-232 serial port; serial communications port; barcode reader port; and audiocassette interface; and optional memory expansion unit with up to 32K RAM and ROM in two configurations.

SYSTEM PRICE: $795.

PROGRAMMING LANGUAGES: Proprietary OS and programming language.

PRINTERS: Built-in dot matrix impact printer; other printers optional.

MODEMS: Optional CX-20 Acoustic Coupler 300-baud modem.

OTHER PERIPHERALS: Bar code readers available from other vendors.

AVAILABLE SOFTWARE: Six types: business and accounting; education and personal development; entertainment and recreation; home management and recordkeeping; personal and professional productivity; and program development. Includes EpsonLink telecommunications software ($49.95). SkiWriter word processing included in ROM.

SALES OUTLETS: Dealer network across the country.

SERVICE AND SUPPORT: Authorized service centers and factory service.

FUTURE DEVELOPMENTS: Epson is fully capable of making smaller and more powerful 16-bit briefcase-sized computers and will almost certainly do so.

GAVILAN COMPUTER CORP.

Gavilan Mobile Computer

BRIEF SUMMARY: Gavilan Computer has a relatively unique product that is aimed squarely at the "mobile professional," people who do most of their work on the road and want to take a lightweight briefcase computer with them and communicate with the computers at their office. Among the unique aspects of the Gavilan Mobile is a touch-sensitive panel called a "capsule," which replaces the cursor keys. It works much like a mouse pointer. Moving your finger around the small panel moves the cursor around the screen to mark text, highlight commands, and control the system. Touch-sensitive buttons next to the panel act as function-control keys. The same buttons function as IBM PC control keys F1-F10 for IBM PC-compatible software.

The "capsule" panel works with "CapsuleWare" programs stored in ROM on plug-in cartridges. These programs are integrated with a common interface and set of commands, and information from one program can be moved to another as long as the needed programs are plugged into Capsule-Ware slots. Other mass storage requirements are handled with Sony 3.5-inch microfloppy disks.

The Gavilan appears to be a remarkable product for its relatively low price. It weighs just 9 pounds and its dimensions are 11 x 11 x 2.7 inches.

CPU: Intel 8088 16-bit processor.

RAM/ROM: 64K CMOS RAM, expandable to 288K with 32K RAM capsules.

MASS STORAGE: CapsuleWare cartridges for Gavilan-produced applications programs; built-in 3.5-inch microfloppy disk drive with 400K capacity; optional IBM PC-compatible minifloppy disk drive for downloading MS-DOS software from minifloppy to microfloppy disks and vice versa.

VIDEO DISPLAY: 16 x 80 LCD display on Ga-

Figure 64. The Gavilan Mobile Computer has a relatively large 16-line by 80-character display, a touch-sensitive panel for cursor control, a built-in microfloppy disk drive, and fully integrated word processing, communications, and spreadsheet software on ROM cartridges. (Courtesy of Gavilan Computer Corporation)

vilan and 8 x 80 LCD on Gavilan SC, a stripped-down and less expensive version.

KEYBOARD: Full travel typewriter keyboard with solid state, pressure-sensitive touch panel.

I/O SLOTS/INTERFACES: RS-232 serial interface; and built-in 300-baud auto dial/answer modem. (Modem not available for SC model.)

SYSTEM PRICE: $3,995, $2,995 for SC model.

PROGRAMMING LANGUAGES: MS-DOS; MS-BASIC: proprietary OS for CapsuleWare.

PRINTERS: Slow correspondence quality printer available from Gavilan ($895). It has its own battery supply and can print about forty pages without recharging.

MODEMS: Built-in 300-baud direct connect auto dial/answer modem in 16-bit model; any 300-baud modem can be attached to SC model.

OTHER PERIPHERALS: None in early 1984.

AVAILABLE SOFTWARE: Five CapsuleWare packages: CapsuleWord; CapsuleCalc; Capsule-Comm; CapsuleForm; and CapsuleOffice. Variety of MS-DOS products available on microfloppy disk, and more being converted from IBM PC minifloppy to Gavilan microfloppy format.

SALES OUTLETS: Business retail stores, computer stores, original equipment manufacturers, systems houses.

SERVICE AND SUPPORT: Factory service and a few authorized dealers.

FUTURE DEVELOPMENTS: Gavilan is likely to introduce a 24-line LCD screen, and variations of the basic machine during 1985, and introduce a 32-bit machine for 1986.

KAYPRO CORPORATION

Kaypro 4 and 10

BRIEF SUMMARY: Kaypro is another superstar of the portable computer market. In 1982, it challenged Osborne with its first model, the Kaypro 2, and quickly dislodged Osborne from first place. (Osborne has since entered bankruptcy proceedings and stopped making computers.) The Kaypro 2 is an 8-bit, dual disk drive model which costs $200 less than the Osborne. Kaypro's newest portable products, the Kaypro 4 and the Kaypro 10, differ from each other only in that the Model 10 has a built-in 10 Mb. hard disk drive and uses the faster Z-80A microprocessor.

Kaypro is also one of the companies that have introduced desktop "clones" of their originally portable models. The new Kaypro Robie desktop unit costs $2,295, and includes dual double-sided, double-density 2.6-megabyte minifloppy disk drives and a built-in 300-baud modem. It is also

Figure 65. The Kaypro 10 is the 10 megabyte hard disk version of the Kaypro 4 model which replaced the Osborne 1 as the leading "transportable" computer with an 8-bit microprocessor. (Courtesy of Kaypro Corporation)

strictly CP/M compatible and can run hundreds of programs with little alternation.

New Kaypro computers introduced in 1984 include the Kaypro II Plus 88 and the Kaypro 4 Plus 88 which add 16-bit coprocessor boards to allow users to select which software—CP/M or MS-DOS—they want to use. The 16-bit CPU board also includes 256K RAM, and MS-DOS OS is included in the purchase price of both units. The Kaypro 4 Plus 88 model sells for about $2,000 while the Kaypro 4 Plus 88 sells for about $200 more.

But the description below applies to the Kaypro 4 and 10 portable models. They weigh 26 and 31 pounds respectively, and the dimensions of both are 8.5 x 19 x 16.5 inches.

CPU: Zilog Z80 for Model 4; and Z80A for Model 10.

RAM/ROM: 64K RAM, not expandable.

MASS STORAGE: Dual double-sided, double-density minifloppy disk drives for Model 4 with 392K capacity per drive; one minifloppy drive for Model 10 with a 10 Mb. hard disk built in.

VIDEO DISPLAY: 9-inch, 24 x 80 green phosphor. Fair graphics.

KEYBOARD: Typewriter-style with four cursor keys, fourteen-key numeric keypad (also act as programmable function keys).

I/O SLOTS/INTERFACES: Two RS-232 serial ports for printer and modem; one Centronics-type parallel printer interface; slot for light pen interface.

SYSTEM PRICE: Model 4, $1,795, including big bundle of applications software; Model 10 $2,795 with hard disk and software.

PROGRAMMING LANGUAGES: CP/M 2.2 OS and M-BASIC, C-BASIC, and S-BASIC for applications programming; and WordStar, PerfectWriter, Microplan, Perfect Filer, PerfectCalc, The Word Plus, Perfect Speller, and Sup'R'Term communications (only for Model 10) included in the purchase price, an amazing bundle of software.

PRINTERS: Any compatible printer from dealers.

MODEMS: Any compatible from dealers.

OTHER PERIPHERALS: KayNet local area network for up to twenty Kaypro models linked through standard telephone cable; KayLink mainframe communications hardware board and software ($750); and Plus 88 16-bit Intel 8088 coprocessor board. Available from outside vendors are: accelerator boards to speed up Z80 CPU processing times; real-time clock calendar; video board for an external monitor; portable battery packs; multiport controller with four serial-port capability.

AVAILABLE SOFTWARE: All packages bundled into system; hundreds of CP/M 2.2-based programs.

SALES OUTLETS: Hundreds of dealers across the country.

SERVICE AND SUPPORT: MAI/Sorbus Service Division handles all post-warranty service contracts.

FUTURE DEVELOPMENTS: Kaypro will continue to fill out its line of transportable computers and complement its existing lines with new products.

MORROW COMPUTER CORP.

Morrow MD3P: Portable Micro Decision Computer

BRIEF SUMMARY: This is the transportable clone of the Morrow MD (Micro Decision) Series. It weighs just 24 pounds and is attractively styled with dimensions of 19 x 15.5 x 7 inches. Its 9-inch screen appears to be somewhat stretched because it is only 5 inches tall; squeezing 24 lines into 5 inches appears to be too tight for easy viewing, but it is still a good machine.

CPU: Zilog 8-bit Z80A processor.

RAM/ROM: 64K RAM, 4K ROM.

MASS STORAGE: Dual double-density, double-sided minifloppy disk drives with 384K formatted capacity per drive.

VIDEO DISPLAY: 24 x 80 green phosphor, but in 9-inch diagonal by 5-inch tall screen.

KEYBOARD: Same as rest of Morrow MD line with thirty programmable function keys.

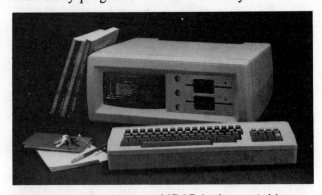

Figure 66. The Morrow MD3P is the portable clone of the company's low-cost Micro Decision series of personal computers. It includes seven software packages in the purchase price. (Courtesy of Morrow Computer Corporation)

I/O SLOTS/INTERFACES: Same as rest of Morrow MD line.

SYSTEM PRICE: $1,899 for all, including bundled software.

PROGRAMMING LANGUAGES: CP/M 2.2 OS; Microsoft BASIC 80 and Morrow PILOT.

PRINTERS: Any compatible models from dealers.

MODEMS: MorrowModem MM300 direct connect 300-baud modem.

OTHER PERIPHERALS: Large line of Morrow-made boards and disk drives.

AVAILABLE SOFTWARE: Bundled in system are seven packages, including OS and programming languages and New Word word processing, Correct-It spelling checker, Personal Pearl data base manager, LogiCalc spreadsheet, and Quest Bookkeeper pegboard replacement system.

SALES OUTLETS: Same as rest of Morrow line.

SERVICE AND SUPPORT: Same as rest of Morrow line.

FUTURE DEVELOPMENTS: This shoud be the first of a line of portables manufactured to accompany Morrow's line of high-quality, low-cost micros. A 11 Mb. portable version of the MDS-11 should be available before mid-1985.

NEC HOME ELECTRONICS (U.S.A.), INC.

NEC PC-8200

BRIEF SUMMARY: NEC Home Electronics is the consumer-oriented division of the giant NEC corporation which also makes the Advanced Personal Computer. The NEC 8200 briefcase computer is actually a more advanced clone of the Radio Shack Model 100. They are made by the same Japanese company, Kyocera, for both companies. At the same price as the Model 100, the NEC has numerous advantages: twice as much initial RAM; three times the RAM capacity (96K versus 32K); bundled software; RAM program cartridges; two more function keys; and additional ports. The only features this briefcase computer lacks that the Epson HX-20 has are built-in printer and built-in microcassette data storage. It uses CMOS RAM cartridges for data storage, a battery-backed, but unreliable and temporary,

Figure 67. The NEC Home Electronics PC-8201 is a powerful briefcase model with fourteen applications programs included in the low purchase price. (Courtesy of NEC Home Electronics (U.S.A.), Inc.)

method compared to cassettes or floppy disks. However, it does have a port for a floppy disk peripheral.

Its bundled software offering includes fourteen applications and utility programs: text and memo editor; telecommunications software, M-BASIC programming language; investment portfolio; linear regression forecaster; loan evaluator; appointment scheduler; bar code reader; memory calculator; music; games; terminal mode selector for communications protocols; and three memory switching utilities.

Its LCD display is adequate—8 x 40—and its dimensions are small—2.5 x 11.5 x 8.25 inches. It weighs just 3.8 pounds. In mid-1984, this was just about the best briefcase portable available for less than $1,000.

CPU: CMOS version of Intel 8085 8-bit CPU.

RAM/ROM: 32K ROM, 16K RAM standard, expandable to 96K RAM (64K internal and 32K external.).

MASS STORAGE: Standard CMOS RAM stores data in RAM cartridges with battery backup for long periods; interfaces built in for optional audio cassette recorder and minifloppy disk drive.

VIDEO DISPLAY: 8 x 40 LCD with reverse white on black possible.

KEYBOARD: Sixty-seven standard keys with five function keys, four cursor keys.

I/O SLOTS/INTERFACES: RS-232 serial port; floppy disk interface; cassette recorder interface; bar code reader interface; system RAM adapter slot; and parallel printer interface, all built in and standard.

SYSTEM PRICE: $799.

PROGRAMMING LANGUAGES: Microsoft BASIC.

PRINTERS: Optional battery-powered 40-character-per-line thermal printer ($170).

MODEMS: Small acoustic coupler modem, 300-baud, from NEC.

OTHER PERIPHERALS: Optional NEC data cassette recorder ($115); AC adapter ($20); 32K RAM cartridge ($395); 8K RAM chip ($120); Printer/Cassette Recorder AC Adapter ($16); optional floppy disk drive interface; optional external RAM storage device; and CRT adapter for 24 x 80 or 24 x 40 video output.

AVAILABLE SOFTWARE: Twenty-seven applications packages available from NEC on RAM cartridges.

SALES OUTLETS: Hundreds of computer stores, department stores, mass market stores, and electronics boutiques across the country.

SERVICE AND SUPPORT: Factory service and some authorized service centers.

FUTURE DEVELOPMENTS: NEC Home Electronics is gradually becoming a force to be reckoned with in the home computer field. Its strategy has evolved to be one of taking market share away from leading companies with somewhat better products sold at the same price. Look for numerous 16-bit briefcase portables before the end of 1985 and 32-bit briefcase portables by mid-1986.

OTRONA ADVANCED SYSTEMS CORP.

Attache Portable Computer

BRIEF SUMMARY: The Otrona Attache was one of the first portable computers introduced after the Osborne 1. During 1983, it appeared to run into competitive difficulty, but was still being manufactured through mid-1984. One of its problems is a relatively small 5.5-inch amber screen; that is much

Figure 68. The Otrona Attache was one of the first portable computers, and it comes with three applications packages. (Courtesy of Otrona Advanced Systems Corp.)

smaller than most of its competitors' screens and had been criticized. Another is its lack of IBM PC-compatibility without the coprocessor board. The company has other lines of business, so it should continue to make the portable and add more to its growing number of optional features. It was one of the first to offer a 16-bit coprocessor board, for example. There are three models: Attache, Attache S, and Attache 8/16. They weigh between 16.5 and 20 pounds, and have the same dimensions: 12 x 5.75 x 13.6 inches.

CPU: Zilog Z80A 8-bit processor with additional processor for disk drive and communication port operations; Intel 8086 in 8/16 model.

RAM/ROM: 64K RAM, 4K ROM in regular and S models; 256K RAM in 8/16 model.

MASS STORAGE: Two 360K double-sided, double-density minifloppy disk drives.

VIDEO DISPLAY: 5.5-inch green phosphor with 24 x 80. Many attributes such as reverse video, bold face, and underline through software selection.

KEYBOARD: Another problem with no independent function keys, but four cursor keys.

I/O SLOTS/INTERFACES: Two identical RS-232 serial ports; slot for multi-function expansion interface board.

SYSTEM PRICE: $2,495.

PROGRAMMING LANGUAGES: CP/M OS and Extended BASIC.

PRINTERS: Any compatible from dealers.

MODEMS: Any compatible from dealers.

OTHER PERIPHERALS: Multi-function expansion card option; bus expansion option; separate battery and charger unit; DC power adapter option; 10 Mb. hard disk subsystem board; system extension board.

AVAILABLE SOFTWARE: Bundled into system are WordStar-Plus, Charton II business graphics; and Multiplan spreadsheet.

SALES OUTLETS: Dealer network and distributors.

SERVICE AND SUPPORT: Authorized service centers and factory.

FUTURE DEVELOPMENTS: Otrona seems to have lost its leading position and has become a follower in this rapidly changing market.

PANASONIC

Panasonic Senior Partner

BRIEF SUMMARY: Panasonic is approaching the microcomputer market in several ways through several divisions. Its consumer division is marketing two low-end home computers which are being replaced by an MSX mode, and its business division is selling an IBM PC-compatible portable called the Senior Partner. This portable computer is distinctive only in that it is one of the few with a built-in printer. The paper is fed and returns through the top of the cabinet. Otherwise, it is very similar to most other IBM PC-compatible portables, but it may become popular because it carries the Panasonic name and the company knows how to aggressively market it. It is also interesting because it has five popular programs bundled into the purchase price.

It weighs 28.7 pounds, somewhat heavy, and is 18.5 x 13.25 x 8.25 inches in size.

CPU: Intel 8088 16-bit processor, 8087 math coprocessor option.

RAM/ROM: 128K, expandable to 512K, 16K ROM.

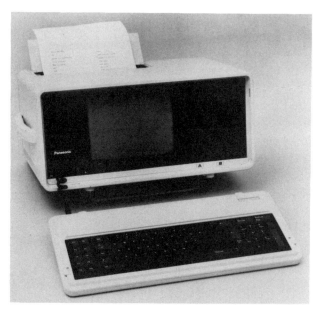

Figure 69. The Panasonic Senior Partner portable computer is an IBM PC-compatible model and comes with five applications software packages. (Courtesy of Panasonic Company)

MASS STORAGE: One 320K double-sided, double-density minifloppy standard; second 320K minifloppy optional.

VIDEO DISPLAY: 9-inch green phosphor CRT with 25 x 80 and high-resolution two-color or color graphics standard.

KEYBOARD: Eighty-three keys with ten-key numeric pad and ten function keys. Accepts IBM PC keyboard overlays for duplication of function.

I/O SLOTS/INTERFACES: One RS-232 serial port; one Centronics parallel printer port; one port for expansion card; and one port for RAM expansion card.

SYSTEM PRICE: $2,495 with one disk drive.

PROGRAMMING LANGUAGES: MS-DOS 2.0 OS; GW-BASIC.

PRINTERS: Built-in 80-character per line thermal printer for rough draft quality; switchable to 132 characters per line.

MODEMS: Any compatible from vendors.

OTHER PERIPHERALS: None in mid-1984.

AVAILABLE SOFTWARE: Bundled in the price are WordStar, VisiCalc, PFS File, PFS Graph, and PFS Report.

SALES OUTLETS: Computer retailers, computer specialty stores, office product dealers.

SERVICE AND SUPPORT: One-year limited warranty; then factory service or authorized dealer service centers. Software support through software houses.

FUTURE DEVELOPMENTS: It is likely Panasonic will be introducing a hard disk drive for this machine. It will tend to follow, not lead, the market in introducing new technology.

RADIO SHACK/TANDY

Radio Shack Model 100

BRIEF SUMMARY: This is the machine that caused a major step forward in the briefcase computer market. It was the first computer to offer a full-sized keyboard in a very lightweight package. It is made by Kyocera of Japan, a world-renowned maker of miniaturized electronics and semiconductors. Since its introduction, Radio Shack has sold hundreds of thousands of these machines through its computer centers and stores. However, as you've seen, the NEC 8200 and Epson HX-20 have improved on the basic idea. Radio Shack will undoubtedly (if it hasn't already) introduce more powerful and functional briefcase portables to regain its lead in this area. Radio Shack's first response was to include five applications programs in its Model 100, something it had not done when the machine was introduced. It weighs just 3.9 pounds and is 2 x 12 x 8.5 in size. One advantage it does have is that you can swap cassette tapes with the Radio Shack Model 4 computer.

CPU: 8-bit CMOS 80C85, a derivative of the Intel 8085 processor.

RAM/ROM: 8K, expandable to 32K, 32K ROM.

MASS STORAGE: Internal CMOS battery-backed storage, and optional cassette tape recorder off-line storage.

VIDEO DISPLAY: 8 x 40 LCD display with upper and lower case letters.

KEYBOARD: Full travel fifty-six-key typewriter keyboard with eight function keys and four cursor keys.

I/O SLOTS/INTERFACES: Parallel printer interface; RS-232 serial communications interface; cassette tape interface; bar code reader interface; built-in 300-baud direct connect modem.

SYSTEM PRICE: $799 for 8K version; $999 for 24K version.

PROGRAMMING LANGUAGES: Model 100 Microsoft BASIC included.

PRINTERS: Any compatible Radio Shack model, but software required. A weakness of this machine.

MODEMS: Built-in 300-baud direct connect auto dial modem; optional acoustic coupler cups for use on the road ($40, cable $20).

OTHER PERIPHERALS: Bar code reader ($100); 8K RAM expansion cartridge.

AVAILABLE SOFTWARE: Bundled with price are TEXT word processing; TELCOM communications; SCHEDL appointment scheduler; and ADDRSS address book. Optional cartridges include Decision-Making ($70); Statistics ($30); Calculator ($20); Function Plotter ($20); Personal Finance ($20); BASIC Language Lab ($30); Executive Calendar ($20); and Starblaze 100 game ($20).

SALES OUTLETS: All Radio Shack computer centers and stores.

SERVICE AND SUPPORT: Radio Shack service centers or factory service after standard warranty.

FUTURE DEVELOPMENTS: Radio Shack will introduce many more applications programs and build an entire produce line around this highly successful concept.

Radio Shack Pocket Computers

BRIEF SUMMARY: Radio Shack also offers the largest line of pocket computers of any company. Its line has three models and a full line of peripherals. The models are the PC 2, PC 3, and PC 4, and the last two are priced at less than $100, but their printers are more expensive than the computers at $119.95. This description will concern just the PC 3, the newest and smallest of the pocket computers. The PC model is similar, but larger and less powerful, although also less expensive. The PC 2 is larger and more powerful with function keys and a larger keyboard. The available software runs on all three of them, although some software for the PC 2 will not run on the other two because its memory is larger.

The PC 3 weighs only 4 ounces and is small enough to put in a coat pocket with dimensions of 3/8 x 5 5/16 x 2 3/4 inches.

CPU: Custom VLSI microprocessor.

RAM/ROM: Small, less than 2K RAM.

MASS STORAGE: Optional cassette interface and tape recorder.

VIDEO DISPLAY: One-line, 24-character LCD display.

KEYBOARD: Nontypewriter calculator-style with numeric keypad and all alphanumeric keys.

I/O SLOTS/INTERFACES: One slot for optional printer/cassette interface peripheral. (PC 4 model [$70] has separate cassette and printer interfaces.)

SYSTEM PRICE: $99.95.

PROGRAMMING LANGUAGES: None; numeric formulas and programs stored in ROM cartridges.

Figure 70. The Radio Shack PC-3 Pocket Computer with its thermal printer/cassette recorder interface peripheral. (Courtesy of Radio Shack/Division of Tandy Corporation)

PRINTERS: PC 3 Printer/Cassette Interface ($120), with 24-character per line thermal printer. Price includes AC adapter.

MODEMS: None with PC 3 or PC 4; RS-232 interface option with PC 2.

OTHER PERIPHERALS: For PC 3, none; PC 4 Cassette Interface ($40) and PC-4 Printer ($80), although list price for PC 4 is just $70; PC 2 Color Graphics Plotter ($220); RS-232 Interface ($200) for PC 2.

AVAILABLE SOFTWARE: For PC 3—twenty cartridges for financial, math, engineering, and games.

SALES OUTLETS: All Radio Shack stores and computer centers.

SERVICE AND SUPPORT: Radio Shack service centers and factory service.

FUTURE DEVELOPMENTS: Expect Radio Shack to continue to expand this line with smaller and larger models with more power and memory as the whole area of pocket computers evolves.

SEEQUA COMPUTER CORPORATION

Seequa Chameleon

BRIEF SUMMARY: Seequa Computer Corp. was founded in 1977 as a computer store. It expanded under the name Computers Etc. to four stores, and then in 1980 started manufacturing private label microcomputers. In 1982, the company saw the success of the IBM PC and the available software for both the PC and the CP/M operating system. Thus, the Seequa Chameleon has dual processors and built-in operating systems to handle both types of software. Seequa has also expanded its line to include the Chameleon Plus and the hard disk Seequa/XT version. Seequa got off to a fast start, but has slowed, although it does have strong financial support.

The Chameleon and Chameleon Plus each weigh 28 pounds and are 18 x 8 x 15.5 inches in size; the Seequa XT is slightly heavier.

CPU: Intel 8088 quasi-16-bit processor and Z80A 8-bit processor. And 8087 math coprocessor optional ($320).

RAM/ROM: 128K on Chameleon standard and 256K RAM on Chameleon Plus standard, expandable to 704K RAM externally; 16K ROM, expandable to 48K ROM.

MASS STORAGE: Dual double-sided, double-density 320K minifloppy disk drives standard on Chameleon and Chameleon Plus; one minifloppy and one 10 Mb. hard disk standard on Seequa/XT.

VIDEO DISPLAY: 9-inch 25 x 40 and 25 x 80 green phosphor screen. Sixteen-color high-resolution graphics available with optional external monitor.

Figure 71. The Seequa Chameleon Plus portable computer comes with seven software packages and is IBM PC-compatible. (Courtesy of Seequa Computer Corporation)

KEYBOARD: IBM PC look-alike keyboard.

I/O SLOTS/INTERFACES: RS-232 serial port; Centronics-compatible parallel port; video output jack; optional expansion chassis with eight IBM PC-compatible slots; optional IEEE-488 bus ($149); second serial port optional ($49); analog-to-digital interface optional ($49); RGB color monitor optional; optional battery pack ($345).

SYSTEM PRICE: $1,995 for Chameleon; $2,895 for Chameleon Plus; $3,995 for Seequa/XT standard versions.

PROGRAMMING LANGUAGES: Standard for Chameleon and Chameleon Plus: MS-DOS OS and M-BASIC-86 with CP/M-80, CP/M-86, and Advanced BASIC as options. Seequa XT features MS-DOS and GW-BASIC as standard.

PRINTERS: Any compatible from dealers.

MODEMS: Any compatible from dealers.

OTHER PERIPHERALS: 64K RAM expansion ($175); game paddles ($35); joystick ($49).

AVAILABLE SOFTWARE: Bundled with Chameleon Plus are Perfect Writer, Perfect Calc, Perfect Speller, Condor I DBMS, and communications software as well as the programming lan-guages. Optional software includes Advanced BASIC ($295); Perfect Speller ($250); Perfect Filer ($495); and Condor 3 ($493) with a Condor 1 to 3 upgrade for $295. Also MicroSoft Windows software environment for mouse pointer systems.

SALES OUTLETS: More than 500 authorized dealers.

SERVICE AND SUPPORT: Ninety-day warranty, then one year extended warranty for $245 with dealer or factory service.

FUTURE DEVELOPMENTS: Seequa is staying abreast of the ongoing developments in the field and is likely to continue to do so.

SHARP ELECTRONICS CORPORATION

Sharp PC-5000 Commuter Computer

BRIEF SUMMARY: As discussed, Sharp manufactures Radio Shack's pocket computers and has introduced its own vastly improved line based on the same hardware. These pocket computers are discussed below. But Sharp caused some real excitement in late 1983 and during 1984 with its new PC-500 portable computer with 16-bit CPU, a

Figure 72. The Sharp PC-5000 Commuter Computer is an impressively packaged and powerful briefcase-sized computer with built-in word processing, communications package, spreadsheet, and executive planner with a built-in 80-column thermal printer. (Courtesy of Sharp Electronics Corporation)

built-in printer and very high-resolution 8 x 80 LCD display. It is also IBM PC-compatible in that it uses the same processor, operating system, and programming language. No disk drive was available for the PC-5000 in mid-1984, but that was undoubtedly in the works so the computer could use off-the-shelf IBM PC software. At the same time, Sharp is encouraging software vendors to convert their programs for its ROM cartridges. It appears Sharp has a very impressive machine with its fold-up display, and small size, and light weight. It weighs less than 14 pounds with the modem, printer, and accessories hooked up. It is 13 x 12 x 4 inches, very small for so much power.

CPU: Intel 8088 16-bit processor.

RAM/ROM: 128K, expandable to 256K, the most in a portable its size, and an enormous 192K ROM.

MASS STORAGE: Optional dual IBM file compatible double-sided, double-density 360K mini-floppy disk drives.

VIDEO DISPLAY: 8 x 80 LCD display.

KEYBOARD: Standard typewriter keyboard with eight programmable function keys.

I/O SLOTS/INTERFACES: RS-232 interface; two slots for 64K memory cartridges; built-in disk drive interface; and printer interface.

SYSTEM PRICE: $1,995 base price.

PROGRAMMING LANGUAGES: MS-DOS OS and GW-BASIC standard.

PRINTERS: Built-in 80-column thermal printer; interface for optional letter-quality printer.

MODEMS: Optional 300-baud direct connect auto dial modem with its own telephone with a touch-tone keypad, and speakerphone for conference calling. The modem is designed to fit into the rear of the display screen.

OTHER PERIPHERALS: 128K bubble memory for permanent data storage; optional cassette recorder.

AVAILABLE SOFTWARE: Built-in word processing, communications package, spreadsheet analysis, and executive planner.

SALES OUTLETS: Nationwide network of dealers.

SERVICE AND SUPPORT: Sharp service centers and authorized dealers.

FUTURE DEVELOPMENTS: Sharp has set the pace for compact briefcase portables and packed its machine with a lot of memory and computing power. Others will undoubtedly follow its lead, but Sharp has the knowhow to become one of the first to produce a 32-bit portable computer and is probably doing so now.

Sharp Pocket Computers
BRIEF SUMMARY: As noted, Sharp makes a line of pocket computers and accessories. It has two basic models, the PC-1500A and the PC-1250A. The PC-1500A model is the more powerful one and is the one described below. It is just 8 x 1 x 3.5 in size, and weighs less than a pound.

CPU: CMOS 8-bit processor.

RAM/ROM: 8.5K RAM, 16K ROM.

MASS STORAGE: CMOS memory battery backup for RAM modules; optional cassette tape recorder.

VIDEO DISPLAY: 26-digit, 1-line LCD.

KEYBOARD: Sixty-five keys, nonstandard, but with ten numeric keys and function keys.

I/O SLOTS/INTERFACES: RAM/ROM module slot; two cassette tape recorder plugs; printer/cassette interface; optional RS-232 serial interface; and optional Centronics parallel printer

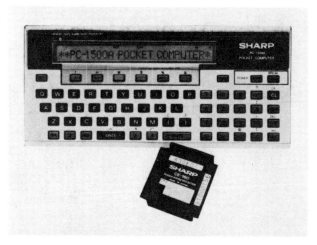

Figure 73. The Sharp PC-1500A Pocket Computer is a handy hand-sized computer with numerous applications routines available in plug-in ROM cartridges. (Courtesy of Sharp Electronics Corporation)

interface. Optional RS-232/parallel expansion box allows connection to other printers and computers.

SYSTEM PRICE: $220 for standard system.

PROGRAMMING LANGUAGES: Most BASIC commands.

PRINTERS: Optional four-color printer/cassette interface ($230); or any printer through RS-232/parallel interface ($225).

MODEMS: Any compatible from other sources.

OTHER PERIPHERALS: 8K RAM expansion module with battery backup ($110); 16K RAM expansion module with battery backup ($170); cassette tape recorder ($80).

AVAILABLE SOFTWARE: ROMWare Library stored on cartridges (all $65 each)—Graphics, Business Graphics, General Statistics, Statistical Distribution, Electrical Engineering, Circuit Analysis, Finance, Math, and SharpCalc spreadsheet.

SALES OUTLETS: Electronics outlets, department stores, thousands of locations across the country.

SERVICE AND SUPPORT: Sharp authorized dealers and Sharp service centers in major cities.

FUTURE DEVELOPMENTS: Sharp will boost the power and capacity of its pocket computers as pocket computers grow in size to meet user needs and briefcase computers shrink to a point where they are actually light enough to carry around and use without special knowledge. Sharp will stay a leader in this field.

TANDY CORPORATION

Tandy Model 4P Transportable

BRIEF SUMMARY: This is the clone of the regular TRS-80 Model 4 computer with significant differences in price and new features. These include: two built-in 184K double-density minifloppy disk drives; 64K RAM, expandable to 128K; 9-inch black-and-white display; optional RAM disk drive setup; detached keyboard; and a new TRSDOS 6 operating system. It will run all Model 4, Model III TRSDOS, and LDOS Model III mode software as well. All of this costs just $1,799, a very reasonable price for a transportable model. An optional integral direct connect 300-baud modem with auto

dial/answer is $150. This appears to be a good buy for the prices and features.

TEXAS INSTRUMENTS

BRIEF SUMMARY: Texas Instruments produces both a portable clone of its TI Professional Computer and a briefcase portable called the TI CC-40, which is also an impressive one of its kind. The TI Portable Professional is almost identical to the desktop Professional with the only differences being RAM, size, display, and price. The machine has attractive packaging, has a 9-inch green phosphor monitor (color optional), comes with 64K RAM and one minifloppy disk drive, and costs $2,395 ($2,695 with color). Software and options are the same as those for the desktop model.

Texas Instruments Compact Computer CC-40

BRIEF SUMMARY: The programmable calculator division of Texas Instruments developed and produced the CC-40 briefcase computer. This machine is designed as a response to the emerging briefcase market when the Model 100 gained prominence, but the TI CC-40 was in the development stages when the Model 100 was announced. It

Figure 74. The Texas Instruments Portable Professional Computer is the clone of its respected TI Professional model. (Courtesy of Texas Instruments, Inc.)

Figure 75. The Texas Instruments Compact Computer CC-40 is an inexpensive and useful briefcase-sized computer with a large supply of available software on both *Solid-State* modules and *Wafertape* plug-in cassettes. (Courtesy of Texas Instruments, Inc.)

is very powerful and equally inexpensive ($250). It has a very large 34K ROM with a BASIC language interpreter, but its RAM is small—6K expandable to only 18K. But a plug-in module port allows up to 128K more ROM for applications software. TI appears to want to keep the applications programs for itself, not the best strategy as has been consistently shown in the field. It also uses a "Wafertape" digital tape drive for optional mass storage, actually a special type of microcassette unique to TI. This is a fine little computer, and even the software is in good supply with more than seventy-five applications packages on a special type of digital cassette storage medium. It is 9.5 x 5.75 x 1 and weighs just 22 ounces.

CPU: TI 16-bit 990 series derivative.

RAM/ROM: 6K RAM, expandable to 18K; 34K ROM. 128K ROM available with plug-in modules.

MASS STORAGE: 48K Wafertape digital tape drive option ($140); CMOS battery backup for RAM storage.

VIDEO DISPLAY: 31-character, 1-line LCD.

KEYBOARD: Typewriter layout with 20-key numeric and cursor keypad. Cross between full travel and calculator-style.

I/O SLOTS/INTERFACES: RS-232 option ($100); plug-in module port; Hex-bus intelligent peripheral interface connector built in.

SYSTEM PRICE: $250.

PROGRAMMING LANGUAGES: TI Enhanced BASIC with calculator functions.

PRINTERS: Optional four-color HX-1000 printer/plotter with 36 characters per line ($200).

MODEMS: TI CC-40 Modem optional.

OTHER PERIPHERALS: AC adapter ($15); Wand input device; black-and-white video monitor.

AVAILABLE SOFTWARE: Seventy-five Wafertape and solid-state module applications packages in business, engineering, science, and finance fields, and more coming.

SALES OUTLETS: Hundreds of department stores, computer specialty and electronics outlets across the country.

SERVICE AND SUPPORT: Texas Instruments' regional service centers and authorized service centers.

FUTURE DEVELOPMENTS: One can expect TI to produce more peripherals and software for this briefcase-sized computer while expanding the line of hardware itself with a 16-bit model. TI has the technical knowhow to stay ahead in this field, but its marketing has lacked pizzazz for years.

XEROX CORPORATION

Xerox 1800 Portable Computer System

BRIEF SUMMARY: Xerox has done well with its Xerox 1810 portable computer because it has a large 64K RAM memory, and includes a built-in speakerphone with automatic dialing capabilities and a 30-number telephone directory. It also includes eight ROM programs. And it includes a built-in 1,200-baud modem. It also has a "base station" peripheral whichs adds a 16-bit processor and two floppy disk drives for a fairly reasonable price.

CPU: NSC 800 8-bit processor, a CMOS version of the Zilog Z80.

RAM/ROM: 64K user RAM, expandable externally to 512K RAM, 32K ROM, and 48K plug-in ROM.

MASS STORAGE: CMOS RAM with battery backup in 1810 briefcase model, and two double-

Figure 76. The Xerox 1810 is a versatile portable computer with a built-in telephone and answering machine as well as a large 64K memory. (Courtesy of Xerox Corporation)

sided, double-density 1-megabyte minifloppy disk drives in the 1850 base station.

VIDEO DISPLAY: 3 line x 80 character LCD; two video monitor plugs.

KEYBOARD: Full travel typewriter keyboard with sixty-three keys, ten function keys, and four cursor keys.

I/O SLOTS/INTERFACES: Telephone port; parallel printer port; data link port; RS-232 port; bus expansion port; TV port; composite video monitor port; and speaker/microphone port for telephone answering machine functions. On base station, the following interfaces are included: telephone port; two data link ports; RS-232 port; expansion port; composite video monitor port; RGB monitor port; bus expansion port; and parallel printer port. Optional for 1850 are hard disk interface; memory expansion port; and printer/plotter port.

SYSTEM PRICE: $2,195 for Xerox 1810 computer with display, $1,595 without, $2,495 for 1850 base station with two disk drives and 16-bit processor, and $1,195 for disk expansion unit.

PROGRAMMING LANGUAGES: M-BASIC with computer; CP/M-80, CP/M-86, or MS-DOS options for 1850 base station.

PRINTERS: Any Xerox printer will work with the system.

MODEMS: Built-in 1,200-baud auto answer/dial modem.

OTHER PERIPHERALS: Variety of Xerox produced peripherals and hard disk drives.

AVAILABLE SOFTWARE: Built-in calendar, calculator, tape recorder, and dictation machine, teletypewrite terminal, typewriter note taker, and M-BASIC language. ROM-based applications packages also available for business and management functions.

SALES OUTLETS: Retail stores, Xerox dealers, Diners' Club, and Carte Blanche.

SERVICE AND SUPPORT: Authorized Xerox service centers and factory service.

FUTURE DEVELOPMENTS: Xerox received a good response to this system's introduction, and it is likely Xerox will move to make it compatible with the rest of its line of personal computers and office automation equipment. Its optional MS-DOS and CP/M-86 compatibility will also encourage conversion of software for the unit.

MISCELLANEOUS PORTABLE COMPUTERS

The following companies also produce portable computers:

Access Matrix: An interesting 8-bit portable with a built-in printer, a built-in acoustic coupler modem, *and* a built-in direct connect modem, and ten bundled software packages, all for $2,495. It has 64K RAM and a 7-inch amber screen.

Columbia Data Products Columbia VP: An IBM PC-compatible portable model of its desktop computer with 128K RAM, MS-DOS, 640K dual minifloppy disk drives, and a very large total of thirteen bundled programs, all for $2,995.

Pronto Computer Series 16 Portable: It is basically a 30-pound clone of the **company's Series 15 IBM PC-compatible model. It does have non-IBM PC** standard 400K disk drives, but it comes with integrated applications software including Executec's word processor, data base manager, and spreadsheet.

STM Electronics STM Personal Computer: An Intel 80186 true 16-bit IBM PC-compatible with 1 megabyte dual minifloppies and 256K RAM standard. The retail price is $2,500 and includes an auto dial/answer direct connect modem.

Televideo Tele-PC TS 1605: An IBM PC-compatible 16-bit portable with all of the standard MS-DOS and IBM PC features for $2,995 for the dual disk drive version, and $4,995 for the 10 Mb. hard disk drive version.

More and More Computers

Part II has discussed dozens of the available computers in every category. But dozens, if not hundreds, more are also being produced. I did not ignore any computer because it was inferior. Space and time constraints prohibit including more than two hundred known microcomputers in an introductory book of this type. As this book was written during mid-1984, new computers were being introduced all the time, practically every day; it was not possible to include the latest specific models and manufacturers. In any case, they, too, will evolve and change over time.

However, this book in general and Part II in particular does identify the most popular and important computers and shows you how to identify and recognize trends in hardware and software development. It takes several years for a trend to take hold—the evolution from 8-bit to 16-bit computers between 1979 and 1984, for example—so you will know what is coming between today when you are reading this book and the end of the 1980s. The names of the computers may change, but their hardware and software will not fundamentally change.

Good luck in your search for hardware. In Part III, you can find hundreds of things to do with your computer. I cannot provide every possible application, but I do hope to stimulate your imagination while providing many ways you can put your computer to good and profitable use right now.

PART THREE

WHAT DO YOU DO WITH A MIND MACHINE?

CHAPTER 11

Putting the World At Your Fingertips—Easily

Twenty-eight of the most important librarians in the United States get together to plan a White House conference on the future of American libraries. They see each other only once during the six months before the conference, yet they hold committee meetings, exchange ideas, plan agendas, and keep in close contact, as often as every day, without making a personal long-distance telephone call.

An independent investor analyzes her portfolio of fifty stocks, bonds, and options every day and instantly compares a stock's current status to six years of price, earnings, and dividend performance, without poring over thick volumes of reports or doing complex research in a faraway library. As a matter of fact, she does it from her den in her home.

A business executive remembers at midnight that he forgot to book theater tickets for an important client in a city one thousand miles away. He gets out of bed, and within three minutes, the reservations and the tickets are paid for. Another few minutes, and the tired executive is fast asleep.

A seven-year-old girl corresponds with a pen pal without ever using a pencil and plays spirited video games with another seven-year-old although the other child lives three thousand miles away.

Children in a cerebral palsy school and senior citizens in a home for the aged talk to each other and with hundreds of other people without ever dialing a telephone.

More than fifty separate committees of physicians and medical professionals hold on-going meetings and the members never have to travel to participate in the group discussions.

A project manager wants to hold a planning meeting for a large group of engineers, marketing staff, manufacturing directors, quality control personnel, and more. Her assistant never places a personnel telephone call to anyone, yet the meeting is planned and the agenda approved in just one day.

These few examples demonstrate the limitless uses that anyone, without knowing anything about computer operations or computer programming, can find for a home computer through those seemingly hard-to-understand information utilities. In fact, the creators of increasing numbers of information utilities want to make them as essential to the home as water and electricity and more useful than television and all other home appliances. Although these information utilities—and even newer electronic mail networks—have not had that kind of impact yet, within ten years, they probably will change the way all of us communicate with each other.

Anyone with an inexpensive home computer

and a telephone modem can join hundreds of thousands of people who use these networks many times a day. When you join the SOURCE, CompuServe Information System, Dow Jones Information Service, MCI Mail, BRS After Dark, Knowledge Index, one of the commercial videotex services, or a network like EIES (Electronic Information Exchange System), you link into a time-sharing network in much the same way that a small business or large corporation may use a time-sharing service or bureau to do its payroll, billing, inventory control, or financial analysis. These networks differ in the means of access and the types and amounts of information to which you are given access. Using any of these information utilities or data bases, you can tap huge amounts of information and very convenient and helpful services.

The networks create new ways of using information and they provide new information in fresh forms to which no one previously had access. For example, a new home computer owner may have access to more than five thousand programs for the Apple IIe computer, several thousand for the TRS-80 series, and more than seven thousand programs for the IBM PC, if he can find them at a local store or find a source for them through mail order. But by hooking up to CompuServe or SOURCE, he can access more than three thousand programs and download them or use them on line. Or through his computer, terminal emulation software, and a modem, he can "converse" with the information network's computer and leave messages for and receive them from anyone in that network regardless of the kind of computer each has, where each is located, or the time of day. And he can do it far more cheaply than he could with a long-distance phone call.

OPENING THE INFORMATION WINDOW

What do you need to know to hook up to these fantastic networks? By now, you know what a modem does; it converts computer signals into audio analog signals a telephone line can transmit. To expand on our earlier discussion, *modem* stands for *modulator-demodulator* and takes digital flows of information from the computer and converts them into low frequency sound waves. As the modulator in the modem "speaks," the demodulator "hears" and converts the audio signals into digital signals. Modems, of course, transmit in a serial fashion, one bit at a time, in a stream of electronic pulses.

All modems for home computers have two modes of operation, "originate" and "answer." The former means it can begin a message, and the latter means it can receive and respond. All standard home computer modems communicate through an RS-232 data communications interface so they are perfectly compatible. Many other kinds of modems exist—answer only, originate only, and others. But they are for special uses and of little concern here. Just remember that to communicate with a home computer you must have an answer/originate modem.

To hook up a home computer to a modem, you attach a communications interface cable to the RS-232 interface port in the back of the modem. Then, you attach the other end of the communications cable to the RS-232 interface port, or a special modem interface port, in the back of the home computer. However, with many computers, including the Apple IIe, the Atari, and the IBM PC, you must first buy the communications interface and plug it in the back of your computer.

As we noted previously, modems transmit data at different rates. Most home computer modems transmit at 300-baud (roughly 300 bits per second) and cost between $80 and $250 (prices which continue to fall). Soon, modems will be built into every home computer and included as "standard equipment"; modems that transmit at 1,200-baud cost between $250 and $700. The cost is related to the "intelligence" of the modem—the number and variety of automatic answer/dial, telephone number memory, and so on, the modem has. A modem with these advanced features is often called a *smart modem.*

Recall, too, that modems are either direct connect or acoustic coupler types, with the former directly plugging into a modular phone, and the latter accepting the ends of the telephone handset.

Once your modem is properly connected to your computer, you will need a software package called a *terminal emulator.* The large computers through which you communicate have programs which allow them to communicate with a variety of popular computers and CRT terminals. Your computer must "pretend" to be one of those terminals; it is said to "emulate" the terminal, hence the name for the software that turns your computer into a terminal.

A few home computers have built-in terminal emulator programs, but the vast majority do not, so you have to obtain one and load it each time you want to communicate. Depending on the computer and the modem's features, the package can cost between $25 and $300 for popular microcomputers. Unfortunately, the often required RS-232 interfaces can cost $200 to $400 or more.

Fortunately, many portable computers already have either the RS-232 interface and the modem built in at no extra charge, or just the communications interface. These added features of the portables are their greatest advantages over regular personal or desktop computers. Consider this factor—and the added cost for those computers that do not have the interface and the modem built in—when you buy a computer.

After you have correctly hooked up the modem, loaded the terminal emulator program, and dialed a local access for an information network, the step-by-step procedures for using the system are very easy. In fact, CompuServe, SOURCE, and MCI Mail, to name just three, require only that you enter your access number and/or a password; you are then given the first menu of services.

HOW TO HOOK UP TO MCI MAIL

When you dial the local access number of MCI on your telephone, you will receive a steady beep from the MCI computer. Connect your modem and make the connection to your terminal emulator program, often by simply pressing RETURN.

MCI Mail will present two lines on the screen:

```
Please enter your user name:
Password:
```

Enter your user name and password, pressing carriage return after each entry, and MCI mail will respond:

```
Connection initiated . . . Opened
Welcome to MCI Mail!

-----------------------------------

Keep informed by typing HELP NEWS

-----------------------------------
```

In a second, another screen will appear:

```
MCI MAIL Version 1.14
Your INBOX has _messages (_PRIOR-
ITY, _RECEIPT)
You may enter:

SCAN      for a summary of your
          mail
READ      to READ messages one by
          one
PRINT     to display messages non-
          stop
CREATE    to write an MCI Letter
DOWJONES  for Dow Jones News/Re-
          trieval
ACCOUNT   to adjust terminal dis-
          play
HELP      for assistance
Command   (or MENU or EXIT):
```

You enter a command, such as CREATE and press RETURN.

MCI Mail responds with a practically blank screen, except for the word:

```
TO:
```

You now have the power to create a free-form electronic message, a business letter, or any type of communication from love poems, to a consumer complaint, to a business appointment, or "conference call," with the same message going to a lot of people.

You enter a name on the same line as the TO: For example, you enter:

```
TO: John J. Jones
```

Press RETURN and the system responds:

```
TO: John J. Jones
(John J. Jones ABCZ Company Any-
town, ME)
```

The system is asking you whether the John J. Jones at that address is the person to whom you wish to send the message. You can also enter the user number, if you know it—for example, JOHN J. JONES 112233—and go directly to the person you know.

Or you can use a Telex number and enter any number of names to receive the same message. MCI staff say any number of names means just that, any number.

However, if the person you are sending the message to does not belong to MCI Mail and cannot receive electronic mail, then MCI Mail sends him or her a letter by regular mail. To do this, press return after the person's name:

```
TO: JOHN J. JONES (RETURN)
TO: (press RETURN)
CC: 10 Oak St.
    Apt. A
    Somewhere, NY 00000
    (Press RETURN and the response is:)
Subject: Vacation plans (Enter why
                        you're writ-
                        ing and press
                        RETURN.)
Text: (Type / on a line by itself to end)
```

Then, you simply enter text any way you want and write as much as you want to write. End the letter with slash and RETURN. Your video screen clears, the message is stored in the MCI Mail main computer, and the system gives you another simple menu:

You may enter:

```
READ        to review your letter
EDIT        to correct your letter
SEND        U.S. mail for paper; in-
            stant electronic deliv-
            ery
SEND ONITE  OVERNIGHT courier for
            paper; PRIORITY elec-
            tronic delivery
```

```
SEND 4HOUR  FOUR-HOUR courier for
            paper; PRIORITY elec-
            tronic delivery
Command (or MENU or EXIT):
```

If you enter SEND, your letter is automatically sent to the electronic INBOX or mailbox of the recipient, or is immediately transmitted for instant printing. If your letter does not go through electronic INBOX, MCI Mail puts the letter into a very conspicuous orange envelope and puts it in the regular Post Office.

THE MCI MAIL ADVANTAGE AND DISADVANTAGE

The best thing about MCI Mail, in my opinion, is that each letter is presorted by zip code and delivered directly to the zip code you want it to go to. Thus, in most cases—depending on the U.S. Post Office—the letter will be delivered within one or two days with regular service. This is a blessing for someone like me; I live in an area where postal service is poor at best.

And that is just how simple using the basic MCI mail system can be. It has many advanced editing features which make it a very powerful communications system for individuals, families, and businesses. Of course, businesses with large volumes of inter-office mail among distant locations, or those businesses and professionals like me whose long-distance telephone bills often resemble the national debt of some small countries, will find immediate application for MCI Mail.

MCI Mail has this major advantage over the other information services: it allows you to send regular mail to the 99.99 percent of the population who do not yet have home computers *and* modems *and* subscriptions to an electronic mail service. Neither CompuServe, SOURCE, Dow Jones, Dialog, BRS, nor any of dozens of professional data base networks nor hundreds of computerized bulletin boards has this capability.

However, at this time, MCI Mail has one major disadvantage. With the exception of access to Dow Jones, MCI Mail does not give subscribers access to any information services. In this regard, the others have MCI Mail beat.

Of course, there's no reason not to belong to at least two or three of them. There is *no* subscription fee for either MCI Mail or Dow Jones, but there are charges which can mount up. These are explained below, but there are subscription fees and hourly use charges ranging from as low as $4.25 for off-hours CompuServe and SOURCE to as high as $120 an hour or more to access highly specialized data bases in Lockheed Dialog or regular BRS.

I advise joining at least two of them, especially those for which no minimum use fee is charged, and getting used to using them.

HOW MCI MAIL FEES WORK

MCI Mail has four levels of service and four kinds of charges:

- ELECTRONIC MESSAGES—Just $1.00 for the first 7,500 characters, about three typewritten pages. Each additional 7,500 characters is another $1.00.
- NEXT DAY DELIVERY—MCI Mail drops the letter, pre-sorted by zip code, into the post office nearest to the recipient, and the cost is $2.00 for the first 7,500 characters and $1.00 for each additional group of 7,500 characters.
- OVERNIGHT PRIORITY—This is an overnight delivery arranged by MCI with Purolator Courier service. Purolator delivers the message by noon the next day. Cost: $6.00 for the first three pages, and $1 each for each additional group of 7,500 characters. Seven pages, therefore, costs just $8. Sending letters or short documents is much cheaper and faster this way than by Express Mail or any of the overnight delivery services.
- FOUR-HOUR SAME DAY SERVICE—The charge is $25 for delivery of the same 7,500 characters to any address within four hours.

The same charges for next day delivery and four-hour delivery hold for a category of electronic transmission labeled PRIORITY. With Compu-Serve or SOURCE, the *recipient* of the letter must pay for it. In the MCI transmission, the sender pays, like he does when he puts a stamp on a letter and sends it through the mail. This method, with the sender being charged, is very familiar and comfortable, and makes a lot more sense. With CompuServe, SOURCE, or any similar electronic

mail service, you must pay for the time you are hooked up to the service and retrieving your messages. This can be costly and is not something we are used to doing.

Other unique advantages of MCI mail are: A) you can store an unlimited number of names on a mailing list (friends, customers, clients, staff members, project team members, and so on); and B) you pay only when you actually send messages. There is no charge for storing drafts or messages before you put them in your OUTBOX.

MCI also offers two similar benefits to the other information services:

1. Twenty-Four-Hour Access to the service;
2. Instant transmission of a message to the recipient's mailbox.

HOW CAN YOU USE MCI MAIL AND SIMILAR SERVICES

MCI Mail appears to be a very good way to reduce your long-distance communications costs. If you make a lot of long-distance telephone calls during the day, you more often than not cannot reach the other person on the first try. You end up playing expensive telephone tag at least several times before you reach the person with whom you wish to speak. With MCI Mail, you can send important, but not absolutely crucial, messages or requests with the next-day regular mail service *if* your correspondent does not have electronic mail. If he or she does have MCI Mail and you know the receiver's user name, you can communicate instantly.

For example, in gathering information and photographs for this book, I made dozens, if not hundreds, of telephone calls trying to reach marketing communications directors of computer companies. And, I had to place those calls when those people were most likely to be there—during regular business hours, the most expensive time of day to call on the phone. However, if I had used MCI Mail overnight mail, I could have sent the same message, explained in greater detail what I wanted, and asked them to send me the material by any of several means: regular mail, USPS Express Mail, or courier delivery service. And I could have asked them to call me back at my convenience, on their telephone bill. Even better, I could have written these messages after working hours when I had more time to think, and I could have sent the same message to anyone I wanted, just by entering their addresses. I could have saved myself a lot of valuable time and a lot of expense.

Of course, not everyone is a writer on deadline, but there are millions of professionals, business people, or just plain folks with families scattered around the country, who can profitably use this kind of service.

TRUE INFORMATION NETWORKS AND THEIR ADVANTAGES

I use the MCI Mail example to show how easy it is to make the telecommunications link to an information or electronic mail service. The best thing is this: making the initial link to any information service is just this simple. Of course, with a plethora of services and data bases, the information networks will take a little practice to learn to use. But, as many frequent users have told me, you quickly learn ways to use shortcuts to get around in the networks. As your experience increases, your finesse increases, so you do not waste money wandering through groups of menus.

Like MCI Mail, the information networks are both menu-based for novices and command-based for experienced users. As your experience grows, you learn to avoid the time-consuming and boring menus, and enter commands you have memorized to quickly reach the service you want.

Given below are brief descriptions of the most popular information services and data bases, and information on how to join them and their costs.

BIBLIOGRAPHIC RETRIEVAL SERVICES (BRS LTD.)

1200 Route 7, Latham, NY 12110; (800) 833-4704; in New York State, (800) 553-5566

Services: The second largest number of bibliographic data bases in the U.S. Includes such data bases as BRS/Pre-Med, current citations of medical journals; BioSciences Information Service (BIOSIS); and National Information Sources on the Handicapped, to name just three for the medical and biological science fields. There are dozens more covering most economic and academic fields.

Charges: $50 subscription fee and $12 monthly minimum. Hourly charges vary for each data base, but often less than $40 per hour.

Hours of Operation: Hours other than 6 P.M. to midnight.

BRS/AFTER DARK

This is the same service outlined above, but it is offered at somewhat lower rates between 6 P.M. and midnight.

COMPUSERVE INFORMATION SERVICE

5000 Arlington Centre Blvd., Columbus, OH 43220; (800) 848-8199

Services: Electronic mail with on-line conversation and conferencing functions; dozens of data bases, including current and historical stock and commodities markets information; special interest groups for various professionals, especially a medical group called MEDSIG, sponsored by the American Association for Medical Systems and Informatics (AAMSI), and a pilots' association. With more than one hundred thousand subscribers, CompuServe is the largest information network.

Charges: $39.95 sign-up kit available from many computer stores and Radio Shack computer centers includes five hours of user time, with a temporary user ID and password. Hourly charges are: $5.00 per hour evenings (6 P.M. to 5 A.M.), weekends, and holidays. In some locations, there is an extra $2.00 per hour charge for access to the long-distance telephone networks, Tymnet and Telenet. Prime-time charges (8 A.M. to 6 P.M. weekdays) are: $22.50 per hour plus $10 per hour for Tymnet or Telenet. Further, some services, such as a pilot association's Flight Plan service, cost extra.

DIALOG INFORMATION SERVICE

3460 Hillview Avenue, Palo Alto, CA 94305; (800) 528-6050; in Arizona (800) 352-0458

Services: This is the largest data base service in the world with more than 150 different bibliographic and information data bases covering almost every profession and industry. The range of information this data base contains is simply astounding, from abstracts of psychological journals to complete Census Bureau information to yesterday's Washington Post newspaper.

Charges: No start-up fee, but manuals and training seminars range from $30 to $135. This system takes some training to use efficiently and properly, and Dialog does provide an hour of free time to get used to the system. You also incur telephone surcharges in areas where direct connections are not provided. Hourly charges vary for each data base and can range from as low as $10 an hour to as much as $150-$180 per hour, depending on the type and scarcity of the information.

Hours of Operation: Regular weekday business hours.

KNOWLEDGE INDEX

Knowledge Index is a much easier to use, boiled-down version of the more complex Dialog services. You use simple menus to access selected data bases within the service.

Services: About half of the data bases of Dialog are available.

Charges: $35 start-up fee includes two free hours and a user's manual. The hourly fee is $24.

Hours of Operation: Evenings and weekends.

DOW JONES NEWS RETRIEVAL SERVICE

P.O. Box 300, Princeton, NJ 08540; (800) 257-5114

Dow Jones News Retrieval Service is the electronic publishing arm of Dow Jones enterprises. Through this service, you can access almost all of Dow Jones' services by paying hourly charges. The charges are levied on the time of day as for the other services. Of course, Dow Jones leans very heavily toward business and financial information. Dow Jones has between fifty thousand and one hundred thousand subscribers, mostly in business and finance.

Services: Dow Jones News and Stock Quote Reporter, the 15-minute delayed stock ticker; *Wall Street Journal,* current and back issues; Barron's; Dow Jones News Service, the long-time electronic newswire which carries up-to-the-minute reports of corporate and government events; and a range of special economic reports and data bases. Dow Jones also has an arrangement with Comp-U-Card for electronic shopping and an electronic mail facility for subscribers. This service is growing steadily, as are the others.

Charges: During prime time, the charges range from 60 cents per minute ($36 per hour) to $1.20 per minute ($72 per hour) with the vast majority at the higher rate. During evening and weekend hours, the charges range from 20 cents per minute ($12 per hour) to as high as 90 cents per minute ($54 per hour) with the majority of services in the lower range. The one-time start-up fee is $75.

Hours of Operation: All day.

BULLETIN BOARDS

Another interesting way you can use your home computer for communications is to connect to a *bulletin board (BBS).* A bulletin board is an electronic message board which anyone with a computer, a terminal emulation program with a response routine, and an automatic answer modem can establish. Hundreds of individuals, hobbyist user's groups, and computer societies, have set up these message centers. To do so, one hooks up a computer to a modem and a telephone in the answer mode. Any call that comes into the telephone number to which the computer is linked will be automatically answered with a steady beep tone from the modem. You connect your modem and you will receive a response from the bulletin board computer.

Existing bulletin boards cover every subject under the sun from particular medical specialties to pornographic subjects. However, some bulletin boards tend to exist for a few months or years and then disappear as quickly as they appeared. And most often bulletin boards can only be reached by long-distance telephone calls. But they can give you an interesting and different perspective on what is happening in the world of the microcomputer hobbyist or professional user.

SPECIAL INTEREST GROUPS

Another and more valuable way to communicate with other people with similar interests, personal or professional, is to join a *special interest group* (*SIG*). For example, CompuServe has numerous special interest groups in addition to the fifty which the AAMSI set up for health and medical professionals. It has about ten groups for users of various kinds of computers and programming languages, including CP/M. This kind of SIG can help with programming problems and help you find: sources of programs, especially esoteric ones computer stores do not carry; and sources of equipment or peripherals you would like to have. Of course, it is also an excellent way to swap knowledge and make friends.

A partial list of the SIGs available just through CompuServe includes: AAMSI, Atari, Commodore, Commodore PET, Commodore 64, Commodore VIC-20, Communications, Computer Art, Cooks Underground (for gourmet cooks), CP/M Group, Educators', Family Matters, HamNet, Health Users Group, IBM-PC, Legal, Literary, MAU G (Apple), Microsoft, MNET 870 (TRS-80),

Multi-Player Games, Music, Programmer's, PUG (Panasonic), Religion, Space, Sports, Travel, TRS-80 Color, TRS-80 Model 100, Veterinarians, and Work-At-Home.

There are certain rules of conduct expected, and a warning or two. First, you are expected to communicate with a civil "tongue" and in a cordial manner. Unlike the often vulgar use of Citizen Band radios, computer SIGs and bulletin boards tend to be more straightforward, even pleasant, and courteous. Second, some SIGs and bulletin boards tend to be full of advertisements or solicitations for various products. In many ways, they are a perfect medium for advertising. Third, many people who use SIGs only take information and do not often try to share with others. The basic idea is to communicate, and reading the listings or messages is not communicating. Replying to messages, getting involved in an electronic discussion, and offering the help when you can are what help make SIGs and BBSes successful and interesting.

There is literally something for almost everyone through home computer communications, and as our discussion of teletext and videotex systems shows, communicating through your home computer will become as much a part of your life as yakking on the phone, or gluing yourself for a blissful hour to your favorite sitcom on the tube.

CHAPTER 12
One Hundred and Five Common Things to Do With a Microcomputer

Now that you have discovered what home computers are and what impact they can have on your life today, you may feel as though microcomputers will dominate you and change you in ways you don't applaud. Let's go back to one of this book's main points. Home computers are no more and no less than all-purpose calculating machines. Without your telling them what to do, they are dumb, stupid, inert, and worthless. *You* control the machine and command it to do what you want it to do; it acts merely as an electronic slave.

What do you want a home computer to do for you? Although you probably gave that question some thought back in Chapter 6 (how to buy a computer), you may still be puzzled. Although you'll think of and find many ways unique to your situation, we'll give your imagination something to chew on and some directions to consider. Before you buy a computer, look over this list and compare these ideas with your own. By the time you have thought it through, you'll be able to answer confidently the nagging question, "What is a home computer good for?"

Almost none of the answers given in this chapter require any programming skills or knowledge at all. All of these uses can be done simply by slipping a cassette, cartridge, or disk into the computer and starting up the system.

In this chapter, we'll briefly describe each of 105 common uses, but we will not mention every possible use, configuration, required interface or computer capable of accomplishing each application. Frankly, the field changes too rapidly. What only one or a few machines can do today, five will be able to do tomorrow and twenty-five the day after.

GAMES, SIMULATIONS, AND ANIMATIONS

1. *Play Preprogrammed Action Strategy Games—* Thousands of game programs are already on the market; game playing was the first and remains the most popular use for home computers, and it continues to grow at a rapid pace. Every computer has some games available for it; the most popular computers have the widest variety of games with thousands of every kind for the Apples, Ataris, and Commodores, and hundreds for the out-of-production TI 99/4A, even the IBM PC, considered primarily a business machine. The number and variety of games for less popular computers depends on the manufacturer's willingness to invest in games and its ability to gain the support of game software companies. See the Appendix for listings of more than one thousand games available now.

2. *Write Your Own Game Programs*—With a simple knowledge of the BASIC language, anyone can write his or her own short game programs in a few weeks. See the Bibliography for many excellent books on how to program in BASIC for a variety of computers. The Bibliography also includes references to books filled with program listings of games you can enter into your computer, play now and save for later. Word and letter guessing games are the simplest to write, action and *Space Invader*-type games the most difficult.

3. *Hold Chess, Checker, Backgammon, and Othello Tournaments*—Computer chess makes up the most popular adult use of home computers. Since the original Microchess program from Personal Software (now VisiCorp) sold fifty thousand copies in less than two years, dozens of good chess programs have been produced. Sargon 3.0 from Hayden remains one of the best.

At a much higher level in universities, computer chess tournaments are very serious affairs with thousands of dollars in prizes often at stake. Serious programmers spent most of their leisure hours trying to find ways to beat each other's computers and develop the quintessential chess program that will beat even the best human players.

4. *Simulate Economic and Political Activity*—Simulations like Muse Software's famous Three Mile Island put you in the driver's seat and construct a hypothetical situation as unpredictable as real life. Other simulations used in education often concern ecological or nature topics—control of rat populations, studies of whale migrations, and so on. Political and economic simulations re-enact for example famous battles, revolutions, depressions, stock market activity, and growth of oil cartels. You must juggle dozens of factors to continue orderly progress, corner a market, or win a war. No easy task, and quite stimulating for teenagers and adults. *President Elect* from Strategic Simulations and *Millionaire* from Blue Chip Software are other good examples of simulations.

5. *Make Three-Dimensional Animations*—Several companies offer interesting programs that demonstrate the principles of animation.

6. *Demonstrate Artificial Intelligence*—Several companies have adapted the famous Eliza program created by Joseph Wizenbaum; the program *seems* to act like a practicing psychoanalyst. In recent years, artificial intelligence experiments have made great progress, and many programs demonstrate these principles.

7. *Create Your Own Stories*—For frustrated writers, Edu-Ware Software has Story Teller, one example of how micros can produce thousands of different stories by combining word menus. I don't think you'll get *Gone with the Wind* or a John Le Carré novel, but it can be fun.

8. *Test Your Skills in Games of Chance*—Other popular programs pit you against the computer or your friends in traditional games of chance: poker, blackjack, roulette, horse racing, go-moku, and many others. They are available for practically every computer.

9. *Compose and Play Computerized Music*—Since the first edition of this book came out, computerized micro music has soared as an applications field. *Song Writer* software for children from Scarborough Systems teaches music scales and composition, and very sophisticated programs and piano keyboard peripherals let adult professionals compose any kind of music they want with microcomputers. If you have any musical interest or talent at all, this application is a real sleeper to stir your interest.

10. *Create Your Own Murder Mysteries*—Several companies introduced games in which you must solve a murder mystery. In some cases, you become the detective and the mystery can be solved any of several ways depending on how you write the script.

11. *Simulate Airplane Flight*—Some of the most exciting games actually have serious educational purposes. *Air Flight Controller* from Creative Computing Software was an instant hit during the air flight controllers' strike of several years ago, and about half a dozen flight simulators are available for the most popular machines. In a combination of quasi-simulation and action game, Atari's very popular *Star Raiders* puts you at the helm of a star fighter; it appears you are sitting in a cockpit with enemy fighters and cruisers coming at you from all directions.

EDUCATION AND INSTRUCTION

12. *Learn Repetitive and Memory Skills*—Home computers are unsurpassed, if very underutilized, in teaching simple math skills with infinite patience. Many home computer makers, led by Atari and Commodore, provide tutorial programs for introductory-level math, spelling, and reading comprehension. They also teach more advanced skills, such as typing and speed reading, to teenagers and adults. Scarborough Systems' *Master Type* combines touch typing lessons and an exciting game. This combination of skill and drill lessons and colorful action and sound can make even the dullest subject more interesting than a classroom lecture.

13. *Learn Computer Languages*—Instructional programs with manuals and books are available to learn all the popular, and many not so common, computer languages from the dozens of variations of BASIC to "C," Pascal, APL, FORTRAN, and COBOL.

14. *Evaluate the Effectiveness of Teaching Methods*—Using a simple home computer, a teacher can evaluate and analyze how effective his tests have been in probing students' knowledge. Numerous statistical programs that instantly analyze multiple-choice or single-answer tests are available.

15. *Improve Children's Perception*—Edu-Ware Software provides programs that test a child's ability to match lines and shapes with other lines and shapes and improve a child's memory of perceived sizes, shapes, and colors. Children's Television Workshop, the creators of *Sesame Street,* also produce a line of preschooler games that has the same effects.

16. *Learn How to Think Logically*—A computer uses perfect logic in a rigorously structured grammar and syntax. Youngsters may learn how logical thought occurs and how to think in the same manner as they learn to use a home computer.

17. *Take College Courses for Credit Through Software and Videotex Networks*—Warner AMEX QUBE has had college courses through its two-way cable system program called "QUBE Campus." And a growing number of educational packages teach college-level courses.

18. *Use a Home Computer for Science Projects and Fairs*—Any child or teenager, with just a little knowledge of programming, can develop impressive presentations to illustrate or solve problems within any area of interest. Home computer programs have been very popular at high school science fairs for several years.

19. *Learn Advanced Mathematics and Science*—Many educational software companies offer disks that teach trigonometry, logarithms, metric systems, and advanced sciences, including physics and chemistry, at relatively low prices, often lower than game prices.

20. *Learn Human Health and Social Relationships*—A Canadian company provides a series of programs for several popular computers in human health and relationships. Half a dozen companies have introduced programs of varying sophistication to improve nutrition. And an increasing number of doctors are using computers in their waiting rooms with educational programs to teach patients about common medical conditions: hypertension, pregnancy, arthritis, and cancer.

PERSONAL INFORMATION MANAGEMENT

21. *Determine Biorhythms and Chart Biofeedback*—Programs to chart biorhythms are available for most computers, and several will measure stress and biofeedback patterns. Serious biofeedback therapists have attached measuring devices to microcomputers for instant analysis of stress tests, blood pressure readings, and so on.

22. *Foretell Personal Fortunes*—Programs for Tarot card readings, the Chinese I Ching, and astrology programs, are commonly available.

23. *Manage Family Diets*—More than merely programming a recipe file, home computers can instantly coordinate each family's weight and health *and* a family's grocery shopping list with desired weight goals to produce a weekly or monthly menu plan.

24. *Serve as a Kitchen Tool*—Home computers can create a kitchen directory, act as a family message center, store measurement and conversion tables, and more.

25. *Establish a Personal Data Base*—Many software houses offer programs that let you establish organized, instantly retrievable files for all kinds of information, from birthdays and anniversaries to the contents of an entire stamp collection, including each stamp's value, date of purchase, and distinguishing characteristics. My wife and I have a simple, though useful, home and office contents inventory we update occasionally for insurance purposes. A physician keeps track of several thousand videotapes of all of the operations he has performed with a simple information manager; he coordinates the videotapes to help him give speeches and lectures and teach courses at a medical college. People with many volunteer or community activities find micros indispensable.

26. *Act as a Personal Secretary*—A home computer can perform all of the duties of a personal secretary and keep track of your appointments, schedules, plans, correspondence, and remind you—with music, graphics, or sounds—when something needs to be done.

27. *Plan for Social Life and Entertainment*—Use home computers with communications to check information utilities for theater, movies, restaurants, airline, and vacation schedules and plan your entertainment and vacations with that information.

28. *Get Shopping Advice*—Using Compu-U-Card electronic shopping service either independently or through the CompuServe Information Network, you can compare prices for more than fifty thousand consumer products and place an order with a major credit card.

29. *Compose Letters and Correspondence*—The most popular home application for computers, besides games, is word processing. The home computer with a word processor and a simple information manager is the perfect repository for all personal mailing lists—Christmas cards, parties, receptions, and so on. Even letter-quality printers have become relatively inexpensive ($495–$895), making the home computer the perfect letter-writing and correspondence tool.

30. *Plan Home Improvement*—A variety of programs available for the most popular and prevalent home computers let you plan your interior decoration with graphics and art programs. Others let you plan and calculate necessary materials for home improvement projects.

HOME FINANCIAL MANAGEMENT

31. *Calculate Income Taxes*—An entire segment of the software market is concerned with income tax preparation and income tax planning. You can easily keep track of all expenses, deductions, credits, and so on for federal income tax. Full- or part-time tax return preparers will find that these programs can increase by six or seven times, at relatively low cost, the number of returns they can do during one tax season. Other "personal tax planning" programs let you work out alternative ways to arrange your taxable income so you can maximize deductions and minimize income.

32. *Coordinate Family Budgets*—Dozens of programs—and at least one for each type of computer—such as Continental Software's very popular *Home Accountant* package can keep line-by-line and running totals of all family budget items, including each expenditure and deposit category, and analyze the ups and downs of monthly and annual budget targets and savings and investment plans.

33. *Plan Home Purchases*—Most home computers can be used to plan all aspects of a home purchase, including mortgage loan calculations.

34. *Figure Loan Interest Rate Comparisons*—A lot of software is available so your computer can calculate and compare all kinds of interest rates for car, appliance, or any other major credit or installment plan purchase.

35. *Analyze Private Portfolios*—Dow Jones offers a full line of software with which you can analyze a private portfolio of stocks. With the Dow Jones Stock Quote Reporter and a free subscription (using time hooked up to the service, however, is charged by the minute) to the Dow Jones News & Information Service can get you instant quotes on thousands of stock issues.

36. *Plan Personal Estates and Retirement*—A variety of programs is available for the popular computers and operating systems (Apple, IBM PC,

Radio Shack, MS-DOS, CP/M,) that can project retirement income, annuities, and savings and pension plans, and coordinate results with personal investment and retirement goals.

37. *Maintain Personal Checkbooks*—Using a computer only to balance your checkbook is like using a cannon to catch a mouse. However, if you not only balance your checkbook, but maintain a budget and keep track of your tax deductions and credits, the checkbook balancer will be a very helpful and handy tool.

COMPUTER GRAPHICS

38. *Design Anything*—With an inexpensive touch tablet from Atari or Koala, or a graphics tablet like the Apple Graphics Tablet, you can design anything at all from new clothes, new rooms, new gardens, or new landscapes to a complete home redecoration. And you'll be surprised at how colorful and interesting the designs will be on the video screen.

39. *"Paint" Computer Pictures*—A home computer creates a new kind of art anyone can do; computer art is dynamic and can change and take on new expressions. The Commodore, Atari, and Apple computers are very well regarded for the quality of their color resolution with inexpensive art programs for children.

40. *Illustrate Mathematics*—Home computers with color can create dynamic, high-resolution graphics that illustrate how algebra, trigonometry, and geometric formulae take shape in the real world.

41. *Display TV Pictures*—Using a home video camera and a special interface, you can use your home computer to permanently store slow-scan television pictures in high-resolution graphics on the monitor display.

42. *Draw Hobby Electronic Circuits*—Thousands of home electronics buffs—and professional electronics engineers, as well—use home computers to draw audio, hi-fi, stereo, or other electronic circuitry.

43. *Create High-Resolution Kaleidoscopes*—A home computer, especially the Apple IIe model, can create an endlessly changing variety of color

kaleidoscopes in a "living" art display with a simple and inexpensive program.

44. *Program Charts and Graphs*—An increasingly popular use of computer graphics for small and home business applications is to draw bar charts, pie charts, scattergrams, line charts, and so forth of business and financial data. Dozens of graphics packages, often integrated with a series of other financial programs, are available for the Apple IIe, Apple III, Apple Macintosh, IBM PC, and IBM PC-compatible computers. Simpler programs are available for the Atari and Commodore home computers which do graphs for home and personal financial information.

45. *Draw With Light Pens*—With an electronic pen or stylus, you can draw on a home computer any shape you want from lines and boxes to complex pictures. These inexpensive light pens have also caught the fancy of young children who do *not* know the alphabet and therefore cannot correctly use a computer keyboard.

47. *Set Up a Moving Signboard*—If you want to make sure your children get an important message, your home computer can act as a moving billboard that will certainly catch their attention. Radio Shack has such a program for less than $10.

HOME AND SMALL BUSINESS

48. *Analyze Cash Flow*—In any kind of economic conditions, cash flow makes or breaks any home-based or small business, and home computers with a simple financial spreadsheet—there are dozens of adequate ones for at-home businesses—let you track cash flow on a daily, weekly, monthly, and annual basis in minutes.

49. *Control Inventory And Stock*—Even door-to-door salespeople can use a computer to keep precise control of their inventories, and a home computer with as little as 32K RAM can do it for a product line with one thousand or more items. Perhaps you run a small mail order catalog business from home: a small desktop computer with a hard disk drive can control an inventory with ten thousand items. Plenty of adequate inventory control software is available, and many of them can

work together with order entry, accounts receivable, and general ledger programs.

50. *Generate Cost Reports*—Home business people often overlook how much doing business actually costs them. A home computer with a simple profit-and-loss statement and a balance sheet can show you a complete picture of your costs in a few seconds.

51. *Analyze Market Surveys*—Even a used 48K Apple II Plus computer can quickiy summarize market surveys or opinion polls of hundreds of people who are asked several dozen questions. This is a very useful application to bring to at-home businesses a sophistication they've never had before. Or if you are very active in your community, you can do your own opinion polls for your PTA, local political committee, or nonprofit volunteer groups.

52. *Perform Accounting Services*—Every home computer has available at least one package, often dozens, with which a bookkeeper, auditor, or accountant can perform small business accounting at home.

53. *Do Word Processing/Text Editing*—Every home business must send out correspondence of many kinds, and a good word processing program and an inexpensive printer can save you 50–60 percent of your drafting and editing time.

54. *Maintain General Ledgers*—Many home business people can adapt home budget management programs to act as simple general ledgers and P & L statements for their budgets, or they can buy simple, inexpensive general ledger software (as low as $69).

55. *Keep Accounts Receivable*—If cash flow is the lifeblood of any small business, then accounts receivable is the heart that keeps the blood flowing. It is essential for any small business to keep accurate track of who owes it money, how much, and when it should be paid. A simple A/R program for the Atari, Commodore, Apple, and similar computers will keep track, print reports, and help write dunning letters. You can also find plenty of packages which integrate A/R with general ledger and order entry.

56. *Keep Accounts Payable*—Like the above, knowing how much you have to spend and when

you should spend it helps you manage your money better and use or invest any excess wisely. There are also plenty of A/P packages that integrate A/P with general ledger.

57. *Keep Payroll And Personnel Records*—Most at-home businesses do not need a payroll program, but if you have more than a couple of part-time employees or family members on whom you pay federal withholding taxes, a simple, inexpensive payroll program can eliminate hours of irritating drudgery filling out forms and doing impossible calculations. It is epecially helpful when filing quarterly tax returns.

58. *Maintain Extensive Mailing Lists*—Door-to-door or party-plan salespeople need a fast, efficient home computer to maintain mailing lists by name, address, zip code, block, phone number, or other category. Useful, but not spectacularly functional mail list programs cost as little as $50 and store up to one thousand names for the Atari, Apple, Commodore, Radio Shack, and similar computers.

59. *Establish Index Card File*—Many business people keep extensive reference or index card files. Using an inexpensive personal information manager such as PFS:File, they can enter all the information into their home computer in their own formats and retrieve it at will by any category they had established. Of course, some of these programs can also be used for simple mailing lists.

60. *Serve Private Investors*—Private investors now have a plethora of programs which analyze and manage every kind of investment from stocks and bonds to put and call options and financial interest rate futures.

61. *Plan Installment Sales*—Mom-and-Pop retail stores can tighten their installment plan sales controls, maintain more accurate records of all installment transactions, and estimate future cash flow from such sales with a microcomputer like the Apple IIe or IBM PC.

62. *Track Sales Calls*—Traveling, part-time, or commission salespeople can keep track of all sales calls, analyze their territories, and more effectively plan travel and sales strategy with a home computer. A portable or briefcase computer with built-in appointment scheduling, memo writing, note

taking, and telephone calling software can be especially valuable.

63. *Keep Sales Expense/Business Entertainment/Business Travel Records*—A variety of personal filing systems and simple spreadsheets allow records of this sort to be kept far more accurately than a scrawled notebook or calendar.

PROFESSIONAL APPLICATIONS

This is by far the biggest category of applications. Since the first edition was published in 1980, the microcomputer has revolutionized the use of time and information among more than 25 percent of the professionals in the United States The list below gives the briefest idea of how professionals can use microcomputers.

64. *Manage The Medical Office*—From appointment scheduling for one doctor to a totally automated, paperless office for a dozen physicians and a dozen nurses, microcomputers can help physicians manage every aspect of their practice. A few suggested applications include:

— *Accounts receivable and patient billing.*
— *Insurance claims/medicare forms processing.* More and more are being automated with direct telecommunications links to the insurance company or Blue Cross/Blue Shield.
— *Word processing.* From sending out recall notices to patients to writing books and journal articles. Word processing is the second most prevalent use of computers in physicians' offices.
— *Patient medical record keeping.* A growing application limited by lack of software and storage, more and more physicians are automating their patient's records and medical histories. More than a dozen systems are available.
— *Computer-Assisted diagnosis and medical decision making.* Known as CAD and CMD, with them, physicians can more accurately diagnose and treat their patients. Long experimental software is now becoming available for desktop microcomputers.
— *Research studies.* Using a home computer and telecommunications, any physician/researcher can use numerous data bases to do detailed bibliographic research on any of thousands of medical subjects.

65. *Assist Attorneys*—Attorneys have been using dedicated word processors for more than a decade, but the microcomputer opens ways they can be more efficient and knowledgeable:

— *EXIS/NEXIS service.* Mead Data Central offers an IBM PC software package for direct links to their data base of all of the legal decisions in the U.S. Attorneys and paralegals are reducing to one-tenth the amount of time they spend searching case histories.
— *Time and billing.* Attorneys' time is their most important asset, and most charge by the fraction of an hour. Now, there are dozens of time and billing programs that let attorneys bill more accurately than ever before.
— *Attorneys' case files.* Attorneys are using even small-screen home computers like the Commodore PET to process case files, store and recall standard contracts, write and edit briefs, and other legal tasks. Any word processor is appropriate for these and dozens of other word processing tasks.

66. *Analyze Real Estate And Property Investments.*—From buying a house to financing enormous skyscrapers, microcomputers can be used in real estate offices and brokerages for dozens of applications.

— *Nationwide referral service.* Several automated property referral services are available to real estate agents—either within their national franchise or private services.
— *Part-time real estate investments.* A home computer with a spreadsheet can quickly tell a part-time real estate investor or property owner the best deal for any prospective purchase. One can also use the same program and computer to do a variety of calculations on depreciation, amortization, mortgage loans, interest rates, net present value of money and so on. A very valuable application is to keep track of construction or restoration contractors' charges and billing.
— *Manage income property.* Many software houses now have programs with which you can manage rental property or apartment buildings and

determine occupancy rates, rents, rates of return, repair and utility costs.

67. *Assist Architects*—A variety of applications for architects are available for the IBM PC. One called MicroCAD helps an architect plan an entire structure, including structural analyses, mechanical engineering, heating, cooling and plumbing systems. Others are computer-aided design programs which let architects do their drawings on the computer screen before they are committed to blueprints.

68. *Assist Engineers*—Similarly, dozens of programs are available, even for pocket computers, to help any kind of engineer with measurement calculations, and statistical analyses.

69. *Calculate Statistics*—Statisticians and other professionals who must use statistics frequently—even market researchers—can use microcomputers with a variety of programs, notably StatPro for the Apple and IBM PC, to speed their computations and comparisons.

70. *Measure Energy/Saving Applications*—Numerous programs are available for solar designers and air conditioning and heating professionals to design and keep track of energy-saving and solar home heating systems. Even homeowners can use some of them to calculate heat loss from windows, doors, and attics to help determine how much insulation and what type to install for maximum savings at the lowest cost.

71. *Perform Teachers' Class Management Tasks*—Teachers, instructors, and professors can use microcomputers for many tasks.

— *Student grade and record keeping.* Enter all your classes' grades and test scores into a record keeping program and the computer will figure out all the averages. It may also keep attendance records.

— *Lesson and curriculum plans.* Some software is available to help teachers plan their lessons on a monthly basis.

— *Graduate studies applications.* Teachers doing graduate studies can use micros for all of their work processing tasks, and can use information managers to keep track of bibliographies, function as notecards, and act as a personal library card catalog. Of course, teachers in many fields

can also use telecommunications to access the enormous data bases for most technical, economic, sociological, and psychological areas of study through Lockheed DIALOG or Bibliographic Research Service (BRS, Ltd.).

HOME CONTROLS

72. *Control Lights With Preprogrammed Timing*—Controlling all of your lights with a home computer is feasible, and many experimental systems in model homes have been developed. However, a $50 system with its own microprocessor can do the job itself, or you can hook it up to a home computer with a special interface. In the future, it appears "dedicated" microcomputers built into the walls of homes like an intercom system will be the way in which microcomputerized home control systems become popular.

73. *Operate Home Security Systems*—Inexpensive microprocessor-based systems are already available to control security systems. They can run independently or be worked through your computer. One hobbyist installed a voice recognition security system that would not open the front door unless it recognized the voice of the person speaking into the microphone.

74. *Sense Remote Areas*—Some computer pioneers have combined off-the-shelf sensors with microcomputers and created computers that can "watch" your children at play, provide perimeter security, and indicate when the lawn needs watering, or turn the sprinkler system on by itself without bothering you.

75. *Operate Home Heating And Air Conditioning*—Numerous solar and energy-saving houses have been developed through which a home computer controls and senses heating and air conditioning, thermostats, heat pumps, solar systems, hot water tanks, oil burners, gas heaters, electric heaters, or any kind of energy device in the home that plugs into a wall socket.

76. *Regulate All Home Appliances*—Using Mountain Computer Corp. or Radio Shack systems, you can program a home computer to turn on or off any home appliance at any specified time of day.

77. *Check And Predict Weather*—Attach a home computer to a Heathkit digital weather station and it will instantly monitor temperature, pressure, and so forth, and indicate future weather conditions.

78. *Control a Home Message Center*—A home computer in the kitchen can replace written bulletin boards or reminder pads, and be programmed to hold all personal and family information.

VOICE RECOGNITION AND SPEECH SYNTHESIS

79. *Learn Conversational Foreign Language Speech*—Many programs help you learn a foreign language, although these products have not been as popular as it was once thought they would be.

80. *Voice Control of Home Management Systems*—Using an inexpensive voice recognition system and interface from Heuristics, many hobbyists have enabled their home control systems to recognize voice commands.

81. *Inform, Instruct, Question, and Prompt*—Texas Instruments has pioneered both talking and listening computers, and now has voice recognition software and boards for its TI Professional model.

82. *Manage Medical Software*—Two companies have developed voice recognition systems that control medical office management as well as accepting spoken codes from nurses and physicians. These systems "hear"—that is, divide spoken speech into digital bits and store them on disk—spoken numbers and letters from standard medical procedure codes.

MUSIC

83. *Learn How To Read Music*—Software which teaches children how to read music and encourages them to compose their own songs is readily available for most home computers, especially Atari, Commodore, Apple, and many others. Scarborough Systems' SongWriter software is one of the best.

84. *Learn Music Appreciation*—Advanced programs for adults teach music history and appreciation.

85. *Learn Basic and Advanced Coomposition*—Many clubs and societies, such as the Computer Music Society in Philadelphia, already encourage home computer owners to hone their skills through advanced music composition programs.

86. *Combine Home Computers With Music Peripherals*—Sophisticated music synthesizers and computerized keyboards can be hooked up to many personal computers. Professional musicians are using these and even more advanced dedicated electronic and computerized music systems, too.

87. *Combine Computer Music and Art*—Many hobbyists are combining the musical and artistic potentials of their home computers to create "multi-media" shows for their own entertainment, or to entertain others.

HELP FOR THE HANDICAPPED

88. *Talking Wheelchair*—With an Apple computer as its brain, a talking wheelchair has been perfected which allows a handicapped person who cannot speak to touch the keyboard, spell words and sentences, and have the computer say the word, phrase, or sentence through a speech synthesizer. The system can store hundreds of words and sentences on a disk drive; these can be recalled with a few keystrokes.

89. *Printing Communicators*—Several hand-held computerized systems allow handicapped people who cannot speak to type out on a printer what they want to say. These computers are specially adapted for people who do not know how to use keyboards. They can, however, be slow and laborious. Some are programmable and can use one letter or symbol on the special keyboard to represent various ideas or sentences.

90. *Talking Communicators*—Dedicated microcomputers with special operating systems, talking communicators have preprogrammed words, phrases, sentences, and speech sounds.

91. *Environmental Controls*—Since many handicapped people cannot move one or more of their limbs—quadriplegics cannot move any—microcomputers have been connected to various control mechanisms and devices, ranging from simple touch or pressure switches to microswitches that

respond to no more than the twitch of a muscle or the blink of an eye. There are many handicapped people in Veterans Administration and other public hospitals now using such devices. One device uses tiny bioelectrodes which amplify eye muscle electrical signals through a digital electro-oculogram transducer. Others enable the handicapped to turn lights, appliances, and televisions off and on, dial telephones, raise and lower electric beds, operate motorized wheelchairs, and do other tasks many handicapped people have never before been able to do for themselves.

92. *Refreshable Braille*—These microcomputer devices record and store Braille symbols in digital form on audio cassette tapes or disk drives in the same way a home computer sends digital signals for cassette storage. The information can be automatically recalled, making them "refreshable." Now any information that can be printed or displayed or stored on another medium—typewriter, calculator, or computer—can be automatically translated into Braille and vice versa.

93. *Terminal Message Centers*—Handicapped patients can use simple home computers hooked up to simple communications systems in a hospital or rehabilitation center to send messages to nurses or medical staff in another room.

94. *National Communications Network*—Experiments using telecommunications to let handicapped people use communications networks to send electronic mail and have on-line "conversations" with other people—handicapped or not—have proven to be very successful outreach programs.

95. *Patient Monitoring Systems*—At least several physicians have hooked up microcomputers to handicapped infants' cribs in their homes. The cribs are equipped with sensors which can tell when a child makes a dangerous or unusual movement.

96. *Captions for the Deaf*—For a number of years, most Public Broadcasting Stations and two major networks have broadcast television programs with teletext captions hidden in the unseen portion of their TV signal. Using a special teletext decoder, more than fifty thousand deaf people can now read the dialog from many of their television programs.

Until it was canceled, "Little House on the Prairie" was one of the many shows broadcast for the deaf in this manner.

97. *Artificial Limbs with Microcomputer Controls*—The Veterans Administration and several private research organizations have been experimenting with microcomputer-controlled artificial limbs and prostheses. These use microcomputer chips attached to simple analog-digital signal convertors to duplicate the movement of a real limb. The battery-operated miniature microcomputers both send and respond to signals in the leg muscles, for example, to make the artificial leg move as naturally as possible.

ODDS AND ENDS

98. *Operate Ham Radio Networks*—One of the major hobbyist uses for home computers is running ham radio networks and controlling transmission and reception.

99. *Track Satellites*—Several programs have been printed in computer magazines that allow you to predict when and where the next satellite will fall to earth.

100. *Learn Amateur Astronomy*—With a home computer program available for most popular computers, you can track stars, predict eclipses, program your own "heavens," and learn astronomical techniques.

101. *Create Your Family Tree*—A very popular use of home computers is to develop one's own family tree and communicate with a network of computerized genealogists. Many magazines have published free genealogy programs.

102. *Organize Car Pools*—Several individuals and companies use home computer models to manage employee car pools; some are even managed on a neighborhood- or city-wide basis.

103. *Run Household Robots*—Home computer "brains" control all of the new, inexpensive robots. Still mostly toys, the inexpensive robots will become useful household servants within ten years.

104. *Produce Flight and Navigation Plans*—Many programs are available for portable and pocket computers which produce and modify flight and

ship navigation plans. One of the most popular features of the CompuServe Information Network are preprogrammed flight plans sold at extra cost by a professional pilots' association.

105. *Think Logically*—Interacting with a computer and software whose operations are based on a very tightly structured system of logic and thought can help the individual learn to think more precisely and logically as well.

These 105 things to do with a home computer only scratch the surface of the thousands of ways people are using computers as their all-purpose pleasure machines each day. So, let your imagination soar and enjoy your computing.

CHAPTER 13

The Three Rs and a C

People learn by doing, whether the task involves learning how to add and subtract or how to program computers in machine-level languages. Home computers provide an extraordinarily promising way for everyone to learn whatever they want to, even though they may gain experience only vicariously on a home computer. As one computer expert has said, if experience is the best teacher, then pseudo-experience is the next best teacher. To this I would add, "as long as the learner recognizes it as pseudo-experience and does not confuse what happens on a video screen with reality." A chemistry experiment that makes a nice, clean textbook reaction on the computer screen could easily become a smelly, messy or even dangerous problem in the laboratory. On the other hand, a child might listen to a teacher explain how to add or subtract, and define what addition and subtraction mean, but that child will not *know* what addition and subtraction really are until he or she manipulates numbers and things. This a computer can easily do, and the result will be both "textbook" and actual. In either case, computer experience can be amazingly helpful.

A home computer can act as a teacher in the home for practically every aspect of a learning experience. It may show a colorful display illustrating what addition and subtraction mean, it may show the process of adding and subtracting as a child interacts with and manipulates numbers and objects. Of course, a simple example such as elementary arithmetic merely introduces the power of a home computer in educating your child and you.

When you buy your first computer, perhaps a simple inexpensive model, you immediately discover what may be the most important fact about computers. This fact often becomes obscured in the distracting excitement of lights, colors, sounds, and captivating displays, but it concerns the fundamental nature of the machine. Simply, computers must operate through *logic,* a precise, ordered set of operations that cannot be changed or challenged without causing the computer to malfunction or do nothing. For example, the most common example given about programming computers begins with the line: PRINT "HELLO." If you don't type in that line exactly as it's shown, the computer cannot understand the instruction and will flash an error message. If you don't exactly follow the grammar and syntax of computer language, it can't understand you. This fact becomes especially apparent when you begin to learn programming. In short, a computer must follow the perfect logic as that logic is given to it by the programmer.

This structure may seem like a minor tyranny, but, in education, especially of young children, a home computer can help them rapidly and thoroughly learn how to think. Young children, often those just learning to read, take to computers like ducks to water. It seems that children inherently want to learn, and enjoy learning in a logical way. Some people may object and say that children like home computers because of the exciting games, sounds, and colors. But that viewpoint doesn't explain why and how many children quickly learn programming—often difficult and complex languages—at an early age (10 or 11).

And that viewpoint runs counter to something Marshal McLuhan said about entertainment and education. To paraphrase: *The person who thinks entertainment has nothing to do with education does not know the first thing about either one.* In the occasional seminars and lectures I teach or attend, my best learning and teaching experiences have also been the most enjoyable ones—in which the teacher or speaker was dynamic, interesting and thus, entertaining. The worst have been when the teacher (including myself) was pedantic, preachy, dull, and long-winded. For parents and teachers to object to computerized learning programs because they are often games or entertainment says more about their Victorian attitudes and fear of being replaced by a computer than the value of computerized learning. It also may say a lot about what the teachers really believe about the quality of their teaching; if they cannot teach as well as a computer game, they have good reason to doubt their choice of profession.

The problem I see with much, if not most, of today's educational software is that it is *not* entertaining enough. This poor-quality type of program takes skill and drill exercises—that is, repeating the multiplication tables over and over again—straight from a textbook or workbook and puts them on a video screen. That merely turns a $1,000–$2,000 computer and a $40 educational program into a $10 workbook, hardly the best way to use a microcomputer for education. However, that is exactly how most schools are using home computers today.

Returning to the discussion of childrens' fascination with programming, there is very little excitement to writing a program until it is completed and works perfectly. The first, second, and often twenty-fifth draft of a program often fail, as any professional programmer will agree. Getting a per-

fectly working program requires repeated refinements. Yet tens of thousands of children are learning to program in fluent BASIC, Pascal, LOGO, and other languages. And they are leaving adults with little training in logic and no training in computers far behind.

What this willingness of children to work hard at a program appears to mean, at least in part, is that many children first enjoy the sense of control they get from a computer. They push the buttons, they make things happen or not happen. Second, children desire and will go to great lengths to obtain a sense of accomplishment. Third, they are willing to put forth the effort if they have a clear sense of their goals. And computer programs, with a definite path laid out in a flowchart and precise steps for them to follow through the language, give them that clear sense of direction and goal orientation. Fourth, children "soak up" positive reinforcement and thrive on it; just as readily, they soak up negative reinforcement and wilt under it.

In many schools today, children enjoy going to computer class because it is an excuse to escape the drudgery of sitting in a class and being lectured to all day. In the average classroom today, it is practically impossible to properly use home computers. Consider that the average class is 50–55 minutes long. If the computers are kept in one location, a whole class may have to troop to the room and get settled; this takes a minimum of 10 minutes. The teacher must set up the various computers and programs—a minimum of 10–15 minutes. The children get to work with the computers for 15–20 minutes, and then they must shut down the computers and return to their regular classroom. Fifteen minutes a day once a week, or even several times a week, won't truly make any child "computer literate."

On the other hand, a home computer can be an excellent tool for "individualized instruction," a buzz word in the public schools for giving some kids the attention and extra effort they need to become adept at a subject. If a child is having trouble with certain concepts, long division or fractions, for example, having the child work with well-programmed software that teaches, reinforces, and tests the child has been shown to be very helpful. The computer as tutor can remove the child from the pressure of the classroom, let her learn at her own pace, perk up her interest with color, sound, graphics, and interesting problems, and give patient, positive reinforcement. In short, a computer tutor never gets tired, never leaves the room, never changes the subject matter. It doesn't have to look after 125 other students. It doesn't go too fast for slow learners or too slow for fast learners. In addition, dozens of these programs are available free through magazine or book listings, various user's groups, or educational texts. Ask the head of the computer program at your children's school for help in finding them.

Many school systems have regular computer literacy and programming classes, which a student may take as electives. But only a handful of schools today have made computer literacy a required part of their curriculum or a requirement for graduation. Yet, the entire structure of American business is evolving very rapidly into one in which more than half of all workers use some kind of computer workstation or terminal. And many of the rest will in some way be connected to the computer industry—building them, servicing them, or writing programs for them. This situation is comparable to the lack of emphasis on typing skills. Although the typewriter was the standard instrument for business communications by the 1930s, typing was not taught in the high schools as a business education subject until more than 20 years later, and only after business pleaded for it. The same thing happened with mainframe computers; few high schools taught data or word processing when the

demand for both was growing during the 1960s and 1970s. This EDP and WP training was considered the province of vocational and private business schools and somehow slightly beneath the dignity of the public education system.

As long as the public school system misapplies or misuses home computers as educational tools, it will be up to the parents and children themselves to take matters into their own hands. In fact, many parents are motivated to buy computers to learn about computing and programming. One professional programmer who bought a home computer for his children has said, "I wanted to educate my family about computers because of the importance computers will have in everybody's lives." That importance, as we've seen, stretches far beyond the bounds most people have even begun to consider. Home computers, or microprocessors, already "inhabit" more than two thousand common devices, and new habitations—from home appliances to solar heating to automobile engine blocks—are added to the list practically every day.

With its emphasis on logic, grammar, and rational structures, home computer-based education could even reincarnate what used to be considered a "classical" education. Experts who devote serious thought to future home computer applications believe that long after every small business has its own microcomputer running its general ledgers, word processing, financial analysis, budgeting, and inventory systems, parents and children

Figure 77. Home computers have found a home in the public schools as tutors for individualized learning and as subjects of study for the new generation of computer-literate youngsters. (Courtesy of Apple Computer, Inc.)

WHAT DO YOU DO WITH A MIND MACHINE?

will still be discovering new ways to learn with home computers.

At present, education with home computers—whether in the school or in the home—can be divided into four broad areas: 1) repetitive skill and drill training; 2) simulations; 3) thought exercises; and 4) problem-solving exercises. (By the way, the current fad for computerized programs to help teenagers or adults prepare for college entrance examinations does *not* appear to give substantially better training than the many printed workbooks on the same subjects. However, they are more profitable for their makers: The basic cost of a computer program of that sort is less than $5.00, about the same as a book, while the sales price of the software is between $30 and $50 or more, three to five times more than the cost of a printed workbook.)

You will find hundreds of educational programs available for each type of popular home computer, especially Apple, Atari, Commodore, IBM, and Radio Shack. Most home computer makers stress educational software. Often these programs are aimed at schools as well as individuals. At the end of the chapter, I will discuss how to find and buy good-quality educational software.

STIMULATING SIMULATIONS

The most fascinating and challenging type of educational use for computers, I believe, is simulation. As you know, many dangerous and essential professions—jet pilot, nuclear power plant operator, oil tanker captain, astronaut, chemical plant operator and so on—cannot use on-the-job training without endangering other people. During the past three decades, huge, complicated, computerized "environments" have trained people for these jobs with very realistic simulations of the actual conditions they will face. These simulators have proved enormously successful in improving the skills of the operators when they actually receive on-the-job training, and as a direct result, have improved the safety records of these employees and the industries.

In business and education, role-playing exercises and management simulation games have become popular in training new supervisors or managers. Sony Management Systems Company, for example, gives seminars in a complex, but fascinating game in which each participant is given control of her own company. The game compresses years of operational experience into a few hours and each player must manage the resources of her own company and compete in free markets against a table full of competitors in the same industry. Sony, the electronics giant, had used this game to train thousands of its own managers and supervisors, and the results were so good, it decided to sell the game as a seminar and training service. The only thing this modern Japanese company hasn't done is computerize its model. The game could easily become a computerized simulation for use in the office or at home; the manager could play against the computer, or a network of other managers within the same company, each at his or her own computer.

Already, however, universities, "think tanks," and economic forecasters are using complicated computer models to predict future economic, social, political, and cultural conditions. These, too, are simulations.

But you don't need a professional seminar or expensive mainframes to learn through simulations. In fact, the second most popular kind of consumer computer game is the simulation game. The new wave of arcade games, led by *Zaxxon* and *Star Raiders* and brought to its current zenith by *Dragon's Lair,* are actually simulations. They put you in the driver's seat, so to speak, and you must act as if you were part of the game itself. In *Star Raiders* and many of its descendants, you are the pilot of a star fighter, and the oncoming alien star ships are firing at you; this three-dimensional simulation is far different from the two-dimensional *Space Invaders* game in which you are an onlooker at the action.

Dragon's Lair takes this simulation concept ever further, and combines the television video of the optical laser video disc with the graphics and programmability of the microcomputer. You are a participant in the action within the Dragon's Lair. And the scenes are not rough computer graphics with quaint figures like Pac-Man, but superior, startlingly colorful animations. They are equal to or better than the animations done by Walt Disney Studios.

And this is just a children's game. The U.S. Army uses the combined power of the videodisc and the microcomputer to train soldiers in how to drive tanks and fire artillery. In the tank simulation, the tank driver sees exactly what he would see if he were inside a real tank, and he must use the same controls to make the right moves, or he gets destroyed. A real incentive to learn to handle a tank properly.

The Israeli Army has taken the simulation concept out of the classroom lab and put it back into real life. During the recent strife in Lebanon, they used armed drones—about six feet long—to bomb Syrian targets. However, these drones had television cameras implanted in their noses and radio receivers inside their bellies. Real Israeli pilots, sitting in front of a television, a radar screen, and hand-operated flight controls in secure bunkers dozens of miles away, "flew" the drones to their targets, avoided enemy fire, dispatched the drones' armaments, and watched them hit and explode. Reports from the field say this new weapon was very effective in bombing hard-to-find positions, but also very hard on the pilots. Why? They had very negative psychological reactions to crashing their drones, which sometimes happened. Of course, they did escape the crashes with their lives.

This discussion is not meant to frighten you, but to show how the synergism of the videodisc and the microcomputer can be used, either as a very valuable tool in the real world, or as a very positive and intensely personal tool in education.

Consider the extraordinary and long-popular *Three Mile Island* game from Muse Software. Running on an ordinary Apple II Plus or IIe computer, it portrays the actual operation of a nuclear reactor in vivid color. The demanding simulation game tests the player's skill at maintaining rapidly changing temperatures and pressures and solving emergencies—which appear both randomly and as a result of a player's mistakes. Other inexpensive commercial programs simulate population explosions, population control, rat infestations, whale migrations, presidential elections, football games, the life and death of kingdoms and empires, and a variety of social and economic challenges. In the latter two, a player acts as "king" or "queen" and must maintain balances among supplies and demands for food and other necessities. Other very popular programs simulate pilot training and air traffic control.

Any real-life situation or occupation can be simulated on a home computer, and any simulation can provide challenging ways for children and adults to learn. And if you think these games are kid's stuff, try some of the war game simulations developed by the software house Strategic Simulations.

USING THE HOME COMPUTER FOR LEARNING AT HOME

My point in this chapter is not only that computers can help improve education in the schools, *if used properly,* which I doubt occurs in most school systems. My point is that home computers used in the home with quality educational programs can *supplement, replace,* and *even improve upon* the quality of education a child receives at school. Child development experts have stated that children learn more between birth and five years of age than they do during the rest of their lives: walking, speaking, and more. Remember, too, that the publicly funded school is a very recent institution by historical standards. And, although it is officially frowned upon, tens of thousands of parents already teach their children at home on a full-time basis.

The home is actually a "learning institution" of far more importance than a public school, and the home computer can be used as an integral tool in learning at home. The best situation for children who go to schools outside the home and use a computer to learn at home would combine two elements: 1) reinforcement of the subjects currently taught at school; and 2) encouragement of any subjects or interests a child may have. For example, most boys, for some reason I have never understood, seem to develop a fascination with chemistry sets at about ages 9–12. Most parents buy them the sets and endure the smells and messes until the fad passes. With a home computer, the children can play with simulations of chemistry sets and chemical reactions and the parents can avoid the stink and mess, or at least lessen the amount. And the chemical simulations can teach a far more detailed and sophisticated type of chemistry than an inexpensive chemistry set. The same holds true for physics, biology, geology, and geography.

These simulations will also pique children's curiosity and encourage them to test what they have learned in the real world. Of course, simulated learning can only go so far; a simulation can explore only a limited number of predetermined variables within any situation. Real life, as we all have learned through often painful experience, tends to involve a practically infinite number of random variables, or variables that cannot be predicted or "programmed" beforehand. For example, one presidential election simulation used only about a dozen variables, including popular vote, available campaign funds, weeks to campaign, and electoral votes. Those are only a few of the thousands of variables that make up an election, but they gave an excellent "taste" of the real thing. Simulations for home computers can only give a "taste." You still have to eat the whole thing to get the "nutritional" benefit.

It is also a good idea to try to work with your children's teachers and find educational software which supplements what they are learning at school. This is especially helpful if a child is having trouble at school in a particular subject or concept and cannot get the individualized attention—from a teacher or a computer—she needs. You and a home computer with a reinforcement program can do much to overcome the shortcomings of the public and private schools.

But make sure that your children's use of your computer is tightly structured. A home computing pioneer who had young children when the revolution began always made his children do something useful with the computer—programming or an educational excersise—*before* they could play games and *after* they had completed their regular school assignments. This appears to be a good method of putting things in their proper order.

HOME EDUCATION FOR ADULTS

Although it is not developing as quickly as I thought it would several years ago, the future of the home computer in education may rest as much with adult education as with the education of children. It seems that adults are more likely to buy computers to educate their children than to improve their own educations. And, with a few exceptions in the self-improvement and pop psychology field, software for adult education remains in very short supply.

But the potential for career development, job improvement, career changes, hobby education, and many more areas for adults remains enormous in my view. You can use home computer software in the same way as correspondence courses, weekend classes, or night school. There is a course of software that offers a complete self-study course in real estate, and the same potential exists for self-study courses for law students, chartered life underwriters (CLU), certified public accountants (CPA), certified records managers (CRM), and dozens of other careers and professions which require or suggest licensing tests or advanced studies. Even Civil Service tests will become a field for home computer software.

In my opinion, adult education and self-improvement programs are two important secrets to showing people how useful home computers can be in their lives. They can then use the same home computer with word processing to write reports, studies, examination papers, term papers, book reviews, and articles. With information manager software, they can keep their notes and bibliographies stored on a magnetic medium. Combined with a videodisc, they can even store encyclopedias, photographs, and pictures of works of art for an instant reference library.

Considering the success of the many aerobics videotapes and records, it is a simple step to combining a videodisc with a computer program to produce an exercise tape with which you can design your own exercise plan. Nutrition and menu programs already allow this with family eating habits and diets; why not family exercises? The main reason is: not many people yet own both a programmable laser videodisc and a home computer. When they do, the programs will quickly be made available. The technology and programming knowledge are both well known and are ready to be turned into this kind of adult education and self-improvement course. Just put Jayne Kennedy's or Jackie Sorenson's name and face on the program and videodisc, and sales should start to happen.

PRESCHOOL EDUCATION EVOLUTION

Home education with home computers does not leave out anyone in the family, not even preschool children who cannot read, write, or use a keyboard.

Great strides were made during 1983 and 1984 in developing simple "interfaces" for young children to work with computers. First Texas Instruments, and more recently Atari, have introduced inexpensive touch tablets that let children under the age of five move the cursor around the screen and press the tablet to execute a function. The AtariArtist program, for example, includes screens full of pre-programmed colorful shapes. A child can choose the shapes with the touch tablet and create drawings on the screen. The same tablet will be used for games for preschool children and learning exercises. Many programs also use colors and shapes to teach both how to use the keyboard and the alphabet.

But more important than the touch tablet is the LOGO programming language designed especially for children. LOGO was developed at the Massachusetts Institute of Technology by Seymour Papert and his colleagues and bases computer programming on a simple "turtle" geometry concept. Children learn computer operations and basic programming skills by instructing and directing a turtle-shaped cursor on the video screen. Turtle geometry teaches spatial relationships, basic geometrical concepts, programming skills, and computer operations, and can be extended to teach math, reading, and more.

LOGO programming language packages are widely available for all popular computers including BBC Acorn, Apple, Atari, Commodore, IBM, and the now out-of-production Texas Instruments and Timex models. It will be one of the first applications languages for the Japanese MSX computers as well. LOGO is very popular in the elementary or grammar schools, but can be very enjoyable for the home, in its inexpensive versions.

TALKING AND LISTENING COMPUTERS IN EDUCATION

The future of home computers in home education, I believe, lies with talking and listening computers. Texas Instruments introduced the educational talking computer in 1978 with its very successful Speak 'N Spell game. This $50 game packed more ROM memory onto a silicon chip (128K ROM) than any other chip at the time. In fact, the game had two chips, both of which were used to synthe-size speech. The game pronounced words, some easy and some tricky, and asked the child to type in the correct letters on a simple keyboard with a one-line video display. If the child typed the correct answers, the game spoke words of praise and played a pleasant little tune. If the child was wrong, the game gently corrected the mistake. Since then, TI has introduced numerous plug-in modules expanding the available vocabulary from 140 words to more than 1,000, and introduced Speak 'N Math and Speak 'N Read.

However, the same capability has not yet been translated into home computer software. The now defunct TI 99/4A had the same speech capability, and it used speech synthesis in its educational command modules for the classroom. But no other company has yet followed through on this technology. In 1981, several toy companies introduced educational toys with speech synthesis chips which taught common words, the alphabet, and spatial relationships to preschool children, but none of them became big hits.

None of the newer computers, the IBM PCjr, for example, has the same speech synthesis capabilities, so it remains to be seen when the existing technology will be used on a consistent and widespread basis for education.

THE EDUCATIONAL NETWORK

While many people will prefer to buy disks and cassettes to take educational courses at home, another way that may be popular in the future is the electronic correspondence school. The first popular electronic campus was "QUBE Campus" in the two-way cable videotex system in Columbus, Ohio. Through the campus, adults can enroll in college courses at one of four local colleges or universities and take college-level courses for credit over a QUBE channel. The college instructor takes attendance by asking those watching to "touch in" and a record is stored on computer.

But the interactivity between QUBE Campus instructor and pupils was limited to multiple-choice questions and a simple interaction. However, the teacher could ask an individual student a question and get an answer—if the student knew it, of course.

QUBE was offering a variety of courses, not just

undergraduate college material, including: update classes for professionals such as physicians who need special information; self-help and self-improvement classes including beginning shorthand and golf.

But compared to an electronic conferencing network with on-line interaction among all participants, QUBE is a limited system. With a conference network, the interaction is not only between student and teacher, but among students in the same class, although they may be miles and hours apart. For example, through a network, students can prepare and submit research papers, conduct discussions, receive replies and criticism, and respond. Other students or instructors can critique the others' work, and carry on academic or professional discussions.

And almost any subject can be taught this way, with the possible exception of those that require laboratory exercises. Even those could be done with simulation programs and manuals sent to the students as part of the course material.

Using conferencing networks means that not everyone has to sit in class at the same time. Students can participate at their leisure within time limits. That would have helped me make better grades in college; I never *could* get up for my 8:00 A.M. classes.

HOW TO BUY EDUCATIONAL SOFTWARE

For the present, we must live with the situation we have. Finding educational software may be difficult; finding good quality software will be even more difficult. Computer stores and department stores are likely to carry some software, but not much and not often the kind of program you need. An exception to this may be the software-only franchises and stores. But unfortunately, they are not as prevalent today as bookstores. However, an increasing number of bookstores now carry software, and in the future—and perhaps at your urging—they will carry educational software.

Your best source of software will be directly from the software houses themselves. But finding them and finding the ones which make the software you want must be done by a process of elimination.

First, ask your children's teachers for help. They especially may know what software generally corresponds to the lessons they are teaching. This will be helpful in using the computer to reinforce what your child is learning in school.

Second, if the teacher does not know, as he or she may not, ask the head of the computer department, or the person in the school most interested in and knowledgeable about home computers in education. This person should know the most about sources of software.

Third, try the school or local library for directories of microcomputer software. Use the listings of programs to call or write for catalogs from the software houses.

Fourth, find a local or nearby user's group which supports the type of computer you have.

Fifth, call the company which makes the computer you own and ask them for their catalog of educational software and a list of software houses that makes educational software for the machine.

Sixth, check local newsstands for computer magazines which include listings of educational programs. Of the magazines, *Creative Computing, Popular Computing, Personal Computing, Micro Kids, Family Computing, COMPUTE!,* and many of the machine-oriented magazines would be the best to find these listings.

How will you know what programs to try? If you buy by mail order, it will be tough to discern whether an educational program is good or not. As you look through these other sources, look for reviews, ratings, or evaluations of programs in which you may be interested. Ask for references from teachers and user's group members. If you subscribe to an information utility, put a message on the bulletin board asking for references. Be aware that the bulletin board approach may elicit sales solicitations, but it may also turn up excellent advice from teachers or knowledgeable users.

Even if you find some evaluations and references, the ultimate decision will still be up to you. If you plan to buy by mail order or from the software house, do not buy unless there is a money-back guarantee. In almost every phase of the mail-order business, the reputation of any reputable seller is built on a guarantee. Of course, if you destroy the disk or cassette, don't expect your money back. But any manufacturer's or seller's error or your judgment that you don't want the program should be enough to get your money back.

Once you've found some possibilities, determine what kind of program each is: skill and drill, simulation, and so on. If it is skill and drill, find out whether it includes any ways to entertain and positively reinforce the child. If it is in black and white and simply presents one problem after another, save your money and buy a colorful workbook instead. If it incorporates sound, music, and color into a varied and interesting framework of lessons, then take a good look at it.

For simulations, determine whether action is shown on the screen. Often, as in some adventure games, the game is all text and no displays, and this can be boring. Most recent simulations use good-quality color displays and sounds to teach the lesson.

Check the background of the developer. Although this is no guarantee a program will not be boring and poor quality, check out the background of the provider. In the early days, most educational software was designed by well-meaning teachers who knew a little about programming. Today, major educational publishers and computer companies are banding together to produce educational software, as are groups or consortia of educators in state school districts and universities. Another major source of educational software in the future will be Control Data Corp's PLATO system; developed over twenty years as a time-sharing, terminal-based system for universities and corporations, PLATO contains 1,500 educational courses in most subjects. CDC is now gradually converting them to microcomputer software.

Finally, as when you buy any software, give it a test drive before you buy it, or accept it from a mail-order house. If it's available, get a demonstration disk (it may cost $5) from a mail-order house and see what the program offers.

In this discussion, we have only scratched the surface of the rapidly developing potential for home education with home computers. And no one really knows what new forms of teaching will evolve through the home computer. For now, however, consider the advice of a teacher who began teaching his first-grade daughter with a home computer. He believes that many people easily tire of their new computer and treat it like a Christmas toy. Once they play too many games, or run out of money for peripherals, they turn the computer into an expensive doorstop. He advises, instead, that parents can keep their home computers "young and active" by using them to help teach their children and themselves. An imaginatively used home computer could be just the thing for you and your children.

CHAPTER 14

Division of Labor: Microcomputers in Your Work

Hundreds of thousands of small businesses and professionals—from part-time salesmen to owner/executives of $10 million companies—have bought microcomputers during the past six years as they sought new ways to overcome the handicaps that every small business faces: too little time; too much paperwork; too much to do with too little help; too little money; and so on, down a long list of adversities.

At the same time, in medium-sized to large corporations, the microcomputer, spurred first by the Apple II Plus and more recently, by the IBM PC, has dramatically improved the lot of the executives, middle managers, and staff professionals who are using micros with spreadsheets and integrated software to reduce by factors of up to 90 percent the time they spend on financial analysis tasks.

Among professionals, accountants have looked to microcomputers to pare the time they spend on paperwork and calculations, doing income tax returns, general ledgers, balance sheets, and so forth. Lawyers want microcomputers to speed up the processing of briefs, standard contracts, collection notices, and routine correspondence, and lower secretarial costs. Small printers use micro-to-micro typesetter telecommunications to slash labor costs and the time typesetting jobs require. Consulting engineers want faster means of sketching initial construction blueprints and calculating bid estimates. Physicians, whether in group practices or individually, want computers to reduce the usually huge amounts of accounts receivable owed by patients and insurance companies; they want to send their insurance and Medicare claim forms by telecommunications to reduce the time they must wait to get paid. Authors want to reduce the time they used to spend typing, editing by pencil, and retyping, and retyping rough drafts. In fact, any small business owner can find many uses for microcomputers that can save him or her time, money, and energy.

A microcomputer can do four general types of tasks for a small business:

1. Sorting, searching, coordinating, analyzing, or preparing information;
2. Receiving or "capturing" information whether through a keyboard, a disk drive, a modem, a touch screen, a light pen, or the spoken voice;
3. Printing out the results, documents, and reports, or talking back, transmitting through a modem, or sending the results to mass storage; and
4. Interacting for special uses such as telecommunications with a remote information utility, or as an industrial processor controller.

Figure 78. Using a peripheral such as the Apple Graphics Tablet shown here allows you to design anything from the interior of an office to a new kind of industrial equipment, or even a work of computer art. (Courtesy of Apple Computer, Inc.)

Any microcomputer—with sufficient RAM, CPU power, and adequate mass storage capacity—can do any or all of these tasks for any small business or professional, if not simultaneously, then one after the other.

The main benefits a microcomputer confers even on someone with a weekend, at-home business involve time savings, increased knowledge and control over business affairs, and money savings. For example, say you have a small business that generates about 100 checks each month and a lot of petty cash vouchers. In the past, how often did you balance your own books? Once a month, once a quarter? How long did it take if you figured out the petty cash vouchers, cash expense receipts, deposits, and so forth once a month? Four hours? Eight hours? Probably the latter over two or three days. Or maybe an accountant does that for you. I reply, "But how much do you pay your accountant or bookkeeper or payables clerk? Or all three?" (If you do it yourself, how much is that time worth to you?)

Between reconciliations, how do you know where you stand in your business? Probably by the status of your checkbook, with comparisons of daily receipts and checking account balances to current bills. But that picture probably doesn't show you where your business is headed.

How long would it take you to complete a thorough financial analysis, including factors such as debt/equity ratios, inventory turnover, days sales outstanding (or average collection period), net profit margin, return on equity, and return on investment?

If you're like most small business people, professionals, or people with at-home businesses, you've never figured out and analyzed these essential business facts. You may think that only big companies need to do that. Or, "I can't do that. I don't have time, I don't know how, and I don't have enough money to pay my accountant to do it regularly." Sound familiar? If it does, you have just discovered only a few of the ways a microcomputer will help your business. Remember, too, that every big business was at one point a small business. Apple Computer exceeded $1 billion in sales during 1983, less than eight years after it was started by two men in a garage with the proceeds of the sale of a used Volkswagen Beetle. Apple, of course, had the help of tremendously rich and powerful men and institutions along the way, but one of the reasons was because Apple's founders understood the meaning of financial controls and demonstrated to potential investors and the public that they understood what was required to make a business grow.

With a microcomputer, you can begin to gather these essential business facts and gain, for the first time, the information you need to develop a precise, clear, and accurate picture of your business. *Control* is the word big companies use to define this helpful procedure. Yet, the formulas and steps to carry out these procedures are both simple and readily available.

For example, I have used a good book, *Financial Keys to Small Business Profitability,* to take many of these steps for my business. The book is written by Edward N. Rausch and published by AMA-COM, 135 West 50th Street, New York, NY 10020, and costs $15.95. I used the budget layouts and formulas and put them into a financial spreadsheet program. I accomplished this over a period of days working late at night, developing my own spreadsheet formats and formulas and testing various row and column combinations. My analysis system is limited to about half a dozen key formulas and my budget uses round numbers and is not exact to the penny. But it works and I can put a few numbers into the formulas and in about half an hour, I get a clear picture of exactly where my business stands. In a couple more minutes, I have a printed copy of my monthly budget report.

In fact, I use an old version of one of the first spreadsheets, and there are dozens of better versions, including programs that integrate word processing and graphics. With these capabilities, you can produce attractive reports and statements that will impress your accountant, your banker, and your investors (current or future).

But there's a catch. In fact, it's more than a catch; it's a difficult, careful process to make sure you buy the right microcomputer software for your situation. First, remember that only a "small" small business can buy a computer for less than $1,000 and use it for basic tasks like accounting or payroll. Many small business people and professionals have failed to understand this principle and have purchased home computers without enough power, memory, available software, or capability to perform the jobs they want to automate.

For example, a few physicians in solo practices have used older Apple II Plus computers and Radio Shack Model IIIs to do their basic billing and accounts receivable for a few hundred patients a month. They've even done some simple word processing with the system and a dot matrix printer. But today, it is generally recognized that it is foolish to computerize a medical office with several thousand active patients without a 16-bit microcomputer with 128K RAM and a 10 Mb. hard disk drive and at least two or three terminals for

accounting, insurance claims, and word processing employees. You can do it with an Apple II Plus and limited software, but it won't be efficient and it won't save very much time or money. A recent poll in which I surveyed fifty medical practices showed that of thirty practices using their computers for billing and accounting, four were replacing older microcomputers simply because they were not adequate to handle the job compared to other models.

DIFFERENCES BETWEEN BUYING A HOME COMPUTER AND A SMALL BUSINESS COMPUTER

Although much of the advice about buying a computer in Chapter Six, "How to Buy a Home Computer," applies to the small business person or professional, there are many specific areas where important differences arise. It's the same kind of qualitative and quantitative difference one has between having no employees or several employees. You may have the same kinds of business and decisions with each, but your surpervisory duties and paperwork are a lot more complicated with larger numbers of employees.

The first important rule for business which does not necessarily apply to home or personal use is to plan for and allow for growth when you buy your system. You probably want your business to grow and expand. So, buy a small system with a RAM that can be expanded beyond 64K, or these days, 128K; a minifloppy disk drive system that can change to a hard disk drive; an operating system that can work with a hard disk drive; a sufficient number of built-in or expansion ports (less than four is too few); and so forth, otherwise you may find in a short time that you are locked into a system you have outgrown before you have either used up its depreciation, amortized it properly, or even paid off the bank loan with which you paid for it. For example, although my system can expand to work with 12 Mb. tape drives, telecommunications, and more than one printer, it cannot share its programs with another terminal. However, my consulting business has grown to the point at which I want a second terminal on my system. Instead, I have to use the serial interface and dumb terminal emulation software on my microcomputer to jerry-rig a dumb link to the computer I use for word processing. This was not easily, efficiently, or comfortably done, and it is not satisfactory. It works, but it is not ideal.

The second rule, which also comes from my experience, is this: Always expect to make compromises in your system purchase and ultimate operations. No system is perfect and no system will perfectly do what you want it to do all the time. Be flexible and look for ways to overcome the shortcomings to get the job done. For example, to me, my system's ability to handle a very sophisticated data base management program is more important than the jerry-rigged link between the main system and the second microcomputer.

A third rule that has held me in good stead for six years has been: Lower your expectations and raise your estimates of how much time and trouble it will require to buy a good system and get it running to your satisfaction. You can expect the process to take two or three times as long as you'd originally planned or would prefer. "Bugs" or "glitches" will appear in small ways, at best. At worst, you may experience system crashes and strong resistance from your employees which can cause its own unhappy variety of difficulties. And you can also expect it to take some time for you

and your employees to learn how to use the system like experts. As I've noted, it took me about three days to get the hang of the basics of my word processing package, but four years later, I am still discovering new functions I did not know it could do.

Compare it to learning to play tennis: at first, it's hard to get the ball over the net. Then, it's hard to develop a good serve, and finally, although it's still difficult, you develop a well-rounded game. To accomplish that requires practice and a lot of it. The same holds true when learning how to use a home computer, especially in a small or at-home business or professional practice. You'll be amazed at how distractions will arise at the worst possible moment. Patience and perseverance are the watchwords if you are to get the best possible use out of a computer in your business.

Despite these difficulties, and as the problems common to any new system are overcome, you'll begin to enjoy the benefits of computerization. Despite shortcomings and foolish errors which I made and which caused some downtime, the benefits I have received far outstrip any minor problems.

In my own experience, the ratio of time and money savings—and vastly increased personal productivity and income—has more than paid for both of my computers the four years I have owned

Figure 79. Even a simple home budget management program, like the Commodore 64 Home Budget Manager, can be used for the budgeting chores of an at-home business or a professional who works at home part- or full-time. (Courtesy of Commodore Business Machines)

WHAT DO YOU DO WITH A MIND MACHINE?

them. That includes maintenance contracts, increased cost of supplies, bank loan interest, and so forth. Have I achieved perfection? No, not even close. Have I achieved greater personal and professional productivity than I ever thought possible? Yes, and I have hardly scratched the surface of the applications of my machinery for me as a consultant and author. I have only rarely used telecommunications, accessed information utilities, or used electronic mail, but I am beginning to do all of these because the available information and services have evolved until I can at last find very productive uses for them at relatively low cost or with definite time and dollar savings.

A fourth rule is: Do not automate any function unless you can foresee or estimate definite savings in time and money. As a born-again capitalist (and proud of it), and as someone who is in the information business, I have learned the high value of my time. And microcomputers, in numerous ways, can save me time and money.

A fifth rule is: Computerize where the greatest *perceived* need lies. I have long advocated adding as many applications as one can to keep a computer as busy for as many hours of the day as feasible. I still do so, but with a tempered viewpoint. A friend of mine showed me that the value of a microcomputer in a small business or to a professional is in the most important *application*. If you can buy a microcomputer to do one task that makes your business life easier and more profitable, do it for that purpose alone. You can add more applications as time passes. My computers sit idle sometimes for days at a time, and I occasionally look at them longingly wondering what someone I could hire to use them could accomplish while I was studying or doing research. But the cost in time, trouble, and money in creating new things to do was never worth the effort.

With the rapid expansion of the information utilites and the availability of an inexpensive (and I emphasize the word *inexpensive* compared to long-distance telephone calls) electronic mail service, such as MCI Mail, I have found ways to improve the quality of my research while saving money on my long-distance telephone bill. It may cost me the same amount of money to send MCI Mail messages, but my productivity will increase: I can send out more messages and obtain more information from more sources for more projects for

the same cost. Or I can reduce my cost for the same number of messages. And, I hope, I can substantially reduce my playing of "telephone tag"—making repeated telephone calls without reaching the person called or receiving a call back.

THE ECONOMICS OF BUYING A COMPUTER FOR SMALL BUSINESS

If you can find similarly useful applications for a computer, the cost becomes basically irrevelant to anyone with a small business or professional practice. You may disagree and think that spending $2,500–$5,000 or more on a computer is a major expenditure. But the economics of buying a computer are almost all in your favor. First, it is smart to borrow the money from the bank to buy the equipment. Since the loan could be secured (although a personal or unsecured loan is far preferred) by the equipment, a bank is likely to loan you the money. Of course, the loan interest will probably be tax deductible for you. If things go reasonably well, you will reap the benefits of improved productivity and increased income *before* you have paid off the bulk of the loan principal.

Second, depending on your tax situation, you can treat the purchase in one of two beneficial ways:

1) Under the 1981 Economic Recovery Act, you can *deduct* up to $5,000 of the system purchase price in the year you bought it during the 1983 tax year (Jan. 1–Dec. 31, 1983). If you are in a 50 percent tax bracket, that translates into a tax savings of $2,500 on your tax return. For the 1984 tax year, that increases to $7,500, and by 1986, the one-time deduction will be $10,000. In any case, you can buy a very powerful 256K RAM, 16-bit microcomputer with a 20 Mb. disk drive, a raft of software, a letter-quality printer, and a 1,200-baud telecommunications modem for less than $10,000. If you do some negotiating and careful shopping, you can get it for less than $7,500. Just five years ago, a similar system would have cost almost $30,000, if not more.

If there is any excess left after you take the deduction, you can use accelerated depreciation and take most of the depreciation during the first three to five years of ownership. In effect, this depreciation deduction will offset most of the money you take out of your pocket to pay back the bank loan. Thus, it may cost you less than $1.00 per hour to own your computer. Compare that to the cost of hiring part- or full-time help to do the same job. Before I bought my computer, I had hired an assistant; although my assistant left under mutually agreeable circumstances, I have not hired another one although my business has doubled in size since that time. The savings there, too, equaled more than I pay for my monthly on-site service contract. And for most microcomputers and most small businesses, on-site service is not necessary, and service costs will be much lower than mine.

2) If you do not want to take the one-time deduction, you can take a 10 percent investment tax credit and use accelerated depreciation on the difference. Thus, if you spend $10,000 on the computer, you can take a $1,000 investment tax credit. That means the $1,000 comes directly *off* the bottom line of your tax return. If you owed $2,500 before the credit, you would only owe $1,500 after taking the $1,000 credit.

The remaining $9,000 would be depreciated. Combining this method with a bank loan is another good way to obtain the benefits of automation *before* you have to repay the bulk of the loan principal.

If the good tax benefits, very great increases in personal productivity, and potentially large savings in time and money are not enough to convince you that your small business or practice can use a computer, consider the chart below. It includes numerous ways you may be able to use a microcomputer in your business.

FIFTY-EIGHT POSSIBLE FUNCTIONS FOR YOUR DESKTOP COMPUTER

Here is a list of fifty-eight common applications for a desktop computer. All of these functions are being done effectively and efficiently in tens of thousands of at-home and small businesses and professional practices today.

Financial Management
Accounts receivable
Accounts receivable reports
Collection and dunning letters
Accounts payable
Payroll and W-2 forms
Quarterly and annual tax returns
General ledger
Merchandise/warehouse inventory management
Profit and loss statements
Balance sheets
Profit-sharing and pension plan accounting
Income and expense statements
Checkbook register and check writing
Daily cash reports
Bank deposit records
Audit trails
Order entry and invoicing
Job cost and bid estimates
Project scheduling
Sales staff productivity management
Sales commission tracking and management
Managerial/executive/staff appointment schedules
Telephone bill management and analysis
Electronic mail transmission and receipt
Electronic data base access and information retrieval

Word Processing
Project proposals
Office memoranda
Mailing labels and envelope addresses
Journal and magazine articles
Research reports
Conference/meeting presentations
General correspondence
Management reports
Mail order solicitations
Public relations and advertising copy preparation
Customer service correspondence
Personnel and employee policy manuals and procedures
Electronic mail through word processing stations

Data Base Decision Making Aids
Market research and survey analysis
Research data bases and analyses
Customer/client relations
Investor relations
Literature data base storage and recall
Computerized office/personnel records

Information network interaction (CompuServe,
SOURCE, MCI Mail, BRS Ltd., Dialog, pro-
fessional data base network)
Office-to-home communications
Office-to-office communications
Office-to-field sales, service, traveling manage-
ment communications
Customer mailing list and data base manage-
ment and sales

Office and Practice Management
Employee productivity reports
Office supplies inventory
Staff vacation, sick-time, and attendance records
and analyses

Personal
Stock market portfolio management
Tax shelter analyses
Real estate evaluation
Sclf-taught programming
Computerized game playing and recreation
Home/personal budget management

Figure 80. An information manager, such as the
one displayed on the screen of the Apple IIe monitor, can keep track of large quantities of facts
and figures which used to take days or weeks to
find and manipulate. (Courtesy of Apple Computer, Inc.)

"USER-FRIENDLY" SOFTWARE

As I advised in Chapter 6, choosing the software
first is the key to a successful purchase and use of a
microcomputer. This is far more important for a
business than for someone who wants to play
games. But you will find that the path to good software is not smooth and is littered with jargon-rid-
dled potholes that can wreck your plans. Every
publication which advises how to buy computers
stresses that you must buy "easy to use," "flexible,"
and "user-friendly" software. These terms are not
rigorously defined, nor do any standards exist
which the software they are supposed to define
must meet. Software vendors wrap their products
in these terms to give them a legitimacy and appeal
they may not deserve.

Some authors have compared these terms to por-
nography: you may not be able to define it, but you
know it when you see it. Thus, like beauty, pornog-
raphy, or any other value based on human judgment, "user-friendly" is in the eye of the beholder.
Or it used to be.

To avoid falling into the user-friendly trap you
need some definitions and guidelines. These definitions and guidelines can serve the same purpose as
an art or literature appreciation course; they cannot tell you what is art, but they can give you a few
tools with which to sharpen your judgment.

First and most important, novices with no computer training or experience should be able to learn
how to apply the package under consideration with
as little personal training as possible. The package
should quickly and permanently overcome the
user's fear of computers. It should make the computer "familiar" and require as little new learning
as possible for an operator to start the machine,
load the programs, and begin working.

Second, the software should have been written
to be learned by novices. Newcomers can hardly be
expected to grasp the complexity of an internal
operating system or the full power of a system
within a few hours. I have been using the same
word processing software for four years and I still
have not explored all of its capabilities, nor do I
need to. Luckily, I didn't have to to get the program up and running. But novices may become
overwhelmed if they have to learn a lot of jargon
and procedures just to get the machine on and load
a program.

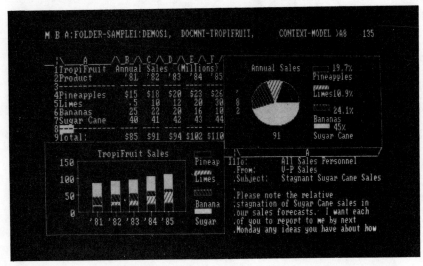

Figure 81. Integrated software, such as the Context MBA shown here, combines electronic spreadsheet, word processing, graphics, data base, and telecommunications into one package. Like many other packages, the MBA screen can be divided into as many as four "windows" through which you can see how the separate functions work together. (Courtesy of Context Management Corp.)

Third, a package should help the user with prompts and simple menus, provide feedback and encouragement, and clearly explain errors. It should also never crash just because an operator hits the wrong key. Unused function keys should be "dead," that is, they should not respond to keystrokes. A help menu or similar set of instructions should be one simple step away. An error should simply send a user back to the previous step or menu.

Fourth, for experienced users, the same features which make a package easy to learn can be annoying and inefficient. Experienced users soon know the procedures and want to avoid repetitious menus and prompts. So, the software should allow experienced users to overrride the prompts and menus they don't want. However, many so-called user-friendly packages do not allow experienced users to avoid the features that were designed to help them in the beginning. Well-designed packages will include functions such as "end menu" which gets rid of an on-screen menu, but allows it to be recalled with a keystroke or two.

And it will provide utilities experienced users can call up as needed, such as file copying and disk copying routines, printing facilities, format alterations, and so on.

Fifth, it should combine both a menu structure and a command structure which novices and experienced users both find useful. A menu structure gives a user a list of choices, usually numbered one through nine or ten, and a main or introductory menu leads a user to a second, third, fourth menu,

and so forth. A command structure gives a list of commands with the proper keystroke required to execute each.

It is essential that these keystrokes relate directly to the name of the function, such as H for Help, I for Insert, W for Write, E for Edit, and S for Save. In complex programs, the commands may have two letters, but they should still relate to the command: EM for End Menu, DE for Delete or Destroy a file or document, RM for Remove a disk, or CA for Catalog the contents of a disk. You will be surprised at how often software violates this seemingly simple, yet elegant, principle.

Sixth, the user's manual, documentation, and reference cards provided with a package should be written so users who read at a high school level can read them and understand them. Of course, they should not be simplistic, nor full of jargon (without clear definitions and explanations). The contents should be marked clearly and the procedures should be discussed in a logical step-by-step fashion. The manuals should have both tables of contents and indices, and error messages should be discussed in great detail. Rare but very helpful features are referrals from one page or section to another page or section where more explanation or definitions can be found.

Seventh, self-teaching programs or tutorials should be included in the package itself, and novices should be able to learn how to use the system through the on-screen tutorials without referring to the manuals. One experienced software publisher has remarked, "No one ever reads the manual anyway, so we have to provide self-teaching programs in a package if they are going to learn how to use our products."

Eighth, the program should provide a menu-based function that allows anyone to set up (also called configure) printers, printing formats, communications devices, and other peripherals as an out-of-the-way utility program. The configuration, once completed and stored on disk, should work automatically with no more operator intervention.

Ninth, the whole mess must work together in a consistently logical fashion. Putting these often contradictory elements together can result in chaos, but a consistent design well executed will practically lead a user through its operations by itself. Essentially, if its organization makes sense, users will find it friendly.

Unfortunately, such well-designed programs are hard to find. Achieving true user-friendliness requires many programming trade-offs and takes up a lot of internal memory. As the new computers provide more internal memory at a lower per-character cost, programmers will have enough room to easily provide all of these features in the next generation of software. You can find such well-designed and executed software today, but you have to look a little harder for it.

FOUR-STEP PURCHASING PROCESS

If you have determined the most important function you want to automate and conducted a thorough analysis of your computer budget and organization, then you can purchase software in a four-step process: comparison, manual evaluation, service and support evaluation, and operation evaluation.

First, draw up two lists, one with all of the features and capabilities you require, and a second with all of the features and functions you *want*. These are called, in purchase negotiations, "must" lists and "wish" lists. Then compare your listed features to those features and functions given in the software vendor's literature. (As you draw up your list, write or call all available software vendors and ask for their complete descriptive literature.) Making this initial comparison will quickly eliminate all packages clearly unsuitable for your requirements. Most packages will be eliminated because their capacities are too small, or they do

not operate on a hard disk drive, or they do not provide information on-line, or similar reasons.

Second, study the user's manuals for the five programs which best fit your requirements. Some companies may loan manuals to you for your appraisal, but expect to pay $20 to $60 for manuals. The manual fee is usually refunded in the purchase price if you buy the software. Do not skip this step although spending $200 on manuals may be half the cost of the entire package. The expenditure will be meaningless after you begin to use the *proper system for you* and accumulate savings of time and money.

Again, good manuals and documentation are crucial. A badly organized and amateurish manual almost always signals a badly organized program. A good manual will be organized along the lines of the software itself. It should proceed step by step from simple, introductory procedures through the more difficult ones.

Next, a good manual will have either a tear-out reference card, or a command summary, or both. The reference card should briefly explain all commands and procedures, and a command summary should discuss all commands in detail and how they relate to each other.

The organization of a good manual will follow these guidelines:

- A complete table of contents.
- An introduction and overview.
- Self-teaching lessons or tutorials beginning with the simple steps in plain English and working through the advanced operations.
- The command summary, including common utilities, such as copy, print, and disk copy, and configurations.
- Technical details for programmers who want to modify the program.
- Error messages or problem-solving section.
- A complete index.

Of course, any manual can have these parts and still be poor. So, make sure your staff can easily understand what the manual says. Make sure the manual is written in correct English and is printed with an attractive, yet legible layout.

Software support is the next area you must investigate. High-quality software support is indicated by six characteristics:

Figure 82. A "friendly" personal computer like the Hewlett-Packard HP-150 with a touch-sensitive screen can make running a small business or working at home more enjoyable and profitable than ever before. (Courtesy of Hewlett-Packard Corp.)

- An 800 number or free hot line for free or low-cost technical support.

- A minimum ninety-day warranty with a six-month or one-year warranty far preferable.

- Inexpensive or free copies of the program disk once you have invested for your initial one. (Or else you could be required to buy a whole new program just because your son spilled his hot chocolate on one you had inadvertently left on the kitchen table.)

- Dealer training for local support of popular business packages, such as VisiCalc, Lotus 1-2-3, and others.

- Free or inexpensive program updates.

- On-site service as an option for multi-user systems.

Finally, you should test drive the software using real documents and information for your business in the way you use it now. Do *not* be persuaded that you can or want to turn the way you do business around 180 degrees for the benefit of computerizing. You may have to change some procedures and adapt to the system, but a good package should not cause severe upheaval or trauma to im-

plement in your operation. If it does, there are two possibilities: the package is not useful, or your business operations are a mess. If the latter, follow my final rule: Straighten out your messy business before you buy a computer

Remember one of the few very useful pieces of computer jargon: **GIGO: Garbage In, Garbage Out.** If you put poor or inaccurate information into a computer, that is exactly what you get out of it.

If you have followed this procedure in obtaining the software, and are satisfied, it is likely most of your hardware purchase problem will be solved, too. You will have automatically eliminated 95 percent of the available computers because the software probably just will not run on them. Choosing them among the remaining 5 percent should come down to key hardware factors:

- *Expandability.* Can you add terminals, more memory, or a hard disk to the existing CPU?

- *Human factors,* also called ergonomics. This concerns whether the hardware is pleasing and comfortable to use. Is the video display easy on the eyes? Does the terminal layout strain your hands, neck, shoulders, or back? Is the printer easy to operate, is the paper easy to load, are the printer ribbons easy to install, does it run quietly? Are the disk drives located within easy reach? As one who sits at a fairly uncomfortable keyboard and terminal for six hours at a stretch, I can tell you from experience that comfort is crucial to your enjoyment and productivity.

- *Excellent response times under peak load conditions.* Although five computers may have the same microprocessor, they will handle heavy-duty processing at different speeds because of the way the operating system handles disk drives and internal operations. Make sure the computer you buy retains good processing times even when floppy disks and RAMs are almost full, and when you are continuously entering and processing large amounts of information, such as during a monthly billing cycle.

- *Printer speed.* Is it fast enough to handle peak loads to your satisfaction? A slow printer can delay mailing of your invoices a day or two, or cause your mailing list solicitation process to bog down.

Using these steps and ideas will take you a long way toward the most productive and beneficial use of a microcomputer in your business.

CHAPTER 15
The Thinking Computer of the Future

Many people have written science fiction stories or futuristic anecdotes about what the home computer will be like twenty or thirty years from now. One of my favorites, written in 1979 by a very famous science fiction writer for a computer company's annual report, described the portable home computer of the year 2025: the computer was the size of today's pocket calculator; it communicated with a built-in modem or digital transmission link through a worldwide satellite network with both voice and data links. With voice recognition, the computer spoke to the business traveler using it. The computer kept track of the traveler's schedules, automatically sent memos and messages, retrieved data and processed it through spreadsheets and a data base manager, and similar tasks.

With the exception of voice recognition, everything the fictitious portable home computer of the year 2025 was supposed to do can be done now—though in somewhat cruder fashion—with the real briefcase computers of today. And today's briefcase computers are more versatile than fiction in that they can handle regular-sized paper printouts and produce graphic black-and-white (and soon color) charts and graphs, and they have built-in telephones for voice calls.

It will not be long—at most five years—before the voice recognition part of the fictitious 2025 computers comes true as well. So, the title of this chapter is somewhat misleading; as a marketing consultant in the microcomputer industry, part of my work is to make predictions about the directions in which the industry is headed. So, I should not feel hesitant to do so, but I do. No one really can accurately predict the future of how home computers will evolve. A lot of assumptions which many very bright people made in the late 1970s simply have not happened. For example, it was thought that using micros to control home appliances and energy systems would be a very popular application. It has simply not happened because the energy crisis subsided and the home control systems simply did not fall in price far enough to offset the public's lackadaisical attitude toward energy consumption. On the other hand, in business and industry, microprocessor-controlled energy management has made great strides and is one of the major reasons this country's use of energy has remained stable or dropped since the oil price shocks of 1973 and 1979.

I, with many others, thought the Japanese would be on their way to dominating the market for home computers by 1985. But, in fact, they have had little impact so far. However, they have dominated certain portions of the market: dot matrix and correspondence-quality printers; color video monitors; hand-held electronic games; intelligent calculators; and briefcase-sized and pocket computers. And the three most popular computers are built by Japanese companies: Kyocera builds the NEC and Radio Shack models, Epson builds its own HX-20, and Sharp builds its own briefcase computer and both its own and some of Radio Shack's pocket computers. But it took much longer than expected for the Japanese to decide on the software standard they have just begun to follow.

And most of us were wrong about whether U.S. manufacturers would be forced to adopt a standard operating system by 1985. De facto standards have emerged because of the IBM PC and MS-DOS, but they have not been formally accepted. In the near future, however, it appears the Japanese proclivity for building inexpensive, attractive, compact, and useful electronic devices will extend to home computers. Timex Computer Corporation's early 1984 decision to drop out of the market was a strong indicator of how rapidly the Japanese can be expected to dominate the market for under $500 home computers.

It appears that Apple and IBM have abandoned any hope of competing in that marketplace. Only Commodore and Coleco appear able to continue in the low-end market for the near (one to two years) future—and don't hold me to that guesstimate. Coleco is known for dropping like hot potatoes products whose sales turn sour, and Commodore can change its mind quickly as well.

The prediction business is treacherous and all too often inclined to portray the future as a new and magical utopia. Look at what the experts of the future predicted at the 1939 World's Fair: they predicted super airways filled with rocket-powered people transporters the size of an automobile by the year 1989. And even science fiction writers, whose business it is to point technological directions, have missed the most important developments of the century: rocketry, nuclear bombs, digital computers, communications satellites, and even the semiconductor chip—the heart of all microcomputers and processors. With all of these caveats under my belt, I will still venture to poke a bit at the future. I do it acknowledging that we all grope in the dark, and I will confine my comments to developments I know are in the laboratories today and which could become consumer products during the next five to ten years from now. And keep in the back of your mind how the future always seems to do what people want it to do. Who

in 1951 would have thought that, in 1984, the average family would watch seven hours of television a day, and that one of the most popular TV programs in the world would be reruns of that then-new show with that Cuban bandleader and funny redhead, "I Love Lucy"?

Voice Recognition

Computers that can easily "understand" anyone's normal speaking voice—called *continuous speech recognition*—have baffled the experts for almost twenty years. Finally, they are slowly, but surely getting there. Today, for less than $500, you can buy voice peripherals for home computers that can understand dozens of words spoken by the same person. I suspect a major breakthrough in continuous voice recognition during the next several years with inexpensive voice-based home computers before 1990. One new executive workstation by Santa Barbara Development Laboratories, for example, does not have a keyboard at all, but uses voice recognition and touch-sensitive keyboards as the only input devices.

Voice recognition may play an important part in home security systems: as in *Star Trek,* you program the computer to release locked doors only if it recognizes your voice patterns or your family's. International Resource Development has reported for several years that IBM has developed an experimental voice-activated typewriter, which, I suspect, will eventually be released as a voice-activated workstation or automated factory device.

Digital Telephone Networks

AT&T and all of the telephone operating companies plan to have 97 percent of the country converted to all-digital telephone switching systems by 1990. That will mean the end of the need for communications modems, and every home computer will be able to communicate with every other computer at the touch of a button and with some built-in software. In fact, the first inexpensive *integrated voice/data terminals* with microcomputer functions are being produced now. These *IVDTs* combine the functions of telephone, intelligent terminal, and microcomputer into a small desktop unit. The Convergent WorkSlate and Xerox 1810 portable computer are crude examples of very sophisticated technology now being sold to major corporations around the country. The price for these IVDTs now ranges from as low as $500 to as high as $2,-500, and most include built-in applications such as calculators, spreadsheets, communications with any mainframe computer, personal information data base, and memo writing word processing.

Within five years, almost every home computer will be an IVDT with a built-in speakerphone.

With all-digital telephone networks, communicating with a home computer through a satellite will happen as a matter of course, and you will not know how you are making a connection between computers. By 1988, at least twenty-five more communications satellites will be launched for voice, data, and combined communications purposes.

I suspect that with the Space Shuttle flights, AT&T, IBM, or a consortium of industrial giants will build a series of huge, football field-sized communications satellites that will allow use of wristwatch-sized telephones for everyone. The new cellular mobile telephone networks have begun to put a telephone in every car within reach of everyone in the middle class. You will also be able to use that carphone for data communications. The mobile phones already for sale around the country include intelligent functions, such as 16-number memory, automatic redialing and the like. It is a very small step to making that carphone into a microcomputer/telephone.

The Trend Toward "Tiny" Continues

As you have seen, the trend toward miniaturization of computers is already in full swing and will continue to its logical vanishing point: wristwatch telecomputers, car computers, and one-inch floppy and hard disks are all fairly inevitable within five years. Whether they will become generally accepted, no one knows. It is easy to assume that there will be a Sony ComputerMan with a television, radio, telephone, and microcomputer in your future.

Just as more than 80 million people now use pocket calculators the size of a credit card, many more than that will soon use pocket micros the size of a credit card for a variety of school, business, and personal tasks.

Home Controls

Although most of us were wrong about the impact of home computer controlled houses, the technology has been developed to do this. I believe that during the next big energy scare, probably in the late 1980s, computerized home control systems will sell very rapidly. You will not have to put new plugs into your outlets or buy new appliances. The computer will be built into new homes and will work with microprocessors implanted as intelligent oil burners, water heaters, solar energy and hot water systems, electric utility meters, and so forth. The construction and utility industries are very conservative, and these changes will come slowly. They will filter from the top down—from large, expensive homes and apartment complexes to middle-class homes to tract houses. They will be inexpensive and unobtrusive, and you won't normally know they are even there.

Videotex

The future of videotex in this country at this time is very shaky. I have predicted, with others, that by 1992 some 7 to 9 million homes will have two-way information services, but progress toward this has been very slow. Teletext services—one-way information services—seem to be falling by the wayside as Time, Inc., dropped a planned service after spending $30 million, and CBS and NBC, both of which obtained permission to establish teletext services, had not done anything about them a year later.

The first commercial consumer videotex services have begun, but acceptance is slow in coming. Cable companies were thought to be the ones to lead the videotex thrust, but most cable companies do not have the money to invest, and most cable systems do not have two-way capability. The major two-way cable TV systems will not be in place before 1988 when huge systems in New York, Boston, and other major cities will finally be in place, but acceptance will be gradual after that.

My own studies of videotex show me that the companies simply are not offering the kinds of services people find useful or entertaining. CBS tested an electronic "Woman's Day" type of videotex service in its 1982-83 test in New Jersey. That approach did not impress anyone. It appears to me that videotex will succeed with information that is very time-sensitive or cannot be *easily* obtained anywhere else. News and weather reports will not suffice because that information is rapidly and constantly available: radio stations give almost constant local weather reports, television makes the news much more entertaining, and a newspaper gives the details of the news in a cheaper and more readable—and portable—fashion. On the other hand, weather reports for travelers, pilots, and truck drivers; up-to-the-second news flashes for professionals; and information not obtainable except by a laborious search through old magazines or libraries will have definite appeal.

The information must also be given free or very cheaply and must be supported by advertising. The crude videotex terminals in use now will also have to give way to sleek, portable, attractive home terminals. AT&T, IBM, Radio Shack, and the Japanese appear smart enough to eventually figure all of this out for themselves. But of the information providers, including CBS, Inc., NBC, Time-Life, Dow Jones, Warner Communications, ABC, and so forth, none has yet figured out what people would use videotex to do in real life, but only in unrealistic tests. I tend to believe that Dow Jones, Meredith Publishing, and Cox Cable Communications will be among the first to find the right mix of services and information.

I feel a first major use would be mail-order advertising and sales, and companies, such as L.L. Bean, Horchow's, Fingerhut, Neiman Marcus, Sears, Montgomery Ward, and Book-of-the-Month Club, would push the systems. But the usual technological chicken-and-egg question loomed large in 1984: there are no terminals in homes, so why start and buy advertising in a videotex service? It is clear to me, anyway, that videotex will have to follow the footsteps of the telephone company. You will have to give people the terminal for a small monthly charge (more than $2 is too much), and give them a lot of things to do with the system simply by pressing a few buttons. Only a company the size of AT&T or IBM, or groups of conglomerates, can afford to finance this system on a national basis. Thus, videotex will first be offered through the telephone lines in a few major cities, and it will spread through other cities.

As quickly as possible, too, each videotex network should hook up to other national data bases as easily as dialing a long-distance telephone number. MCI could end up with something like that with MCI Mail if the electronic mail portion makes any money. Then, MCI could expand the available services beyond mail and Dow Jones. People have very diverse interests and they want easy ways to pursue those interests and will do so through telecommunications if the price is right (that is, low) and the benefit high, even if the perceived benefit is simply entertainment.

Optical Laser Video Disc

Videotex information services will be threatened by the optical laser video disc. The video disc looks like an aluminum record sealed in clear plastic, with digital impulses substituted for audio impulses. The consumer video disc for movies sold very poorly compared to expectations during the early 1980s. But in the laboratories, major strides have been made in using the optical laser video disc for digital information storage. And the capacities are staggering: 1.2 *billion* bytes on each side of one video disc. That's enough to store all the text of any encyclopedia series on one side of one disc. (Note the use of video *disc* and floppy *disk;* these are de facto industry standard spellings.)

Of course, with video disc, you can mix digital storage with video storage on the same disk, and create video encyclopedias. Imagine a 5-minute video sequence showing and discussing the life of the alligator, and then a lengthy article filling in the details after the video. Of course, you could even print out the article for future reference. You can access any article or listing in any video data base as rapidly as you can access data on a mini-floppy disk, if not faster.

The implications for data storage—replacing hard disk drives and the huge tape and disk storage systems for the world's mainframes, and substituting optical laser disc boxes the size of an Apple IIe computer—are mind-boggling. Yet, both the video encyclopedia and the optical laser disc as computer storage devices are already realities, just a few months or a year from being commercial products.

Electronic Mail Networks and Electronic Funds Transfers

MCI Mail is the first of what must become numerous electronic mail networks for consumers. AT&T must make some response to this challenge to its bread-and-butter phone service, or face a desperate future. The U.S. Postal Service also faces a dismal future, as electronic mail and electronic funds transfers (in the shape of home banking) begin to reduce the volume of first class mail, the USPS's own bread and butter. Now that sending digital bits and bytes through the telephone system is almost as cheap as, or in business, already cheaper than, sending a first-class typed or printed letter, or placing a voice telephone call, it will dawn on businesses and consumers to start using them. Acceptance is slow, but the systems are almost in place, and the critical mass of public approval is being reached.

You can expect AT&T to eventually rise to the challenge and introduce an electronic mail network as easily accessible as the long-distance network. Dial 2 instead of 1 to make an electronic mail connection, or something like that. And you can hope that, however unlikely it is, the Postal Service cannot convince Congress to save its bacon at our expense. The whole trend of the early 1980s has been for Congress to force the USPS to survive on its own and compete with the delivery services for business. Electronic mail is a direct threat to the USPS's first-class mail business, and so far, Congress has not listened to its entreaties to prevent it. It would seem that Congress could not prevent electronic mail networks if it tried, so these electronic alternatives will grow haltingly, but eventually with great impact on your daily life. Look for AT&T to take major steps toward all of these electronic alternatives after 1985 as it prepares to enter the information business it is prohibited from actually entering until 1990.

These are just a handful of the possibilities that may occur during the next *five* years. I would not be so foolish as to speculate on the situation in 1995, much less 2025. But one thing is for certain: in extraordinary ways no one has yet thought of, the home computer will help you live your life more easily, more pleasurably, more intelligently, and with greater prosperity than ever before.

Thirty-Two Questions to Ask When Buying Software and Hardware

SEVENTEEN QUESTIONS ABOUT MICROCOMPUTER SOFTWARE

These seventeen questions will serve as guideposts along the path to selecting the right software for your business.

1. How long has the package been in use in actual businesses? How many times has it been updated? If a package is a year or two old and has been implemented in numerous businesses, you can be fairly sure no serious problems or bugs remain.

2. With this software, can the same date be entered once and used a number of ways? Determine whether an accounts receivable package can share its information with a general ledger package, or data base management package? If not and you plan to add these functions during the next three to five years (the average lifetime of a system), think again.

3. What is the ultimate capacity of the software, its upward limitations on volume and function? Is it adequate for your anticipated growth?

4. Do the software manuals and documentation meet the standards outlined in Chapters 6 and 14?

5. During interviews with the vendor, how often did he use vague phrases of reassurance when confronted with what you consider a serious concern? If more than once, look elsewhere.

6. What are the warranties, money-back guarantees, and similar vendor commitments to its products?

7. Is the package menu-driven, and if so, can experienced users take advantage of a command structure? How well does the package meet the user-friendly standards described above?

8. How many levels of support does the vendor provide? Free of charge? For a monthly or annual maintenance fee?

9. How does the vendor handle package enhancements or upgrades? Free of charge? Small update fee? Trade-in allowance? Or full charge?

10. Is the package programmed in modules which can be added in stages? Are separate packages available which can be integrated—that is, easily swap information among applications—with your primary function? Does the package already include major integrated functions, such as Context MBA, Lotus 1-2-3, or a host of others?

11. Does the software store information with "virtual memory"? *Virtual memory* means that information entered into the computer is automatically stored on a disk storage device. Most small computers first store information in a temporary internal memory (RAM). But this temporary memory can be small and fill up quickly. Then, users must frequently save data on a disk to empty the temporary memory so it can accept more information. Virtual memory, on the other hand, is limited only to the amount of data a disk can store. For example, in a 48K computer, a regular package may store only 16,000 characters at a time, but with virtual memory, the same computer can store ten or twenty times that much information at one time. You will find that virtual memory for microcomputer software is hard to come by, but during the next several years, as the available storage and RAM increase to four or eight times their current sizes, that virtual memory will become a standard feature of quality software.

12. Does the software allow "spooling," or simultaneous printing and data entry? Add-on devices are now available for the popular personal computers which allow spooling. This is a significant timesaver if a staff member can work at the computer at the same time it is printing out a month's worth of bills or insurance forms.

13. Will the software work with a hard disk? Most older business packages will not work with a hard disk without significant modifications, but almost all major packages have hard-disk versions or updates available with more in the future. With almost all desktop computers sold with hard disks as standard equipment in the near future, all software will have this feature. But you are in a transitional period now, so be careful. With what kinds of hard disks will the software run? Many packages only work with certain hard disks, limiting your choice of hardware.

14. What kind of printer is required? Does the software allow one to use many types of printers, or does it limit the choice to a few? Does it allow the user to easily modify the printer configuration without the vendor's, dealer's, or a programmer's help?

15. Can the software adapt to changes in the size and form of your account numbers, the number of clients, or especially changes in your order forms and required reports? Positive answers to these questions are essential and finding them will probably be rare.

16. How does the software handle security? Through the operating system? With easy-to-change passwords? How many levels of security are there? Two, three, or more?

17. Does the software provide "friendly" disaster recovery techniques and routines. Never think that it won't happen to you because it will, and at the worst possible time.

FIFTEEN QUESTIONS ABOUT MICROCOMPUTER HARDWARE

1. How many peripheral ports does the central processing unit have? Four is a minimum, eight or more is good.

2. Is the system open-ended, that is, are their any upper limits to the number of accounts, files, records, and so on the system can process?

3. Can floppy disks be replaced or supplemented with a hard disk drive without major internal or software modifications?

4. Are there any upper capacity limits to the size of hard disk drive the CPU can handle?

5. What are the upper limits of the size of RAM the CPU can operate? 64K, 128K, 256K, 512K, 640K, 768K, 896K, 1 megabyte or more?

6. How much does the system response time degradate when the system is operating at peak capacity?

7. Is the system large enough—in total capacity, internal memory, printer speed, and such—to process your applications at peak loads?

8. Does the system expand in a modular fashion and can it accommodate all of the growth you expect in your practice during the next three to five years?

9. How reliable is the hardware? Can the vendor give you test results, published reports, or user testimonials concerning the reliability of any little-known equipment? What is its mean time between breakdowns and similar measurements of performance?

10. Is the hardware "ergonomically" designed to be comfortable and safe for users?

11. Can you obtain all of the hardware from one vendor at reasonable prices compared to prices others are charging?

12. What is the reputation and financial status of the hardware manufacturers? Can you find out who originally produced each piece of equipment for the company whose name is on the computer?

13. What is the preferred and available method of permanent, backup, or archival storage?

14. Does the hardware require any special environmental considerations, such as power supplies, electrical outlets, and surge protectors?

15. Does the software you choose limit you to only one or at most a few choices of hardware? Can you accept those limitations?

Of course, these are just a few of the possible questions you may want to ask as you purchase a microcomputer. Use these as a starting point for your own list before you begin your search.

APPENDIX B

More Than 2,500 Computer Programs

Given in this appendix are listings of more than 2,500 computer programs available for various home, personal, and desktop computers, and specific operating systems. Program names may be repeated because they run on different machines or operating systems. This is not to show favor to these software packages, but to reflect their wide availability for various microcomputers. This organization will also make your task much easier when you look for software to use on the computer you want to buy or have recently purchased. Note also that these lists are not meant to be exhaustive because dozens of new packages are introduced and new software companies go into business each week. They are meant to serve as an aid in your search for software.

Quality Software
6660 Reseda Blvd.
Suite 105
Reseda, CA 91335

Programs for the Atari 400/Atari 800 Computers

CATEGORY: UTILITIES

QS Forth
Assembler
6502 Disassembler
Character Magic

CATEGORY: GAMES

Fastgammon
Name That Song
Starbase Hyperion

Tari Trek II
Combat Zone
Tank Trap
QS Reversi
Ali Baba

Programs for the Apple II Computer

CATEGORY: UTILITIES

Bag of Tricks
Linker
Cross-ref

CATEGORY: ADVENTURE

Ali Baba
Fracas
Beneath Apple Manor

CATEGORY: GAMES

Meteoroids in Space
Fastgammon
Battleship Commander
QS Reversi
Astro-Apple
Babble

CATEGORY: BUSINESS

GBS
Spellwright
US Mail
Satellite Tracking

Broderbund Software, Inc.
Entertainment Software Division
1938 Fourth Street
San Rafael, CA 94901

*Programs for the Apple II or II+
Computer*

CATEGORY: BUSINESS

Payroll
General Ledger with Payables
Accounts Receivable

CATEGORY: HOME

Bank Street Writer Word
   Processor

CATEGORY: GAMES

Seafox
Deadly Secrets: Adventure #1
Serpentine
Choplifter
Arcade Machine
Labyrinth
Dueling Digits
Star Blazer
Track Attack
David's Midnight Magic
Apple Panic
Red Alert
Genetic Drift
Space Quarks
Galactic Empire
Galactic Trader
Galactic Revolution
Tawala's Last Redoubt
Galaxy Wars

*Programs for the Atari 400/Atari
800 Computers*

CATEGORY: GAMES

Genetic Drift
Apple Panic
Choplifter
Labyrinth
David's Midnight Magic
Star Blazer
Stellar Shuttle
Track Attack
Seafox
Serpentine

*Programs for the TRS-80
Computers*

CATEGORY: GAMES

Galactic Empire
Galactic Trader
Galactic Revolution

**EPYX/Automated Simulations
1043 Kiel Court
Sunnyvale, CA 94086**

CATEGORY: GAMES

Alien Garden (for Atari 400/800)
PlatterMania (for Atari 400/800)
Monster Maze (for Apple,
   TRS-80, Atari 400/800,
   Commodore VIC 20)
King Arthur's Heir (for Atari
   400/800 with Disk 32K)
Escape from Vulcan's Isle (for
   Atari 400/800 with Disk 32K)
Crypt of the Undead (for the
   Atari 400/800 with Disk 32K)
The Nightmare (for the Atari
   400/800 with Disk 32K)
Temple of Apshai (for the Apple,
   TRS-80, Atari 400/800, IBM)
Upper Reaches of Apshai (for the
   Apple, TRS-80, Atari 400/800,
   and IBM PC)
Curse of Ra (for the Apple,
   TRS-80, Atari 400/800, IBM)
Hellfire Warrior (for the Apple,
   TRS-80, Atari 400/800)
Danger in Drindisti (for the
   Apple, TRS-80, Atari 400/800)
The Keys of Acheron (for the
   Apple, TRS-80, Atari 400/800)
Dragon's Eye (for the Apple,
   Atari 400/800 with Disk 32K,
   Commodore)
StarFleet Orion (Commodore)
Sword of Fargoal (Commodore)
The Datestones of Ryn (for the
   Apple, TRS-80, Atari 400/800)
Morloc's Tower (for the Apple,
   TRS-80, Atari 400/800)
Sorcerer of Siva (for the Apple,
   TRS-80)
Crush, Crumble & Chomp! (for
   Apple, TRS-80, Atari 400/800,
   Commodore VIC 20)
Star Warrior (for the Apple,
   TRS-80, Atari 400/800)
Rescue at Rigel (for the Apple,
   TRS-80, Atari 400/800,
   Commodore)
Ricochet (for the Apple, TRS-80,
   Atari 400/800, Commodore)
New World (for the Apple,
   TRS-80)

Jabbertalky (for the Apple,
   TRS-80, IBM)
Oil Barons (for the Apple, IBM)
Invasion Orion (for the Apple,
   TRS-80, Atari 400/800)
Armor Assault (for the Atari
   400/800 Disk 32K)
Tuesday Morning Quarterback
   (for the Apple, TRS-80)
FORE! (for the Apple)
3-Pack (Commodore)

**Strategic Simulations, Inc.
465 Fairchild Drive
Suite 108
Mountian View, CA 94043**

*Programs for the Apple II+, IIe,
III Computer*

CATEGORY: GAMES

Cytron Masters
Galactic Gladiators
The Cosmic Balance
S.E.U.I.S.
GuadalCanal Campaign
Computer Air Combat
Torpedo Fire
Napoleon's Campaigns: 1813 &
   1815
The Road to Gettysburg
Computer Bismarck
Operation Apocalypse
Southern Command
The Warp Factor
Pursuit of the Graf Spee
Computer Conflict
The Shattered Alliance
The Battle of Shiloh
The Battle of the Bulge: Tigers in
   the Snow

CATEGORY: SPORTS SIMULATIONS

Computer Quarterback
Computer Baseball

CATEGORY: SIMULATIONS

Cartels & Cutthroats
President Elect

*Programs for the TRS-80
Computer*

CATEGORY: GAMES

The Battle of Shiloh
The Battle of the Bulge: Tigers in
the Snow

*Programs for the Atari 400/800
Computer*

CATEGORY: GAMES

The Battle of Shiloh
The Shattered Alliance
The Battle of the Bulge: Tigers in
the Snow

*Programs for the IBM PC
Computer*

CATEGORY: GAMES

The Warp Factor

Sirius Software, Inc.
10364 Rockingham Drive
Sacramento, CA 95827

*Programs for the Apple II+ or IIe
Computer*

CATEGORY: GAMES

Lemmings
Borg
Phantoms Five
Pulsar II
Orbitron
Gorgon
Epoch
Cops and Robbers
Dark Forest
Hadron
Twerps
Computer Foosball
Jellyfish
Bandits
Fly Wars
E-Z Draw 3.3
Space Eggs
Autobahn
Gamma Goblins
Sneakers
Pascal Graphics Editor
Outpost
Beer Run
Joyport
Snake Byte

Audex
Kabul Spy
Minotaur
Cyclod

*Programs for the IBM Personal
Computer*

CATEGORY: GAMES

Call to Arms

Muse Software
347 North Charles Street
Baltimore, MD 21201

*Programs for the Apple II+ or IIe
Computers*

CATEGORY: WORD PROCESSING

Super-Text 40/80 Column Word
Processor
Super-Text 40/56/70 Column
Word Processor

CATEGORY: BUSINESS
    APPLICATIONS

Form Letter Module
Data Plot
The Address Book

CATEGORY: EDUCATIONAL

Know Your Apple
U-Draw II
Appilot II Edu-Disk
The Elementary Math Edu-Disk

CATEGORY: EDUCATIONAL GAMES

The Voice
Robotwar

CATEGORY: GAMES

ABM
Castle Wolfenstein
Firebug
Frazzle
The Cube Solution
The Best of Muse

Artworx
150 North Main Street
Fairport, NY 14450

CATEGORY: EDUCATIONAL GAMES

Hodge Podge (for the Atari,
Apple)
Teacher's Pet (for the Atari,
Apple, TRS-80, PET, North
Star, and CP/M-M-BASIC)

CATEGORY: UTILITIES

Drawpic (Atari)
A Text Display Device (Atari)

CATEGORY: BUSINESS

Mail List (for the Atari, Apple,
and North Star)

CATEGORY: GAMES

PM Editor (Atari)
Rocket Raiders (Atari)
Forest Fire! (Atari)
Giant Slalom (Atari)
The Predictor (Apple, Atari,
TRS-80, North Star, and
CP/M-M-BASIC)
Pilot (Atari)
The Vaults of Zurich (Atari,
Commodore)
Bridge 2.0 (Atari, Apple, TRS-80,
Commodore, North Star, and
CP/M-M-BASIC)
Encounter at Questar IV (Atari)
Hazard Run (Atari)
Beta Fighter (Atari)

Microcomputer Games
A Division of The Avalon Hill
Game Company
4517 Harford Road
Baltimore, MD 21214

CATEGORY: GAMES

Draw Poker (Atari 400/800,
TRS-80, Apple II, Commodore,
IBM)
Knockout (Atari 400/800)
RoadRacer (Atari 400/800,
Commodore)
Bowler (Atari 400/800,
Commodore)
ShootOut at the OK Galaxy
(Atari 400/800, TRS-80, Apple
II, Commodore)
Bomber Attack (Atari 400/800,
Apple II, Commodore)

Galaxy (Atari 400/800, TRS-80, Apple II, Commodore, IBM PC)

Voyager I (TRS-80, Atari 400/800, Apple II, Commodore, IBM PC)

Computer Stocks & Bonds (TRS-80, Commodore, Atari 400/800, Apple II, IBM PC)

Midway Campaign (TRS-80, Apple II, Commodore, Atari 400/800, IBM PC)

Computer Foreign Exchange (TRS-80)

Empire of the Overmind (Apple II, TRS-80, Atari 400/800)

Controller (Atari 400/800, Apple II)

Tanktics (Apple II, TRS-80, Commodore, Atari 400/800)

Dnieper River Line (Apple II, TRS-80, Commodore, Atari 400/800)

Guns for Fort Defiance (TRS-80, Commodore, Atari 400/800, Apple II)

Computer Football Strategy (TRS-80, IBM)

Computer Baseball Strategy (Atari 400/800, Apple II, Commodore, TRS-80)

Tank Arcade (Commodore, TRS-80, Atari 400/800)

Lords of Karma (Apple II, Commodore, Atari 400/800, TRS-80)

Computer Statistics Pro Baseball (TRS-80, Apple II)

B-1 Nuclear Bomber (TRS-80, Apple II, Commodore, Atari 400/800, IBM)

North Atlantic Convoy Raider (TRS-80, Apple II, Commodore, Atari 400/800)

Conflict 2500 (Apple II, TRS-80, Commodore, Atari 400/800)

Planet Miners (Apple II, TRS-80, Commodore, Atari 400/800)

Nukewar (Atari 400/800, Apple II, TRS-80, Commodore)

Acquire (Atari 400/800, Apple II, TRS-80, Commodore)

Legionnaire (Atari 400/800)

Andromeda Conquest (Apple II, TRS-80, Commodore, Atari 400/800, IBM PC)

Telengard (Atari 400/800, Apple II, TRS-80, Commodore)

G. F. S. Sorceress (Atari 400/800, Apple II, TRS-80)

Moon Patrol (Atari 400/800)

V.C. (TRS-80, Atari 400/800, Apple II)

ATARI
Home Computer Division
P.O. Box 50047
San Jose, CA 95150

CATEGORY: HOME EDUCATION

Atari Speed Reading
Scram
Music Composer
My First Alphabet
Conversational French, German, Spanish, Italian
Energy Czar
Kingdom
Touch Typing
An Invitation to Programming 1: Fundamentals of Programming
An Invitation to Programming 2: Writing Programs One and Two
An Invitation to Programming 3: Sound and Graphics
States & Capitals and European Countries & Capitals
Hangman

CATEGORY: HOME OFFICE

Personal Financial Management System
TeleLink I
TeleLink II
The Communicator I Kit
Investment Analysis Series
Bond Analysis
Stock Analysis
Mortgage & Loan Analysis
Stock Charting
The Bookkeeper
Mailing List
Graph It
Statistics I
Atari Word Processor
The Home Filing Manager

CATEGORY: HOME ENTERTAINMENT

Space Invaders
BlackJack
Basketball
Super Breakout
Missile Command
Asteroids
Video Easel
Star Raiders
Centipede
Pac-Man
Caverns of Mars
3-D Tic-Tac-Toe
Computer Chess
Biorhythm

Synapse Software
820 Coventry Road
Kensington, CA 94707

Programs for the Atari 400/Atari 800 Computers

CATEGORY: BUSINESS

FileManager 800

CATEGORY: UTILITIES

DiskManager
SYN Assembler
Page 6

CATEGORY: GAMES

DodgeRacer
Protector
Nautilus
Slime
Chicken

Dynacomp, Inc.
1427 Monroe Avenue
Rochester, NY 14618

Programs for the Atari Computer

CATEGORY: GAMES

Baccarat
Poker Party
Go Fish
Management Simulator
Flight Simulator
Valdez

Backgammon
Forest Fire!
Space Evacuation!
Monarch
Chompelo
StarTrek
Lil' Men From Mars
Space Tilt
Escape from Volantium
Alpha Fighter
The Rings of the Empire
Intruder Alert
Midway
Triple Blockade
Games Pack I
Games Pack II
Moon Probe
Super Trap
Super Sub Chase

CATEGORY: BUSINESS & UTILITIES

MailMaster
Personal Finance System
Family Budget
InterLink
Shopping List
Turnkey and Menu
Stockaid

CATEGORY: EDUCATIONAL

Talk To Me
Teacher's Aide

CATEGORY: STATISTICS AND
ENGINEERING

Digital Filter
Fourier Analyzer
Transfer Function Analyzer
Harmonic Analyzer
Regression
Regression II
Multilinear Regression

CATEGORY: MISCELLANEOUS

Crystals

Programs for the Apple II

CATEGORY: GAMES

Gin Rummy
Poker Party
Go Fish
Flight Simulator
Valdez

Black Hole
Space Evacuation
StarTrek
Games Pack I
Games Pack II

CATEGORY: BUSINESS AND
UTILITIES

Family Budget
PayFive
Util
Shape Magician

CATEGORY: EDUCATIONAL

Hodge Podge
Teacher's Gradebook

CATEGORY: STATISTICS AND
ENGINEERING

Digital Filter
Data Smoother
Fourier Analyzer
Transfer Function Analyzer
Harmonic Analyzer
Regression I
Regression II
Multilinear Regression
Anova
Basic Scientific Subroutines,
    Volumes 1 & 2
Softnet
Active Circuit Analysis
Logic Simulator

Programs for the Commodore

CATEGORY: GAMES

Poker Party
Go Fish
Flight Simulator
Valdez
StarTrek
Games Pack I
Games Pack II
Chirp Invaders

CATEGORY: EDUCATIONAL

Pharmacology Update

CATEGORY: STATISTICS AND
ENGINEERING

Digital Filter
Data Smoother

Fourier Analyzer
Transfer Function Analyzer
Harmonic Analyzer
Regression I
Regression II
Multilinear Regression
Basic Scientific Subroutines,
    Volumes I & II

*Programs for the TRS-80
Computer*

CATEGORY: GAMES

Poker Party
Go Fish
Blackjack Coach
Flight Simulator
Valdez
Chess Master
Space Evacuation
StarTrek
Games Pack I
Games Pack II

CATEGORY: STATISTICS AND
ENGINEERING

Digital Filter
Data Smoother
Fourier Analyzer
Transfer Function Analyzer
Harmonic Analyzer
Regression I
Regression II
Multilinear Regression
Anova
Basic Scientific Subroutines,
    Volumes I & II
Matchnet
NumberKruncher
Statsort
Stattest

*Programs for the North Star
Computer*

CATEGORY: GAMES

Bridge Master
Poker Party
Go Fish
Management Simulator
Flight Simulator
Valdez

Backgammon
Chess Master
StarTrek
Games Pack I
Games Pack II
Moon Probe
Cranston Manor Adventure
Gumball Rally Adventure
Uncle Harry's Will

CATEGORY: BUSINESS & UTILITIES

Personal Finance System
Tax Optimizer

CATEGORY: STATISTICS AND
 ENGINEERING

Digital Filter
Data Smoother
Fourier Analyzer
Transfer Function Analyzer
Harmonic Analyzer
Regression I
Regression II
Multilinear Regression
Anova
Basic Scientific Subroutines,
 Volumes I & II

**North Star Software Exchange
Library**

*Programs for the CP/M
(M-BASIC–C-BASIC)*

CATEGORY: GAMES

Poker Party
Go Fish
Management Simulator
Flight Simulator
Valdez
Backgammon
StarTrek
Games Pack I
Games Pack II
Chirp Invaders
Cranston Manor Adventure

CATEGORY: EDUCATIONAL

Hodge Podge

CATEGORY: STATISTICS AND
 ENGINEERING

Digital Filter
Data Smoother
Fourier Analyzer
Transfer Function Analyzer
Harmonic Analyzer
Regression I
Regression II
Multilinear Regression
Anova
Basic Scientific Subroutines,
 Volumes I & II

*Programs for the Osborne
Computer*

CATEGORY: GAMES

Poker Party
Go Fish
Management Simulator
Flight Simulator
Backgammon
StarTrek
Games Pack I
Games Pack II

CATEGORY: STATISTICS AND
 ENGINEERING

Digital Filter
Data Smoother
Fourier Analyzer
Transfer Function Analyzer
Harmonic Analyzer
Regression I
Regression II
Multilinear Regression
Anova
Basic Scientific Subroutines,
 Volumes I & II

**Piccadilly Software
89 Summit Avenue
Summit, NJ 07901**

*Programs for the Apple II & Apple
Plus*

CATEGORY: GAMES

Star Blaster
Falcons
Warp Destroyer
Survival

Suicide!
Succession

**Commodore Business Machines
Software Group
681 Moore Road
300 Valley Forge Square
King of Prussia, PA 19406**

CATEGORY: BUSINESS

Ozz—The Information Wizard
Dow Jones Portfolio Management
 System
Information Retrieval &
 Management Aid (IRMA)
LTA Legal Time Accounting
Tax Preparation System

CATEGORY: WORD PROCESSING

Wordcraft 80

CATEGORY: UTILITIES

Integer BASIC Compiler
Assembler Development Package
TCL Pascal Development System

CATEGORY: GAMES

Lunar Landing
Wumpus
Jumbo Jet Lander
Draw Poker
Concord Lander
Wrap Trap
Super 9 x 9
Black Jack
Glider
Awari
Reverse
Polaris
Rotate
3-D Tic-Tac-Toe
Target Pong
Galaxy Games
Off the Wall
Space Trek
Formula 1
Space Talk & Space Flight
Life
Backgammon
Crypto

Creative Software
P.O. Box 4030
Mountain View, CA 94040

Programs for the Commodore Computers

CATEGORY: BUSINESS

Accounts Receivable
General Ledger
Inventory
Accounts Payable

CATEGORY: WORD PROCESSING

Petword

CATEGORY: UTILITIES

Isam

CATEGORY: GAMES

Tag
Seawolf
Bounceout
Star Wars
Road Race
Space War II
Life
Sketchipad and Maze

Computer House Division
1407 Clinton Road
Jackson, MI 49202

Programs for the Commodore Computer

CATEGORY: BUSINESS

Real Estate Listing
Accounting
Inventory
Mailing List
Legal Accounting
Legal Accounting Demo

CATEGORY: UTILITIES

Sof-BKUP 2.0
Super-Ram
Vari-Print
Docu-Print
Screen Dump/Repeat
Trace-Print
Scrunch Plus
Sorter

CATEGORY: TECHNICAL AIDS

Beams
Trig/Circle Tangent
Bolt Circle
Spur Gears
Machines Part Quoting

United Software of America
750 Third Avenue
New York, NY 10017

Programs for the Commodore Computer

CATEGORY: BUSINESS

Kram & Super Kram
Thinker
Request

CATEGORY: PERSONAL AIDS

Decorator's Assistant
Finance
Checkbook
Stock Options
Mortgage
Annual Reporter Analyzer

CATEGORY: GAMES

Jury/Hostage
Space Intruder
Kentucky Derby/Roulette
Alien I.Q./Tank
Submarine Attack
Midway
Super StarTrek
Baseball
Swarm
Super Gomoku
Laser Tank Battle

Briley Software
P.O. Box 2913
Livermore, CA 94550

Programs for the Commodore Computer

CATEGORY: BUSINESS

Business Researcher

CATEGORY: PERSONAL AIDS

Home Addresser
Deluxe Addresser

Inventory
Shopper
Grocery Mart
Dinner's On
League Bowl-24
Archive Bowl
Tournament Bowl
RNAV3 Navigator

CATEGORY: GAMES

Mansion!
Museum!
Pentagon!
High Seas
Fur Trapper

Instant Software, Inc.
Elm Street & Route 1
Peterborough, NH 03458

Programs for the Commodore Computer

CATEGORY: BUSINESS

Accounting Assistant

CATEGORY: GAMES

Penny Arcade
Casino I
Casino II
Trek-X
Arcade I
Arcade II
Code Name Cipher
Tangle/SuperTrap
BaseBall Manager
Chimera
Santa Paravia and Fiumaccio
Turf and Target
Mimic
Pet Demo I

Programs for the Pet Computer

CATEGORY: GAMES

Mimic
Dungeon of Death
Quibic 4/Go Moku
Code Name Cipher
Santa Paravia and Fiumaccio

CATEGORY: UTILITIES

PetUtility I

Programs for the TRS-80 Computer

CATEGORY: GAMES

Dr. Chips
Perfect Pong
Ball Turret Gunner with Sound
Danger in Orbit
Alien Attack Force
Space Shuttle
Night Flight
The Flying Circus
Jet Fighter Pilot
Air Flight Simulation
Swamp War
Cosmic Patrol
Airmail Pilot
Flight Path
Mimic
Ramrom Patrol
DareDevil
The Domes of Kilgari
Temple of the Sun
Mind Warp
House of Thirty Gables
Dragonquest, The Princess Has
   Been Kidnapped
Master Revers!
Oil Tycoon
Battleground
All The Stars
Sparrow Commander
Kitchen Sink
Z80-Checkers
Life
Who-Dun-It?
Investor's Paradise

CATEGORY: BUSINESS

The WordSlinger
The One-D Mailing List
Mail/File
Find-It-Quick
Bowling League Statistics System
Omni-Calculator
General Ledger Mod. II

CATEGORY: HOME/PERSONAL

Money Manager
Personal Bill Paying

CATEGORY: UTILITIES

Ultra-Mon
Dynamic Device Drivers

Utility II
Label
Super Terminal
The Communicator
TRS-Tests
Cassette Scope
OmniConverter
Basic Programming Assistant
QSL Manager
Enhanced Basic
TLDIS & DLDIS
RENUM/Compress
IRV
Disk Editor
Master Directory
Disk Scope
Programmer's Primer
Compression Utility Pack
The DisAssembler
Programmer's Converter

CATEGORY: EDUCATIONAL

Polyfona
Teacher's Aide
The Elements
Beginner's Russian
Everyday Russian
Russian Disk
Easy-Calc
MathMaster
IQ Test
Archimedes' Apprentice
Grade Book
Video Speed Reading Trainer
WordWatch
Typing Teacher
Geography Explorer: USA
Surveyor's Apprentice
The Electric Breadboard
Climate-Comp
Music Master
Kids Gallery

Programs for the Apple Computer

CATEGORY: GAMES

Air Flight Simulation
Apple Fun
Paddle Fun
Dr. Chips
Golf
SkyBombers II
Sahara Warriors
Mimic

Jet Fighter Pilot
Oil Tycoon

CATEGORY: BUSINESS

Client Records/Bill Preparation

CATEGORY: UTILITIES

Ham Package I
The Apple Clinic

CATEGORY: EDUCATIONAL

Capitalization
Solar Energy for the Home
Astrology
Russian Disk

Programs for the North Star Computer

CATEGORY: MISCELLANEOUS

Traffic Accident Analysis and
   Reconstruction

Programs for the Heath Computer

CATEGORY: MISCELLANEOUS

Mental Gymnastics

Adventure International
Box 3435
Longwood, FL 32750

CATEGORY: GAMES

StarFighter (TRS-80)
Space Intruders (TRS-80)
Frog (TRS-80)
Color Computer Games #1
   (TRS-80)
Planetoids (TRS-80, Apple)
ShowDown (TRS-80)
Mean Checkers (TRS-80)
Galaxy Gates (Apple)
Back-40 III (TRS-80, Apple)
Armored Patrol (TRS-80)
Lunar Lander (TRS-80, Atari)
3-D Tic-Tac-Toe (Atari)
Sunday Golf (Atari)
Mountain Shoot (Atari)
Deflection (Atari)
Missile Attack (TRS-80, Apple)
Tunnel Terror (Apple)
Sea Dragon (TRS-80)

Sky Warrior (TRS-80)
Mean Craps (TRS-80)
Z-Chess III (TRS-80)
Stone of Sisyphus (TRS-80,
Apple, Atari)
Balrog (TRS-80)
Adventure Special Sampler
(TRS-80, Atari)
The Eliminator (TRS-80, Apple)
Galactic Trilogy (TRS-80)
Galactic Revolution (TRS-80)
Galactic Trader (TRS-80, Atari)
Galactic Empire (TRS-80, Atari)
Escape From Traam (TRS-80)
Rear Guard (Apple)
Combat (TRS-80, Atari)
Silver Flash-Pinball 1 (TRS-80)
Strip Dice/Concentration
(TRS-80)
Treasure Quest (TRS-80, Atari)
Conquest of Chesterwoode
(TRS-80)
The Curse of Crowley Manor
(TRS-80)
Death Planet: The Dog Star
Adventure (TRS-80)
Quad Pack Special (TRS-80)
Interactive Fiction (TRS-80,
Apple)
Reign of the Red Dragon
(TRS-80)
EarthQuake-San Francisco, 1906
(TRS-80)
Adventure #1 Adventureland
(TRS-80, Apple, Atari)
Adventure #2 Pirate Adventure
(TRS-80, Apple, Atari)
Adventure #3 Mission Impossible
(TRS-80, Apple, Atari)
Adventure #4 Voodoo Castle
(TRS-80, Atari)
Adventure #5 The Count
(TRS-80, Atari)
Adventure #6 Strange Odyssey
(TRS-80, Atari)
Adventure #7 Mystery Fun
House (TRS-80, Atari)
Adventure #8 Pyramid of Doom
(TRS-80, Atari)
Adventure #9 Ghost Town
(TRS-80, Atari)
Adventure #10 Savage Island
(Part 1) (TRS-80, Atari)

Adventure #11 Savage Island
(Part 2) (TRS-80, Atari)
Adventure #12 Golden Voyage
(TRS-80, Atari)
Adventure 12-Pack (TRS-80,
CP/M)
Adventures #1, 2, 3 (Apple,
Atari)
Adventures #4, 5, 6 (Atari)
Adventures #7, 8, 9 (Atari)
Adventures #10, 11, 12 (Atari)
Classic Adventure #1 (Apple)
Pro-Pix (TRS-80, Apple, Atari)
Morton's Fork (TRS-80, Apple)
War (Apple)

CATEGORY: BUSINESS

Maxi Mail (TRS-80)
Business Analysis: Oracle-80
(TRS-80)
Cash Register Inventory System
(Atari)

CATEGORY: HOME/PERSONAL

Personal Check Manager
(TRS-80)

CATEGORY: UTILITIES

Floppy Disk Maintenance
(TRS-80)
Maxi Start (TRS-80)
ST80-UC (TRS-80)

CATEGORY: EDUCATIONAL

Twas The Night Before Christmas
(TRS-80)
Little Red Riding Hood (Apple)

**Acorn Software
634 North Carolina Avenue
Washington, DC 20003**

*Programs for the TRS-80
Computer*

CATEGORY: GAMES

Pinball
Word Wars
Quad
BasketBall Game
TenPins
AstroBall

Lost Colony
Mysterious Adventure, Arrow of
Death (Part 1)
Pigskin
Duel-N-Droids
Invaders from Space
Space WR
Space War

CATEGORY: UTILITIES

Sort/Search
Disassembler 1.4
System Savers
SuperScript I/III
Aterm
Structured Basic Translator

CATEGORY: EDUCATIONAL

Spanish I
Spanish II
German I
German II
Italian I
French I
French II

CATEGORY: MISCELLANEOUS

BasketBall Handicapper
Everest Explorer
Your Family Tree

**Discovery Games
936 W. Highway 36
St. Paul, MO 55113**

CATEGORY: GAMES

Chennault's Flying Tigers
(Commodore, TRS-80, Apple,
Atari)
RAF: The Battle of Britain
(Commodore, TRS-80, Apple,
Atari)
Winged Samurai (Commodore,
TRS-80, Apple, Atari)
Migs and Messerschmitts
(Commodore, TRS-80, Apple,
Atari)
Jagdstraffel (Commodore,
TRS-80, Apple, Atari)
Dawn Patrol (TRS-80)

Big Five Software
P.O. Box 185
Van Nuys, CA 91409

*Programs for the TRS-80
Computer*

CATEGORY: GAMES

Meteor Mission II
Attack Force
Galaxy Invasion
Super Nova
Stellar Escort
Defense Command
Robot Attack
Cosmic Fighter

Edu-Ware Services, Inc.
22222 Sherman Way
Canoga Park, CA 91303

Programs for the Apple Computer

CATEGORY: EDUCATIONAL

Algebra II
Algebra III
Rendezvous
SAT Word Attack
PSAT Word Attack
Perception 3.0
Compu-Read 3.0
Statistics 3.0
Spelling Bee
Compu-Math, Fractions
Algebra I
Compu-Math, Decimals
Compu-Math, Arithmetic Skills
Counting Bee
Compu-Spell System

Programs for the Atari Computer

CATEGORY: EDUCATIONAL

Compu-Math, Fractions
Compu-Math, Decimals
Compu-Read

H & E Computronics
50 North Pascack Road
Spring Valley, NY 10977

*Programs for the TRS-80 and
Apple Computers*

The following 100 programs are
on one disk.

CATEGORY: BUSINESS AND
PERSONAL FINANCE

Checkbook Maintenance
Time For Money To Double
Federal FICA & Withholding Tax
Computations
Home Budget Analysis
Annuity Computation
Unit Pricing
Change From Purchase
Nebs Check Printer
Days Between Dates
Mortgage Amortization Table
Inventory Control
Portfolio Value Computations
Value Of A Share Of Stock
Sales Record Keeping System
Future Value Of An Investment
Effective Interest Rate (Loan)
Present Value Of A Future
Amounts
Rate Of Return—Variable Inflow
Rate Of Return—Constant Inflow
Regular Withdrawal From
Investment
Straight Line Depreciation
Sum Of Digits Depreciation
Declining Balance Depreciation
Break Even Analysis
Salvage Value Of Investment
Payment On A Loan
Future Sales Projections
Credit Card File
Economic Order Quantity (EOQ)
Inventory Model
Value Of House Contents
Text Editor
Monthly Calendar
Day Of Week
Cash Flow vs. Depreciation
Complete Mail System
Interest Rate On A Lease

CATEGORY: STATISTICS AND
MATHEMATICS

Random Sample Selection
Anglo-Metic Conversion
Mean, Standard Deviation,
Maximum, and Minimum
Simple Linear Regression
Multiple Regression Analysis
Geometric Regression
Exponential Regression
Simple Moving Average

Simple T-Test
CHI-Square Test
Normal Probabilities
Binomial Probability
Poisson Probability
Matrix Addition and Subtraction
Matrix Transpose
Matrix Inverse
Matrix Multiplication
Solution Of Simultaneous
Equations
Quadratic Formula
Linear Equation Solutions
Root Half Interval Search
Roots Of Polynomials
Roots—Newton's Methods
Prime Factors Of Integers
Least Common Denominator
Radian-Degree Conversion
Numerical Integration

CATEGORY: UTILITIES

Quick Sort Routine
Program Storage Index
Multiple Choice Quiz Builder
Form Letter Writer
Shell Sort
Cassette Label Maker
Codes Messages
Merge Two Files
Sort With Replacement

CATEGORY: GRAPHICS

Draws Bar Graph
Draws Histogram
Moving Banner Display

CATEGORY: GAMBLING AND
GAMES

Random Sport Quiz
Government Quiz
Horse Race
Magic Square
Arithmetic Teacher
High Low Gamble
Unscramble Letters
Hangman
Game of Nim
Russian Roulette
Roulette Game
One-Armed Bandit
Hit The Target
Walking Drunk
State Capital Quiz

Tic-Tac-Toe
Dice Game
Lunar Landar Game
Biorhythm
Horse Selector (Class Calculator)
Random Dice Roll
Random Roulette Roll
Random Card Dealer
Guess The Number
White Out Screen

Avatar Software
691 Corinthia
Milpitas, CA 95035

Programs for the Atari Computer

CATEGORY: PERSONAL FINANCE

Family Expenses
Datagraph
Budget
Number Graph

CATEGORY: WORDPROCESSING

Personal Editor

JMH Software of Minnesota, Inc.
4850 Wellington Lane
Minneapolis, MN 55442

Programs for the Atari Computer

CATEGORY: EDUCATION

Math—Speed Facts
Math—Timed Facts
ABC's
Alphabetize
Dictionary Use
Vowel Sounds
Money Change
Stars Number Guess
Bagels Supreme
Rocket Spell
Scramble Spell
Tic-Tac-Toe Spell
Spelling Practice
Bookshelf
Calendar
Math—Number Sequence
Number Sequence
Math—Diving Facts
Math—Place Value
Math—Numerical Names

Math—Tens and Hundreds
Math—Race Car Facts
Math—Tic-Tac-Toe
Math—Counting

C.E. Software
238 Exchange Street
Chicopee, MA 01013

Programs for the Atari Computer

CATEGORY: PERSONAL FINANCE

CCA Data Management

CATEGORY: WORD PROCESSING

The Letter Writer

CATEGORY: GAMES

Helicopter Battle
Tag
Tractor Beam
Musicgame
The Mad Marble
War At Sea
Horse Racing
Keno
Light/Bolts & React
SuperMaster

T.H.E.S.I.S.
P.O. Box 147
Garden City, MI 48135

Programs for the Atari Computer

CATEGORY: EDUCATIONAL

Math Facts Level III
Preschool Fun
Spatial Relations
Hidden Words
Fishing For Homonyms
Math Facts Level I
Word Scramble
Math Facts Level II
Word Mate
Spellbound
Cribbage
Casino I
Computation
Wanted
Guessword

Softswap
333 Main Street
Redwood City, CA 94063

Programs for the Atari Computer

CATEGORY: EDUCATIONAL

Geography
Meet The Romans
States & Capitals
Fancy Rose
Sine Waves
Hangman For One
Bourreau
Multiplication Bingo
Math Quiz
Scrambled Word
Name the States
Bagels
Trap

Santa Cruz Educational Software
5425 Jigger Drive
Soquel, CA 95073

Programs for the Atari Computer

CATEGORY: RECORD KEEPING

Mini-Database/Dialer
Automatic Dialer
Bob's Business
Bowler's Database

CATEGORY: WORD PROCESSING

Mini-Word Processor

CATEGORY: EDUCATIONAL

Player Piano
Tricky Tutorials
Kids' 1
Kids' 2P

P.S. Software House
P.O. Box 966
Mishawaka, IN 46544

*Programs for the Commodore
Computer*

CATEGORY: UTILITIES

Toolkit Mover
6502 Disassembler and Peek A
   Boo

Machine Language Utility Pack
Ultra-Mon

CATEGORY: PERSONAL AIDS

Mail List
Home Utilities

CATEGORY: GAMES

Mad Libs
Computer Derby
Bounce
StarTrek
Mortar
Race Car
Numberama

Dorsett Educational Software
Goldsby Airport Box 1226
Norman, OK 73078

Programs for the Atari Computer

CATEGORY: EDUCATIONAL

Reading Comprehension
Carpentry
General Shop Practice
Independent Solid-State
    Electronics
Digital Electronics
Vocational Reading
    Comprehension
Math
First-Aid Safety
Health Services Career
Philosophy
Auto Mechanics
Math Electronics
Spanish/English

Program Design, Inc.
11 Idar Court
Greenwich, CT 06839

Programs for the Atari Computer

CATEGORY: GAMES

Astro Quotes
Kross 'N Quotes
Sammy the Sea Serpent
Bowling
Captivity
Word Search/Spanish
Word Search/French
Minicrossword

CATEGORY: EDUCATIONAL

Do It Yourself: Spelling
Memory Builder: Concentration
Spelling Builder
Code Breaker
Let's Spell
Cash Register
Story Builder/Word Master
Addition With Carrying
PreSchool IQ Builder
PreSchool IQ Builder 2
Reading Comprehension
Analogies
Vocabulary Builder 1: Beginning
Vocabulary Builder 2: Advanced
Quantitative Comparison
Number Series

Zapata Microsystems
P.O. Box 401483
Garland, TX 75040

Programs for the Atari Computer

CATEGORY: PERSONAL FINANCE

Personal Loan Analysts
Personal Banker
200 Year Calendar

CATEGORY: GAMES

Blockade
Pursuit
Super Le Mans
Road Race

CATEGORY: EDUCATIONAL

Spanish Word Guide

H.E.L. Laboratories, Inc.
95A Halls Croft
Freehold, NJ 07728

Programs for the Atari Computer

CATEGORY: PERSONAL FINANCE

Mailing List Version 1.0
Mailing List Version 2.0

CATEGORY: EDUCATIONAL

Codeword
Math Duel/Basic Math
Stumper (Hangman)

Krell Software
21 Millbrook Drive
Stony Brook, NY 11790

Programs for the Atari Computer

CATEGORY: GAMES

Time Traveler
The Sword of Zedek
Superstar Baseball and All Time
    Superstar Baseball
Odyssey In Time

CATEGORY: EDUCATIONAL

College Board SAT Preparation
    Series
Pythagoras and The Dragon
Alexander the Great
The War of The Samurai
Micro-Deutsch

APX
P.O. Box 427
155 Moffett Park Drive
Sunnyvale, CA 94086

Programs for the Atari Computer

CATEGORY: PERSONAL FINANCE &
    RECORD KEEPING

Bowler's Database
Computerized Card File
Data Base/Report System
Data Management System
Family Budget
Family Cash Flow
Family Vehicle Expense
Financial Asset Management
    System
Newspaper Route Management
    Program
Recipe Search 'n Save
Weekly Planner

CATEGORY: BUSINESS &
    PROFESSIONAL APPLICATIONS

Calculator
Decision Maker
Diskette Mailing List
Enhancements to Graph It
Hydraulic Program (HYSYS)
Isopleth Map-Making Package
RPN Calculator Simulator
Text Formatter (FORMS)

CATEGORY: PERSONAL INTEREST &
    DEVELOPMENT

Advanced Music System
Astrology
Banner Generator
Blackjack Tutor
Going to the Dogs
Keyboard Organ
Morse Code Tutor
Personal Fitness Program
Player Piano
Sketchpad

CATEGORY: EDUCATIONAL

Algicalc
Atlas of Canada
Cubbyholes
Elementary Biology
Frogmaster
Hickory Dickory
Instructional Computing
    Demonstration
Lemonade
Letterman
Mapware
Mathematic-Tac-Toe
Metric and Problem Solving
Mugwump
Music 1: Terms & Notation
Musical Computer—The Music
    Tutor
My First Alphabet
Number Blast
Polycalc
Presidents of the United States
Quiz Master
Starware
Stereo 3-D Graphics Package
Three R Math System
Video Math Flashcards
Wordmaker

CATEGORY: ENTERTAINMENT

Alien Egg
Anthill
Attack!
Avalanche
Babel
Blackjack Casino
Block Buster
Block 'Em
Bumper Pool
Castle
Centurion

Checker King
Chinese Puzzle
CodeCracker
Comedy Diskette
Dice Poker
Dog Daze
Domination
Downhill
Eastern Front
Galahad and the Holy Grail
Graphics/Sound Demonstration
Jax-O
Jukebox #1
Lookahead
Memory Match
Midas Touch
Minotaur
Outlaw/Howitzer
Preschool Games
Pro Bowling
Pushover
Rabbotz
Reversi II
Salmon Run
747 Landing Simulator
Seven Card Stud
Sleazy Adventure
Solitaire
Source Code for Eastern Front
Space Chase
Space Trek
Sultan's Palace
Tact Trek
Terry
Wizard's Gold
Wizard's Revenge

CATEGORY: SYSTEM SOFTWARE

ATARI Pascal Language System
ATARI Program-Text Editor
BASIC Cross-Reference Utility
    (XREF)
BASIC Program Compressor
    (MASHER)
BASIC Renumber Utility
    (RENUM)
BASIC Utility Diskette
BLIS
Chameleon CRT Terminal
    Emulator
Cosmatic ATARI Development
    Package
Developer's Diskette
Disk Fixer (FIX)

Diskette Librarian
Dsembler
Extended fig-FORTH
Extended WSFN
GTIA Demonstration Diskette
Insomnia
Instedit
Instedit (Microsoft BASIC
    version)
Keypad Controller
Load 'n Go
Microsoft Cross-Reference Utility
Player Generator
Screen Dump Utility
Sound Editor
Speed-O-Disk
Supersort
T: A Text Display Device
Ultimate Renumber Utility
Utility Diskette II
Variable Changer
Word Processing Diskette

Apple Computer, Inc.
20515 Mariani Avenue
Cupertino, CA 95014

Programs for the Apple II and IIe
Computer

CATEGORY: BUSINESS
    MANAGEMENT

Agenda Files
APM
Order Tracking System
VT-100 Emulator
Dow Jones News & Quotes
    Reporter
Dow Jones Portfolio Evaluator
Plan 80
Senior Analyst
VisiCalc Real Estate Templates
Comm-Pac
P Sort
Personal Finance Manager
Utopia Graphics Tablet System
Datatree
Formulex

CATEGORY: EDUCATIONAL

Geometry & Measurement Drill
    & Practice
Musicomp

SuperMap
Speed Reader
Hand Holding BASIC
Topographic Mapping
Math Strategy/Spelling Strategy
PILOT Animation Tools
Designer's Toolkit
GoodSpell

CATEGORY: GAMES &
  ENTERTAINMENT

The World's Greatest Blackjack
  Program
Bridge Tutor
Galactic Wars
The Wreck of the B.S.M. Pandora
Artist Designer
Musicomp
Moptown
Magic Spells
Bridge Tutor

CATEGORY: PERSONAL

Diet Analysis

CATEGORY: UTILITIES

Circuit Analysis
Stepwise Multiple Regression
Apple III Pascal Utility Library

CATEGORY: WORD PROCESSING

Apple Writer II
Apple Writer III
Apple Access III
Apple III Business Graphics
Script II
Script III

Monument Computer Service
P.O. Box 603
Joshua Tree, CA 92252

Programs for the Apple Computer

CATEGORY: BUSINESS
  MANAGEMENT

Paysystem Accountant
Personnel Office
Project Boss
Office Manager
Dental Secretary
Inventory

Legal Clerk
Mailroom
Medical Secretary
Paymaster
Personal Accountant
Tax Advisor

CATEGORY: PERSONAL FINANCE

Asset Manager

CATEGORY: GAMES

Mind Games
War Games

CATEGORY: HEALTH

Executive Fitness

CATEGORY: EDUCATIONAL

Scientist

CATEGORY: WORD PROCESSING

Letterite
Letter Master

Edutek Corporation
415 Cambridge #14
Palo Alto, CA 94306

Programs for the Apple Computer

CATEGORY: EDUCATIONAL

Hand/Eye Coordination
A Clock Game
Finger Abacus
Write It In Color
Counting Programs
Basic Arithmetic Skills
Crazy Sentences
Vocabulary Quiz
Syllabication
Game of Synonyms and
  Antonyms
Vowel Exercise
Syllabication Tutorial
Syllable Count
What Was That Word?
Game of Hard/Soft Consonants
Word Break Up
Short Vowel Box
True or False Syllabications
Basic Reading Skills
Musical Staff Drill

Find the Key
Piano Keyboard Drill
Make a Tune
Poly-Choice
Akan

CATEGORY: GAMES

Alien Contact
Take 'em

Inst Sys/School District of
  Philadelphia
5th & Lucerne Streets
Philadelphia, PA 19140

Programs for the Apple Computer

CATEGORY: EDUCATIONAL

Atom
Chem
Period
Molar
Molar 1
Element
Area of Triangles
Fren 1
Span
Spiel
Clouds
Space
Bar Graph

CATEGORY: PERSONAL

Saving

CATEGORY: GAMES

Jigsaw
TicTac
Golf
Clocks
Chase
Bljack
Batnum
Bagel 2
Guess
Footbl
Teaser
Towers
Bagels
Trajectory
Nim
Guess the Number
Maze 1

Paul's Electric Computer
P.O. Box 42831
Las Vegas, NV 89116

Programs for the Apple Computer

CATEGORY: BUSINESS

Employee Profile (Evaluation)

CATEGORY: EDUCATIONAL

Adding Machine
Color PI

CATEGORY: GAMES

Tic-Tac-Toe
Watch It
Race Track
Petals Around the Rose
Herm the Worm
Simon Says
Legal Advice
Merry Mix-ups
Nine Bars
Mini-Casino
The Big Whale
Tag It (word game)
Skipper the Robot
Knock-Knock Jokes
Mr. Backwords
Frogs in the Pond
Super Nim
Acey-Ducey
Hangman
Space Klutz
Palm Reader
The Beer Game
The Race Track (Nevada
   Version)
Sin Palace
Sin Palace II

CATEGORY: GRAPHICS

Dee-Zigns
Zapper
Sound Etcher
Wild Sign
Fancy Border
Bounce/n'/Bars
Scotch Plaid
Tapestry

CATEGORY: PERSONAL

Life Expectancy
Honesty Test

I Ching
BlackJack "21" Strategy
California Driver's Test (2 Parts)
L.U.S.T.

CATEGORY: UTLITIES

Lucky Disk

Micro Music Inc.
P.O. Box 386
Norman, IL 61761

Programs for the Apple Computer

CATEGORY:
   MUSIC/ENTERTAINMENT

Name That Tune
Arnold
Mode Drills
Key Signature Drills
Music Composer
Micro Music Digisong Paks
Sir William Wrong Note
Pitch Drills Without Accidentals
Pitch Drills With Accidentals
Rhythm Drills
Envelope Shaper
Auto Digisong Player
Music Lover's Guide For
   Teachers
Envelope Construction
Music In Theory and Practice
Harmony Drills: Set 1
Doremi
Experimenter's Package
Melodious Dictator
Chord Mania
Interval Mania
Harmonious Dictator
Rhythmic Dictator
Music Lover's Guide to Musical
   Instruments
Music Lover's Guide to General
   Music Terms
Music Lover's Guide to Musical
   Symbols
Music Lover's Guide to
   Composers
Music Lover's Guide to Italian
   Terms
Music Lover's Guide to Foreign
   Instrument Names

Milliken Publishing
1100 Research Boulevard
St. Louis, MO 63132

Programs for the Apple Computer

CATEGORY: LANGUAGE ARTS

Grammar Problems For
   Practice—Homonyms
Grammar Problems For
   Practice—Verbs
Grammar Problems For
   Practice—Pronouns
Grammar Problems For
   Practice—Modifiers
Grammar Problems For
   Practice—Spelling
Reading Comprehension—Level
   D (Reading Level 4)
Reading Comprehension—Level
   E (Reading Level 5)
Reading Comprehension—Level
   F (Reading Level 6)
Reading Comprehension—Level
   G (Reading Level 7)
Reading Comprehension—Level
   H (Reading Level 8)
Reading Comprehension—Level I
   (Reading Level 9)
Reading Comprehension—Level J
   (Reading Level 10)
Reading Comprehension—Level
   K (Reading Level 11)
Reading Comprehension—Level
   L (Reading Level 12)
Reading
   Comprehension—Combined
   Levels J-K-L
Language Arts: Study Skills

Hartley Courseware, Inc.
P.O. Box 431
Dimondale, MI 48821

Programs for the Apple Computer

CATEGORY: EDUCATIONAL

Clock
Calendar Skills
Math Concepts
Metric Drill
Expanded Notation
Prescriptive Math Drill

Integers/Equations
Vocabulary—Elementary
Vocabulary—Dolch
Who, What, Where, When, Why
Create—Vocabulary
Create—Spell It
Word Families
Homonyms/Antonyms/Synonyms
Verbs
Multiple Skills
Number Words—Level I
Number Words—Level II
Nouns/Pronouns
Letter Recognition
Wordsearch
Roots/Affixes
Consonants
Vowels
Capitalization
Word Families (Phonograms)
Create Skills—Elementary
Create Skills—Intermediate
Create—Fill In The Blank

Charles Mann & Associates
55722 Santa Fe Trail
Yucca Valley, CA 92284

Programs for the Apple Computer

CATEGORY: BUSINESS

Construction Accounting Systems
Job Cost Accounting
Project Planning and Budgeting
Personal Secretary Package
Reprogrammable Data Base
    Program
Scientific Data Base
Dental Office Management
Dental Office Management II
Print Check Accounting System I
Asset Record Program
Stock Portfolio Program
Inventory Pac
Professional Secretary Package
Billings Management
Disk Mailing List
Mailing List Management
Medical Office Management I
Medical II
Medical Office Management IIC
Personnel Record Program
PayRecord I
Payroll I
Paycheck I

Retail Management System
Attendance
The Electric Grade Book
Grading System Program
The Teacher Plus
The Class Scheduling System
The Light Pen Quiz
Statistics Pac

CATEGORY: PERSONAL

Programmed Exercises
Personal Accounting System

CATEGORY: WORD PROCESSING

Docuwriter
Personal Text Processor
Master Text Processor

Sensational Software
39 E. Hanover Avenue
Morris Plains, NJ 07950

Programs for the Apple Computer

CATEGORY: GAMES

Action Games
Space War
Outdoor Game
Ecology Simulations II
Voodoo Castle, The Count, and
    Ghost Town
Air Traffic Controller
Torax
Tsunami
Milestones
Super Invasion
3 Adventures
Bumping Games
Haunted House
Brain Game
Sports Games I
Space Games I

On-Line Systems
36575 Mudge Ranch Road
Coarsegold, CA 93614

Programs for the Apple Computer

CATEGORY: GAMES

Thrilogy
Bustout
Smashup
William Tell

Missile Defense
Hi-Res Cribbage
Pegasus II

MSA/Peachtree Software
3 Corporate Square
Suite 700
Atlanta, GA 30329

Programs for the Apple Computer
with CP/M

CATEGORY: BUSINESS

Accounting System
General Ledger
Accounts Payable
Accounts Receivable
MagicCalc
Magic Messenger
Inventory
Sales Invoicing
Mailing List
Magic Address
Payroll
PeachPay
PeachTax (Tax Assistant Service)

CATEGORY: WORD PROCESSING

PeachText 5000
Magic Wand 2.0
Magic Spell

Avant-Garde Creations
P.O. Box 30160
Eugene, OR 97403

Programs for the Apple Computer

CATEGORY: EDUCATIONAL

The Definite Article, German
    Language
Poetry
Phrases and Clauses
Sentence Diagramming
The Relationship Life Dynamic
The Responsibility Life Dynamic
The Aliveness Life Dynamic
The Conditioning Life Dynamic
The Environment Life Dynamic
The Life Dynamic
    Transformation Experience

CATEGORY: UTILITIES

Action Sounds and Hi-Res
    Scrolling

CATEGORY: GAMES

Race For Midnight
5 Great Games
5 More Great Games

CATEGORY: GRAPHICS

Hi-Res Secrets
The Creativity Life Dynamic
    Package
Super Shape Draw
Super Shape Animate
Ultra Plot
Block Shapes for Applesoft or
    Assembly
Super Draw and Write

CATEGORY: BUSINESS

The Mailing Label and Filing
    System
The Mailing Label and Filing
    System Supplement
The Mailing Label and Filing
    System Adjunct
Z.E.S. System of Computer Aided
    Instruction

TCS Software
3209 Fondren
Houston, TX 77063

Programs for the Apple Computer

CATEGORY: BUSINESS

Client Ledger System
General Ledger
Total Payables
Accounts Receivable
Total Receivables
Total Ledger
Accounts Payable
Inventory Management
Total Payroll
Payroll

High Technology Software Prod.
2201 N.E. 63rd Street
Oklahoma City, OK 73113

Programs for the Apple Computer

CATEGORY: BUSINESS

Practical Basic Programs
Some Common Basic Programs

The Order Scheduler
Job Control System
Data Master
Data Base Management System
Information Master
Transit
Client Billing System
The Store Manager
Doctor's Office Companion
    (Billing System for Doctors)

CATEGORY: EDUCATIONAL

Chem Lab Simulations 1:
    Titrations
Chem Lab Simulations 2: Ideal
    Gas Law
Chem Lab Simulations 3:
    Calorimetry
Chem Lab Simulations 4:
    Thermodynamics

CATEGORY: PERSONAL FINANCE

Disk-O-Check

CATEGORY: UTILITIES

The Tool

Beagle Brothers Micro Software
4315 Sierra Vista
San Diego, CA 92130

Programs for the Apple Computer

CATEGORY: GAMES

Game Pack #1
Game Pack #2
Game Pack #3
Game Pack #4

CATEGORY: UTILITIES

Dos Boss
Utility City

Computer Games
511 Iowa Avenue
Iowa City, IA 52240

Programs for the Apple Computer

CATEGORY: GAMES

Green Beret
The High Priest
Tomcat vs. Mig
Beowulf

Humbaba Will Get You
Gunship

Datasoft Inc.
19519 Business Center Drive
Northridge, CA 91324

Programs for the Apple Computer

CATEGORY: GAMES

Mychess
Dung Beetle
Bishop's Square
Maxwell's Demon
Micro-Painter

CATEGORY: UTILITIES

Lisp: The Language
Datasm/65 Editor/Assembler

Sensible Software
6619 Perham Drive
West Bloomfield, MI 48033

Programs for the Apple Computer

CATEGORY: UTILITIES

Applesoft Program Optimizer
    (APOT)
Disk Recovery
Appleguard
The Bug
Pascal Lower Case
Original Quickloaders
Build Using
Disk Organizer II
Image Printer (EPSON)
Super Disk Copy III
Dos Plus
Applesoft-Plus Structured Basic
    (APLUS)
Amper-Sort II
Back It Up II

CATEGORY: WORD PROCESSING

The Apple Speller

Apple Macintosh and Lisa
Apple Computers, Inc.
20525 Mariani Avenue
Cupertino, CA 95014

The following is a list of available
    or announced Macintosh or

Lisa 2 software during Spring, 1984. Many new packages were being announced weekly at this time, so you can anticipate hundreds of programs for the Macintosh and Lisa 2 computers will be available during 1984 and beyond.

MacWrite (Apple)
MacPaint (Apple)
MacDraw (Apple)
MacTerminal (Apple)
MacProject (Apple)
Multiplan (Microsoft)
BASIC (Microsoft)
Microsoft Budget (Microsoft)
Microsoft Cash Budget (Microsoft)
Microsoft Chart (Microsoft)
Microsoft File (Microsoft)
Microsoft Financial Statement (Microsoft)
Microsoft Personal Finance (Microsoft)
Microsoft Word (Microsoft)
LisaCalc (Apple)
LisaList (Apple)
LisaGraph (Apple)
LisaWrite (Apple)
LisaDraw (Apple)
LisaProject (Apple)
Lisa QuickDraw (Apple)
Lisa QuickPort (Apple)
Lisa Workshop (Apple)
Lisa Toolkit/32 (Apple)
Macintosh BASIC (Apple)
Macintosh Pascal (Apple)
Macintosh LOGO (Apple)
Macintosh Assembler (Apple)
Macintosh C Compiler (Apple)
ThinkTank (Living Videotext, Inc.)
SolarSoft Energy Design Series (Kinetic Software)
Real Estate Investor II (Rems Software)
Rems Financial Package (Rems Software)
Real Estate Appraiser 1004 (Rems Software)
Real Estate Rent Versus Buy (Rems Software)

LisaMediCard (CMA Micro Computer Division)
Bank President Game (Lewis Lee Corp.)
High-Tech Entrepreneur Game (Lewis Lee Corp.)
Venture Capitalist (Lewis Lee Corp.)
LisaUNIX Operating System (UniPress Software)
TessStar Medical Office Software (Tess Enterprises)
The Quest Adventure (Penguin Software)
Transylvania Adventure (Penguin Software)
The Coveted Mirror Adventure (Penguin Software)
Business Strategy Software (Human Edge Software)
—The Communication Edge
—The Leadership Edge
—The Management Edge
—The Negotiation Edge
—The Sales Edge
How To Use Your Macintosh (ATI)
MAC/3270 mainframe communications (Persyst Products)
MAC/3770 mainframe communications (Persyst Products)
MicroPlan Spreadsheet (Chang Labs)
MicroPlan Consolidation Module (Chang Labs)
MicroPlan Link Module (Chang Labs)
FilePlan (Chang Labs)
GraphPlan (Chang Labs)
MemoPlan (Chang Labs)
DocuPlan (Chang Labs)
NPL Information Management System (Desktop Software Corp.)
Telofacts 2 (Dilithium Software)
SEACAS Auditing Software (Peat Marwick Mitchell & Co.)
pfs:FILE (Software Publishing)
pfs:REPORT (Software Publishing)
Murder by the Dozen Game (CBS Software)

Lisa COBOL Compiler (Micro Focus)
Idol Applications Development Tool (Science Management Corp.)
PIMS—Profile Impact of Market Strategy (Strategic Planning Institute)
IFPS/Personal (Execucom Systems Corp.)
Personal Composition System (Compugraphic Corp.)
The Tax Machine (AMI)
The Personal Tax Machine (AMI)
The Profit Center—21 accounting packages (Orchid Technology)
Art Department (BPI/BPS Software)
Professional Tax Planner (Aardvark Software)
Estate Tax Planner (Aardvark Software)
dBase II (Ashton-Tate)
CRTplus Decision Support (Aurora Systems)
General Accounting (BPI Systems)
Accounts Receivable (BPI Systems)
Accounts Payable (BPI Systems)
Payroll (BPI Systems)
Client Management System (Compulaw)
Q-Office office automation tools (Quadratron Systems)
SuperCalc integrated package (Sorcim)
DeskTop Calendar time manager (Videx, Inc.)
StatPro (Wadsworth Professional Software)
Business Accounting Control Systems (American Business Systems)
Condor I and III (Condor Computer Corp.)
Horizon Word Processing and Spreadsheet (Horizon Software)
Horizon Word Processing (Horizon Software)
Horizon Spreadsheet (Horizon Software)
Software Fitness Program (Open Systems, Inc.)

R Word word processor (R
 Systems, Inc.)
Real World Business Software
 (Real World Corp.)
RM/COBOL (Ryan-McFarland
 Corp.)
RM/FORTRAN
 (Ryan-McFarland Corp.)
XENIX Operating System (The
 Santa Cruz Corp.)
XENIX Software Development
 Environment (The Santa Cruz
 Corp.)
XENIX Test Processing System
 (The Santa Cruz Corp.)
The Office Manager (Tom
 Software)
Distributor Business Manager
 (Tom Software)
Public Accountant Business
 Manager (Tom Software)
Restaurant/Food Service
 Management Information (Tom
 Software)
Property Management Business
 Information (Tom Software)
Not-for-Profit Operations
 Management (Tom Software)
Speed I software application
 utility (Tom Software)
EZ Speed records management
 (Tom Software)
UNIFY relational data base
 management system (Unify
 Corp.)
Single-user UniPlus+ operating
 system (UniPress Software)
Multi-user UniPlus+ (UniPress
 Software)
C Development Environment
 (UniPress Software)
Text Processing (UniPress
 Software)
SVS FORTRAN (UniPress
 Software)
SVS Pascal (UniPress Software)
SVS BASIC-Plus (UniPress
 Software)
ADA/COBOL (UniPress
 Software)
Lex word processor (UniPress
 Software)
UniCalc spreadsheet (UniPress
 Software)

**Tano Microcomputer Products
Corp.
4301 Poche Court West
New Orleans, LA 70129**

CATEGORY: CHILDREN'S
PROGRAMS

Number Gulper
Number Puzzler
Circus Adventure
School Maze
Hide and Seek

CATEGORY: ACTION GAMES

Shark Treasure
Flag
Quest
Calixto Island
Black Sanctum
Moonhopper
Robottack
Cave Hunter
Berserk
Astroblast
Cosmic Invaders
Ghost Attack
Doodlebug

CATEGORY: UTILITY PROGRAMS

Graphic Animator
Computavoice
Dream Screen Editor and
 Assembler
Pixel Editor

CATEGORY: SELF-HELP/BUSINESS

Typing Tutor
Timescript (Speed Writer)
Personal Finance
Word Processor

**Coleco Industries, Inc.
945 Asylum Avenue
Hartford, CT 06105**

These programs have been
 specifically modified to run on
 the Coleco ADAM computer.
 Some are written by other
 companies, whose names are
 given in parentheses.

CATEGORY: LANGUAGES AND
PROGRAMMING AIDS

SmartLOGO
SmartLOGO Step-by-Step
SmartBASIC II
SmartBASIC
Electronic Guide to Smart BASIC
Personal CP/M
CP/M Programmer's Tool Kit
AdamLink Telecommunications
 Package
GR BASIC (Hesware)

CATEGORY: HOME INFORMATION
MANAGEMENT

Word Processing Packages:
 SmartWriter
 SmartWordbase/Spelling
  Checker
 SmartWriting Checker
 SmartLetters & Forms
 Omniwriter (Hesware)
Information Processing:
 SmartFiler
 SmartSheet
 SmartMoney Manager
 Supercalc 2 (Sorcim)
Graphics:
 SmartPicture Processing
Other Publishers:
 The Home Accountant
  (Continental)
 The Tax Advantage
  (Continental)
 F.C.M.—Filing, Cataloging,
  and Mailing (Continental)
 Family Organizer
  (Sierra-On-Line)

CATEGORY: FAMILY LEARNING

Adventures In Learning:
 Dr. Seuss' Word Factory
 Richard Scarry's Electronic
  Workbook
 Richard Scarry's Right
  Thing/Right Place
 Smurf Paint 'N Play Theatre
 Dr. Seuss' Fix-Up The Mix-Up
 Telly Turtle
 Brain Strainers
World Shapers:
 World Game
 Entrepreneur
 Presidential Campaign

Time Travel
Fortune Builders
Homework Helpers:
Electronic Flashcards
Self-Improvement:
Type Write
Other Publishers:
Spinnaker Software:
Facemaker
Alphabet Zoo
Fraction Fever
Delta Drawing
Snooper Troops
Trains
In Search of the Most Amazing
Thing
Harcourt Brace Jovanovich:
HBJ's Computer Preparation
for the SAT
Sierra-On-Line:
Wiz Type
Wiz Math
Story Maker
Learning with Fuzzy Womp
Learning with Leeper
Hesware:
Turtle Toyland Jr.
Turtle Graphics
Scarborough Systems, Inc.:
Songwriter

CATEGORY: ENTERTAINMENT

The Official SUB-ROC
Dragon's Lair
Star Trek
The Official Zaxxon
The Official Buck Rogers Planet
of Zoom
Front Line
Donkey Kong
Donkey Kong Junior
The Official Congo Bongo
Roc 'N Rope
Mr. Do!
Mr. Do!'s Castle
Stern's Frenzy
Time Pilot
Victory
Omega Race
Pepper II
Looping
Gorf
The Official Space Fury
Venture

Lady Bug
Space Panic
Exidy's Mouse Trap
The Official Carnival
Cosmic Avenger
Slither
Super Action Baseball
Super Action Football
Rocky's Super Action Boxing
Expansion Module #2 with the
Official TURBO
The Dukes of Hazzard
Destructor
Smurf Rescue in Gargamel's
Castle
WarGames
Cabbage Patch Kids
Tarzan
Ken Uston Blackjack/Poker
Tunnels & Trolls
Family Feud
Password
Jeopardy
The Price Is Right
The Joker's Wild
Tic-Tac-Dough
Wheel of Fortune
$25,000 Pyramid
Choplifter (Broderbund)
A.E. (Broderbund)
Hard Hat Attack (Electronic Arts)
Pinball Construction Set
(Electronic Arts)
Neomancer (Synapse)
Rainbow Walker (Synapse)
Jawbreaker II (Sierra-On-Line)
Troll's Tale (Sierra-On-Line)
Capture the Flag (Sirius)
Gruds In Space (Sirius)
Type Attack (Sirius)
Zork I, II and III (Infocom)
Deadline (Infocom)
Starcross (Infocom)
Suspended (Infocom)
Witness (Infocom)
Planetfall (Infocom)
Enchanter (Infocom)
Infidel (Infocom)
Temple of Aphsai (Epyx)
Upper Reaches of Aphsai (Epyx)
Gateway to Aphsai (Epyx)
Curse of Ra (Epyx)
Pit Stop (Epyx)
Rootin' Tootin' (Hesware)

Gridrunner (Hesware)
Oubliette (Hesware)
Sierra Boxing (Sierra-On-Line)
The Prisoner (Sierra-On-Line)
B.C.'s Quest for Tires
(Sierra-On-Line)
Sammy Lightfoot
(Sierra-On-Line)
Apple Cider Spider
(Sierra-On-Line)
Oil's Well (Sierra-On-Line)
Threshold (Sierra-On-Line)
Frogger (Sierra-On-Line)
Lode Runner (Broderbund)

Commodore Business Machines
1200 Wilson Drive
West Chester, PA 19380

The following are programs
published or licensed by
Commodore for its home and
small business computers.

VIC 20 Software

CATEGORY: CHILDREN'S LEARNING
SERIES

Zortek and the Microchips
Chopper Math
Home Babysitter
Visible Solar System
Speed/Bingo Math

CATEGORY: ARCADE GAMES

Jupiter Lander
Mole Attack
Radar Rat Race
Raid on Fort Knox
Road Race
Super Alien
The Sky Is Falling
VIC Avenger
Cosmic Cruncher
Money Wars
Star Post
Tooth Invaders

CATEGORY: SCOTT ADAMS
ADVENTURE SERIES

Adventureland
Pirate Cove
Atomic Mission

The Count
Voodoo Castle

Commodore 64 Software

Commodore 264 Software

IBM
Entry Systems Division
P.O. Box 1328
Boca Raton, FL 33432

This is an initial listing of
    IBM-provided software for the
    IBM PCjr home computer. In
    parentheses is the name of the
    software house, if it is a
    non-IBM-written program.

Juggles' Butterfly (The Learning
  Company)
Bumble Plot (The Learning
  Company)
Casino Games 1.05
Adventures in Math
Adventure 1.0
Adventure in Serenia 1.0
Arithmetic Games
Fact Track 1.0

CATEGORY: HOME MANAGEMENT

HomeWord word processing
  (Sierra-On-Line, Inc.)
Personal Communications
  Manager
Home Budget, Jr
EasyWriter (Information
  Unlimited Software, Inc.)
pfs:FILE (Software Publishing
  Corporation)
pfs:REPORT (Software
  Publishing Corporation)
Time Manager 1.05 (The Image
  Producers, Inc.)
Dow Jones Reporter 1.0 (Dow
  Jones)
MultiPlan 1.10 (Microsoft)
PeachText 1.0 (MSA Peachtree)
VisiCalc 1.2 (VisiCorp)
Word Proof 1.0

CATEGORY: PROGRAMMING

IBM PCjr BASIC (cartridge)
Turtle Power
Fixed Disk Organizer
DOS 2.10
BASIC Program Development
  System
BASIC Compiler 1.0
COBOL Compiler 1.0
Diskette Librarian 1.0
File Command 1.0
LOGO 1.0
Macro Assembler 1.0
Personal Editor 1.0
Professional Editor 1.0

IBM
(Same address as above)

This listing covers IBM Personal
  Computer software both

endorsed by IBM and labeled
with the IBM name, although
most of them are written by
other companies mentioned
elsewhere.

CATEGORY: BUSINESS

VisiCalc 1.2 (VisiCorp)
VisiCalc 1.1 (VisiCorp)
Word Proof
Mailing List Manager
Inventory Control
  (MSA/Peachtree Software)
Dow Jones Reporter (Dow Jones)
Time Manager (Microsoft)
EasyWriter 1.1 (IUS)
EasyWriter 1.2 (IUS)
IBM Payroll (MSA/Peachtree)
IBM Payroll (BPI Systems)
IBM Job Cost (BPI Systems)
MultiPlan (Microsoft)
pfs:FILE (Software Publishing)
pfs:REPORT (Software
  Publishing)
IBM Personal Editor
PeachText (MSA/Peachtree)
The Accounting System
  (MSA/Peachtree)
IBM General Ledger 1.1 XT
  (MSA/Peachtree)
IBM Accounts Receivable 1.1 XT
  (MSA/Peachtree)
IBM Accounts Payable 1.1 XT
  (MSA/Peachtree)
IBM Inventory Control 1.1 XT
  (MSA/Peachtree)
IBM Payroll 1.1 XT
  (MSA/Peachtree)

CATEGORY: GAMES

Decathlon (Microsoft)
Casino Games
Fact Track
Arithmetic Games Set 1
Arithmetic Games Set 2
Typing Tutor
101 Monochrome Mazes
Adventure in Serenia
  (Sierra-On-Line)
IBM Strategy Games

CATEGORY: HOME MANAGEMENT

The IBM PC Home Budget
  Program

CATEGORY: EDUCATION

Private Tutor
Learning DOS 2.0
Multiplication Tables
Learning to Program BASIC

CATEGORY: PROGRAMMING
  LANGUAGES

IBM PC-DOS 2.0 (XT version)
IBM BASIC 2.0
CP/M-86
IBM COBOL Compiler
IBM LOGO
APL, A Programming Language
BASIC Primer
IBM Macro Assembler
IBM FORTRAN Compiler
UCSD p-System with Pascal
UCSD Pascal Compiler
UCSD p-System with
  FORTRAN-77
UCSD FORTRAN Compiler
UCSD p-System Runtime
  Support
IBM FileCommand
IBM Professional Editor
BASIC Programming
  Development System
IBM Diskette Librarian

CATEGORY: COMMUNICATIONS

Bisynchronous 3270 Emulation
  1.0
SNA 3270 Emulation and RJE
  Support
IBM 3101 Emulation

Hewlett-Packard
3000 Hanover Street
Palo Alto, CA 94304

This was one of the first lists of
  software for the HP-150 touch
  screen desktop computer. More
  compatible software is being
  added on a regular basis.

CATEGORY: WORD PROCESSING

WordStar (MicroPro)
MailMerge (MicroPro)
SpellStar (MicroPro)

WordStar/MailMerge/SpellStar
(MicroPro)
MemoMaker

CATEGORY: BUSINESS

MicroPlan (Chang Labs)
MicroPlan Consolidation Module
(Chang Labs)
MultiPlan (Microsoft)
Context MBA (Content
Management)
Lotus 1-2-3 (Lotus Development)
Personal Card File
VisiCalc (VisiCorp)
Condor 20-1 (Condor Corp.)
Condor 20-3 (Condor Corp.)
Condor 20-1 to 20-3 Upgrade Kit
(Condor Corp.)
BPI General Accounting (BPI
Systems)
BPI Personal Accounting (BPI
Systems)
BPI Accounts Receivable (BPI
Systems)
dBase II (Ashton-Tate)
Personal Business Calculator
pfs:FILE
pfs:REPORT
pfs:WRITE
pfs:GRAPH

CATEGORY: PROGRAMMING

HP-150 BASIC
Compiled BASIC (Microsoft)
Pascal (Microsoft)
COBOL (Microsoft)
FORTRAN (Microsoft)

CATEGORY: GRAPHICS

Picture Perfect (Computer
Support Corp.)
Diagraph (Computer Support
Corp.)
Series 100 Graphics
GraphWriter Basic (Graphwriter
Communications)

CATEGORY: COMMUNICATIONS

DSN/Link

CATEGORY: GAMES

Temple of Aphsai (Epyx, Inc.)
Ricochet
Type Attack (Sirius Software)

MS-DOS 2.0
Microsoft Corporation
10700 Northrup Way
Bellevue, WA 98004

These packages are written by
other companies to run with
Microsoft's MS-DOS 2.0
operating system. This is the
operating system that is directly
compatible with the IBM PC.
Many computers, including
Compaq Computer Corp.,
Corona Data Systems, and
Eagle Computer Corp., have
MS-DOS 2.0 as their standard
operating systems and can run
most, if now all, of the
following programs. Of course,
most will also run on the IBM
PC without modification.

CATEGORY: WORD PROCESSING

PeachText 5000 (MSA/Peachtree)
pfs:WRITE (Software Publishing)
WordStar 3.3 (MicroPro)
MailMerge 3.3 (MicroPro)
SpellStar 3.3 (MicroPro)
SuperWriter 1.0 (Sorcim)
Select 3.0 (Select Information
Systems)
Select 2.2 (Select Information
Systems)
StarIndex 1.0 (MicroPro)
Spell-It 1.08 (Bersurk Systems)
The Word Plus 1.21 (Oasis
Systems)
Word Plus-PC (Professional
Software)
Multimate 3.11 (Softword
Systems)

CATEGORY: SPREADSHEETS

UltraCalc
MultiPlan 1.06 (Microsoft)
VisiCalc 1.4 (VisiCorp)
VisiCalc 1.1 (VisiCorp)
SuperCalc 2 (Sorcim)
The Financial Planner
(Ashton-Tate)
CalcStar 1.46 (MicroPro)
PlanStar 1.0 (MicroPro)
Lotus 1-2-3 (Lotus Development)
SuperCalc 3 (Sorcim)

CATEGORY: ACCOUNTING

Peachtree Accounting 2.0
(Peachtree Software)
Home Accountant Plus
(Continental Software)
Software Fitness Program (Open
Systems)
RealWorld Accounting (MBSI)
ADS General Accounting (ADS)
Multi-Journal Accounting
(American Datacom)
Total Accounting System 2.3
(TCS)
Client Ledger System (TCS)
Total Materials (TCS)
CYMA Accounting (CYMA)
Small Business System (CYMA)

CATEGORY: DATA BASE
MANAGEMENT

dBASE II (Ashton-Tate)
pfs:FILE (Software Publishing)
pfs:REPORT (Software
Publishing)
Personal Pearl 1.6 (Relational
Systems)
Data Base Manager II (Alpha
Software)
Office Filer 1.0 (Digital
Marketing)
InfoStar 1.02 (MicroPro)
DataFax 2.7 (Link Systems)
VersaForm 2.7 (Applied Software
Technology)
Optimum Document Tracking
System (International Red Hot
Software)
TIM III (Innovative Software)
Friday 1.0 (Ashton-Tate)
QuickCode (Fox & Geller)

CATEGORY: COMMUNICATIONS

Crosstalk 3.0 (Microstuf)
Relay 1.2 (VM Personal
Computing)
ASCOM 2.2 (Dynamic
Microprocessor Associates)

CATEGORY: VERTICAL MARKETS

Small Bookkeeping Services &
Public Accountants (ADS)
Retail Florists (ADS)
Churches (ADS)
Private Membership Club (ADS)

Veterinarians (ADS)
The Campaign Fund Tracking
  System (International Red Hot
  Software)
The Advocate (Alta Sierra)
Dental Orthodontic Practice
  Management (CYMA)
Medical and Chiropractic
  Management (CYMA)
Construction Management
  (CYMA)
Client Accounting (CYMA)
Real Estate Strategy 1.0 (Real
  Estate Computer Center, Inc.)

CATEGORY: GENERAL BUSINESS

TK! Solver 1.2 (Software Arts)
Bottom Line Strategist
  (Ashton-Tate)
Personal Calendar 1.1 (Peachtree
  Software)
The Ultimate 2.2 (Computer
  Creations)
Stock Portfolio Reporter (Micro
  Investment Systems)
Confidence Factor (Simple
  Software)
Milestone 1.09 (Digital
  Marketing)
Optimum System Search System
  (International Red Hot
  Software)
Optimum Sales Tracking System
  (International Red Hot
  Software)
Optimum Label Package (Intl.
  Red Hot Software)

CATEGORY: GRAPHICS

VisiTrend/Plot (VisiCorp)
pfs:GRAPH (Software
  Publishing)
Fast Graphs 2.0 (Innovative
  Software)
Caddraft 1.0 (Personal CAD
  Systems)
Cadplan 1.3 (Personal CAD
  Systems)
uGRAF 1.2 (Transparent Data
  Systems)
Drawing Processor (Graphics
  Systems)
AutoCAD 1.4 (AutoDesk)

CATEGORY: PROGRAMMING LANGUAGES

GW-BASIC (Microsoft)
C Compiler (Lattice)
C-Food Smorgasbord (Lattice)
FORTRAN (Microsoft)
Pascal (Microsoft)
BASIC Compiler (Microsoft)
PL/1-86 (Digital Research)
Pascal MT+86 (Digital Research)
CIS COBOL (Digital Research)
Level II COBOL (Digital
  Research)
Dr. LOGO (Digital Research)

CATEGORY: UTILITIES

Race 1.04 (Robec)
VSI 2.05 (Amber Systems)
Smartkey (Heritage Software)
CP+ 2.0 (Taurus Software)

CATEGORY: GAMES

Decathlon (Microsoft)
Flight Simulator (Microsoft)
Zork I (Infocom)
Zork II (Infocom)
Zork III (Infocom)
PC-Man (Orion Software)
Paratrooper (Orion Software)
J-Bird (Orion Software)
Pits and Stones (Orion Software)
Question (Alpha Software)
Night Mission PINBALL
  (subLOGIC Corp.)
Enchanter (Infocom)
Starcross (Infocom)
Suspended (Infocom)
Planetfall (Infocom)
Deadline (Infocom)
Witness (Infocom)
Space Strike (Datamost)
Market Mogul (Datamost)
Creature Creator (DesignWare)
Spellicopter (DesignWare)
Crypto Cube (DesignWare)
Eliza 3.0 (Artificial Intelligence
  Research)

CATEGORY: EDUCATIONAL AND TRAINING

HyperTyper (Summit Software)
Teach Yourself Lotus 1-2-3 (ATI)

Teach Yourself Peachtree
  Accounting (ATI)
Teach Yourself MS-DOS (ATI)
Teach Yourself dBASE II (ATI)
Teach Yourself SuperCalc (ATI)
Teach Yourself MultiPlan (ATI)
Teach Yourself VisiCalc (ATI)
Teach Yourself WordStar (ATI)
Software Sampler (ATI)
Vocabulary Building I (Resource
  International)
Vocabulary Building II (Resource
  Intl.)
Vocabulary Building III
  (Resource Intl.)
Verbs Past Tense/Past Participles
  (Resource Intl.)
Verbs II/Linking Verbs (Resource
  Intl.)
THINK PLUS (Resource Intl.)
Subtraction I (Resource Intl.)
Subtraction II (Resource Intl.)
Simple Addition (Resource Intl.)
Simple Division (Resource Intl.)
Sentences I (Resource Intl.)
Sentences II—Classification
  (Resource Intl.)
Multiplying Single Digits
  (Resource Intl.)
Letter-Writing (Resource Intl.)
Let's Have Fun Subtracting
  (Resource Intl.)
Let's Have Fun Counting
  (Resource Intl.)
Let's Have Fun Comparing
  (Resource Intl.)
Learning and Practicing with
  Money (Resource Intl.)
Learning and Practicing with
  Percentages (Resource Intl.)
Learning and Practicing with
  Fractions (Resource Intl.)
Learning and Practicing with
  Discounts (Resource Intl.)
Learning and Practicing with
  Equivalent Fractions (Resource
  Intl.)
Learning and Practicing with
  Decimals (Resource Intl.)
Adding Two-Digit Numbers with
  Carrying (Resource Intl.)
Adding Two-Digit Numbers
  without Carrying (Resource
  Intl.)

MS-DOS 1.25

The following list of software uses the 1.25 version, *not* the MS-DOS 2.0 version of this popular 16-bit operating system. All of the software in the above list, with a few exceptions, will also run under MS-DOS 1.25.

CATEGORY: BUSINESS

25th Hour (Softrend, Inc.)
Accounts Payable (MSA/Peachtree, IBM)
Accounts Payable (Information Unlimited Software [IUS])
Accounts Payable (MBSI)
Accounts Receivable (MSA/Peachtree, IBM)
Accounts Receivable (IUS)
Accounts Receivable (MBSI)
Benchmark Word Processing (Megasoft Corp.)
Benchmark Spelling Checker (Megasoft Corp.)
Benchmark Mailing List (Megasoft Corp.)
Business Forecasting Model (VisiCorp)
Canadian Payroll (IUS)
CanTax (Atlantic Research)
Client Strategist (Dynamic Business Software)
Correspondence Control (Domus Software)
Courtney Data Base (Courtney)
Data Fax (Link Systems)
Data Reporter (Synergistic Software)
Datakeep (Mathtech, Inc.)
Datasafe (International Microcomp)
DeskTop Plan (VisiCorp)
EasyCalc (Norell Data Systems)
EasyEdit (Norell Data Systems)
EasyFiler (IUS)
EasyProof (Norell Data Systems)
EasySpeller (IUS)
EasyText (Norell Data Systems)
EasyWriter 1.1 (IBM, IUS)
EasyWriter II 64K (IUS)
EasyWriter II 96K (IUS)

Electronic Webster (Cornucopia Software)
F.C.M. (Continental Software)
Financial Analysis (ExecuWare)
Financial Planning Language (Ashton-Tate)
General Ledger (IBM, MSA/Peachtree)
General Ledger (MSBI)
General Ledger & Financial (IUS)
HAI Accounting (Holland Automation)
Homestead Farm Management (Homestead Computer Co.)
Inventory Control (MSA/Peachtree, IBM)
Inventory Control & Analysis (IUS)
The Landlord (Systems Plus)
List Manager (MSA/Peachtree)
Loan Planner (Generic Transforms)
Memoplan (Softlink)
MicroGantt (Westico, Inc.)
Microplan (Softlink)
Money Decisions I (Eagle Software)
Money Decisions II (Eagle Software)
Money Meastro (Innoysys Software)
Multi-State Payroll (CYMA)
Order Entry and Invoice (IUS)
PDS Financial System (Prairie Data Systems)
Personal Equity Management System (Personal Equity Computing)
Payroll (MBSI)
PeachCalc (MSA/Peachtree)
Perfect Calc (Perfect Software)
Perfect Filer (Perfect Software)
Perfect Speller (Perfect Software)
Perfect Writer (Perfect Software)
Perfin (Digital Engineering Group)
Perfmaster (Westminster Software)
Power Planner (Starware)
Project Scheduler (Scitor Corp.)
Proofwriter (Image Processing Systems)
Quotrix (Insoft, Inc.)

Random House Proofreader (Aspen Software)
Real Estate Analyzer (Howardsoft)
Real Estate Investment (Datamost)
Select Word Processing (Select Information Systems)
Sideways (Funk Software)
Spellbinder (Lexisoft)
Spelling Proofreader (MSA/Peachtree)
StatPack (Northwest Analytical)
The Survey System (Creative Research)
Tax Decisions (Eagle Software)
Tax Preparer (Howardsoft)
VisiCalc IV (VisiCorp)
VisiFile (VisiCorp)
VisiDex (VisiCorp)
Volkswriter (Lifetrcc)
Volkswriter International (Lifetree)
Word Perfect (Satellite Software)
Word Plus (Oasis)
Word Wand (Tanda Software)
Wordix (Emerging Technology)
WordMater (Software Systems)
Wordtrix (Insoft, Inc.)

Texas Instruments, Inc.
P.O. Box 2909, MS 2013
Austin, TX 78769

The following is a list of software available for the Texas Instruments Professional Computer. Many more MS-DOS 2.0 programs are available as well, especially the most popular programs, but this list only includes these programs *not* mentioned above.

CATEGORY: ACCOUNTING

Accounts Payable (State of the Art)
Accounts Receivable (State of the Art)
General Ledger (State of the Art)
Inventory Control (State of the Art)
Job Cost (BPI Systems)

Accounting Plus (ASK Micro)
Budget & Financial Reporting
  (State of the Art)
Magis Plus (Management
  Accountability Group)
Sales Invoicing (MSA/Peachtree)
Tax Program (Micro-Tax)
Tax Program (Plenary Systems)

CATEGORY: COMMUNICATIONS

ASCOM (Lifeboat Assoc.)
TI 940 Emulator (Houston
  Computer Services [HCS])
ADDS Emulator (HCS)
Televideo Emulator (HCS)
VT100 Emulator (HCS)
3780 Communications (TI)
NaturalLink Access to Dow Jones
  News Retrieval (TI)
TTY Communications (TI)

CATEGORY: DATA BASE
  MANAGEMENT

Access Manager (Digital
  Research)
EntryPoint (Datalex)
FCM—Filing/Cataloging/Mailing
  (Continental Software)
UltraFile (Continental Software)
The Formula + G.A.S. (Lifeboat
  Assoc.)

CATEGORY: FINANCIAL MODELING
  AND SPREADSHEETS

The Executive Package (Alpha
  Software)
Investment Evaluator (Dow
  Jones)
Market Analyzer (Dow Jones)
Market Microscope (Dow Jones)

CATEGORY: GRAPHICS

Display Manager (Digital
  Research)
DR Graph (Digital Research)
GSX-86 (Digital Research)

CATEGORY: WORD PROCESSING

The Final Word (Mark of the
  Unicorn)
MicroSpell (Lifeboat Assoc.)
PMATE (Lifeboat Assoc.)
SuperSpellGuard (Sorcim)
VisiWord (VisiCorp)

VisiSpell (VisiCorp)
Samna Word II (Samna Corp.)

CATEGORY: VERTICAL MARKET

EasySpeller Legal 1.2 (IUS)
EasySpeller Legal II (IUS)
EasySpeller Medical 1.2 (IUS)
EasySpeller Medical II (IUS)
Lexiter Legal Office Management
  (Contract Research)
PASS Client Write-Up (Plenary
  Systems)
PASS TWO Time & Changes
  (Plenary Systems)
TAX II (Plenary Systems)

CATEGORY: OPERATING SYSTEMS

Concurrent CP/M-86 (Digital
  Research)
CP/M-86 (Digital Research)
UCSD p-System Development
  (SoftTech Microsystems)

NEC Information Systems
Five Militia Drive
Lexington, MA 02173

This list contains packages
  endorsed and sold by NEC for
  its Advanced Personal
  Computer.

CATEGORY: OPERATING SYSTEMS

CP/M-86
MS-DOS
Concurrent CP/M-86
UCSD p-System Runtime OS

CATEGORY: LANGUAGES

RM/COBOL
MS-BASIC Interpreter
MS-BASIC Compiler
MS-FORTRAN Compiler
MS-Pascal Compiler

CATEGORY: ACCOUNTING PLUS

General Ledger
Accounts Receivable
Accounts Payable
Inventory Control
Sales Order Entry
Purchase Order Entry
Payroll

CATEGORY: WORD PROCESSING

Benchmark Word Processor
Benchmark Telecommunicator
Benchmark Mailing List Manager

CATEGORY: MICROPLAN
  SPREADSHEETS

Business Planner
Spreadsheet-to-Planner Upgrade
Consolidator
Spreadsheet

CATEGORY: DATA BASE

dBASE II

CATEGORY: COMMUNICATIONS

ASYNC-86
BISYNC-86/3780
BISYNC-86/3270

CATEGORY: BUSINESS

Milestone project management
The Firm Solution legal time and
  billing

CATEGORY: GRAPHICS

GraphPlan
GraphWriter
VIDEOGRAPH Update Module
VIDEOGRAPH VGTYPE
  Module
VIDEOGRAPH Keyboard
  Version
VIDEOGRAPH

Convergent Technologies
Advanced Information Products
  Division
2441 Mission College Blvd.
Santa Clara, CA 95050

This list includes *only* Taskware
  templates for the company's
  WorkSlate briefcase computer.

Inventory
Accounts Receivable
Accounts Payable
Real Estate
Job Costing
Insurance Analyzer
Consultant

Auditing
Time/Project Management
Data Base
Personal Tax
Business Travel

Sales Reporter
Loan Analyzer
Portfolio Analysis
Estate Planning

Financial Statements
Cash Management
Marketing Management
Business Tax

Glossary

Access time Amount of time it takes data to be read from or written to a disk or cassette tape

Accumulator A register inside a microprocessor that receives, totals, and holds information in the form of bits for arithmetic and logic operations

Acoustic coupler modem A communication device that has two rubber or plastic cups to accept the ends of a telephone handset

Address register Exact location in microprocessor memory where an address is held

Address Spot in CPU memory identified with specific binary digit. Used as a verb, *address* means to refer to an address register or location in storage

Algorithm A set of standard procedures or rules for solving a problem

Alphanumeric Description of letters (alphabetic), number (numeric), and punctuation marks used in computer languages

ALU Arithmetic Logic Unit

APL Acronym for A Programming Language

Applications package A group of programs which carries out a user's task or job

Applications program A set of routines and instructions through which a user executes tasks or jobs with a computer

Architecture The physical structure of a microcomputer's internal operations, including memory, registers, ALU, and so forth

ASCII Acronym for American Standard Code for Information Interchange. It gives a unique 7-bit code for each letter, number, symbol, and punctuation mark to create compatibility among different computer systems and languages. In its basic form, it has 128 codes; in its graphics form, 256 codes

Assembler A computer program which converts into machine language (see below) another computer program written in a high-level English-like language

Assembly language A program language, which uses mnemonics, that breaks high-level languages into digital codes. It is one step more English-like than machine language, but more symbolic than a high-level language

Bank switching A technique that allows a computer to effectively use more internal memory than it normally could be moving among different "banks" of internal memory. For example, although an 8-bit computer normally can only access 64K RAM, bank switching increases that to 96K, 128K, even 256K RAM

BASIC Acronym for Beginner's All-Purpose Symbolic Instruction Code. This English-like language is the most popular language in which computers are being written for personal computers and microcomputers

Baud A measurement of the rate of data transmission. A unit of signaling speed which is equivalent to a

229

rate of one unit-time per second. Thus, 300-baud would mean 300 unique signaling events per second

Binary digit The smallest unit of electronic information processed by a computer

Bit Computer jargon for binary digit, the smallest unit of electronic information processed by a computer

Bit stream A flow of binary digits in serial fashion

Block diagram An easy-to-understand drawing that outlines the functions and relationships within a computer system or the components of computer devices

Boot Computer jargon for starting up a computer and/or loading a program from tape or disk. Also, *booting a disk, boot the system,* and *system boot* are common jargon

BPS Acronym for Bits Per Second

Briefcase computer A type of self-contained microcomputer that includes a CPU, keyboard, display (usually liquid crystal), RAM, ROM, applications software, and often a printer and a communications modem in a cabinet small enough to fit into a regular briefcase. See *lap computer*

Buffer Within microcomputers and their peripherals, an area of RAM memory set aside for temporary storage of data to prevent an overload of data transmission. Most often used in microcomputers to store a file for printing while the regular internal memory remains free for further processing. Often found in printers as well

Bug Computer jargon for an error in a program

Bulletin board Electronic message center accessible through the telephone lines. Often set up by hobbyists or user's groups for general communications

Bus Circuits or a group of circuits that provide a path between a microprocessor and any other part of a computer. The three types of buses are data, address, and control, each of which move digital signals and information in the form of bits

Byte A group of 8 bits which a computer processes as a single unit. One byte generally corresponds to one character. Information stored in a computer is measured in bytes. One thousand bytes equals a kilobyte, called a Kbyte or K

CAD Acronym for at least two phrases: as it applies to manufacturing and industrial design, Computer-Assisted Design, or as it applies to medicine, Computer-Aided Diagnosis

CAI Acronym for Computer-Assisted (or Aided) Instruction

Cartridge A plastic case in which ROM-based applications programs implanted on chips are perma-

nently stored. Most often used for video games and software for inexpensive home computers

Cassette interface The physical circuit that connects a cassette tape recorder and a home computer

Cassette recorder Any device which uses audio or digital cassette tapes to store digital signals from a microcomputer

Cathode ray tube A video tube used to show "output": letters, numbers, symbols, and graphics, on its screen. Abbreviated to CRT

CEEFAX The British Post Office's name for its teletext system

Character Letters, numbers, symbols, and punctuation, each of which has a specific meaning. Roughly, one byte is equal to one character

Character printer A computer printer which prints one letter, number, symbol, or punctuation mark at a time

Character printer Any printer which strikes one character, symbol, letter, or number at a time, as opposed to a line printer

Chip Common term for an integrated circuit etched on a tiny piece of silicon or germanium

Clock card A plug-in board which contains on integrated circuitry a real-time clock and RAM memory

COBOL Acronym for "COmmon Business-Oriented Language." A high-level programming language designed during the 1960s for business applications. Used most often in the past for minicomputers, now is being more frequently used with the second and third generation personal computers

Compatibility The ability of different computers or peripherals to work together without extraordinary physical connections of software modifications

Compiler A computer program which, like an assembler, converts a program written in an English-like language into machine language instructions (see below). However, a compiler is more complex than an assembler because it may analyze the high-level program, actually direct computer operations, and include sets of its own programs, none of which an assembler or interpreter can do

Computer language Any group of letters, numbers, symbols, or punctuation marks, or phrases and sentences made up of these which enable a user to instruct or communicate with a computer

Configuration Any assemblage of computer equipment and software arranged in a functional group. Often used to describe required groupings of hardware and software

Continuous feed In printing, using a continuous roll or

attached sheets of paper to print page after page without stopping

Control key The key on a computer keyboard that, when used with another key, instructs the computer to execute a command

Correspondence-quality printer Any printer or printing method that produces print quality similar or equal to that produced by an office typewriter

Courseware Name for computer programs used in educational or teaching applications

CP/M Acronym for Control Program/Microcomputers operating system and its more recent derivatives. The most popular operating system for microcomputers based on the 8080, Z-80 and 8085 families of microprocessors and their more recent 16-bit cousins, Z-8000, 8086, and 8088. More recent versions are called CP/M-80 and CP/M-86

CPS Acronym for Characters Per Second, the measurement of a printer's speed

CPU Acronym for Central Processing Unit, where all data processing occurs within a microprocessor. CPU is commonly used as an acronym for the entire microprocessor

CRT Acronym for Cathode Ray Tube, it has come to mean a CRT terminal which includes a video screen and a keyboard in one unit

Cursor Dot on a video screen that indicates where the next character will be shown; also used to indicate move or search operations on the screen

Cybernetics The study of artificial intelligence

Daisywheel printer A character printer which produces correspondence-quality type with a typing element on which each spoke contains one character. The element's spokes resemble the petals on a daisy, thus daisywheel.

Data Any kind of information a computer processes. The singular for one piece of information is *datum*

Data base Any organized collection of information

Data transmission rate Baud rate

DBMS Acronym for Data Base Management System, a collection of programs that organizes and processes any given group or collection of information

Debug Computer jargon for removing errors from software

Dedicated A computer structured or programmed for one specific purpose—a dedicated word processor

Desktop computer A system with all of the basic elements of a computer which fits onto the top of a desk. As used in this book, it describes a class of more expensive microcomputers most often found on the desk of managers and staff members of busi-

nesses, professional practices, corporations, and large organizations

Device Any type of computer hardware

Direct connect modem A communications device which plugs directly into the telephone line

Disc 1. As commonly used in the electronics industry, a round, aluminized, metallic oxide, plastic-coated plate used for storing video images and digital data which can be read by an optical laser videodisc player. 2. Often used mistakenly as synonymous with *disk*

Disk A thin, plastic-coated metallic oxide plate on which computer data is stored as magnetic impulses. See *floppy disk, minifloppy disk, microfloppy disk,* and *hard disk*

Disk drive An electromechanical device that operates the process of storing digital data from a computer and retrieving data from a disk and loading it into a computer's internal memory and CPU

Disk operating system A collection of programs that controls the interaction between the CPU and the disk drive

Diskette Synonym for a 5.25-inch diameter or smaller floppy disk. Often used as opposed to an 8-inch floppy disk or any size hard disk. Diskette is not the term preferred in this book or by this author

Documentation 1. The printed or written record of program codes and instructions. 2. The package of printed manuals and materials that show users how to operate computers and programs

DOS Disk Operating System, which controls the operation of any computer with a floppy or hard disk as the primary mass storage device

Dot matrix printer A relatively high-speed character printer which uses a matrix of wires to strike a ribbon and produce the impression of a number, letter, or symbol on paper

Double density A process by which twice as much data as normal can be stored on one side of a floppy disk

Double sided The ability to store data on both sides of a floppy disk; in this, a disk drive has two read-write heads

Downtime Computer jargon for periods in which a computer or program malfunctions

Dual disks A device in which two floppy disk drives are mounted in one cabinet and operated by one controller

Dump Jargon for sending data from a computer to a mass storage device, a printer, or other output device

Editor A program that lets a user correct, change, or manipulate text or programs within a computer system. Also called a *text editor*

EIES Acronym for Electronic Information Exchange System. A leading computer conferencing network begun at the New Jersey Institute of Technology

Electronic mail Messages sent through or received by automated or computerized devices, usually through the telephone lines, but through any electronic communications medium, including satellite and microwave

Electrostatic printer A type of printer that uses special paper and imprints or creates characters by an electric discharge between the print element and the paper

EPROM Acronym for Erasable Programmable Read Only Memory

Erasable Programmable Read Only Memory A type of "permanent" memory that can be erased by exposure to ultraviolet light and permanently reprogrammed

Ergonomics Also called *human factors engineering,* the science and technology of making computers easier and more comfortable for people to use

Error messsage The message a computer produces when a user has made a mistake in an entry or computer "grammar"

Execute A command that tells a computer to carry out a user's instruction or program

External memory Any mass storage device outside the microcomputer itself; a disk drive, hard disk, or cassette recorder is always external memory as in any RAM memory board stored in a cabinet separate from the microcomputer

Facsimile An exact reproduction of printed material. In modern communications, computers and automated devices are used to transmit facsimiles through large networks

Fetch An instruction to call up an instruction or information from a computer's memory and process it through the CPU

Field Any coherent or organized unit of information within a file. For example, in any account, a person's name is a field, her address is another field. The whole group of information centered around one topic, such as an account, is called a *record*

File A group of records or information that the user considers a unit, such as a file of all mail order customers or all of the chapters of a book

Firmware Programs stored inside a computer's ROM; as compared to software, programs stored on media outside the computer itself

Fixed memory See *ROM*

Floppy disk Standard term for an 8-inch-in-diameter round, metallic oxide, plastic-coated plate on which digital data is stored as magnetic impulses. See *minifloppy disk* and *microfloppy disk*

Floppy disk drive An electromechanical device which receives data from a computer and stores them on a round, flexible, metallic oxide-coated plastic disk. It also retrieves data from this disk and transmits them into the computer's internal memory

Flowchart A simple outline using standard logical functions, boxes, and symbols that helps a programmer write a program more efficiently and accurately

FORTRAN Acronym for FORmula TRANslator, a high-level programming language developed in the 1950s by IBM for mathematical, engineering, or scientific applications

GIGO Computer jargon for Garbage In, Garbage Out, meaning that you cannot put inaccurate data into a computer without getting inaccurate data out

Glitch Computer jargon for an electromechanical error or problem in the hardware

Graphics tablet A rectangular tablet layered with printed circuits with which a user can create drawings and art works through a microcomputer. The drawings can be displayed on a video display, stored in memory as digital information, or printed out on paper, often in more than one color

Hard copy Printed information produced from a computer for permanent storage. Term coined by computer pioneer Ted Nelson

Hard disk drive A mechanism in which is permanently sealed a metallic oxide platter. On this platter is sorted relatively large quantities of computerized information. The drive works like, but much faster than, a floppy disk drive retrieving and transmitting data from and to a computer

Hardware A generic term describing any physical equipment used in a computer system

High-level language A language developed to make computer programming easier for large numbers of people. Such languages use English-like commands, instructions, and syntax. BASIC, FORTRAN, COBOL, Pascal, and MUMPS are examples

Home computer Any microcomputer used primarily in the home. As used in this book, any microcomputer costing less than $1,000 and designed for use by a family

Home information system An electronic service of many kinds of data bases, programs, electronic mail, and message facilities offered by outside companies or corporations for use by families and individuals who have home computers with communications or home communications terminals

IC Acronym for Integrated Circuit, a tiny silicon or

germanium slice onto which are etched thousands of transistors, capacitors, and other electronic components

Icon A graphic symbol used in the most advanced operating systems and program menus to represent a specific function. Pioneered by Apple Computer with its Lisa Technology and Macintosh computers

Information provider Any company that supplies information to a computer network, such as CompuServe or SOURCE, and makes that information available to the public for free or a fee

Input Any kind of information or instructions one enters into a computer

Input device Anything used to enter information or instructions into a computer, most commonly a keyboard, disk drive, light pen, graphics tablet, touch-sensitive screen, and so on

Instruction A group of bits that determines one computer operation

Integrated circuit See *IC*

Integrated package Type of software which incorporates at least several functions onto the small disk and allows them to easily interchange information. Integrated functions usually include spreadsheets, word processing, graphics, communications, and information management

Integrated video terminal Any microcomputer that combines a computer, telephone, communications modem, printer, and other devices into one modem communications/information appliance

Integrated voice/data terminal A desktop microcomputer terminal that can simultaneously transmit and receive voice and data along the same wires. Used more and more often for communications between a microcomputer and a mainframe for retrieving information and program. Will be the heart of any home information system used with videotex networks

Intelligent terminal A terminal that has its own microprocessor and can execute some functions on its own, saving the processing time of the central computer. It has limited internal memory and processing power, and most often, no mass storage device

Interface Any hardware/software system that links a microcomputer to any other device

Interpreter A computer program which interprets and executes a program written in a high-level language into machine language one instruction at a time.

I/O Acronym for Input/Output

I/O port A connection between a microcomputer's CPU and any external devices, including video monitors and peripherals

IVDT See *integrated voice/data terminal*

IVT See *integrated video terminal*

Jack Any plug socket on a computer through which an external device, such as a cassette recorder, can be connected to a microcomputer

Joystick An instrument, usually with a lever, a knob, or rotating disk, with which to play video or computer games, or move a cursor or pointer around a display screen. Some believe it will be used extensively in the future as an input and cursor control device

K, kilo represents one thousand in normal counting. Stands for 1,024 bits or bytes in computerese: 16K stands for 16,384 bits or bytes

Keyboard Any input device through which you enter data into a computer by pressing buttons or keys or executing keystrokes. For microcomputers, it usually is laid out like a standard typewriter, but other types are often used in specific applications

Kilobyte 1,024 bytes. See *byte* and *kilo*

LAN Acronym for Local Area Network

Language The defined and logical group of characters which make up the means by which people give instructions to computers

Lap computer Synonymous with "briefcase computer"

Large Scale Integration See *LSI*

LCD Acronym for Liquid Crystal Display, which makes letters, numbers, or symbols appear by reflecting light and placing electrical charges on a special crystalline substance. Often used in watches, calculators, electronic games, and now especially briefcase computers

Letter-quality printer Synonymous with daisywheel printer

Library A collection of programs that serve one general purpose

Light pen An electric stylus with which a user can enter instructions or data through the video screen

Line printer Any printer which produces one line at a time, as opposed to character printers

Local Area Network A system of interconnections built around a standardized interface through which various kinds of computers and devices can communicate through one common pathway

Logic The organized way in which a microcomputer's CPU and circuitry performs various functions

LOGO A high-level, easy-to-learn computer language developed at Massachusetts Institute of Technology to help children learn to program and understand computer operations without knowing how to read or use a keyboard. Based on the concept of "sprite" and "turtle" graphics

Loop A series of program instructions that are repeated a certain number of times

Low-level language A type of computer language which is close to a computer's "native" language. As opposed to an English-like or high-level language

LSI Acronym for Large-Scale Integration, the method by which ten thousand or more logic elements are etched onto one square inch of an integrated circuit or chip. *VLSI* stands for Very Large Scale Integration, through which at least one hundred thousand elements are etched onto a one-square-inch chip

Machine language A computer's unique language written in digital code that its control unit accepts without translation or interpretation. It is represented as string of 1s and 0s, representing the off-on states of the electronic switches inside the computer

Mass storage Any place or device in which large amounts of digital information or programs are restored, such as a floppy disk, hard disk, or cassette tape

Megabyte Term for one million bytes, most often used when applied to the amount of storage in a disk drive system or RAM memory

Memory The location in a microprocessor that stores information and instructions; each bit of information or instruction has a unique location assigned to it within a memory

Memory board A board on which RAM chips (integrated circuits) are placed and which is inserted into an expansion port inside a computer to increase the size of its internal memory

Memory capacity Amount of available storage space, given in kilobytes or megabytes

Menu A list of choices within a program that allows a user to choose which part to work with. Menus allow users to easily and quickly move around within programs or packages without technical knowledge

Microcomputer An entire computer system with a microprocesor as its central processing unit, memory, and input/output devices

Microfloppy disk Any floppy disk under 4 inches in diameter. It appeared that the Sony 3.5-inch floppy disk was becoming the generally accepted standard for this size disk, but Hitachi and others were supporting disk sizes of 3.25 inches, 3.0 inches, and 3.8 inches

Microprocessor The "intelligent" part of a microcomputer which holds a complete arithmetic logic unit and central processing unit on a single chip of silicon

Minifloppy disk A 5.25-inch in diameter floppy disk.

This size is the universal standard for minifloppy disks. In this book, it is the term preferred over *diskette*

Modem Accepted term for the MOdulator-DEModulator device which allows a computer to communicate with another computer through the telephone lines. It turns digital signals into analog signals the telephone line can carry and converts analog signals into digital signals a computer can understand

Monitor software Internal ROM program that governs the process of starting a computer and operating its video display and other internal operations

Motherboard The layered plastic plate that provides space and connections for the CPU, I/O circuitry, buses, memory, display, and peripheral control chips

MPU Acronym for microprocessor

MSX Acronym for standard high-level language and operating system developed by Microsoft for a large group of Japanese computer manufacturers. Programs written in MSX for one computer will run on any other computer designed to accept MSX

Nibble Popular term for a 4-bit group of bits; half a byte

Nonvolatile Computer memory that is fixed or permanently etched onto a silicon chip

OCR Acronym for Optical Character Recognition, a type of device that scans the printed word and translates the letters, numbers, and symbols into digital signal for storage inside a computer system

Operating System: A computer's internal "traffic cop" which directs the flow of information and instructions into and out of the various parts of the computer

OS Acronym for Operating System

Output Any data or information a computer displays, prints, or transmits after its processes input. See *input* and *I/O*

Output device Any device that displays, prints, or transmits digital information after it is processed

Packet-switching In data communications, the process through which groups of bits are sent in bursts in between other digital signals

Packets The groups of bits sent through by packet-switching

Package Jargon for any collection of programs which carry out a specific function

Parallel interface A device through which a computer transmits information in groups which are the same size as its internal bus. An 8-bit CPU, for example, with a parallel interface would send 8 bits through the interface at one time

Pascal Popular, symbolic, and versatile high-level programming language named after seventeenth century mathematician Blaise Pascal

PC 1. Acronym for Personal Computer. 2. Often used as shorthand to describe the IBM Personal Computer

Peripheral Any external I/O device that communicates with a microcomputer, such as light pens, printers, and disk drives

Personal computer 1. Any microcomputer used primarily for individual purposes. 2. As used in this book, any microcomputer costing more than $1,000 primarily for individual purposes at home or in business or management

Plotter A printing device that uses special pens to draw charts, graphs, histograms, and other designs in printer form, often in numerous colors

Pocket computer An inexpensive microcomputer with limited memory that is small enough to be carried in a hand or a coat pocket

Port Physical connection between a computer and any add-on equipment

Portable computer Any complete microcomputer small enough to be carried by hand. See *transportable, briefcase,* and *pocket computer*

Printout Any information from a computer printed on a sheet of paper

Printer Any device that transfers data from the computer to a sheet of paper. See *character printer, dot matrix printer, line printer, electrostatic printer, daisy-wheel printer, letter-quality printer, correspondence-quality printer,* and *thermal printer*

Program A set or collection of instructions that causes a computer to carry out or execute a given function or operation. See *software*

Program step Each procedure with a program

Programmable Read Only Memory A type of permanent memory that can be reprogrammed with extraordinary means

PROM Acronym for Programmable Read Only Memory. See above

Prompt Any symbol on a video screen requesting a user to enter information at that location

QUBE The trademarked name of Warner AMEX Communications' interactive videotex service in Columbus, Ohio, and numerous other cities

QWERTY Abbreviation for the layout of a standard typewriter keyboard, taken from the first six letters in the third row

RAM Acronym for Random Access Memory

RAM disk A type of internal memory which stores information and responds like a disk drive

RAM card A small plastic board on which extra chips are fitted and used to expand the available internal memory of a microcomputer

Random Access Memory Any volatile memory into which you can "read" or call up data, or "write" or enter information or instructions. Any memory in which you can gain direct access to a memory location at any time. But it is volatile, that is, temporary, and all data and programs are destroyed when the power source is removed

Read Only Memory Any memory in which data or programs have been permanently fixed. ROM cannot be changed without special efforts

Read-write The process of sending data to a CPU or receiving data from a CPU. A *read-write head* is the stylus within a disk drive which picks up magnetic impulses stored on a disk and sends them to a CPU or receives them from a CPU and stores them on a floppy or hard disk

Record Any organized group of data. In a billing program, all of the information on a given person is a record

Refresh The process by which electric power is continuously fed to video displays, RAMs, and other components of a microcomputer to keep them working

Register One circuit or location within a CPU that holds or stores one bit

Removable cartridge tape A type of mass storage drive that uses high-capacity magnetic tape as a storage medium. Often used in minicomputer and microcomputer systems for permanent or backup storage of essential information

Resolution The total number of elements on a video screen through which displays are shown. One element is called a *point* or a *pixel* and is defined as the intersection of the vertical and horizontal axes on a video display. The more points on a screen, the higher the resolution, and the more clarity and definition the display provides

Response time The time it takes a computer to carry out instructions and process data.

ROM Acronym for Read Only Memory

Routines Logical groups of steps within a program

S-100 bus A standard bidirectional bus for microcomputers based on the the 8080, Z-80, and 8085 CPU

Scratch-pad memory Small RAM that temporarily holds information or instructions

Semiconductor Solid material, usually germanium or silicon, that allows a variable flow of electricity depending on temperatures and pressures applied to it. The material from which integrated circuits are made

Serial Fetching or executing instructions one-by-one

Serial interface A standard device that transmits digital data one bit at a time. The microcomputer standard is called the RS-232C serial interface

Serial interface port The physical connection between a microcomputer and any serial device

SIG Acronym for Special Interest Group

Simulation The creation of a model that reflects or imitates a real occurrence, event, or system

Slot Any special connection inside a microcomputer through which peripherals or add-on devices are attached. Also called *peripheral slot* or *expansion slot*

Smart modem Any communications device, using the telephone lines, with a built-in microprocessor executing intelligent functions such as automatic answer/dial, redialing of busy numbers, self-diagnostic tests, telephone number memory, and so on

Soft copy Opposite of *hard copy;* any letters, numbers, symbols, or words shown on a video screen or any device in an unprinted form

Software The term for any group of programs or sets of instructions which direct computer hardware

Solid-state Any electronic component made of solid materials that conduct electricity. As opposed to vacuum tubes, which conduct electricity through a vacuum

Special Interest Group Any group of computer users dedicated to a single purpose; the term has been popularized through the CompuServe Information Network

Speech synthesis Process of using a computer to create artificial speech. Also called *voice synthesis*

Spooler A device that allows simultaneous printing and processing with a microcomputer that normally can only do one operation at a time

Storage The process or location for holding information or instructions inside a computer memory

String A list of words or statements in a computer program

Syntax Set of rules dictating the "grammar" or logical structure of a computer language

Telecommunications Process of long-distance communications between computers most often through the telephone system, but also through any independent, noncomputer communications medium

Teletext Generic name for a one-way television broadcast system that flashes printed text on a TV screen while the regular broadcast continues; the system uses a portion of the "blank space" in the TV video signal

Temporary internal memory See *Random Access Memory* and *RAM*

Terminal Any device that allows a person to communicate with a computer: a video display with a keyboard, for example

Terminal emulator A software and hardware combination that enables a computer to act like any one or several common terminals and communicate with other computers

Thermal printer An inexpensive output device that uses a heated element to create characters on a special type of heat-sensitive paper

Time-sharing 1. A computer's capability of working with more than one terminal at a time. 2. Usually applied to minicomputers and large computers, a system through which various companies or individuals pay for access to different programs and applications

Touch screen A type of input device which places a special screen over a video display. The special screen has elements within it which are sensitive to human touch or near-touch. The Hewlett-Packard HP-150 is the first personal computer to popularize the concept

Trackball An input controller which uses a movable, round sphere to control a cursor, enter data, or execute commands within a computer. Most often used for computer games, trackballs were developed to help control the Lunar Landers during the Apollo moon landing program.

Tractor feed A mechanism and device through which continuous feed paper is guided through a printer

Translator A type of programming language which convert a high-level language program into a machine language program

Transportable computer Most often used to describe portable computers which weigh more than 10 pounds and less than 50 pounds and can be carried with a handle or their own carrying cases. It is too big to fit inside a briefcase or be carried in a coat pocket

UNIX Popular operating system and high-level programming language developed by Bell Laboratories to run supermicrocomputers and minicomputers

User's group A regular gathering of hobbyist computer owners and users who share information, programs, and assistance

Utility Any program which operates independently of an operating system and executes auxiliary functions, such as printing or making copies of data from one disk to another

VCR Acronym for Video Cassette Recorder

Video display Any device that shows computer output on a televisionlike screen. Also called *videoscreen* or *video monitor*

Video monitor Any video tube used as an output device for computer signals

Videotex Generic term for an interactive information network that works through the telephone lines, but displays its input and output on a video display and contains its own microprocessor and keyboard

Virtual memory A type of computer operation in which the data stored on a disk acts like it is "resident" or temporarily stored in a computer's RAM or internal memory. This allows faster access speeds and response times as well as greater storage capacities per record or file

VLSI Acronym for "Very Large Scale Integration." See *LSI*

Voice recognition The process through which a computer creates artificial human speech. Also called *speech recognition*

Volatile memory Any computer memory which is destroyed by a loss of electricity

Wafer The thin round piece of semiconductor material from which integrated circuits are made

Winchester disk drive Another term for *hard disk drive,* it comes from the code name IBM used in 1973 when it developed the first hard disk drive

Window The portion of a display showed at any given moment on a video screen

Word A basic unit or group of bits processed together. Microcomputers use words of 8, 16, or 32 bits long

Word length Also called "word size." The length of a rational grouping of bits. A byte has a word length of 8 bits; the word length for a 16-bit microcomputer is 16 bits

Word processing The process of using a computer to write, edit, and manipulate text

Bibliography

Albrecht, Bob; Finkel, Leroy; and Brown, Jerald R. *BASIC for Home Computers, A Self-Teaching Guide.* New York: John Wiley & Sons, Inc., Publishers, 1978.

Buckwalter, Len. *The Home Computer Book.* New York: Wallaby Books, 1978.

Covvey, H. Dominic, and McAlister, Neil Harding. *Computer Consciousness, Surviving the Automated 80s.* Reading, Mass.: Addison-Wesley Publishing Co., 1980.

Dwyer, Thomas A., and Critchfield, Margot. *BASIC and the Personal Computer.* Reading, Mass: Addison-Wesley Publishing Co., 1978.

Eischen, Martha. *CompuGuide, A Consumer's Guide to Small Business Computers.* Beaverton, Ore.: Dilithium Press, 1982.

Foster, Caxton C. *Programming a Microcomputer: 6502.* Reading, Mass.: Addison-Wesley Publishing Co., 1978.

Gilmore, Charles M. *Beginner's Guide to Microprocessors.* Blue Ridge Summit, Penn.: TAB Books, 1977.

Herbert, Frank, and Bernard, Max. *Without Me You're Nothing, The Essential Guide to Home Computers.* New York: Simon and Schuster, 1980.

Hiltz, Starr Rozanne, and Turoff, Murray. *The Network National: Human Communications via Computers.* Reading, Mass.: Addison-Wesley Publishing Co., 1978.

Koff, Richard M. *Home Computers, A Manual of Possibilities.* New York: Harcourt, Brace and Jovanovich, 1979.

Martin, James. *Viewdata and the Information Society.* Englewood Cliffs, N.J.: Prentice-Hall, Inc., 1982.

McCunn, Donald. *Computer Programming for the Complete Idiot.* San Francisco: Design Enterprises of San Francisco, 1979.

McGlynn, D. R. *Personal Computing: Home, Professional, and Small Business Applications, (First Edition).* New York: Wiley Interscience, 1979.

Microprocessor Lexicon, Acronyms and Definitions. Berkeley, Calif.: Sybex, Inc., 1978.

Miller, Merl K., and Sippl, Charles A. *Home Computers: A Beginner's Glossary and Guide.* dp Series in Hardware no. 3. Portland, Ore.: dilithium Press, 1978.

Nelson, Ted. *The Home Computer Revolution.* South Bend, Ind.: self-published, 1977.

Papert, Seymour. *MINDSTORMS, Children, Computers, and Powerful Ideas.* New York: Basic Books, Inc., 1980.

Sippl, Charles A., and Sippl, Roger J. *The Personal Electronics Buyers' Guide.* Englewood Cliffs, N.J.: Prentice-Hall Spectrum, 1979.

Solomon, Leslie, and Veit, Stanley. *Getting Involved with Your Own Computer.* Short Hills, N.J.: Enslow-Ridley Publishers, 1977.

Tydeman, L.; Lipinski, H.; Adler, R.; Nyhan, M.; and Zwimpfer, L. *Teletext and Videotex in the United States.* New York: McGraw-Hill Publications Co., 1982.

Veith, Richard. *Talk-Back TV: Two-Way Cable Television.* Blue Ridge Summit, Penn.: TAB Books, 1976.

Weik, Martin H. *Standard Dictionary Computers and Information Processing, (Revised Second Edition)*. Rochelle Park, N.J.: Hayden Publishing, 1977.

Willis, Jerry, and Miller, Merl. *Computers for Everybody, 1984 Buyer's Guide*. Portland, Ore.: dilithium Press, 1984.

Willis, Jerry, and Miller, Merl. *Computers for Everybody, (Third Edition)*. Portland, Ore.: dilithium Press, 1984.

Zaks, Rodney. *An Introduction to Personal and Business Computing*. Berkeley, Calif.: Sybex, Inc., 1978.

Zaks, Rodney. *Microprocessors, From Chips to Systems*. Berkeley, Calif.: Sybex, Inc., 1977.

SOFTWARE DIRECTORIES

These software directories contain thousands of additional listings of software available from several thousand software houses and software vendors. They can be very helpful to anyone looking for a package one thinks does not exist or is practically impossible to find. And they are updated at least twice a year. In addition, several magazines, such as *PC World,* also publish annual software catalogs.

The Software Catalog—Microcomputers
Elsevier Science Publishing Co., Inc.
52 Vanderbilt Avenue
New York, NY 10017

(This lengthy catalog has almost ten thousand programs in its fall, 1983 edition. It is derived form the data base of the company listed next.)

International Software Data Base
Imprint Software Ltd.
1520 South College Avenue
Fort Collins, CO 80524

LIST
The Personal Computing Software Magazine for Business Applications
Redgate Publishing Company
3381 Ocean Drive
Vero Beach, FL 32963

(This is a monthly magazine listing hundreds of programs in each issue, and more than five thousand listings and descriptions in its annual bonus issue.)

MAGAZINES

BYTE Magazine
70 Main Street
Peterborough, NH 03458

Creative Computing
Box 789-M
Morristown, NJ 07960

InfoWorld
1060 Marsh Road, Suite C-200
Menlo Park, CA 94025

Interface Age
McPheters, Wolfe & Jones
16704 Marquardt Ave.
Cerritos, CA 90701

PC World
555 De Haro Street
San Francisco, CA 94107

Personal Computing
50 Essex Street
Rochelle Park, NJ 07662

Personal Software
50 Essex Street
Rochelle Park, NJ 07662

Popular Computing
70 Main Street
Peterborough, NH 03458

Of course, there are more than 125 computer magazines for general applications or aimed at users of specific computers. It is a good idea to read one or two issues of machine-specific magazines before you buy your computer.

CONSULTING REPORTS BY THE AUTHOR

Published by:

International Resource Development
30 High Street
Norwalk, CT 06851

1. *Non-Keyboard Data Entry Devices,* spring, 1984.
2. *Evolving Keyboard Markets,* summer, 1984.
3. *Integrated Voice/Data Terminals,* January, 1984.
4. *Micro-To-Mainframe Communications,* November, 1983.
5. *PC's versus CWP's in the Clerical workstation of the Future,* July, 1983.
6. *Teleshopping,* April, 1983.
7. *Business Forms, Furniture, Disc Media, and Ribbons for Personal Computer Systems,* January, 1983.
8. *Microcomputer Software Packages,* April, 1981.

About the Author

Robert L. Perry is publisher of *Micro Decision Systems,* a semimonthly newsletter on financial analysis and decision support system applications for microcomputer systems. He is also consulting senior editor for *Computing Physician,* a monthly newsletter on microcomputer applications in the field of medicine. He also writes monthly computer columns for three medical journals, *Primary Cardiology, Group Practice Journal,* and *Hospital Physician.* He was founding editor of *Microcomputer Software Letter,* a monthly newsletter evaluating applications software for major corporations.

For five years he was consulting editor to CBS Publications' computer magazine, *Computers '84.* He has written extensively about microcomputers and home computers for a variety of national magazines, including *Better Homes and Gardens, Creative Living, Datsun Discovery, BOYS' LIFE, Popular Mechanics, Science and Mechanics,* and many more. He is also former Electronics Editor for *BOYS' LIFE* magazine.

In addition, he is author with his partner, Bryce Webster, of *The Complete Social Security Handbook,* published in 1983 by Dodd, Mead.